D1688132

Louis I. Kahn
The Idea of Order

Klaus-Peter Gast

Louis I. Kahn
The Idea of Order

With Forewords by
Harmen H. Thies and
Anne Griswold Tyng

Birkhäuser
Basel · Berlin · Boston

All photographs are by the author, unless otherwise noted.

Figures 65a, 80–83, 85–97, the sketch on p. 157 and the photographs on pp. 114, 126 and 195 are from the Louis I. Kahn Collection, University of Pennsylvania and Pennsylvania Historical and Museum Commission, and are identified more closely in the notes in most cases.

Translation from German: Michael Robinson

Design and Production: Bernd Fischer, Berlin
Typesetting: LVD GmbH, Berlin
Lithography: LVD GmbH, Berlin; Bildpunkt GmbH, Berlin
Printing: Messedruck Leipzig GmbH
Binding: Kunst- und Verlagsbuchbinderei Leipzig

This book is also available in a German language edition (ISBN 3-7643-5860-2)

A CIP catalogue record for this book is available from the Library of Congress, Washington D.C., USA

Deutsche Bibliothek Cataloging-in-Publication Data
Gast, Klaus-Peter:
Louis I. Kahn : The Idea of Order / Klaus-Peter Gast. With forewords by Anne Griswold Tyng and Harmen Thies. [Transl. into Engl.: Michael Robinson]. – Basel ; Berlin ; Boston : Birkhäuser, 1998
  Dt. Ausg. u.d.T.: Gast, Klaus-Peter: Louis I. Kahn
  ISBN 3-7643-5659-6 (Basel ...)
  ISBN 0-8176-5659-6 (Boston)

This work is subject to copyright. All rights are reserved, whether the whole or part of this material is concerned, specifically the rights of translation, reprinting, re-use of illustrations, recitation, broadcasting, reproduction on microfilms or in other ways, and storage in data banks. For any kind of use, permission of the copyright owner must be obtained.

© 1998 Birkhäuser Verlag, P.O.Box 133, CH-4010 Basel, Switzerland
Printed on acid-free paper produced from chlorine-free pulp
Printed in Germany
ISBN 3-7643-5659-6
ISBN 0-8176-5659-6

9 8 7 6 5 4 3 2 1

Contents

6	Foreword by Harmen H. Thies
7	Foreword by Anne Griswold Tyng
8	Introduction
10	Explanation of the Method
13	**Ahavath Israel Congregation**
	1935–37 Philadelphia Pennsylvania USA
17	**Oser House**
	1940–42 Elkins Park Pennsylvania USA
21	**Weiss House**
	1947–50 East Norriton Township Pennsylvania USA
25	**Yale University Art Gallery**
	1951–53 New Haven Connecticut USA
29	**Trenton Bathhouse**
	1955 Trenton Pennsylvania USA
37	**Alfred Newton Richards Medical Research Building/ David Goddard Laboratories**
	1957–64 Philadelphia Pennsylvania USA
45	**Margaret Esherick House**
	1959–61 Philadelphia Pennsylvania USA
53	**First Unitarian Church**
	1959–62 Rochester New York USA
61	**Salk Institute for Biological Studies**
	1959–67 San Diego California USA
73	**Fisher House**
	1964–67 Hatboro Pennsylvania USA
81	**Phillips Exeter Academy Library**
	1965–71 Exeter New Hampshire USA
89	**Kimbell Art Museum**
	1966–72 Fort Worth Texas USA
99	**National Capital of Bangladesh**
	1962–83 Dhaka Bangladesh
113	**Indian Institute of Management**
	1962–74 Ahmedabad India
	Exemplary Building Analysis
131	Indian Institute of Management
	School Complex
157	Indian Institute of Management
	Student Dormitories
173	Indian Institute of Management
	Modular Origin
185	**Kahn's Design Principles**
192	**"Order is"**
196	Geometrical Principles
197	Bibliography

Foreword by Harmen H. Thies

Louis I. Kahn's œuvre is essential for the development of architecture in the second half of the 20th century. In this respect as well it is comparable with the work of architects like Frank Lloyd Wright, Ludwig Mies van der Rohe, Walter Gropius or Le Corbusier. The work of these architects shaped the twenties and early thirties of this century, in other words the Modern period that was to end after 1950. Structuralism, New Rationalism and fundamental features of Post-Modernism owe no less to Louis Kahn's concepts and buildings than the International Style owed to the models and key works of those protagonists of the movement called Modern or, in German, "klassische Moderne".

The more clearly we see Louis Kahn's work in terms of historical development, the more important it becomes to think about and present it in historical and conceptual terms, to show its origins both in the historical and the logical meaning of the word. This should not be done in terms of an abstract conceptual structure attempting to classify the ramifications of architecture since the fifties, but should address the image and understanding of concrete designs and buildings. Insights, reconstructed in conceptual terms, into the genesis of individual, obviously important buildings acquire crucial significance when building up a considered, critical and rational history of architecture.

The only way to provide an appropriate picture of architecture and its history in the second half of this century is by systematical compilation, mutual examination and critical comparison of building monographs. It will be based not so much on the handy pithy catch-phrases of architectural journalese but on careful examination of the works themselves. The succession of works will then make it possible to recognize the genetic series that are to be integrated into the traditions and history of recent modern architecture.

The present book is committed to this methodological approach. It works on a meticulous analysis of Louis Kahn's design and realization process for individual projects. It is less concerned with the general requirements of each design, those that are subject to external laws, than with the immanent factors and elements that determine the nature of every piece of architecture – "what it wants to be" (Kahn) – and that can thus substantiate and secure its autonomy.

The results are surprising and revealing. They show Louis Kahn's buildings, of which the most important examples are collected in this book, in an entirely new light, as the inner laws of their structure are shown more clearly than had ever been possible before. Working on primary propositions, a whole sequence of restructuring, shifting, metamorphosis and retrospective connection is revealed that have to be described as stages in the design process. The result can be understood from the genesis, and from the process of coming into being, the realized presence of the building itself, sensually and vividly comprehensible. Here a particular tool for examination and presentation, the analysis of plans and elevations ("*Rißanalyse*"), has been applied to Kahn's design method. If "the same" result was to be achieved by gradual reconstruction of the design process, then one could be sure of having acquired an insight into Louis Kahn's actual design process.

This opens up valuable possibilities for comparison, both for better understanding of Kahn's individual designs and buildings and for linking them back in a variety of ways to concepts and principles of modern and Modern architecture. Analogies and metamorphoses, reinterpretations and new formulations can be discerned. They make it possible to understand the individuation of Kahn's architecture, which seems committed only to itself and its own laws, as an act of socialization. Like every "major figure" in Western history, this architecture places itself in the continuum of history of its own accord. By deliberately setting itself apart, it relates to something that is definitely other; its own qualities are measured against this other, and enter the process of "history". It is not only ancient Roman and medieval Mediterranean architecture that have left crucial stimuli behind: the notions of the *Idea della architettura universale* in the Italian Renaissance are coming into view in just as new and surprising a way as the work and writings of Giovanni Battista Piranesi, which helped to shape the architecture of the modern ages. "Mannerist" architecture and art with their double structures and ambivalences are also evoked to explain specific Kahn phenomena. References to Sedlmayr, Wittkower, Rowe and Venturi identify fields in which it must seem extremely rewarding to dig more deeply in terms of both architecture and academic history.

In our century the continuing influence of the Ecole des Beaux-Arts is very properly referred to a great deal. But the inner laws of the work of Le Corbusier, its affinity with the pictorial organization of Cubism and, even more, Purism, turn out to be similarly important. Here too the chosen method of plan analysis has given insights into autonomous design processes that positively demand comparison with Louis Kahn's design methods. Thus we see again that, following on from the key position ascribed to Le Corbusier in the first half of the century, Louis Kahn can equally lay claim to a corresponding position in the second half. In both bodies of work the removal of historical architectural traditions results in architectural visions and figurations whose autonomy determines their quality. Thus they should then become the starting-point for correspondingly new and entirely independent traditions. Structuralism, Post-Modernism and architecture beyond Modernism with their different variants are deeply indebted to Louis Kahn's complex and significant work – directed at the "existing will of something" and at vivid "realizations", perceptions of things that have become real.

Foreword by Anne Griswold Tyng

Klaus-Peter Gast's geometric analysis of buildings by Louis Kahn may offer greater understanding of the creative process. Abstract shapes and proportions in geometry transcend limitations of time and space, yet geometry describes spatial relationships at all scales from subatomic particles to star systems. It can free us from superficial applications of "style" by offering profound sources for making space. The essential and most fundamental ordering principles of geometric form eliminate redundancy and at the same time offer infinite tangible variations for natural evolution and human creativity.

Louis Kahn experienced a breakthrough from the architecture of his early Beaux Arts training and the minimal International Style of his low-cost housing projects to free himself from conflicting polarities of style toward the realization of profound truths and universal syntheses in the essences of three-dimensional geometry.[1] Kahn saw that four quite different projects grew from the same geometric order: my 1949–51 octet truss elementary school that grew additional layers toward three tapering supports from the same geometry, Kahn's 1951–53 Yale Art Gallery with its visibly hollowed concrete octet ceiling, my 1951–53 house of wood – the first built totally triangulated space frame hollowed out for living space – and our 1952–57 City Tower project that grew vertically in dynamic undulations.

On December 18, 1953 Kahn wrote to me in Rome of his theory of a three-phase creative process – first "Nature of the Space", next "Order" and finally "Design."[2] As an introverted architect, Kahn began with the phase most introverted and difficult to understand. But before plunging into that phase, two earlier phases are necessary – first receiving the challenge or commission, next to look at precedents and history. From there many architects make a quick shallow return to the Design phase. Kahn's dissatisfaction with students who took such an approach lead to his realization of the "Nature of the Space", involving a more profound probe beyond history and *beyond memory* of any specific form. This phase also involves being open to all the possibilities of time and space, giving up some ego to ask "what the space wants to be." It is a phase of disorientation and chaos. If one is fortunate, the most *improbable* phase of creative breakthrough to "Order" occurs unpredictably as an abstract conceptual geometry with its own autonomous life force. Kahn called it "the seed" and in trying to describe Order, simply said, "Order is." The abstract energy form Order then evolves in the extroverted Design phase into tangible realization of circumstantial requirements of site, structure, materials, budget and specific program needs. As Nietzsche wrote in *Thus Spoke Zarathustra:* "One must feel chaos within to give birth to a dancing star."

The numinous power of the geometry of a "dancing star" is its simultaneity of randomness and order.[3] The resonant energy of simultaneous geometries may combine two kinds of order or order with randomness. Klaus-Peter Gast's uncovering of layered geometries in 1 to root 2 and 1 to 1.61803 (the Divine Proportion) may be examples of such resonance. Rectangles of 1 to root 2 proportion may be infinitely halved or doubled and still maintain consistent 1 to root 2 proportion. The "golden rectangle" maintains the same proportion with the addition or substraction of squares. Such resonant energy is derived from laws of probability. Pascal's triangle illustrates the accumulation of repeated tosses for heads or tails, a binary progression of probable randomness and improbable order. Sums of cross-sections cut diagonally through Pascal's triangle produce the Fibonacci summation series: 1, 1, 2, 3, 5, 8, 13, 21, 34, 55, 89,144, 233 ... 233/144 = 1.61805. The Divine Proportion is 1.61803. Ratios between consecutive terms get closer and closer but never reach the mathematical precision of the Divine Proportion. A Divine Proportion series is unique in being both a summation and logarithmic series. Its connecting potential offers order and contained energy to otherwise dissolving randomness. I am convinced that the Divine Proportion is a safety net to catch chaos in the universe. I have discovered some compelling examples of this.[4]

In 1959, I discovered that a four-phase geometric sequence from simple to complex – bilateral to rotational to helix to spiral – correlates with underlying geometric cycles in natural forms.[5] It was even more exciting to discover a similar correspondence with the sequence of geometric archetypes underlying the four-phase cycle of psychic individuation proposed by Carl G. Jung. Just as the underlying archetypal geometry describes different stages of psychic orientation in the development of the individual, similar shifts of collective orientation and attitude occur in larger cycles of history. The shifts of orientation mark changes of form of empathy that underlie changes of architectural styles. The continuous development of consciousness and creativity in four-phase cycles creates great works of art out of the resonance of randomness and order. The greatest works of art that evoke our deepest wonder and empathy have been described by Abraham Moles as having both "redundancy and originality", by Edwin Lutyens "inevitability and surprise" and by Louis Kahn "commonality and singularity", "desire and means" and "silence and light." The simultaneous randomness and order of the universal Fibonacci-Divine Proportion Matrix is as prevalent as grains of sand between the toes and as unique as the diamond in a crown.

---

[1] Tyng, A. G., "Synthesis of a Traditional House With a Space Frame", International Journal of Space Structure, editor J. F. Gabriel, Multi-Science Publishing Co. Ltd., Brentwood, Essex, England 1991, vol. 6, no. 4, pp. 267–273.
[2] Tyng, A. G., "Louis I. Kahn's Order in the Creative Process", *Louis I. Kahn, l'huomo, il maestro*, editor Alessandra Latour, Edizioni Kappa, Rome 1986, pp. 277–289; and *Louis Kahn to Anne Tyng, The Rome Letters 1953–1954*, edited with commentary by Anne Griswold Tyng, Rizzoli 1997, pp. 71–75.
[3] Tyng, A. G., *Simultaneous Randomness and Order: The Fibonacci-Divine Proportion as a Universal Forming Principle*, PhD dissertation, University of Pennsylvania 1975, University Microfilms International, Ann Arbor, Michigan.
[4] Tyng, A. G., "Inner Vision Toward an Architecture of Organic Humanism", *Morphology and Architecture*, editor Haresh Lalvani, International Journal of Space Structure, vol. 11, no. 1 and 2, 1996, pp. 71–77.
[5] Tyng, A. G., "Geometric Extensions of Consciousness", *Zodiac 19,* editor Maria Bottero, Edizioni Communità, Milan 1969, pp. 130–162.

Introduction

Louis Isadore Kahn's work represents a turning-point in 20th century architecture. Functionalist-Modernism and historical principles for finding architectural form meet in his designs. In the mid fifties his new understanding of *form* enabled him to transcend the empty functionalism that was particularly prevalent in America at the time. Kahn's approach still affects us at the end of the 20th century.

A number of publications[1] have appeared since Kahn's work started to make an impression, in the early sixties. They have to be sifted carefully to find works that do more than provide a mere record. Taking them in order of appearance: Vincent Scully's reflections dating from 1962 are important; here Kahn's innovative contribution is recognized and made accessible to a wider public, with passion. It was followed by the publication of selected sketches and written notes by Richard Saul Wurman and Gene Feldman in the same year. Robert Venturi's well-known polemic "Complexity and Contradiction in Architecture" appeared in 1966; it places Kahn's work directly in its historical context and identifies *ambiguity* as a key principle in Kahn's architecture for the first time. The categories chosen by Romaldo Giurgola to characterize Kahn (1969, expanded in 1975 after Kahn's death) seem somewhat questionable; he provides succinct documentation of essential projects from Kahn's complete *œuvre*, using hitherto unknown sketches and drawings. It was not until the early eighties that Kahn's daughter Alexandra Tyng enabled us to look at her father's work and also his person in some detail; she adopted a very individual point of view and stressed the importance of a philosophical approach. Wurman's extensive, though incomplete and unfortunately uncatalogued collection of spoken and written material by Kahn appeared in 1986, complemented by comments from and interviews with people who knew Kahn personally, or worked with him. The most recent noteworthy publications are Jan Hochstim's drawings, paintings and sketches by Kahn, compiled in 1991, and very well reproduced, and David B. Brownlee's and David G. De Long's 1991 exhibition catalogue, which commendably sheds light on the pre-fifties creative phase, which had previously been neglected. Attention should also be drawn to a first, if not absolutely correct German translation of important thoughts and essays by Kahn; it was published in 1993 and includes his 1955 article "Monumentality" and his important lecture to the CIAM Congress in Otterlo in 1959, based on an English version by Alessandra Latour.

With the exception of Venturi's important and vivid expositions of Kahn's work, most of the publications are based around interpretative and speculative observations – except where the authors' works are mere compilations or records. Although Scully pointed out the mathematical precision of Kahn's figurations as early as in the sixties and the architect himself always spoke in poetic circumlocution about ordering principles, there has been no serious examination of the way his architecture is structured on a basis of dimensions and geometry.

This book attempts to approach Kahn's work in terms of concrete analysis. Kahn's work is obviously dominated by geometrical structures, which leads one to question their complexity. The key here is the search for an inherent *order* as a *system* that drives the designs and thus the architecture as a whole.

Despite the clarity and simplicity of the ground plan and elevation figures in Kahn's architecture their structure is not directly evident: it has to be decoded. *Plans* have been specially drawn to this end and provide the necessary basis; they are also a starting-point for further, more involved observations.

The *plan analysis* will follow a specific method for dissecting the dimensional and geometrical basic structure of architecture. It was used by Harmen Thies for his investigations of ground plans by Balthasar Neumann (1980) and Michelangelo's Capitol (1982).[2] The rational, lucid and comprehensible *genesis* of the design is presented in a cumulative *sequence* of steps in *figurative* geometry – as circular, square or rectangular figures. This method lets us take a fresh look at Kahn's work from a very different – and vivid – point of view. This method – plan analysis – focuses on ways in which design ideas can be implemented rationally, following guiding principles, alongside intuitive development of solu-

---

[1] All the publications named in the introduction are in the context of the following work:
– Vincent Scully, "Louis I. Kahn";
– Richard Saul Wurman and Gene Feldman, "The notebooks and drawings of Louis Kahn";
– Robert Venturi, "Complexity and Contradiction in Architecture";
– Romaldo Giurgola, "Louis I. Kahn";
– Alexandra Tyng, "Beginnings";
– Richard Saul Wurman, "What will be has always been";
– David Brownlee/David De Long, "Louis I. Kahn, In the Realm of Architecture";
– Alessandra Latour, "Louis I. Kahn – Writings, Lectures, Interviews" and
– Jan Hochstim, "The Paintings and Sketches of Louis I. Kahn".

[2] Harmen Thies, "Grundfiguren Balthasar Neumanns: Zum maßstäblich-geometrischen Rißaufbau der Schörnbornkapelle und der Hofkirche in Würzburg", Florence 1980.
Harmen Thies, "Michelangelo, Das Kapitol", published by the Art-Historical Institute in Florence; Bruckmann Verlag, Munich 1982. Thies uses the concept of "plan analysis" *(Rißanalyse)* for the first time here (p. 48, 58, 62).

tions in the design process. But both these approaches – intuition and rationality – are seen as interdependent processes, each affecting the other.

Kahn's complex work is driven by extremely significant individual aspects, for example his virtuoso use of daylight to characterize a specific spatial quality; a linking of architectural elements that was innovative in its days; or particularly noteworthy detailing and selection of materials. These qualities of his work will be mentioned only peripherally in this discussion, as they have already received a lot of attention, with different weight allotted to them.

The book is in three sections: to prepare for the later and more complex work, architecture in Kahn's important early phase is dealt with first of all. The first examples are buildings that already carry the seeds of individual characteristics of the later mature work, but that can also be seen as hybrids, using different views of architecture. After this, nine selected works by Kahn are considered in detail with newly reconstructed ground plans; this acts as a step-by-step introduction to the plan analysis method and makes it possible to discover principles affecting Kahn's design that had not been dealt with previously and to present them in a simple sequence. The final section is a detailed and exhaustive analysis of the Indian Institute of Management in Ahmedabad, India, a training institute for leading figures in the world of commerce and one of Kahn's most important designs. The complexity of the Indian Institute of Management means that analysis by the above-mentioned method does justice to the particularly interesting element of the *disposition* of the parts: the central issue is the relation of the individual figures to each other and to the whole, and the interplay between the two within a general *order*. But this presentation does not just illuminate the *system of figurative geometry*, in other words the rational aspect of the architecture. It goes beyond this and provides further insights into designs by Kahn with a philosophical or spiritual element. Local characteristics and some that have nothing to do with the place show that the Indian Institute of Management occupies an unusual position because it *links Western and Eastern ways of thinking*. It also becomes clear that a far-reaching historical context is built in. All this shows that Kahn was attempting to develop *permanently valid architecture that is not related only to its time*.

However, it should be pointed out that investigations using plan analysis do not aim to fathom the design process as an exclusively rationally determined "mathematical construct": *intuitive* processes are still required for the application of rational principles.

A verification of the dimensions of the project as originally intended but not completely built, set against the built architecture of the Indian Institute of Management, made it possible to reconstruct the ground plans as a basis for this analysis. This was done with the assistance of numerous plan documents from the "Louis I. Kahn Collection" in the University of Pennsylvania in Philadelphia and the office of Anant Raje, Kahn's former colleague in Ahmedabad.

Documents from the Kahn Archive were also available for the analysis of the other projects, but as well as these Ronner/Jhaveri, "Louis I. Kahn, Complete Work 1935–74", was very helpful. The designs for the Salk Institute and the Parliament complex in Dhaka in particular are so large that they have been analysed only on a large scale, without detail, but this process has still produced well-founded statements. This could be seen as a reason and stimulus for more extensive research. The book intends to investigate and analyse the work of the most important architect in the second half of the twentieth century in a new way, but also to provide a stimulus for the expert reader's own design work. The intention is to translate the results of the method of analysis introduced here for the first time into practice. I have to thank Julia Moore Converse, the director of the "Louis I. Kahn Collection" and her staff for their generous help while I was working in the archives in Philadelphia. Thanks to Anant Raje and his wife for making the original plans available and for his time spent in long conversations, and also Esther Kahn, Robert Venturi, Donald Judd and all the other people I interviewed[3] for answering my

---

[3] The following were interviewed by the author, mainly in 1988, but some in 1993; they gave information about Louis I. Kahn's office situation and the circumstances of his personal life:
– Esther Kahn, Louis Kahn's widow;
– Sue Ann Kahn, daughter of Esther and Louis Kahn;
– Dr. Anne Griswold Tyng, architect (mother of Alexandra Tyng), former colleague;
– Carles E. Vallhonrat, architect, former colleague;
– Robert Venturi, architect, former assistant to Kahn at the University of Pennsylvania;
– Henry Wilcots, architect, former colleague;
– G. Holmes Perkins, architect, former director of the architecture department; (all resident in Philadelphia).
– Dr Jonas Salk, director of the Biological Research Institute in San Diego;
– Balkrishna V. Doshi, architect in Ahmedabad;
– Anant Raje, architect in Ahmedabad.
Notes on Kahn as an individual and his architecture given to the author by:
– Bob and Lynn Gallagher, owners of the Esherick House, Chestnut Hill;
– Doris Fisher, owner of, and commissioned, the Fisher House, Hatboro;
– Steve Korman, owner (son of the client) of the Korman House, Whitemarsh;
– Donald Judd, artist in New York and Marfa, Texas.

Explanation of the Method

questions so patiently. I should also like to thank all the people in India who helped to make this book possible, especially Ramesh Nair, Joseph Pulikkal, Ashish Shah and Bibin Skaria. Thanks to Michael Robinson in London for his sensitive translation of the book into English. Thanks also to Bernd Fischer and his assistants in Berlin for their passionate graphic design and to Andreas Müller in Berlin for his great support in preparing the book and for his editorial work. Special thanks to Harmen Thies for introducing me to the method that forms the core of the work, for his encouragement and for his careful corrections.

"Free flowing lines are most fascinating.
The pencil and the mind secretly want to make them exist.
A stricter geometry lends itself to direct calculation
and puts aside the willful particular,
favoring simplicity of structure and space
good for its continuing use in time".[4]

Thinkers like Plato or Pythagoras would consider that the cosmic world as a *harmonious structure* is built on a dependent sequence of numbers.[5] They contend that each part of this world can be grasped abstractly and rationally in its relationship to the next one and its proportions in terms of numbers. Number and proportion, as factors that are entirely dependent on each other, form the basis of an awareness of harmony, changing throughout history, in the creation of architecture as a copy of that *world order*,[6] that man strives for in his work, with very different degrees of success. Countless attempts to transform a world order into the artificial products of the builder's art can be seen in the history of architecture. *Consistently valid quality* is to be produced by the use of geometrical basic principles that are not subject to change.[7] Many studies aim to prove the existence of geometrical structure in nature as an image of this order, as already presented by Villard de Honnecourt in the Middle Ages,[8] and, since conscious application of rational principles to design in the Renaissance, architecture itself has been used to investigate and *interpret* its possibly symbolic structure. Rudolf Wittkower's work on the architecture of Alberti and Palladio[9] analyses the consistent use of rational principles during the Renaissance. As well as this, Harmen Thies's work on Michelangelo's architecture for the Capitol[10] shows the existence of a comprehensive *system* of geometrical order that confirms that the individual parts of the complex were designed by Michelangelo as an entity. Schematic ordering principles appear in the late

Fig.1

---

[4] Quotation by Louis Kahn in: Architectural Forum, July/August 1966, p. 43.
[5] Plato, "Timaeus".
[6] Aurelius Augustinus (St. Augustine; 354–430), "De Ordine": "Order is the means by which everything is determined that God has prescribed". For this see the section on order in Kahn, p. 185.
[7] Paul von Naredi-Rainer, "Architektur und Harmonie", Du Mont Verlag, Cologne 1982/89. A brief survey of attempts to impose order upon architecture throughout architectural history.
[8] Hans Rudolf Hahnloser, "Villard de Honnecourt", Graz 1972, first edition Vienna 1935.
[9] Rudolf Wittkower, "Architectural Principles in the Age of Humanism", London 1949 und London und New York 1952. Detailed survey of the use of proportional principles in Italian Renaissance architecture with extensive bibliography.
[10] Thies, "Michelangelo, Das Kapitol", see note 2.

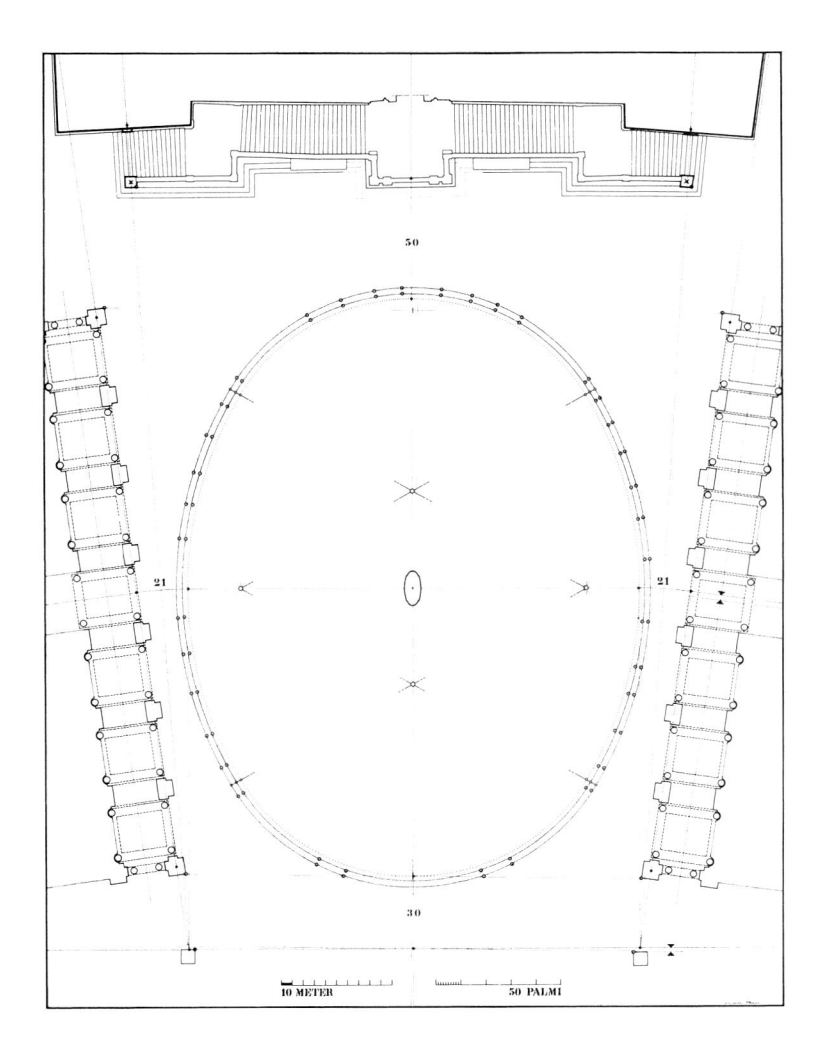

Fig.1
Drawing of the ground plan of Michelangelo's Capitol by Harmen Thies; with measuring points and relations identified

18th century, especially in the case of Jean-Nicolas-Louis Durand,[11] which have to do justice to aspects of economy and construction as grid structures and are robbed of their complexity. Colin Rowe seeks to establish direct links with 20th century architecture in comparative studies of Palladio and Le Corbusier with the aid of proportional diagrams.[12] More recent studies by Stefan Germer and Achim Preiß on the structure of Guiseppe Terragni's architecture (1991)[13] and by Lionel March and Judith Sheine on Rudolf Michael Schindler (1993)[14] provide evidence of the existence of order principles that are inherent in architecture and shape its structure, using the architecture of this century to demonstrate its geometrical complexities.

An anthropometric approach is often used as the basis, with man in the centre as a reference point for scale, just as Leonardo da Vinci, by superimposing a human figure on the basic geometrical forms of circle and square,[15] identifies the human being as a "module" and scale for the creation of architecture and the relationship between man and God.

When attempting to examine architecture precisely, assumptions and observations that seem justified as a result of collating information from many different sources must be substantiated by making statements that are as unambiguous as possible. Here the available material often turns out to be an interpretation, in other words the views taken are individual and expressed from highly personal points of view, and by no means "objective".[16] This information, usually descriptive, and to an extent filtered or alienated, has to be handled by juxtaposing it with things that can be understood concretely, that prove to be "logical" and that thus come close to what is actually there. It can be asserted that what is comprehensible to the uninvolved observer in its illustrated version is more likely to be correct than something that is merely assumed or interpreted. *Logic* as a successive process proves and does not interpret, it presents what is to be examined to the observer as a cumulative sequence, and here it means the internal logic of architectural structure. An architectural design as a whole assembled from parts carries the dependent sequence of its creation, its *genesis*, expressed as it becomes an image, in the *plan*, the drawing made by the designer. His thoughts, brought together as an entity, are illustrated most directly in architectural drawings, which are also instructions for action and actual implementation of what has been devised: if what is drawn is precise, what is built should be precise. In contrast with a vague sketch of a possibly fleeting idea, the plan, as an anticipation of what is later to be realized, requires precision of line and scale. The drawing "constructed" to scale as a working plan already provides an image of what is to be built, represents a basis for understanding and examining the architectural design and now offers the possibility of dissecting the whole that has been assembled from individual figures. Therefore the plans and elevations, the drawings, form the basis for an examination of the architecture. They are the most concrete and usually also the most precise abstraction of what is built or to be built, entirely

---

[11] Jean-Nicolas-Louis Durand, "Précis des leçons d'architecture", Paris 1805.
[12] Colin Rowe, "The Mathematics of the Ideal Villa and Other Essays", Massachusetts Institute of Technology Press, Cambridge und London 1982.
[13] Stefan Germer and Achim Preiß, "Giuseppe Terragni 1904–1943", Klinkhardt und Biermann Verlag, Munich 1991.
[14] Lionel March and Judith Sheine, "RM Schindler, Composition and Construction", Academy Editions, London 1993.
[15] Leonardo da Vinci, Proportionsschema der menschlichen Gestalt nach Vitruv (1485/90), Galleria dell' Accademia, Venice.
[16] For this see for example Juan Pablo Bonta, "Architecture and Its Interpretation", London, 1979.

comparable with the notation in a musical score. The plan, or elevation, is an image of the design, indeed of the design process – what is meant here is the definitive "working plan": all the designer's deliberations about the various parts are finally condensed into an overall solution. This condensed mass has to be unravelled in order to arrive at the *structure* of the architectural design, which has necessarily been prepared in interdependent stages. A logical process has a beginning within its structure: the beginning of the design. It is this starting-point or *starting figure* that has to be reached, and, defined as a *set position*, presented as vividly as possible.

In order to establish that the drawn design corresponds precisely with the realized building it is necessary to check the measurements, although they admit only measurements of the realized building as a comparison. A comparative study of plan and architecture leads to justified statements about the concrete, realized, full-scale implementation. It also shows for the first time where there have been deviations and things left incomplete, as well as changes that may have been recorded in the plans. The structure of architecture is based on rational principles, which reveal their *system* in a comparative examination of the plan and the realized building, and this system seems sound and comprehensible – and thus justified. Thies calls this *Rißanalyse* (plan analysis)[17], and shows how to dissect the basic structure of a building in this way: examples are examined, and the process by which a design was found for the plans and all the interdependent component figures is fathomed.

On closer examination, Louis Kahn's architecture is seen to be ambiguous and mysterious. It can quickly be established that he did not give any precise explanations about his designs, on the contrary, "mere" definitions are all that exist. In the work of many authors concerned with Kahn's work and person this "veiled" linguistic expression leads to very individual interpretations. In contrast with this, a previously unknown starting-point is selected here, which places what evidently exists – as a basis for further observations – at the centre of the approach.

The analyses that follow, as interpretations, work on the premise that an order exists – as a postulate, as hitherto not proved – in the architecture of Louis Kahn. The geometrical structure of the ground plan figures, the disposition of the component figures and the presumed integration of all parts into a greater whole are examined in two-dimensional contexts. Here the orthogonal structure of the designs is helpful: geometrical relations are established – through the relations of the edges of the individual areas, the way in which their corners are connected (usually diagonally) – that bind all the parts into the *network* of the ordering structure as square or rectangular *frames*. One quickly realizes that a system of frames exists that is shaped by overlaps and grids that are proportionally interdependent. Breaking this existing net down into individual geometries produces a sequence of cumulative, and thus hierarchical steps that makes it possible to identify the starting-point of the structure. The intention is to distil a geometry of origin, the *figure at the beginning of the geometrical order*. Thus we discover that Louis Kahn's design principle is to build architecture up by using a dimensional and geometrical structure.

Kahn's method of joining parts and making them relate to each other, their disposition, is thus revealed, but also, well beyond this, the imaginary effect of forces that trigger *movement processes* through tensions and antagonisms. A system of inherent order, supported by scaled geometrical figures, is revealed, right down to similar growth processes in nature, from the germ cell to the organism as a whole.

It should be noted, as an aid to understanding the graphic abstraction of the analytical drawings, that in each case the most important "generated" structure, in other words the figure developed from the preceding image, is emphasized by the use of a thicker line. This characterizes the cumulative development stages of the analytical sequence, within which lines of lesser weight are to be read either as a memory of figures that have appeared before or an indication of those that are still to come.

---

[17] Thies, "Michelangelo, Das Kapitol", p. 48, 58, 62.

Ahavath Israel Congregation
1935–37 Philadelphia Pennsylvania USA

The first building Louis I. Kahn planned and realized independently was a community centre for the "Ahavath Israel Congregation"; it is still standing in roughly its original state, and functioned in its intended role until 1982.

Kahn's fascination with abstract architecture within early American Modernism can already be clearly sensed in this building. But the building is also fascinating because of its "brutality": the fact that the surrounding terraced buildings – admittedly not of very high quality – are completely ignored in favour of a simplified *block* shows how crudely the new architecture was preceived in the period when early Modernism was developing on the American East Coast. But the building, a more or less unarticulated cube, is already a manifesto for Kahn. The decisiveness with which he chose form and position shows that he was determined to explode customary ways of looking at things, and to lay himself open to new ways of understanding. The block is an undifferentiated rectangle, and forms a stark contrast with the existing, intricately articulated housing, additive and hierarchized in the best imported English manner; it defines a *set position*, a self-relating, generally valid form that does not directly illustrate its functions on the outside.

But Kahn does distinguish between the principal and secondary façades: the entrance side and the south-west side are given homogeneous brick cladding, so that on the diagonal we seem to see a brick building, standing out in sharp outline. Thus the centre anticipates a fundamental characteristic of later years in the honesty of its material. "Holes" are punched in the main façade of the entrance area on the street side. They follow functional principles as openings wherever they are needed as such, one to provide light on the stairs, and the other as an entrance. However, structural "purity" in terms of the chosen material is not a feature of these façades: prefabricated lintels over the openings are clad with bricks hung in front of them. Kahn completely abandons classical articulation patterns like symmetry or hierarchy; the building, particularly on its entrance side, is open to interpretation as a personal "act of liberation" because it is so rigid. But there are reminiscences of the Ecole des Beaux Arts influence in Kahn's training: despite the asymmetrical "random façade" the brick wall is concluded at the top by an articulating cornice band. Kahn makes essential protection against the bitter winter climate of Philadelphia a defining design element, and so betrays his spiritual origins. He does not detach himself entirely from the principles of his training, although the other façades, on the north and the north-east sides, seem to fall unambiguously into the modern vocabulary of the "International Style". Here Kahn used rendering (probably white) combined with a perforated façade and windows with small divisions and (probably dark) metal frames. Glass bricks are used at the back, so that the building looks industrial on its less conspicuous sides, and this is additionally underlined by stairs in prefabricated steel sections and tubular steel with very coarse detailing. This is reminiscent of European models in the twenties like the Dessau Bauhaus or villas by Le Corbusier, whose façades include metal bars and particularly filigree metal stairs,

Street and side view with adjacent buildings and passageway

Main entrance façade

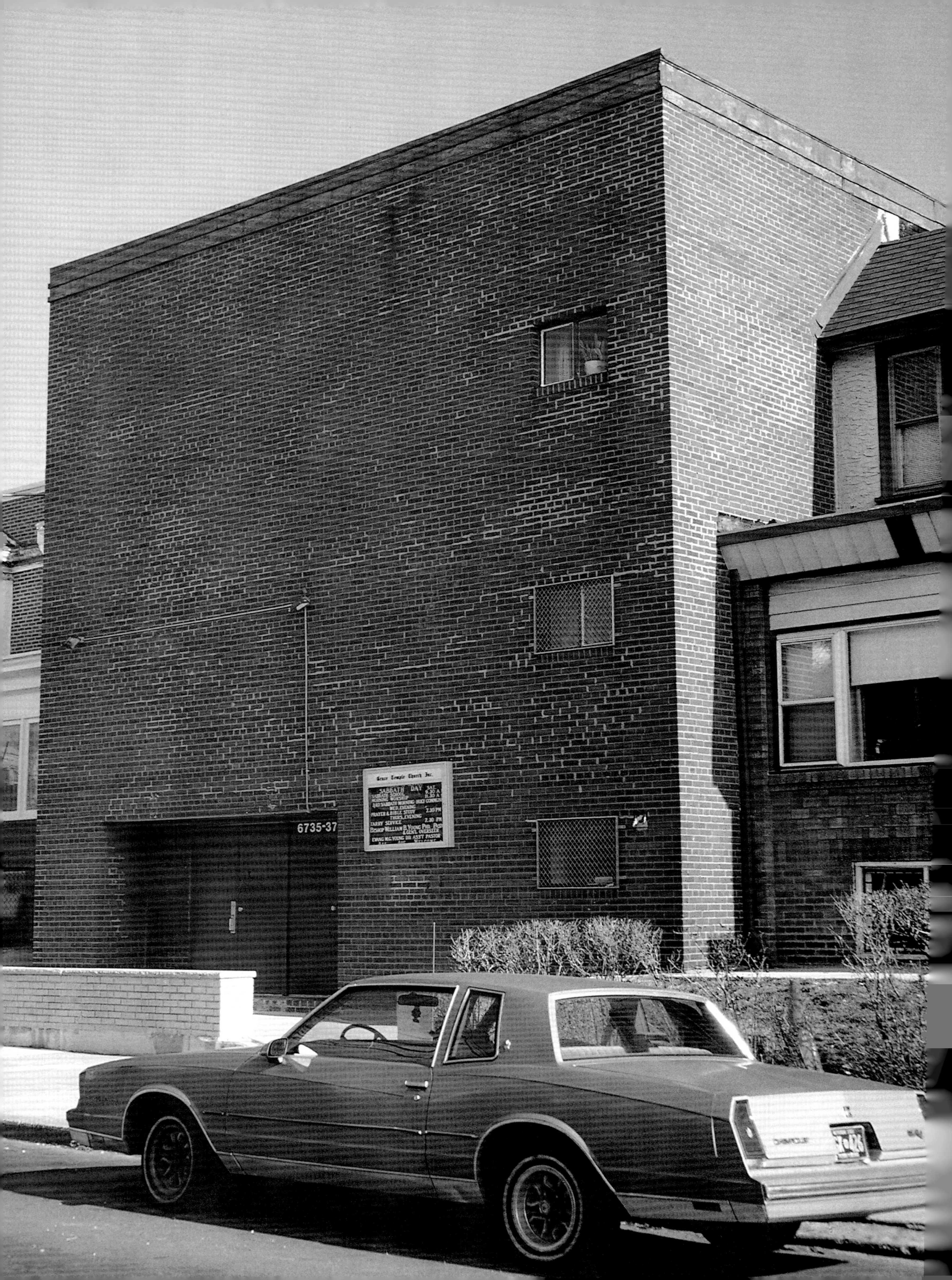

or, as in the case of Le Corbusier, tubular steel banisters, in other words industrial building elements. Here it is clear that Kahn, after the "International Style" exhibition by Hitchcock and Johnson in the Museum of Modern Art in New York and in Philadelphia in 1932,[18] and his earlier joint practice with George Howe, is aware of this revolutionary movement's design principles and tries to apply them to his first independent building. The fact that he places the supports within the façade as pilaster-like articulating elements on the long side also shows that Kahn wanted to identify construction as an industrial building principle in the exterior, and to give the impression that the building has two completely different sides: an L-shaped brick shield covers the "true" body of the building, which is concealed behind it and provided with structural elements. There are also two impressions to be had of the brick wall: from the south-west it forms a closed volume, but from the north the end of this section it is clearly discernible as a wall.

The brick wall as a shield facing the public space and contrasting with a quite different rear façade will be taken up again in a later and much more important design by Kahn: this feature occurs again in the Yale Art Gallery, 1953, in New Haven.

Rear view with rendered façade and glass brick wall

Stairs to the caretaker's flat

Corner of brick wall and staircase windows

[18] Henry-Russell Hitchcock, Philip Johnson: "The International Style, Architecture since 1922", The Museum of Modern Art, New York 1932.

Corner view with timber façade and drive to garage

Oser House
1940–42 Elkins Park Pennsylvania USA

For this house on the edge of Philadelphia Kahn designed a building whose block-like cuboid quality is reminiscent of the Ahavath Israel Synagogue, built only a few years earlier. The entrance side is formed by the sharply defined edges of the building. The south-facing rear façade is differentiated and partially broken up by a single-storey living-room extension and generously glazed areas on the garden side. There the prismatic simplicity of the building is varied by dissolving the volume, with filigree banisters for the terrace of the upper storey and a pergola-like area for the living-room entrance.

The choice of material shows a contrast between two dominant surfaces: Kahn uses undressed stone for the body of the building, then horizontal timber for a secondary section that thrusts forward towards the entrance; this material is also to be found on the rear – south – side of the building. As in the Ahavath Synagogue this produces a double L-shape made up of different surface textures. When viewed from the corner, these suggest volume, but turn out to be two-dimensional at the point at which they meet. The secondary section of the building thrusts forwards and protrudes above the base of the lower storey, apparently keeping itself to itself, but it then reintegrates itself into the rear outline of the building as a whole. We observe therefore that Kahn is building up *double relations* that make it difficult to understand the design concept at a glance: they require more precise consideration. The format of the openings also varies considerably, although it is clear that larger dimensions were chosen within the timber façade, for example a band of windows running round the corners of the protruding section on the ground and first floors, though the corners themselves are not glazed. But this is the case for the back living-room window, a kind of linking zone between the timber façade in the upper storey, the timber cladding on the balcony, and the masonry base on the ground floor. The windows in the undressed stone façade of the entrance and in one of the short sides are stamped in as holes with different formats; their lintels are formed either by a ceiling joist or by a concrete facing structure. As in the Ahavath Congregation building honesty of construction, so important in Kahn's later work, is not yet a key feature of this design.

The ground floor plan is conventionally "functionalistic" and tries to indicate the hierarchy of main and subsidiary spaces in a differentiated way outside the building. Here we see the first signs of a "spatial continuum": main entrance area, corridor zone and living-room flow into each other, and additionally the glazing on the south side suggests that nature is emphatically included in the main living area, with the fireplace as a linking element. The carefully overlaid design of the

Fig.2

Main entrance side with small bridge

Corner view with natural stone façade

Fig.3

exterior space forms a contrast with the angular quality of the ground plan figure. Its heterogeneous lack of symmetry – in particular the polygonal slabs on the terrace – is a mixture of a free, organic concept, still planned in clear outlines, in tune with the fashionable trends of the period. Here we see Kahn's less than secure handling of exterior geometrical composition, which will persist for several years. One corner of the livingroom is dissolved entirely into glass, also separated by the floor covering, and held in position only by the massive fireplace block. But it is not that this area was added as a later design idea. On the contrary, it was a key feature of the outlines from the start: the position of the support in the entrance roofing of the terrace reveals the geometry of a square that is an integral part of the ground plan; this can be seen as the initial figure for the design, and it includes the outline of the "glass corner". The geometry of the pure square is *distorted* only retrospectively: a corner of the square is "cut out" and made part of the exterior as a roofed terrace. The timber-clad, thrusting-out section is also added; thus the separation of material that is so clear in the façade agrees with the found geometrical figure and is justified from within this context. The chosen "shift" of this body in relation to the exterior line corresponds with the shift of the fireplace block south into the exterior space in relation to the outline of the inner square.

For the first time in this early design we see square geometry as a *set position* and possible initial figure within Kahn's design process. It is a first indication of the geometry that is to dominate his ground plan arrangements in future.

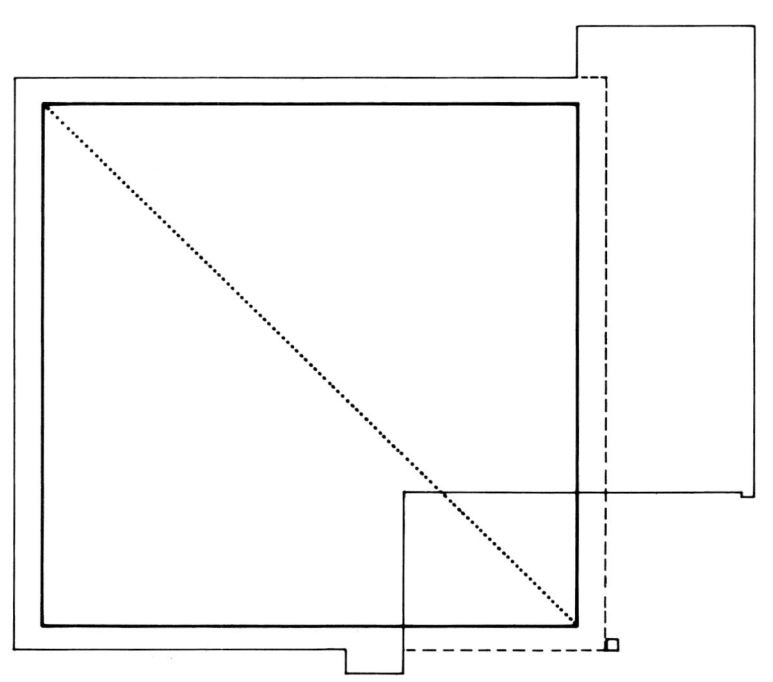

Fig.3
The square as the design starting point for Oser House

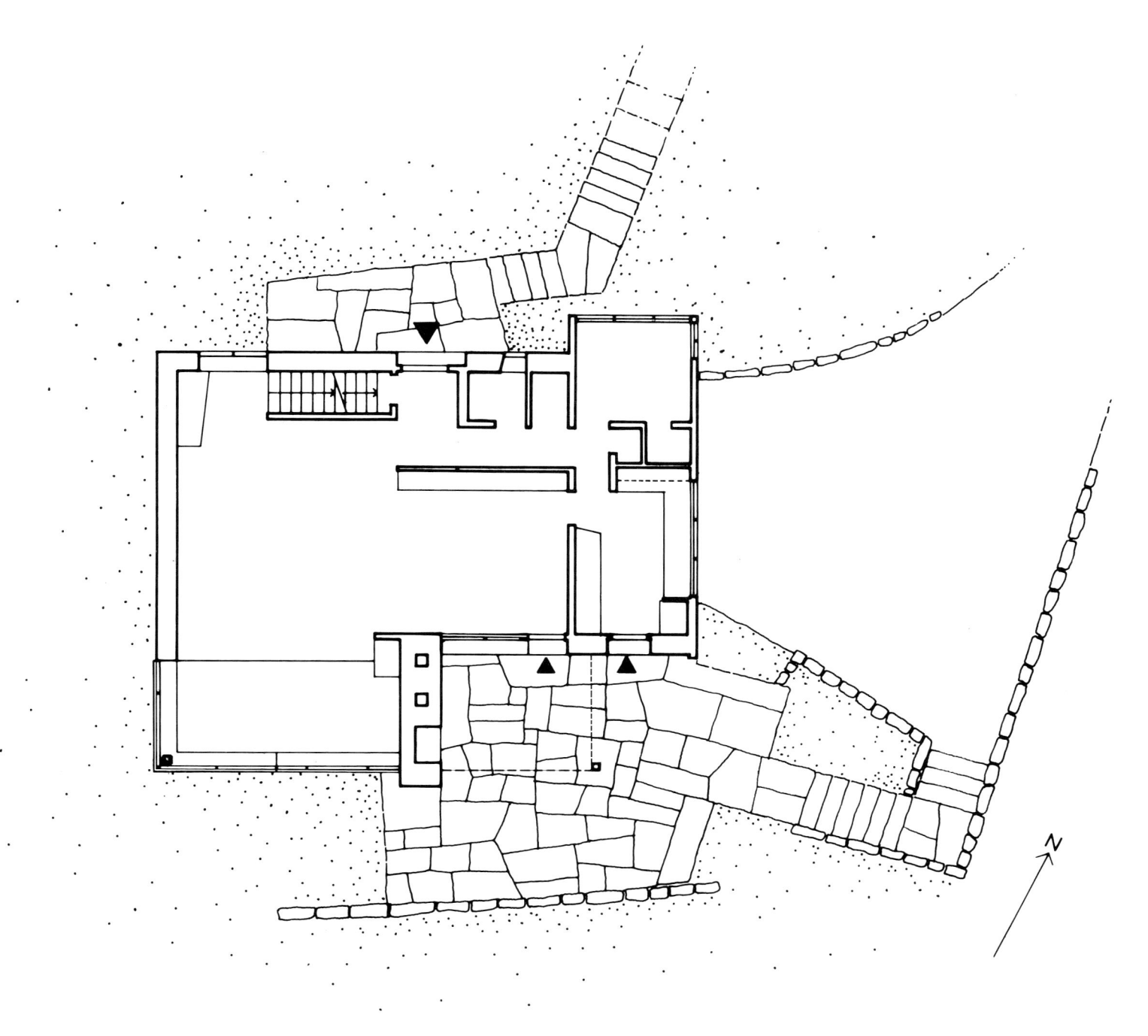

Fig.2
Ground floor plan
of Oser House with
outbuildings

Sliding wooden panels to regulate incident light

Weiss House
1947–50 East Norriton Township
Pennsylvania USA

After Oser house, Kahn produced private house designs whose asymmetrical and functional ground plans indicate an intermediate phase in his development. He abandoned the "pure" cube of a block-like, essentially closed, almost primitive body in favour of dissolving, almost picturesque architecture, marked by filigree-structural sections and large glazed areas.

Kahn returns to clear outlines for the Weiss House in the northern, rural outskirts of Philadelphia. With a great deal of support from his colleague Anne Tyng he designs an additive structure of two volumes meeting under a common roof line, which represents an end of sorts for this development. The division into two equally deep areas, relating to each other in shape and thus again linked together, is derived from each of their functions: the living-room with central fireplace and a kitchen incorporated in the outline with side room is linked to the separate sleeping area by an access corridor. *Hierarchy* emerges as differentiation in the body of the building that can be read from the outside, with the secondary rooms in each volume, the kitchen in the living area and the bathroom in the sleeping area, projecting outwards. This division into three forms the basic structure of the design, anticipating the "servant/served" idea that was so precisely implemented later (for explanation see Richards Building). Secondary rooms, connecting corridor and the fireplace block with its sunken sitting area form a kind of backbone to a central "track" that lengthens towards the outside. It gives the ground plan figure the extraordinary rigidity that was to be such a strong characteristic of Kahn's later designs, lending stability to the ensemble with its separate garage.

Axes and symmetries of the component figures appear in this design; the ground plan does not develop from a random structure but is subject to an *order* that ties all the parts together. Unlike earlier designs, contrasting, asymmetrical polygonal figures within the ground plan are considerably reduced in their weighting; this affects the fireplace block, the furnishings and the draught-excluding wall along the long outdoor sitting area beside the fireplace. They are now almost fully graphic in character and represent relics of previous designs, the exterior of Oser House, for example; Kahn has already recognized that this building was merely a reflection of its time.

A protruding, inward-sloping folded roof slab, interpreted by Brownlee/De Long as reminiscent of Marcel Breuer's designs,[19] certainly follows the contemporary tendency to break volumes down into elements, but Kahn's massive undressed stone walls demonstrate his desire for solidity and mass. The general impression is that he does not feel at home with this formal language; this view is supported by the somewhat unbalanced articulation of the façade, where the proportion of massive to open section is not quite correct. The building's position in a less densely populated area and the open view of the landscape, which slopes slightly to the south, justify the façade solution Kahn chose for the Weiss House: it opens up generously inside the living-room from floor to ceiling, with individually moveable wooden elements to provide a view shaped by ambiance and by the state of the light.

The unbroken line of the roof, which springs back slightly at the side of the exterior fireplace, dissolves into a pergola-like frame in the entrance areas on both sides and emphasizes the point of division between the two parts of the building. A particular characteristic of future designs appears for the first time in the Weiss House: it is not

View from the garden

Corner view with exit to fireplace area

[19] David B. Brownlee/David G. De Long, "Louis I. Kahn, In the Realm of Architecture", Rizzoli International Publications, New York 1991, p. 39.

absolutely clear whether Kahn has "cut out" the volume from an overall body on both sides within the central dividing zone, or whether two independent figures were put together. We will return to this aspect of *contradictory ambiguity* in greater depth in later detailed analyses.

The Weiss House is certainly the most successful design in this phase of Kahn's work, and its austerity and order point forward to the next, very significant period in the architect's œuvre.

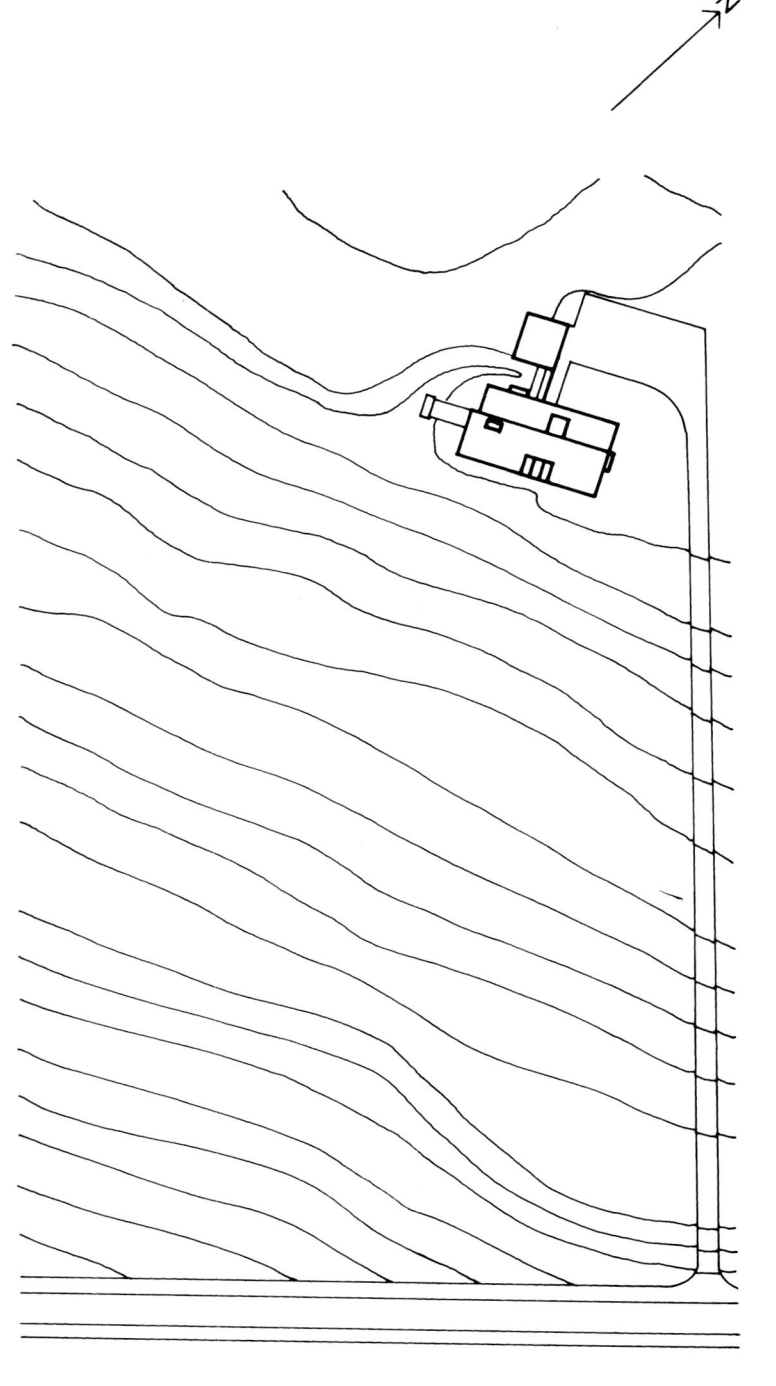

Fig.5
General plan of Weiss House with site sloping to the south

Division between the rubblestone masonry and the timber sections of the building

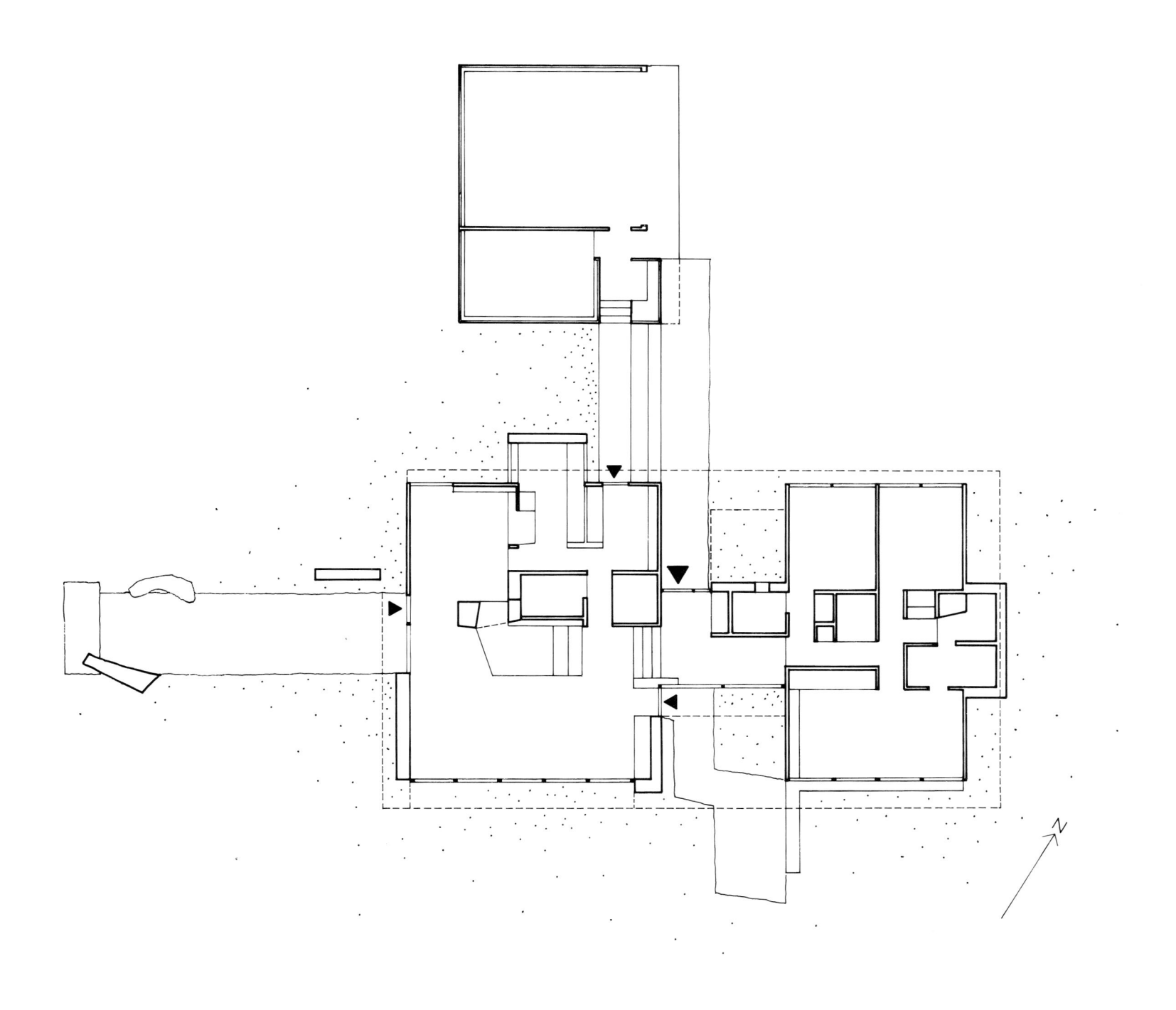

Fig.4
Ground floor plan of
Weiss House with
garden fireplace
area

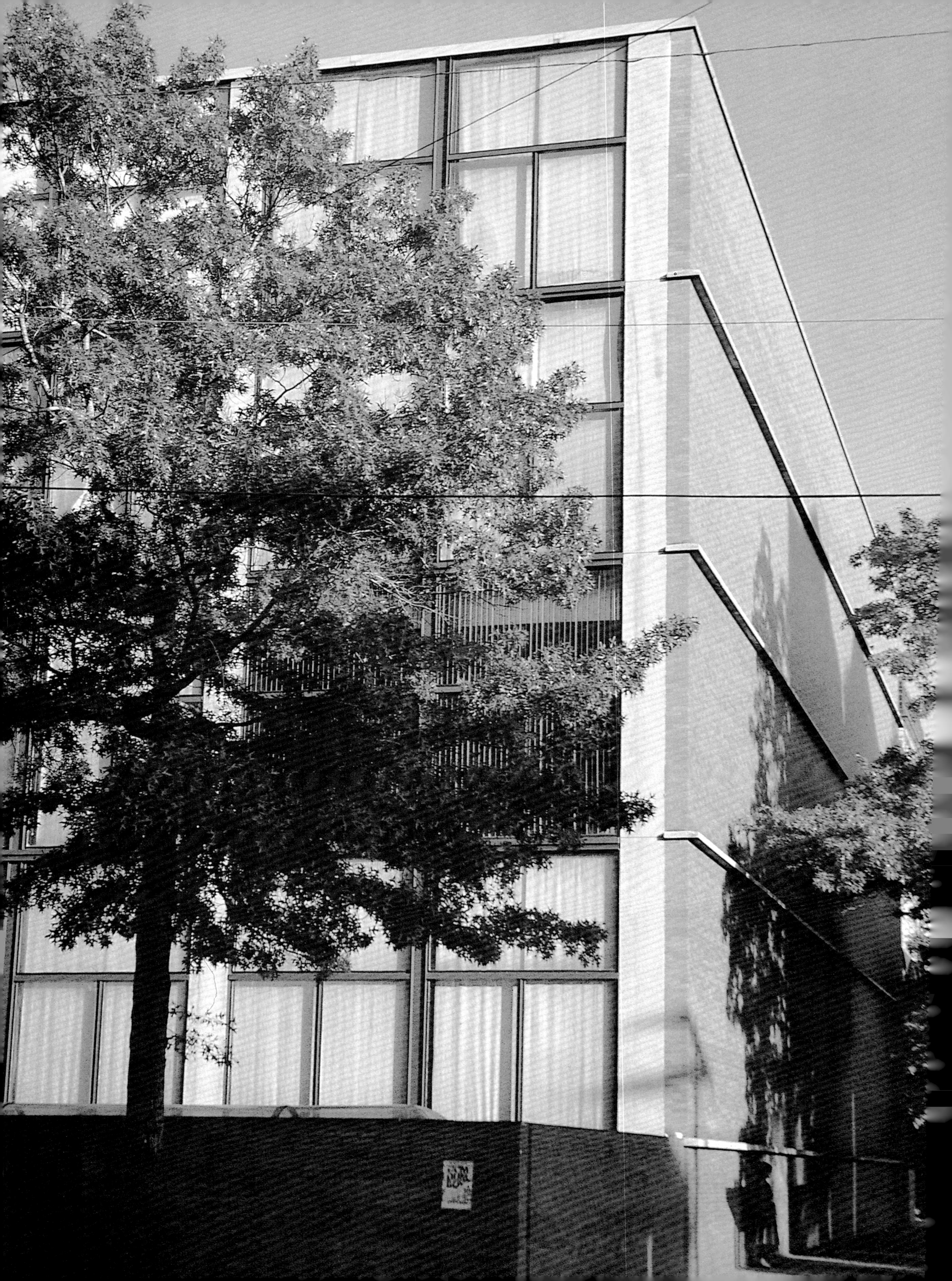

Yale University Art Gallery
1951–53 New Haven Connecticut USA

Fig.6

Kahn was commissioned to extend the Art Gallery in New Haven while teaching at Yale University, and returned to a theme that was familiar from his first building in Philadelphia, the Ahavath Synagogue: a simple block with clear outlines. As the old building was to be included in the exhibition area, a small connecting area was created; this indentation on the street side made the main entrance possible. This connecting element is reminiscent of the Weiss House with its similarly indented corridor, but there it did connect two buildings of the same kind. But here it is perfectly clear that this is an additional area, as the new façade completely ignores the old building's divisions and parts, though it does pick up its outlines.

Kahn also creates two contrasting façades in this design, with their character dependent on external conditions. On the road and access – south – side the impressive brick wall appears as a completely closed façade on both the main and connecting buildings. The other three sides of the building, with the exception of a closed wall for the staircase, are broken down almost entirely into glass. The articulation of the striking brick wall with horizontal, light bands of concrete that protrude on the exterior is particularly new, and is here, in terms of abstract interpretation, reminiscent of *ancient models*. They do serve to illustrate the division of the floors on the exterior of the building, but above all they represent themselves and extend round the corner, meaning that the impression they make shifts between a brick *wall* and a brick *body*. This wall design now demonstrates Kahn's interest in monumentalizing architecture in a new and unaccustomed way, and also in including archaic features. This façade is the first successful integration of historical models in Kahn's work, and is evidence of his ability to synthesize contradictory expressive forms. But the transparent façades, especially the one in the rear courtyard, pick up Mies van der Rohe's formal language, which was predominant in America at the time: they have telltale dark, carefully profiled metal frames. Thus this building can be described as the last hybrid form in which Kahn mixes his deep desire for mass and volume with a high level of transparency, which is not his own, but "borrowed".

The constructive framework of the supports is illustrated on both sides of the building by cladding with light-coloured natural stone. But this gives the impression of articulation by pilasters (similarly to the side façade of the Ahavath Synagogue), which is used here negatively, in other words shifting back behind the glazed façades or flush with the surface at the front. The horizontal load of a concluding attica or similar element is missing, which again questions the credibility of these façades with supports and reduces the supports to the status of façade profiles. Externally they become components of the façade, not of the support structure. This effect is made possible by the famous concrete tetrahedral spaceframe for the floors, whose broad span rests on the inside ends of these supports, maintaining a separation from the glass/metal façade and making an even more dramatic effect in the interior. So much has already been written about it that I shall not discuss it any further here.

The disposition of the ground plan for this building is very important; the floor/ceiling construction makes it possible to provide exhibition spaces without intrusive supports. This produces a "multi-purpose space", divided into three (as in a Mies concept), with side rooms, reduced to clear body outlines, inserted as access elements into the central area. This composition is uncompromisingly dominated by symmetry for the first time in Kahn's work, with inserted "containers", providing vertical access, as independent design figures. Alongside a rectangle for shafts and lifts, the main staircase of the Yale Art Gallery is a particularly striking feature: it is three flights of stairs in the form of a *triangle*, placed inside a *circular* section – the function fits into the form. This staircase is the *first autonomous design figure realized by Kahn*. It acquires independence as an exclusively self-referential form and represents Kahn's most important step into a new dimension of experience and design that is the hallmark of all his subsequent work.

Corner view with brick wall on Chapel Street

The point at which the brickwork with articulating strips meets the completely glazed façade on the short side

Detail of the stairwell skylight

The rear of the building on the courtyard side, reminiscent of Mies van der Rohe

Skylight in the circular stair well with triangular flights of steps

The geometrical proportions of the exterior shape depend on the outline of the old building. A double square based on the width of the old building is added to the existing perimeter; this double square has two characteristic diagonals and is clearly framed. Thus the overall length of the new building includes the position of the exterior outline of the supports on the courtyard side, while on the street side it is the inner line of the supports which relates to this geometrical outline. The choice of width for the supports on the basis of structural necessity now determines the width of the interior (dashed outline in the figure) so that a new interior square can be formed from this width. A simple geometrical construction using the arc of a circle is used to project the diagonal of this square on to one long side, thus generating the right-hand limit of the outline of the main section of the building. The resulting rectangle has the so-called 1-to-root-2 proportion:[20] its short side relates to its diagonals in a ratio of 1 to 1.414. This geometrical figure is extremely significant in Kahn's work; it is a kind of key dimension, and will be discussed in detail below.

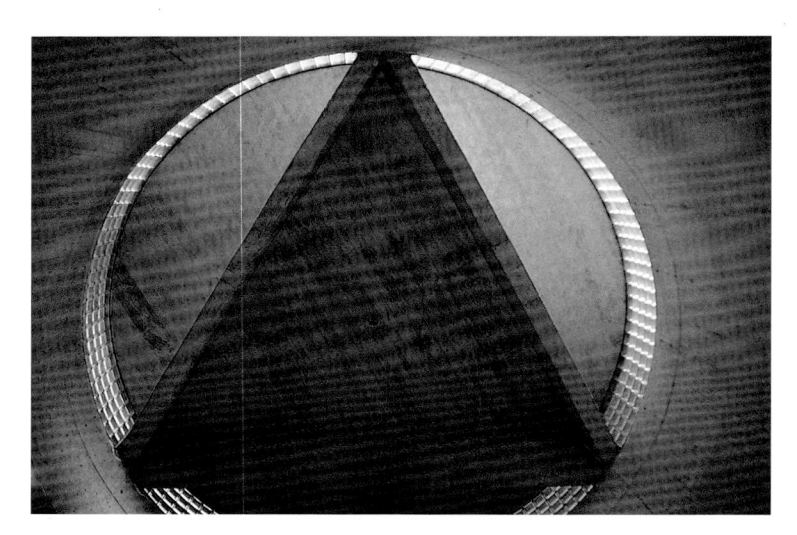

Fig.7

[20] The note is at the end of the book.

Fig. 6

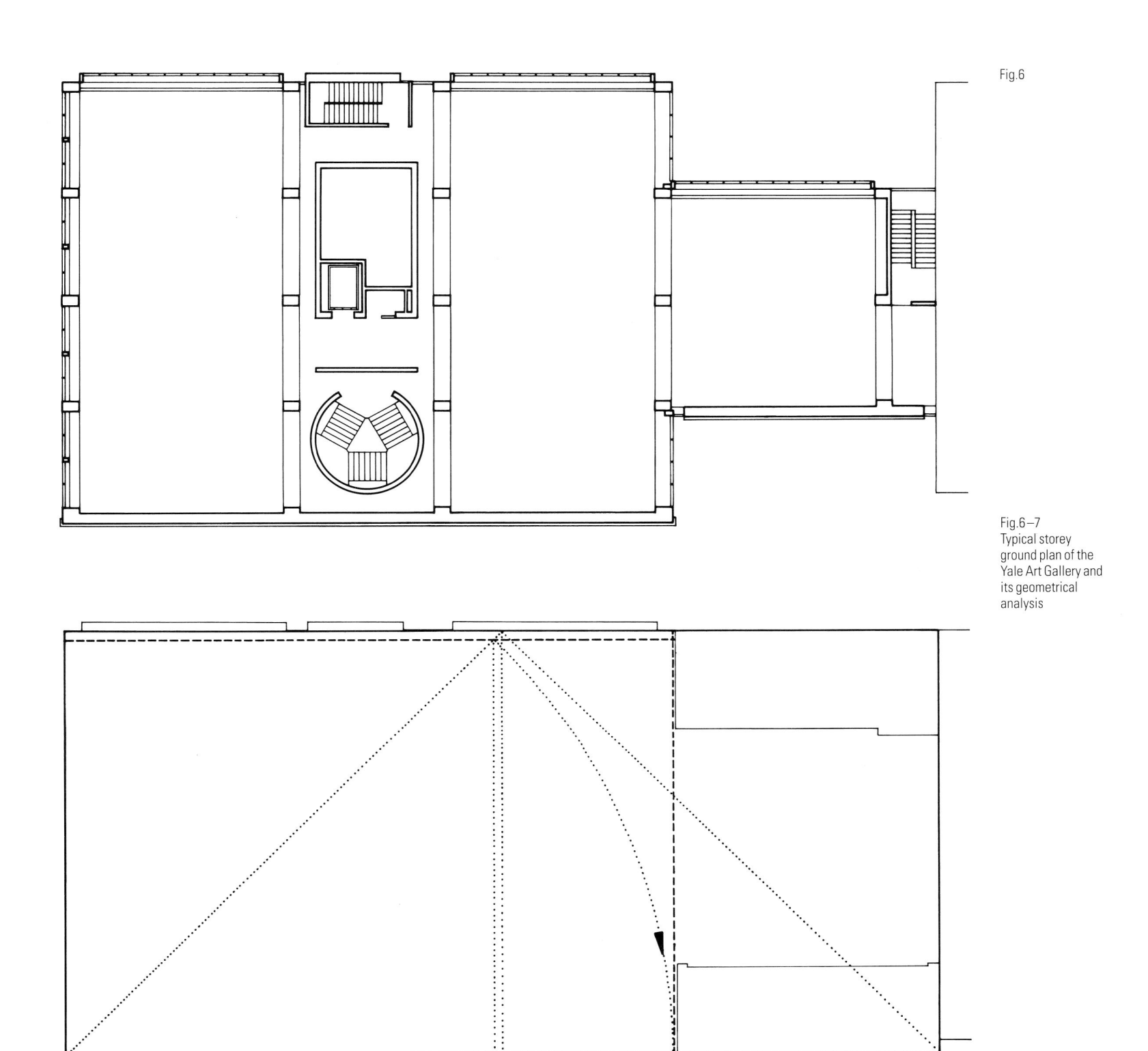

Fig.6–7
Typical storey
ground plan of the
Yale Art Gallery and
its geometrical
analysis

Fig. 7

Bearing point on the "hollow column"

Trenton Bathhouse
1955 Trenton Pennsylvania USA

Fig.8 and 9

Fig.10 and 11

This is not a large building in terms of volume. It is part of a planned but unrealized leisure complex with sports, play and meeting facilities for the "Jewish Community Center" in Ewing Township near Trenton, about 60 km north-east of Philadelphia. It is slightly confusing that it should be called "Bathhouse", as it is in fact only the changing and sanitary area for an adjacent open-air swimming pool; it was designed by Kahn in its final form in April 1955.[21] It consists of four double-axial-symmetrical squares linked by hollow cubic parts; this plan, reminiscent of Jean-Nicolas-Louis Durand's schemes, is so rigid as to reject any "picturesque" composition.

In 1954–55, shortly before the final concept for the Trenton Bathhouse in spring 1955, Kahn had been carrying out experiments in arranging "autonomous units" within ground plans in house projects, which remained unbuilt, for the Adler and Weber-De Vore families, both on the outskirts of Philadelphia; they were structured "freely", in other words not on a grid pattern, and must be seen as crucial preliminary stages.

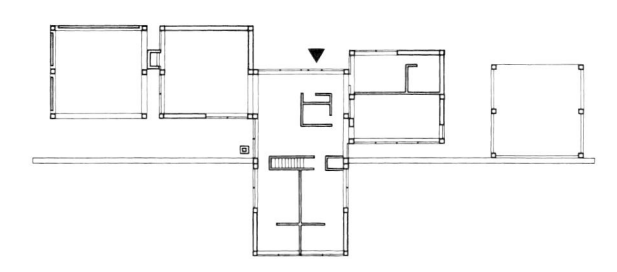

In the case of the Bathhouse, the basic figure is a Greek Cross, and it remains rigid in a way that is unaccustomed and innovative for Kahn in this phase. The ground plan shows five square areas of equal size; they differ in the placing of their dividing walls, which is dependent on the width of the hollow bodies, in order to express different functions: the entrance courtyard, the centre as a meeting-place, a changing and a sanitary area on each of two facing sides and the corridor-hall leading to the swimming pool.

The form seems to have been completely detached from the logic of an "automatic" choice of size and allocation for space resulting from specific functions. Thus for the first time we have concrete evidence that the "form follows function" concept that had imposed functionalism for generations has finally been overcome; the new thinking is realized with extreme consistency in this building, whose spaces define *autonomous entities* of the same kind. The problem of dividing functional areas is solved without creating a "maze"[22] – Kahn's expression for conventional functionalist ground plan arrangements. This building, with its links and the similar pyramid roofings for each unit, emerges as one of the key pieces of innovative architecture of the 20th century.

Vincent Scully describes the Bathhouse as the "starting-point for structural design"[23] in Kahn's work; by "fundamental" significance he obviously does not mean the clearly illustrated structure, but the integration of a constructive and a space-creating structure that in addition creates

Fig.10
Ground floor plan of Weber De Vore House

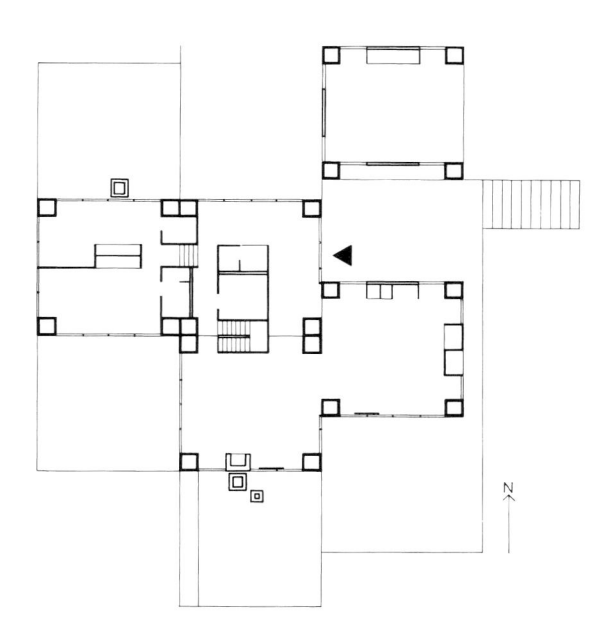

Fig.11
Ground floor plan of Adler House

Model elevation (from: Louis I. Kahn, In the Realm of Architecture, exhibition in the Centre Pompidou, Paris 1992)

[21] Brownlee/De Long, "Louis I. Kahn, In the Realm of Architecture", p. 420.
[22] Richard Saul Wurman, "What will be has always been – The words of Louis I. Kahn", Rizzoli International Publications, New York 1986, p. 130.
[23] "Architecture and Urbanism, Louis I. Kahn", essays, here p. 287; Scully: "Works of Louis I. Kahn and His Method", Tokyo 1975.

Fig.8
Trenton Bathhouse
roof from above

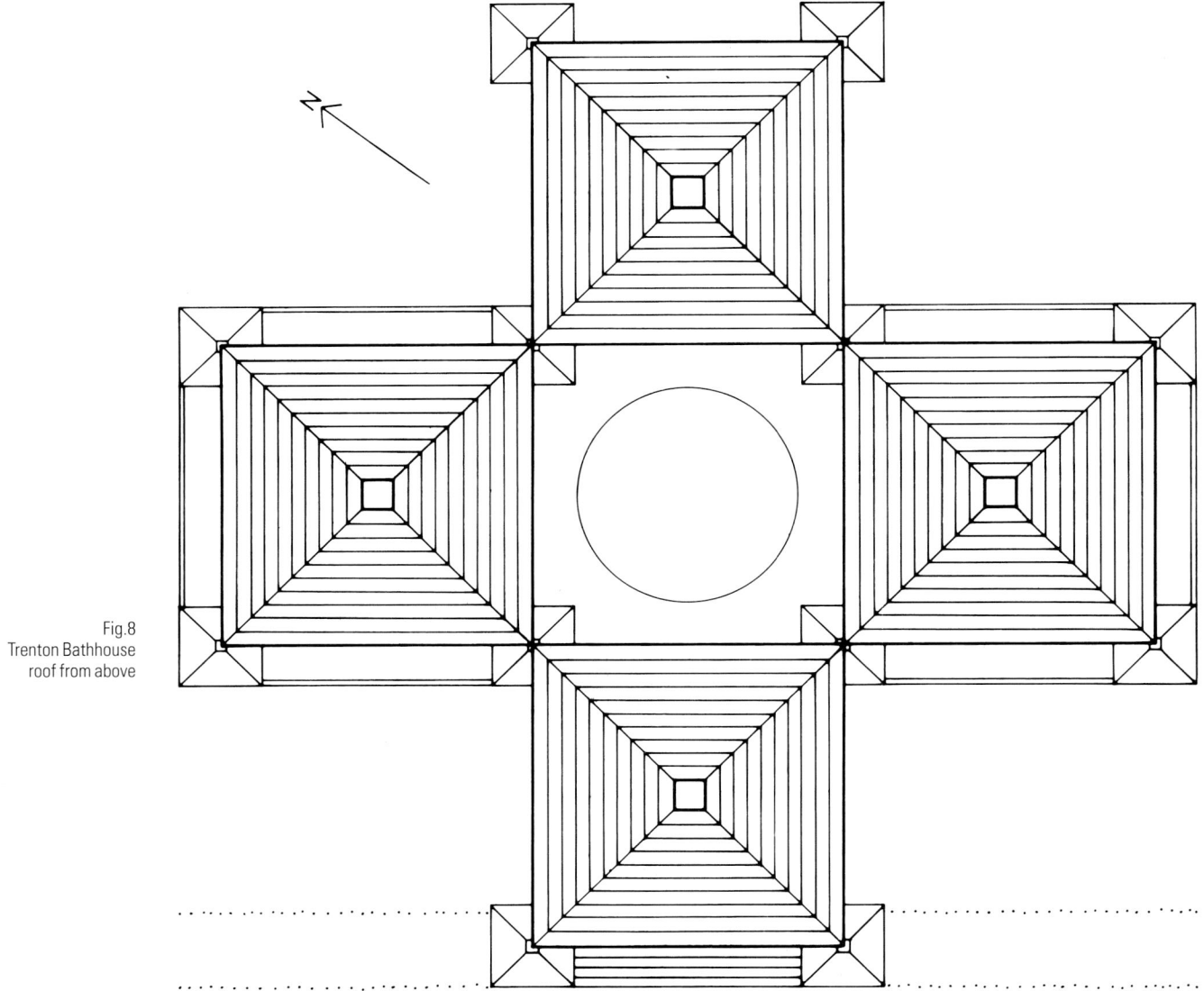

Overall view

30

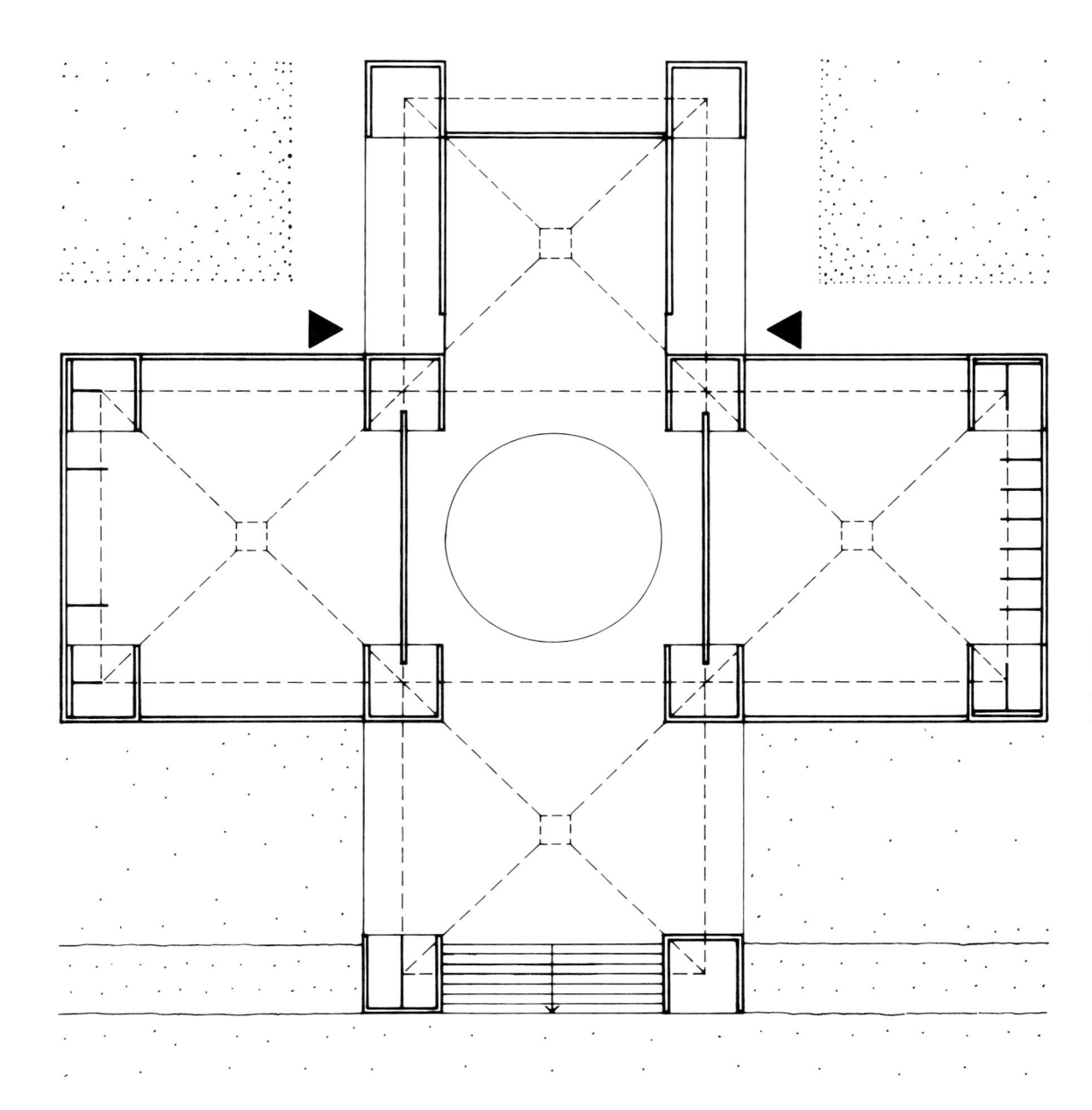

Fig.9
Ground plan of the Trenton Bathhouse with site level difference

View of the entrance to the baths complex

31

order and brings a hierarchy into being, which is to shape all subsequent designs in different ways. A formula that illustrates the hierarchical element particularly well is Kahn's notion of "servant and served spaces". In condensed form, this defines the relationship between subordinate spaces – for services and access areas, for example – and more important spaces, the actual use areas. It appears here in the joint effect of hollow spaces as supports for the roof structure and as an entrance area (servant), and then as the changing area (served). However, despite its subordination, the servant space as access is revalued within the functional context because of its dramatically three-dimensional corporeality, thrusting forward partially at the corners and almost physically dominating. Kahn uses the phrase "hollow column" to describe this. Alexandra Tyng asserts that the practical idea and the phrase "hollow column" date from about 1950, and became a recognizable component of his designs from the time when Kahn was working on the Adath Jeshurun Synagogue in 1954.[24] The concept is first implemented to consolidate the "servant and served" theory in the Trenton Bathhouse.[25]

It remains striking, given their supposedly secondary role, that the "hollow columns" are set in such a stringent grid, with their positions used as markers for the edges of the space. *Thus the existence of the served spaces is evoked only by the servant spaces*. Their thrusting accumulation enhances their presence and thus questions the subordinate nature of the hollow bodies, which is inherent in the servant concept. On the contrary, they seem to dominate because we experience their corporeal quality. Clearly the structure and the two hierarchically defined links between the spaces are completely integrated. It could be said that Kahn allots a servant function to the structure itself. Kahn himself distinguishes between structure that is created "… because you like it …" and applied structure, whose task in the realized architecture is to be clearly demonstrated to the user. He says that structure functions as an element of integration in architecture, even as a stimulus for human activity, whose actions legitimize their value. It follows from this that the quality of architecture can be evaluated only from the interaction of people, space and structure.[26] According to Kahn structure also creates light, creates alternately the columns as negative light and the spaces between them as positive light, and thus "selfishly" enhances itself. It has to relate the light to the chosen space and in the case of a square ground plan, as here in the Bathhouse, provide it with light that makes it a square.

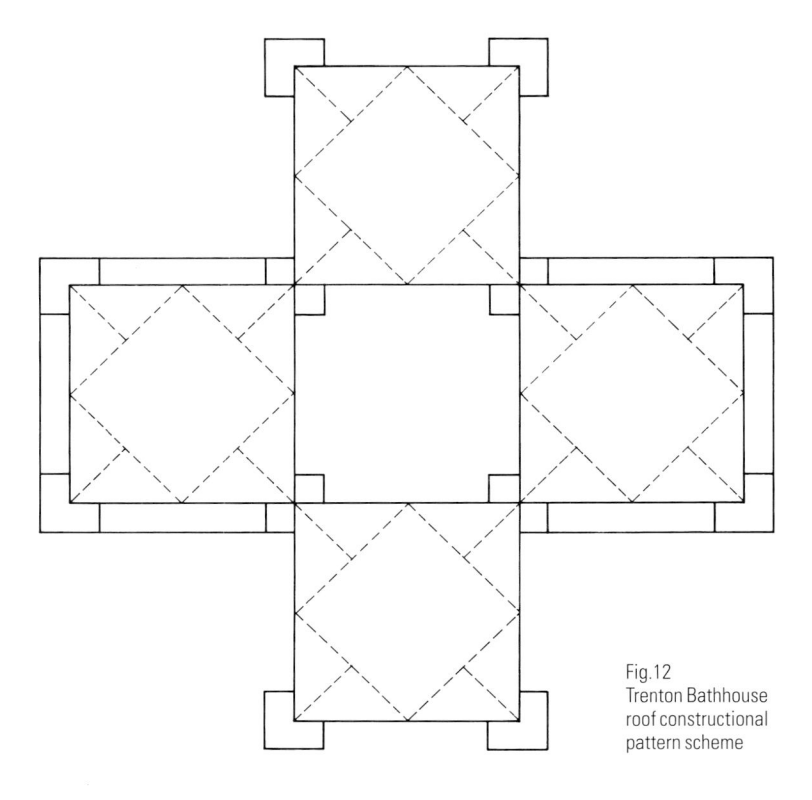

Fig.12
Trenton Bathhouse roof constructional pattern scheme

The shape of the roof, a cumulative entity uniting light-volume and space, is presented succinctly as a truncated pyramid. Surprisingly, it does not cover the functional area in the ground plan, which extends in the first place along the outside wall, but only the centre of the room. This zoning of space is the beginning of the layering of walls that is so important in Kahn's later work, leading to a "space wall" on the periphery of a building and to a "zone of transition" between exterior and interior. In this context the roof pyramid detaches itself and in this independence underlines its symbolic character as a consciously placed "primeval form", which tries to harmonize the unity and totality of the figure as a whole with the simplest possible geometry. Scully asserts that Kahn's visit to Egypt in 1951, which included a visit to the pyramids of Giza, triggered his absolute mastery, that the visit's effects are expressed for the first time here.[27]

The roof top view of this building (figure 8) also shows an element appearing for the first time that is to be found in later designs by Kahn and will have a far-reaching effect. This is the crea-

---

[24] Alexandra Tyng, "Beginnings, Louis I. Kahn's Philosophy of Architecture", Wiley and Sons, New York 1984, p. 35.
[25] Ibid., and Wurman, "What will be …", p. 130.
[26] Wurman, "What will be …", p. 222.
[27] Scully, "Travel Sketches of Louis Kahn", Philadelphia 1978.

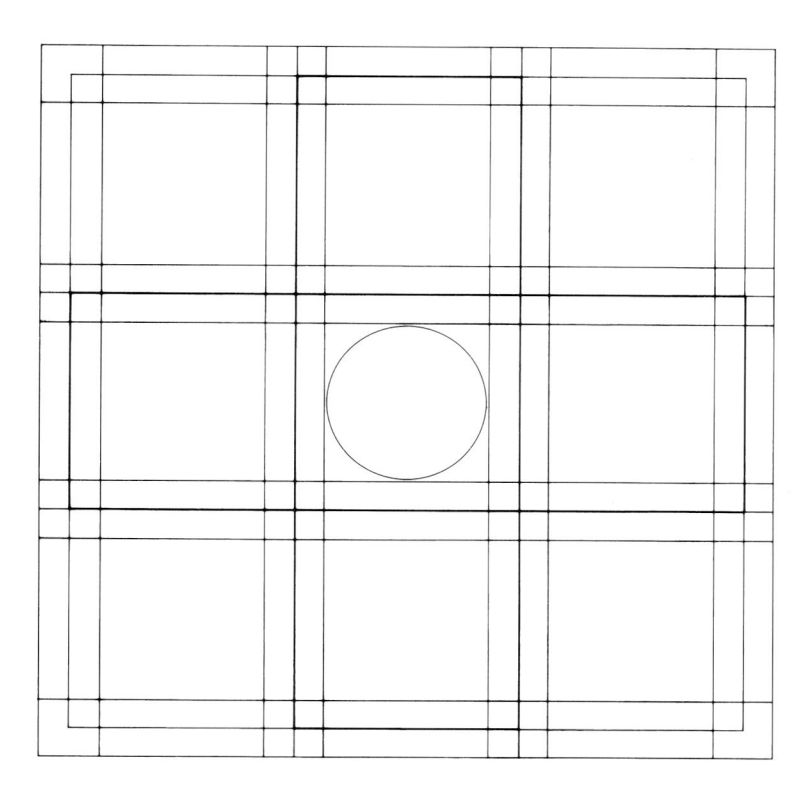

Fig.13
Diagram of the geometrical structure of the Trenton Bathhouse

tion of a *diagonal quality*. Linking the pyramid roof forms automatically generates the diagonal square figure that surrounds the centre, the courtyard square, and indeed "grows" out of it. This "enclosing square" is in direct proportion to the courtyard square and represents the so-called root 2 major proportion, which can be developed simply geometrically and produces a ratio by calculation of 1 : 1.414.

This is the point at which the diagonal quality begins to assert itself in Kahn's design, from here he uses it quite consciously. Seen from below, there are diagonal framing spars in the pyramid roofs, which serve to strengthen the pyramid frame and are additionally joined to it via the corners. Inscribing squares into more squares in a diagonal arrangement, in other words reducing, or vice versa an outer frame of squares as an enlargement is first used in Kahn's work in the Trenton Bathhouse. The root 2 proportion associated with this figuration is particularly worthy of mention; as a pre-existing set position it embodies one of the most important ordering principles in subsequent designs, and is thus a key element in Kahn's rational design principles.

Fig.12

This structure is apparently simple at a first glance, but in fact astonishingly complex. When looking at the *ambivalence* of the figurative appearance of the unity of form in both space and roof and its hollow bodies forming column and space, reference has to be made to Hans Sedlmayr's methodical approach to *Strukturanalyse* (analysis ot the structure).[28]

Sedlmayr uses Borromini's San Carlo alle Quattro Fontane as an example to describe selective seeing, which dissects the building as a whole in order to understand the *structure* on which the architecture is based. The core of this kind of *Strukturanalyse* is a process, akin to plan analysis, of dissecting architecture into component figures and their role within the whole. When dissecting the Bathhouse it is striking that the central hollow bodies of the columns assembled under the pyramid roof that draws them together do not just belong to a particular unit in each case, but also to the adjacent one. This linking blurs the unambiguity of unity; the component figure "hollow column" acquires a dual significance and isolates itself on this basis almost as a "third" figure. This element is defined by Sedlmayr as *Doppelstruktur* (double structure) and by Rudolf Wittkower as *Doppelfunktion* (double function).[29] The impression of a dual function for the central hollow

[28] Hans Sedlmayr, "Gestaltetes Sehen", essay 1925, in: "Belvedere 8" magazine. Also: Sedlmayr, "Die Architektur Borrominis", Olms Verlag, Hildesheim 1986, pp. 17–38.
[29] Rudolf Wittkower, "Das Problem der Bewegung innerhalb der manieristischen Architektur", Art-Historical Institute of Florence, no. C 1109 q (made available by Harmen Thies).

bodies is reinforced by two equal square zones, obviously belonging to and opposite each other and with the same function. One is for the access units, the other for the changing units. Thus differing adjacent squares, each to be ascribed to a different unit category, are linked via the "third" figure. Wittkower defines the dual function of a component figure, its ambiguity, as a *Bewegungsmoment* (movement element):[30] the intended combination of parts within an apparently rigid architectural structure suggests dynamics and its inherent condition of indecisiveness is to be described as "unstable".

As an expression of unstable movement, double function is a fundamental characteristic of Mannerist form-finding. For this reason, even in this early design by Kahn it is clear that he is striving for Mannerist principles. The architecture of the Trenton Bathhouse itself, with its parts, without rhythm, the same in size and spaced on an equal grid, is not a direct expression of movement. But the empty centre *(axis mundi)* with the circular marking on the floor could be interpreted as the centre of a group of figures rotating regularly around it. However, even this suggestive rotation is brought under control: at the entrance to the swimming-pool the building is connected firmly to the ground at a break in the terrain, it is anchored between two columns by the steps. The Bathhouse stands as a centred, almost autonomous figure, not randomly placed within the terrain, but growing into its surroundings in a position that can be seen as carefully related to the community centre that was originally planned.

Kahn becomes aware of the importance of the complex concept "structure" in completing this building. In this sense, structure develops with great variety but as a constant in the subsequent work, always following the principal thrust of the design brief. This, combined with the pair of concepts "servant and serving space", has "generative force"[31] for Kahn, and this can be seen in every building that he later designed.

Fig.13 The figure of the greatest possible integration of structure and form makes up the almost diagrammatic scheme of the basis for the Trenton Bathhouse. It shows a square divided into nine, its blurring, framing peripheral zone and traces of cruciform overlapping. It thus becomes clear that it is not the cross that brings the structure into being, but the square, as the figure that binds the whole building together with its positive and negative areas, in other words the zones that are with and without building on them. The empty centre is to be seen in the context of the four surrounding empty areas at the corners, and immediately invokes the scheme represented as an "ordering image" of figurative geometry that is not immediately perceptible, but definitely present. It is, as will be explained in greater detail later, related to the Indian image of contemplation and means the integration of the perceptible and the not immediately perceptible world, called the *mandala*.

Main entrance

[30] Ibid.
[31] Wurman, "What will be ...", p. 130.

View of the inner zone

Detail view of the joint between hollow column and bordering wall

Ventilation shafts
in the rear section
of the building

**Alfred Newton Richards Medical Research Building/David Goddard Laboratories
1957–64 Philadelphia Pennsylvania USA**

Fig.14   Kahn started to design the Medical Research Building on the University of Pennsylvania campus in Philadelphia in 1957; it was completed in 1961; the biological research facilities were added later and completed in 1964. For this commission Kahn once more – similarly to the Trenton design – groups independent, double-axially symmetrical, square units containing the actual laboratories around a central supply building with a square core and adjacent secondary uses. In the subsequent phase he added, on the axis of one laboratory unit, two more, slightly differing square units for the so-called "Goddard Laboratories" for biological research with a separate access and sanitary unit attached. The main entrance to the medical laboratories is in a raised empty storey, and is accessible by diagonal stairs and a short ramp, while access to the biology building is via a dip below its first laboratory tower.

In contrast with the Trenton Bathhouse design, supporting elements are not related to the corners of a unit: the load is carried by two supports at each of the points along a third of the length of one side. The intention is to make the corners seem particularly weightless as cantilever structures, so that the spatial conclusion can be executed transparently in glass. The units are surrounded in their axes by side rooms or side areas for access and services. Their isolated position has to be defined as "added", as the integration of construction and servant building section as in the Bathhouse was consciously rejected. They stand in front of the laboratory building in emphatic independence; their secondary nature is visually unclear because of the way they are massed and their height: they rise well above the labs.

The servant towers in the Medical Research Building are derived from the hollow columns of the Bathhouse; here they lose their original load-bearing function and now exist as independent figures. Alexandra Tyng takes this as a reason for extending the principle of the hollow column to all components of the design, and even declares that the laboratory building itself is a hollow column.[32]

In the ground plan, which is reconstructed here for the first time from documents in the Kahn Collection in Philadelphia, we see the difficulty of dividing up the spatial depth of the proposed lab squares, which were intended for open-plan use, in a functionally meaningful way. Kahn did not feel that this was particularly significant, as the rooms were planned as units for flexible use.

Overall view within the University of Pennsylvania site with Philadelphia's industrial area in the background

The ground plan of the labs shown here comes from Kahn's office and shows an asymmetrically arranged system of corridors that questions the centred figure of the square and creates a conventional system of offices on either side of a corridor.

The service towers, formally different appropriately to their function, are also clear in the ground plan as quasi autonomous units. But there are inconsistencies: there is an additional vertical access system within the central section of the building, consisting of staircase and lifts; it is not identified independently, even though it "serves". Also, the different dimensions of the service towers by the labs with larger staircases and smaller ventilation shafts is called into question by a large shaft element corresponding to the size of the steps at the link-point with the biological section. In fact, in the ground plan in general the heterogeneous nature of the linking elements, from the central medical research section down to the access tower at the end of the biology laboratory, seems to blur the focus and logic of the original concept without extension. But when one looks at the disposition of the buildings in the realized architecture the different functional areas are still intelligible and the form of the connecting elements is comprehensible. Here we are particularly struck by Kahn's ability not to let the two parts of the design fall apart, but ultimately to develop them as a unit. The "wholeness" of the composition of the buildings is achieved by using the same kind of element with slight variations, and also by geometrical structure and careful attention to their proportions.

In the general plan,[33] the way in which the extension buildings for the biology labs are inte-   Fig.15

---

[32] A. Tyng, "Beginnings", p. 37.
[33] This analysis of the Richards and Goddard Laboratories is based on a seminar by the author at the Institute of Building History at the Technical University, Braunschweig in 1991, together with the Institute for Architectural Design Prof. Ostertag, with P. Teicher, using results arrived at by Jochen Brinkmann and Henning Pohl, who were students at the time.

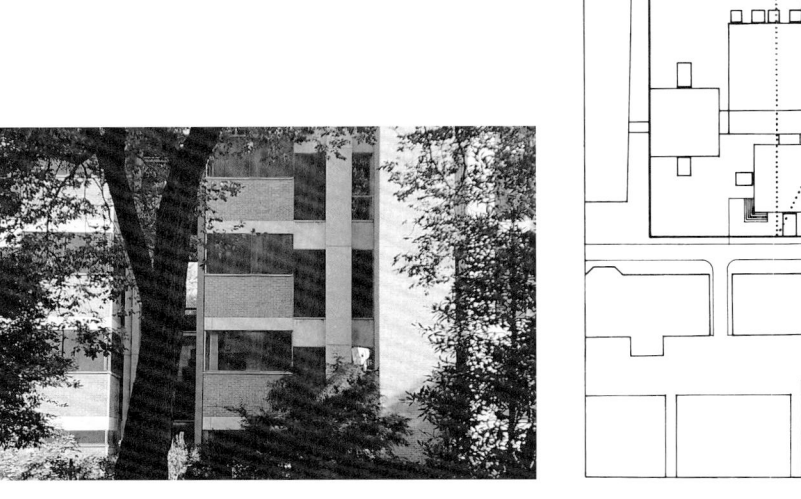

Façade detail in the biology labs

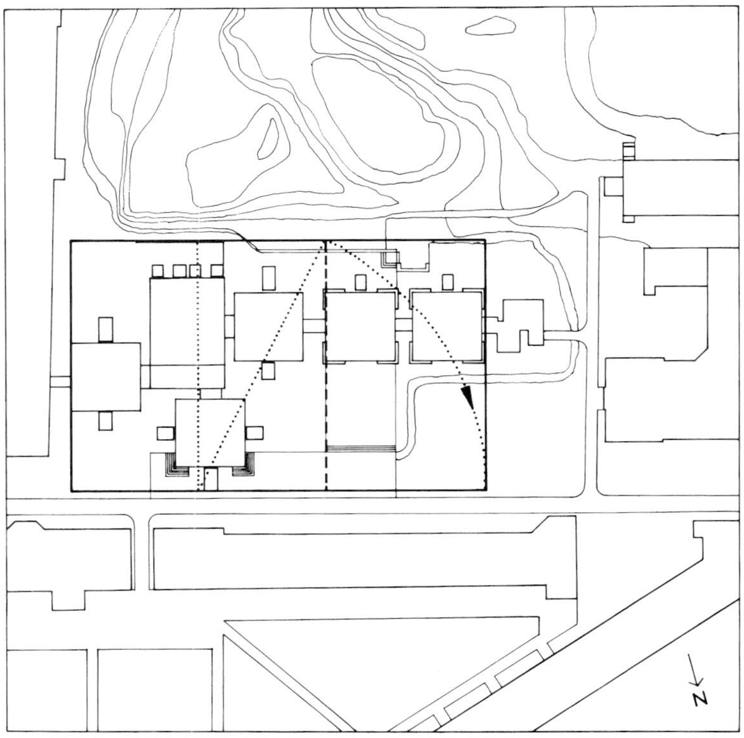

Fig.15
General plan of the Richards and Goddard Laboratories with their framing geometry

Laboratory tower with stairwell

Façade detail with biology labs as connecting elements

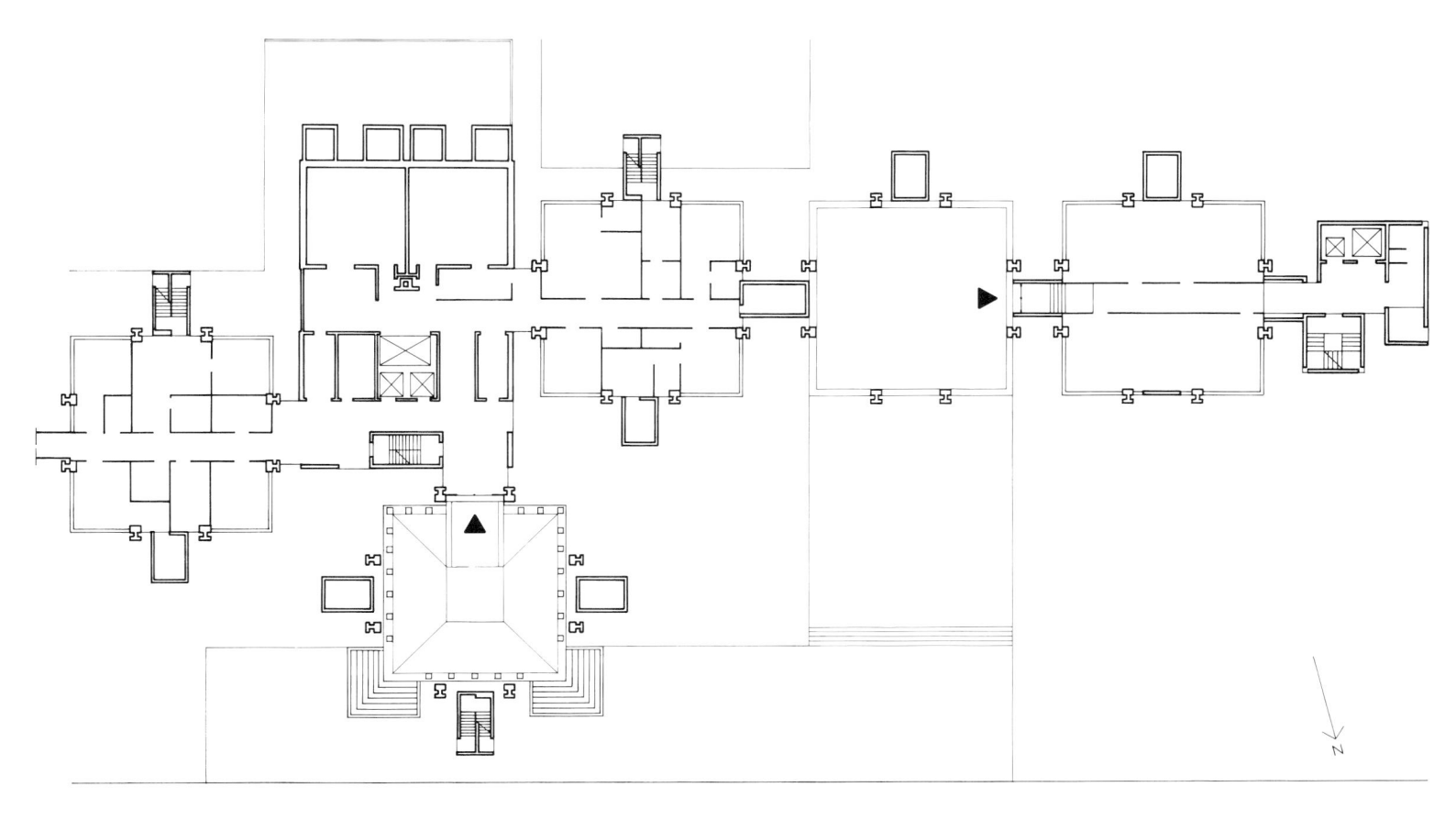

Fig. 14
Ground floor plan of the Richards and Goddard Laboratories

View of the medical laboratories in the background with the biology laboratories on the right

grated is shown with the aid of geometry: the closed "system" of laboratory squares "circling" around a centre is inscribed within an enclosing square, a *frame*. This is the defined starting-point for the design. The extension buildings, which were added during the detailed design phase for this figure, are now tied into a frame that extends in the same way. Here, as can be seen from the general plan, the key is the geometrical construction called the Golden Section,[34] which is developed from the square enclosing the medical laboratories. This framing square forms the initial figure for the proportionally bound extension: the diagonal of half the square is projected by arc on to the lower extended line. The point of intersection produced defines the new Golden Section frame for the figure as a whole.

The right-hand edge of this rectangle marks the boundary of the biology building and fixes the ratio of longitudinal to transverse dimensions for the laboratory buildings in the figure as a whole. As the extension buildings need ventilation shafts only in the rear section the length of their connecting element remains flexible. Thus all parts of the overall design can be fitted into the framing geometry quite effortlessly. These framing figures represent an important ordering principle in Kahn's architecture.

Structure and construction are integrated in the laboratory buildings, whose supporting columns by the service shafts – like tree-trunks – carry tapering cantilever arms as "branches" and shape the appearance of the façade. Thus it is possible to speak of something that is unique in its expressive force within Kahn's *œuvre*: a *structure* that entirely determines, indeed *creates* the form. The detachment of the servant sections is additionally underlined by narrow concrete bands in the joints next to the supports. Kahn's consultant engineer, August Komendant, helped the structure to make this dominant effect, and spoke of an "significant innovation in the construction of multistory concrete buildings using precast members",[35] while critics gave credit to the "truthful" overall appearance of the building: Moholy-Nagy called it an "archetype" that exudes "the inspiration of a pure conscience",[36] Peter and Alison Smithson recognize "meaningful order of spaces, meaningful order of structure",[37] Huxtable senses that it expressed "honesty, integrity, trust" [38] and Giurgola sees its as architecture that has the sense of permanency and of newness.[39]

The material structure of concrete and brickwork as material that is absorbing forces and providing covering can be called a *composite order*, which appears intelligibly in the façade and vividly demonstrates that form is determined by structure. At the same time, a dramatic quality is lent to the mutually defining relation of hierarchically determined sections of the building. This relation should be seen as an interpretative reaction to the existing buildings, whose brickwork and light natural stone set the tone for the site. These surrounding buildings date from the previous

Round-the-corner glazing in the biology labs

century; they are student accommodations, with three storeys and six storeys at the corners. They play in a variety of ways with combinations of an irregular, "romantic" brick, dark red to bluish black, as was customary at the time, and contrasting window reveals, framed gables, articulating mouldings for the different storeys and decorative elements in light natural stone. The precise, smoothly cut, dark red brick of the laboratory building and the light concrete certainly accept the particular qualities of the place, but make the ensemble look independent.

[34] The note is at the end of the book on p. 196.
[35] August E. Komendant, "18 Years with Architect Louis I. Kahn", Aloray Publisher, Englewood, USA, 1975, p. 19.
[36] Moholy-Nagy, "The future of the past", in: Perspecta 7, The Yale Architectural Journal, Yale University, New Haven 1961.
[37] Peter und Alison Smithson, "Louis Kahn", in: Architects Yearbook no. 9, 1960.
[38] Ada Louise Huxtable in: The New York Times, 1970, quoted by: Susan Braudy, "The Architectural Metaphysics of Louis Kahn", in: The New York Times Magazine, 15 Nov. 1970, p. 92.
[39] Romaldo Giurgola, "Giurgola on Kahn", in: American Institute of Architects Journal, Washington, August 1982.

Window detail in the medical labs

The laboratory towers in the context of the neighbouring buildings

Ventilation shafts

The cumulative chain of laboratory towers leaves each unit as an isolated structure connected to the centre by a glazed corridor, and surrounded by its "servants". And then the fact that the storeys of the laboratories are equal in height, and that the towers are of the same height as the central building, as already described, draws all the parts together into a homogenous whole.

Fig.16 Despite the accumulation of figures of the same kind the composition does not seem rigid: unlike the double axial symmetry of the Trenton Bathhouse the parts are linked asymmetrically around a centre, and the figure of the Medical Research Building is itself set in *motion*. Bound into the framing geometry of an embracing square formed by the edges of the buildings and the boundary of a rear delivery yard, the "windmill sails" seem to "rest" in their position. And yet centrifugal forces give an impression of turning and evoke a lively fluctuation in the various parts, especially from the point of view of strolling passers-by. This is reinforced by the different depths of the masonry-clad service towers, whose functions are clearly illustrated on the outside: either as a longer stairwell volume with parallel wall slabs as an upper conclusion with a "true" concrete core visible on the inside, or as a service shaft. The movement described as rotation is once more "braked", with the concluding wall slabs remaining parallel. The linear biology wing also cancels the dynamics of the volume of the first building phase.

Fig.17 It is clear that Kahn does not just choose a square frame to establish the dimensions of the figure, but develops all parts of the design within a grid. This is an 8 foot grid, which defines the outline of the central building and its rear towers, the laboratory areas and the linking corridors, but also all important interior wall positions.

In his design for the Richards Building, Kahn holds without exception to the general grid, as this scheme shows; this is not the case in his later designs. The grid still dictates the design as a corset-like ordering structure. Deviations and conscious breaks that create complexity are merely hinted at and develop only in subsequent years. But there is a large number of contradictions: served main sections of the laboratories, the "primary figures" of the chosen hierarchy, have broken corners, which make them seem immaterial and transparent, and yet their glazed areas, flush on the outside, do suggest a certain immaterial corporeality with their reflections. In contrast with this we have serving "secondary figures" that are heavy and solid, towering well above the laboratories, so that the linking of former contrasting pairs causes inner tension and poses questions about actual primary and secondary figures. This impression is reinforced when looking at the laboratories by their corners: they are edged with supporting columns, which isolate them as almost independent bodies and make them seem "humbly" second-rank and low between the soaring brick towers, while the glass corners of the biology wing rise vertically as gravity-resisting dynamic figures. If the labs are considered on the diagonal only, a broken symmetry can be discerned because of the differences in the flanking service sections. The interplay of symmetry and asymmetry is extremely subtly and powerfully expressed on the rear side of the central brick volume: the four ventilation and service shafts that are blended into the rear wall of the central volume are of *unequal* width, following a scarcely perceptible rhythm of a-b-a-b, working against the first impression of clear centring, and forming overlapping symmetrical figures in the relation of a to a and b to b. But in terms of the function of the interior spaces a1 belongs to b1 and a2 to b2, so that there are clear multiple links between these four elements, and unrest – in other words movement – and insecurity soften the rigidity of the symmetry. Here in particular Kahn's interest in the *contrast of a form swinging between rest and movement* becomes obvious and comprehensible.

Fig.18 A figure that is very similar to the Trenton Bathhouse scheme can be seen in the construction diagram of a laboratory tower. The main double-crossing Vierendeel support structure 16 feet apart directs the forces outwards and creates a support-free interior. In between are the secondary elements, also cruciform and constructed in the same way. An edge beam with tapering cantilever arms (tree branches), invoking the succinct façade figure, frames the square. But we should not concentrate on structural peculiarities here, even though the Richards Medical Research Building is the realized structure by Kahn most impressively determined by construction. We should note that Figure 18 once more represents a square divided into nine, and this, reaching far beyond structural requirements, embodies for Kahn the abstract, universal *integration symbol* for all essential aspects of architecture.

Fig.16

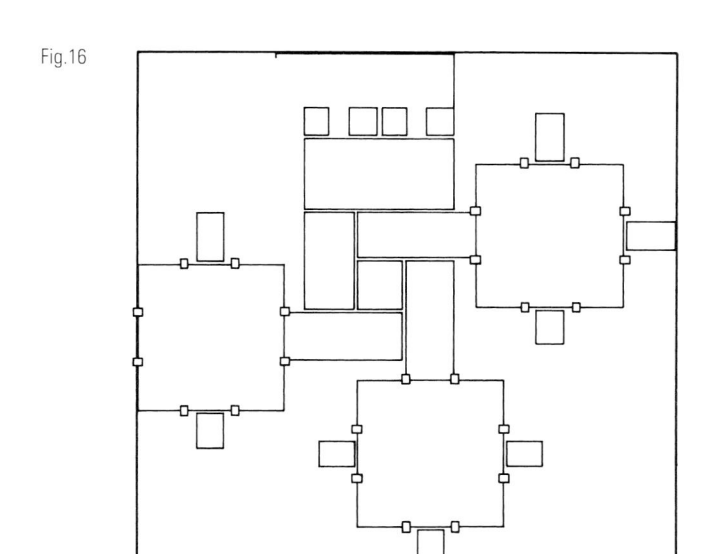

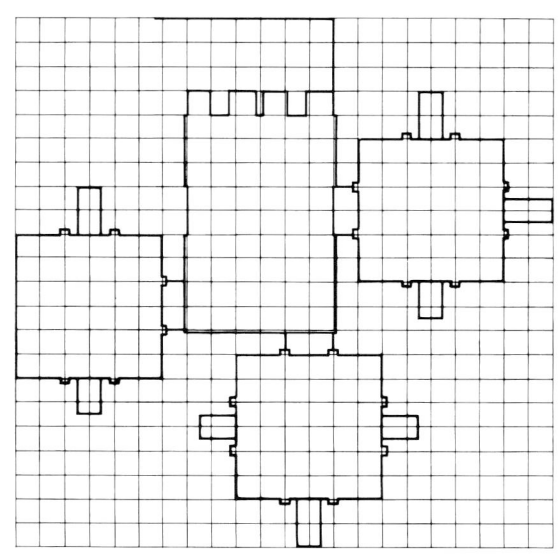

Fig.17

Fig.18

Fig.16–17
Analysis of the geometrical structure of the Richards Laboratories

Fig.18
Constructional pattern of a floor plan element

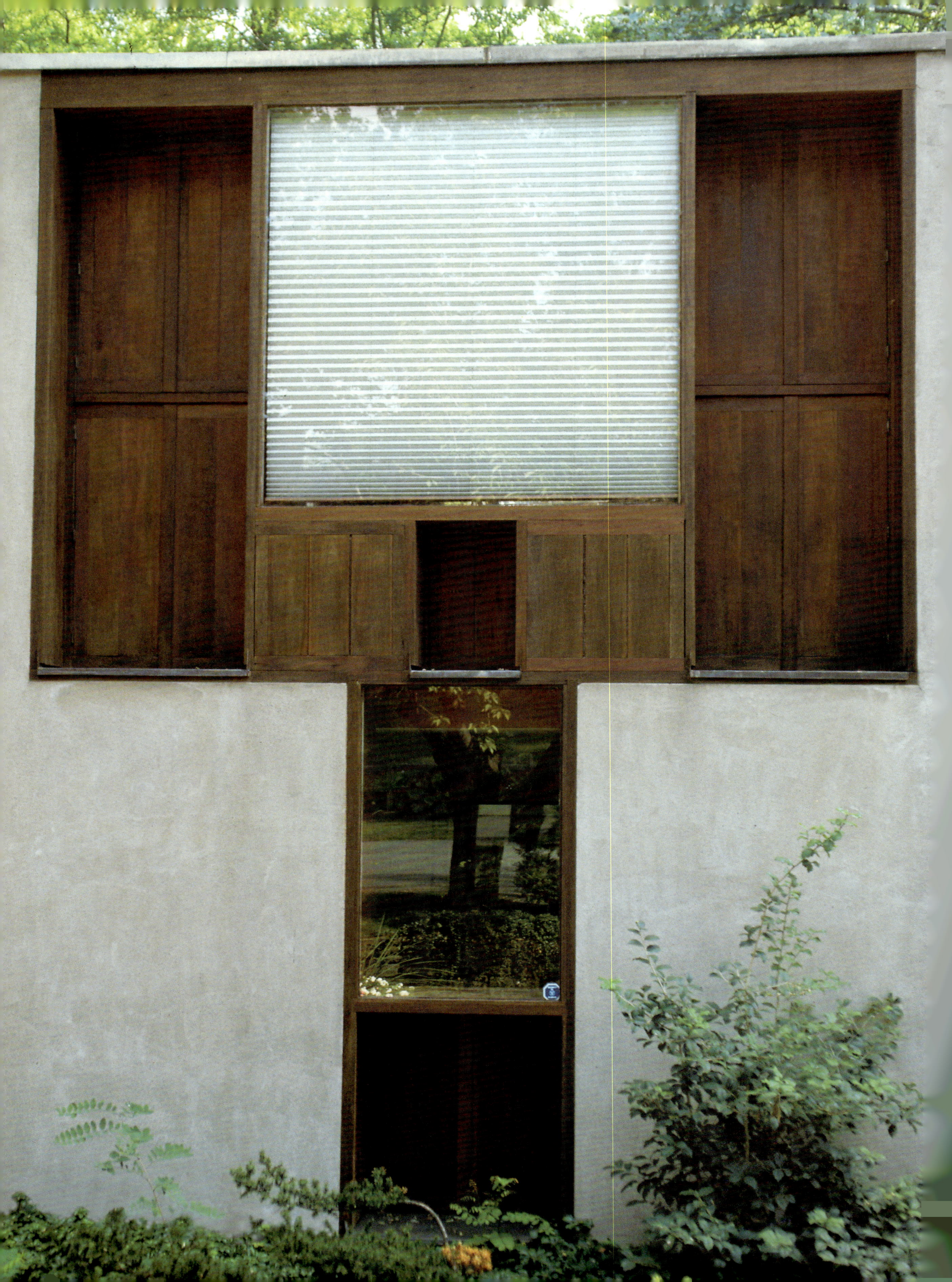

Margaret Esherick House
1959–61 Philadelphia Pennsylvania USA

Kahn's first really significant private house developed from his own typical language dates from a period of many commissions, 1959 to 1961. It was in Chestnut Hill, a residential quarter of Philadelphia, and was commissioned by Mrs. Margaret Esherick, who required a house in which to live on her own. She in fact lived in it for only a few years, and then sold it.

Fig.19 The design envisages a rectangular, block-like building whose longitudinal axis runs parallel to the access road. The entrance side is kept relatively closed, while the garden façade has generous openings. The ground plan is divided into three, following the functional hierarchy of the rooms: a two-storey living-room, then the dining-room on the ground floor, bedrooms upstairs and adjacent in the upper storey the "service block" with kitchen, side-rooms and bathroom. Later owners of the house added an additional dividing wall between the entrance and eating areas, thus blurring Kahn's original concept. The first striking feature is that Kahn did not divide the building unambiguously in this design, in the manner celebrated in the Richards Building, but fused the main and the subsidiary space together in an ambiguous relationship. Here we can see some rethinking by Kahn: he was no longer primarily concerned to accumulate units in a way that is clearly demonstrated in the structure, but is concerned to relate corporeal elements to each other with a complexity and ambiguity that respond to a higher order. This is a radical change in Kahn's work which was to have a far-reaching effect on all subsequent designs. The fact that the inherent geometrical structure is more complex here than in previous designs and that Kahn formulates his perception of "order" more comprehensively will be the main component of the analysis that follows.[40]

It is possible to discern symmetrical axes both in the ground plan and the views, and yet the different parts upon which symmetry has been imposed lose their "striving for autonomy". They are firmly blended into the building as a whole, but their "desire" for independence remains a latent presence: two indentations, like notches, mark the entrances and divide the living-room from middle-ranking rooms, producing two zones of equal size following an axis. These indentations are corporeal structures, independent spaces, *hollow volumes* that seem to be borrowed from the hollow columns of the Trenton Bathhouse. They could be called negative hollow columns, and in their entrance function "serve" the adjacent main rooms. The complex structure of the design is revealed when this service figure is integrated into the outline of the main rooms, so that both division and connection are illustrated. The subsidiary kitchen and bathroom zone remains an independent element despite being integrated, especially because of the clearly outlined contour, again providing visual separation, of the windows in the rear façade – a contradictory contrast.

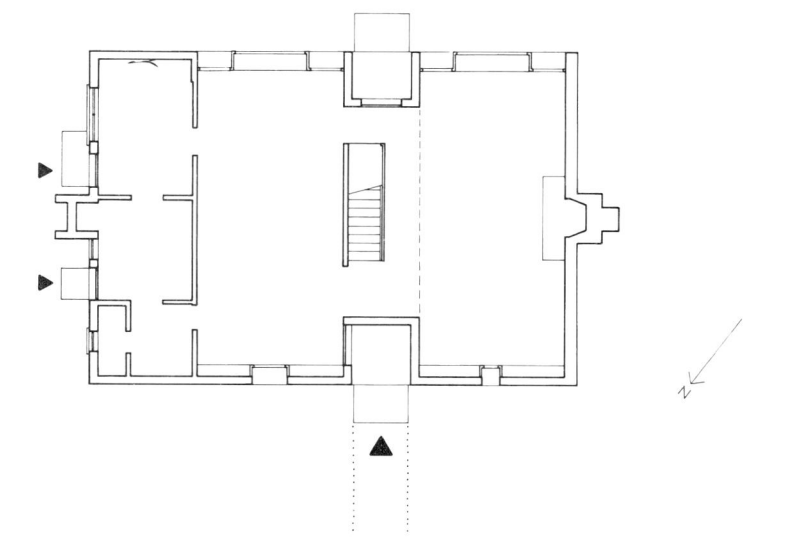

Window in the entrance façade

Fig.19
Ground floor plan of Esherick House

View from the main access road

[40] This is based on copies of the original working plans from the "Louis I. Kahn Collection" in Philadelphia and Ronner/Jahveri's "Louis I. Kahn – Complete Work 1935–1974", Basel/Boston 1987.

As we have already seen in the Trenton Bathhouse, the periphery of the building increasingly emerges as a complex element in Kahn's work. Here Kahn's concern to give the exterior wall a sculpted quality conveyed by two spatial layers is revealed. Protrusion and indentation within a dimension that is fixed and defined in the geometry of the design becomes a driving force behind the design. In the Esherick House this zone acquires a definite material quality: it is not made of solid stone, but of "soft" wood. The wood curves to and fro like a membrane, largely filled with glass, and creating a close relationship between the interior and exterior space by means of the light-modulated transition zone. This sculpting effect also helps to integrate the component figures, which tend otherwise to be separated by the hollow entrance bodies; thus the clear division is blurred.

Entrance façade

A varied and yet constant T-motif can be seen in the entrance façade. It is not just the window figures that are developed as formations of this kind: the metal banister on the upper floor, which is unusually filigree for Kahn's work, is also T-shaped. Even the concrete roofs over the entrance areas can be interpreted as T-shapes lying on their sides, as Kahn maintains their legibility in the surface of the rendering. The T-window has an entirely functional reason, as the narrow slit shape of the lower part is a protection against unwelcome peering-in from public areas. While the left-hand window element clearly reflects the division into two storeys, the very tall slit in the living area "explains" that this can only be a single-storey room. The "window shutters", in other words lighting flaps, allude to the 1947 Weiss House with its sliding wooden panels to regulate the incidence of light, while the rendered cubes with their tall walls without an upper conclusion, in which the timber sectioning provides darker areas, are reminiscent of the motif of the Richards staircase towers with their walls that also thrust up at the sides.

Scully[41] was quick to recognize the window set at the edge of the ceiling and characterizing the whole short side of the living-room as Kahn's intention to "fill the room to the brim with light". The transverse window is probably to be seen as a ceiling reflection light, bathing the ceiling in daylight as another "façade" for the room and emphasizing the limiting area of the high, narrow room, in other words its proportions. There is also a possible stimulus from the work of Le Corbusier, whose 1926 Villa Cook also had a transverse window set at the edge of the ceiling with a narrow, central, vertical window below it.

Positioning these windows within different volumes sounds a new theme in Kahn's work: *similar, but differing component figures are juxtaposed*, working in the same direction. The result of these considerations is a consciously introduced unrest when looking at the façade. Linking the two symmetrical component figures with an asymmetrical overall building causes *movement* for the eye. In the entrance façade the T-windows seem to rise or fall within the static mass of the building, while the different width of the cubes suggests horizontal shifts, supported by different distances from the relevant main volume of the building for the two fireplaces flanking the short sides.

The following analytical sequence, using the plan analysis method described above, reveals the geometrical system that orders the design. In parallel with purely intuitive development it binds all design considerations into a rational structure. Ideas that are still vague, sketched by hand, become fixed *figures* translated into measurements and numbers, presented proportionally, in other words as ratios. These squares or rectangles that can be understood geometrically and arithmetically, determine the whole structure of the building and show Kahn's intention to apply universally valid principles of geometrical form-finding to his designs. It is also possible to show that these figures are interdependent, so that the *system of figurative geometry* leads to an original figure, which in the case of Kahn is usually expressed as a square.

---

[41] Scully, Vincent, "Louis I. Kahn", from the series "Architects of Today", New York 1962.

Window figures on
the entrance side

Corner view with
openings and fireplace on the short
side with kitchen
entrance

Overall view of the
garden side

Here the *genesis* of the ground plan in terms of its rational principles is to be developed, thus arriving step by step at the complete ground plan. The analysis is based on the reconstructed ground floor plan for the original concept of Esherick House.

Window figures on the garden side with entrance and balcony

Window detail on the garden side

Fig.20   The starting-point of the design is a square. It forms the exterior line of the left-hand boundary wall and the distance – relating to the drawing – between the upper and lower internal lines of the long walls.

Fig.21   The diagonal of the square is used by simple geometrical construction to form the radius of an arc of a circle that cuts the extension of the lower side of the square. This intersection point can be used to form a new rectangle whose short side is in a ratio of 1 : 1.414 of the long side. Its 1 to root 2 proportion will further prove its importance within Kahn's work. For reasons of simplification a rectangle of this kind will be called simply a "root 2 rectangle" or a "root 2 figure". This new rectangle is shifted to the right out of the prescribed dimension by the thickness of a wall defined by constructional requirements. The particular significance of the right-hand side of the initial square will be more fully explained in the next step.

Fig.22   The entire interior outline of surrounding walls of the building is defined by the position found by the shifted root 2 rectangle. This outline is a kind of frame, which as a set position fixes the disposition of the component figures. And yet the outlines of both the inner and outer walls are equally significant for the following developmental stages.
The above-mentioned right-hand edge of the initial square defines wall lines for indentations that provide access on each side, but it is also the line of the borders of the two-storey living-room with its gallery above. This line translated into built architecture is an unambiguous indication of the existence of the original square.

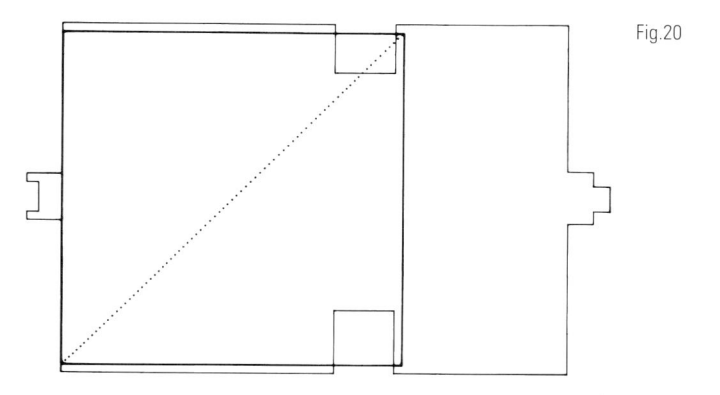

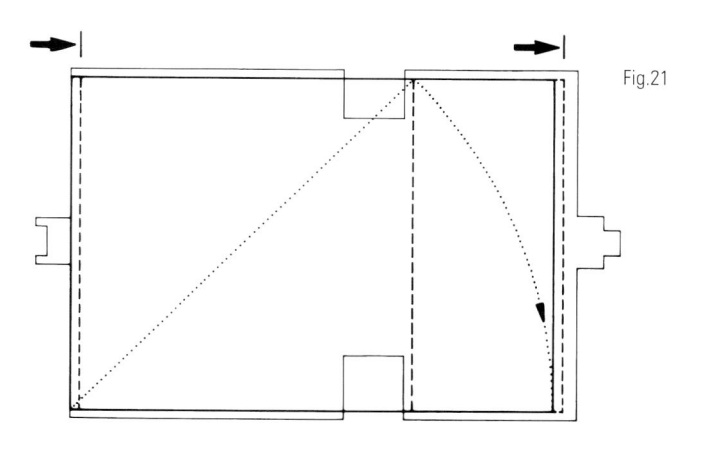

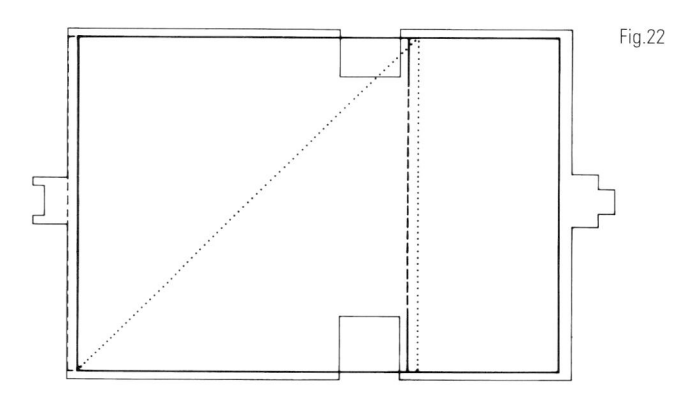

Fig.20–22
Ground plan analysis of Esherick House with a square as starting figure

Fig.23 A new proportional rectangular format defines crucial ground plan positions: a further rectangle can be inscribed using the left exterior wall outline to start the square, the right interior wall outline as root 2 border from the previous step and the newly applied exterior wall in the given dimension on the lower longitudinal side. Dividing it into the square on the left and the narrow rectangle on the right determines an axial position that fixes the width of the access indentations. Dividing the rectangle shows its geometrical structure: an arc of a circle is drawn with the diagonals of half the square to the extension of the lower square outline, similarly to the root 2 construction. The ratio of short side to long side of the rectangle created by this point of intersection is known as the Golden Section and is another extraordinarily important proportional figure in Kahn's work. It can be described by the irrational ratio value of 1 : 1.618 and has already appeared in a framing figure in the Richards Buildings (see Figure 15).

The right-hand line of the stairs in the upper storey is then fixed with this axis. Finally, the upper outline of the Golden Section frame fixes the boundary of the garden entrance indentation depth.

Fig.24 The axis from the Golden Section construction is a crucial element for determining the main rooms. It is a mirror axis of the living area, which has already been clearly outlined; its line is now transferred precisely to the left-hand side and identifies the entrance area and the dining-room or the bedroom area in the upper storey. The mirrored line marks the room wall's inner outline as a border with the side-room zone, the service-block.

Square dimensions describe the indentation for the main entrance and also the upper staircase border in relation to the axis and the garden entrance.

Fig.25 Square figures are generated within the symmetrical room areas, and they fix the dimensions of the double-walled window zones, in other words their depth, in relation to the exterior outline. They are produced with the aid of the horizontal symmetrical axis and define firstly left-hand and secondly right-hand wall outlines in each case, which in the central area relate to wall projections of the indentation figures. At this point it becomes particularly clear how Kahn uses a clear configuration of solid geometry, resulting from a dependent sequence, to determine subordinate parts.

All the essential spatial dimensions of the Esherick House are now determined with the assistance of geometrical analysis. The hierarchy of the rooms is now clear in their trisection, and status is developed in terms of mutual dependence. The final important elements are the fireplaces, which are found on the short sides, and fixed in position by the horizontal axis. They too can be tied into the system on their outer edge with familiar geometrical figures that have already been used.   Fig.26

The square described as the starting-point in figure 20 is now taken up in its previous dimension on the axis of the access figures and, working from this, fixes the external edge of the kitchen fireplace with its left-hand side. Here it becomes clear that it is only necessary to shift the initial square from its original position on the edge of the gallery to the axis to define the fireplace. This suggestive *shifting* of a geometrical figure, causing it to *oscillate* by an identical separating distance, is also a conscious disturbance of the observer's eye and demands heightened awareness.

The analysis of the Esherick House will conclude with the first position of the starting square from Figure 20. The diagonal of the half square when projected on to the lower extended line leads to the Golden Section frame on the right, which finally determines the external outline of the second fireplace.   Fig.27

As can be seen from this first example of a complete sequential analysis, the Esherick House is a complex structure in which Kahn abandons the path from merely additive structures of identical elements. Alongside the precise geometry, which binds all parts of the design into a system, we find here for the first time suggestive processes of movement as a design principle in façade and ground plan.

The first analytical step in Figure 20 also shows that the symmetrical figure of the living and dining area does not contain the dominant geometrical starting figure, as it appears at first sight: in fact the subordinate and the main space are linked geometrically, and it is here that the genesis begins. Thus here too Kahn's continuing interest in the ambiguous treatment of the component figures is revealed, in *contradiction* in the linking of architectural elements.

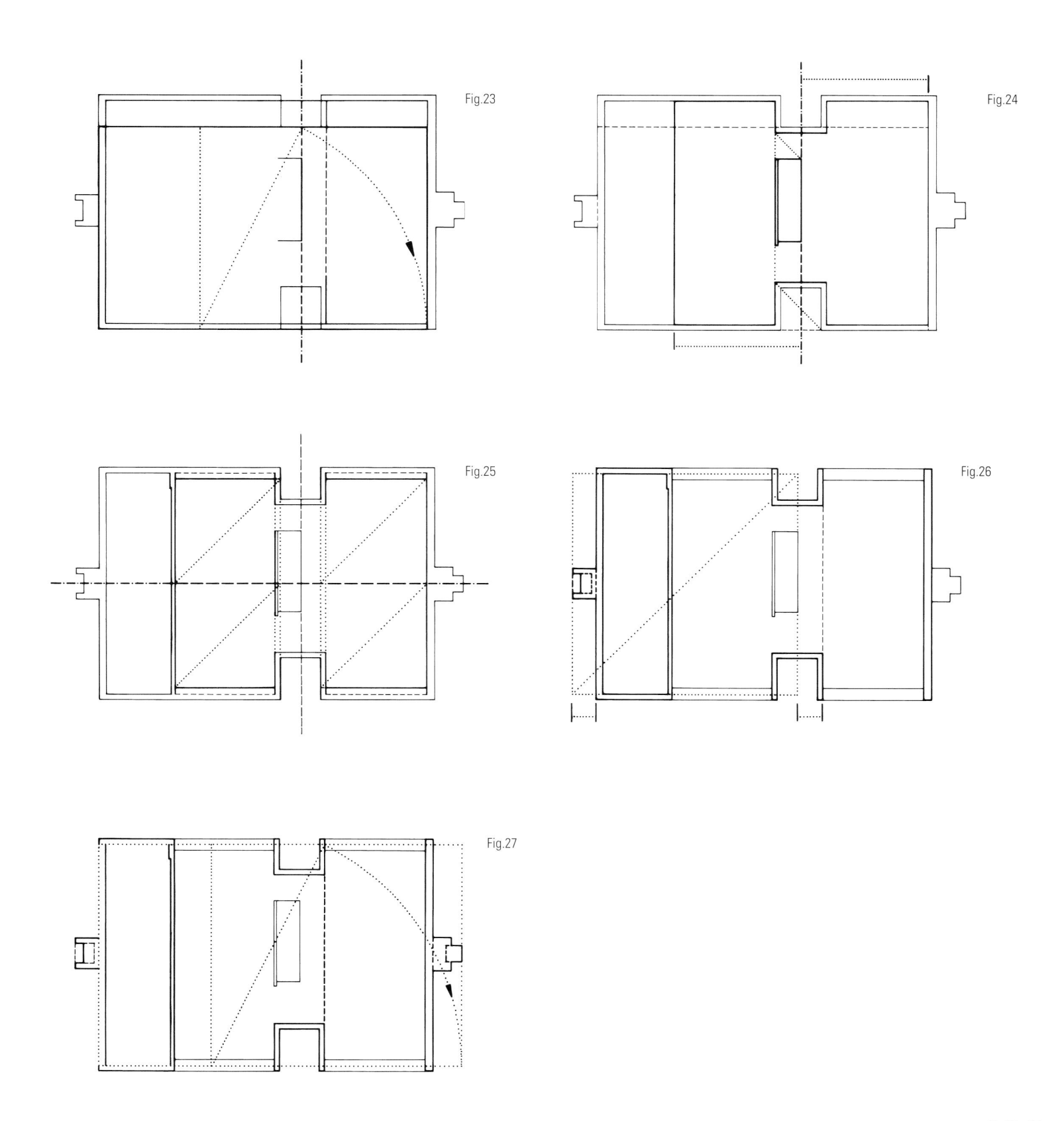

Fig.23–27
Ground plan analysis
of Esherick House
up to the complete
final figure

Cubatures of the sections arranged in a circle around the "sanctuary"

First Unitarian Church
1959–62 Rochester New York USA

Fig.28　Kahn completed the first sketches for the design for the First Unitarian Church in Rochester, in the northern part of the state of New York, in June 1959. The final version was finished in January 1961, the building was quickly realized by December 1962 and required an extension (not discussed here) in 1966–69.

Community rooms, a kindergarten and offices were needed as well as a place of assembly in the form of a church, and so the selected concept was a core room as a centre, the actual church, with functional areas surrounding it. Similarly to the Esherick House, it is again noticeable here that the structure is not cumulative, using units of the same kind, but more differentiated, using the symmetry of component parts. Their axes agree with those of the central space. Parts of different width and length, each belonging to a particular side, are linked together by a surrounding corridor, but the overall configuration is subject to an order of geometrical and proportional dependencies that binds everything together. An important factor when describing the physical appearance of the church is the discovery of *light as a shaping medium*, creating volumes through the penetrating effect of shadow and giving a new value to the periphery of the building. Its external outline – multi-layered – is a moving and massive continuum, conveying an impression of strength and permanence, but more particularly of introversion and concentration on the centre. Scully recognizes a "new and unaccustomed massing of the building",[42] in other words, Kahn's work is acquiring a new and voluminous quality. Emphasis on its external appearance reveals that the façade comes close to being an independently designed figure, with the components light/shade leading to the form; then *the form "invokes function"*. As an experience of a three-dimensionally shaped exterior wall the additively structured spaces have niches with seats, and the light that impinges on the interior is given its own frames. Thus in the case of the alcoves in the window areas Kahn speaks of the result of a "wish to express"[43] and not of the programme. Thus the design process's claim to autonomy takes comprehensible shape in the façade of the church building and makes light into an extraordinarily significant factor. This is impressively increased in the equivalent of the central space with four tower-like corner skylights as light bodies. These skylights, called "mystical corners" by Kahn's design engineer Komendant, are indeed corner positions in the rectangular church interior. The roof is a reinforced concrete shell that is kept low, in contrast with customary church spaces, so that man is not made small in relation to God.[44] This can be seen as a Greek cross when viewed from below by visitors to the church. Just as the interior draws life from the light bodies at the corners and the dark cross of the ceiling, the surrounding façade of the building acquires its appearance from light surfaces and dark shaded openings. This gives the interiors a subdued light similar to shaded sunlight. The result of these thoughts about the façade is the building's three-dimensional sculpture which is anticipated in the rear side of the Richards Building with its row of ventilation shafts, but here with the *doubling* of its peripheral outline as a integral part of the interior, leading to a new architectural statement by Kahn. A direct preliminary stage for this, as mentioned above, is the façade of Mrs. Margaret Esherick's house. The shadows cast on the multi-layered façade of the Unitarian Church is built

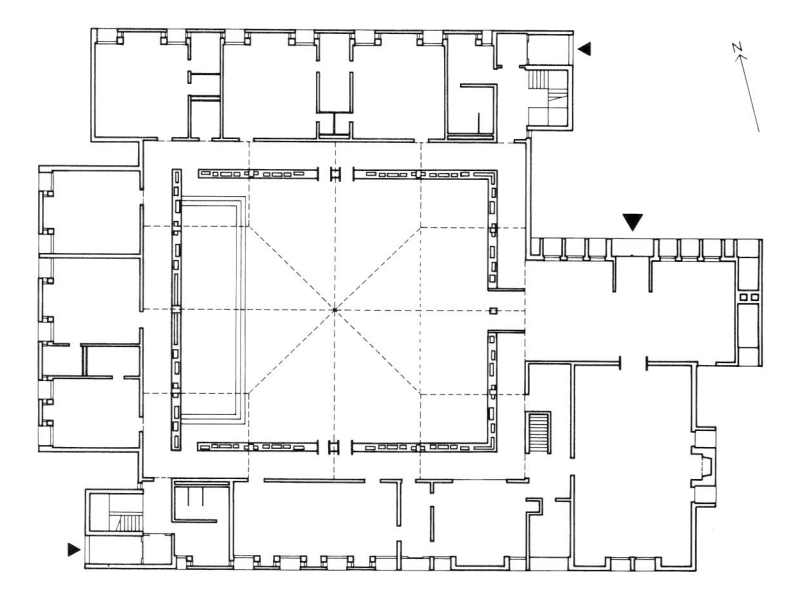

Fig.28
Ground floor plan of the First Unitarian Church (without extension)

Overall corner view from the street

[42] Scully, "Light, Form and Power", p. 164 and Scully, "Works of Louis I. Kahn and his method", pp. 292–293.
[43] Wurman, "What will be ...", p. 192.
[44] Komendant, "18 Years with Architect Louis I. Kahn", p. 40.

up by the alternating protrusion and indentation in its two external planes, which blend into each other, producing positive and negative, in other words solid and hollow bodies. Their wall slabs and volumes flow into each other, and for the first time provide light, which is expressed by its shadow, its own spaces in front of the plane of the windows. Each side of the building develops articulation that is differentiated and depends on the spatial dimension. Thus because of the differing distances of the window frames and a variation in the width of the windows and of their frames, façade images presented as linked cubes are created and held in extended tension. Bernd Foerster speaks of the "prototypical" nature of each detail of this architecture,[45] meaning the development of the entrance, of the windows, of the fanlight, of all parts of the design as an attempt by Kahn to give each part its own expres-

Detail view with side entrance

sive force, but yet to reduce the formal canon to the permanently valid simplified "ancient" element of the prismatic block to create a whole that is complete in itself.

Thus the concept of the *monolithic building sculpture* can be used to describe the Unitarian Church; everything seems to form an integrated whole, and this is the first time we come across such a homogeneous material quality in Kahn's work. The unison of the brick in this dramatic staging in Rochester drives everything else "into the background", i. e. it forces the timber of the windows into the second level of the façade. Kahn went so far in homogenizing the outward appearance that he even had the concrete roofing of the façade niches coloured red. Today these are almost completely covered by a band of zinc sheeting, but in the original plan this was a scarcely visible narrow strip, and did not spoil the prismatic shape of the volumes as much as it does today, after the refurbishment of the roof.

It is easy to make out that the built version of the ground plan is not symmetrical, in the form of a pure square, but is a rectangular, in other words a directed space with figures "circling" round the periphery. Diagonally placed end points in the form of staircases mirror the peripheral zones, but the axial relations again link centre and the peripheral areas closely together. The movement of the parts of the building around an empty centre, as already observed in the Richards Building, which gives an effect of rotation, is resisted by tying it into outlines and picking up common axes, so that here too the polarity of movement and rigidity determines the disposition of the ground plan. The façade is also set in motion by changing rhythms, but its "flow" is halted by partial symmetries within the coherent whole. The protrusion and indentation of its planes gives nothing for the observing eye to hold on to, and this blurs a defined main outline of the kind that can be observed in the Esherick House. As well as this, the vertical articulating elements in the façade contrast with the horizontal quality of the peripheral area.

The peripheral parts of the building and the "sanctuary" of the centre fuse together, and yet in some positions underline their own value as almost independent figures by separating joints: indentations between the functionally separated parts are solid walls without openings, showing the centrally located volume. At the point of contact with the ends of the bar-like peripheral zones, diagonally opposite staircases separate themselves off by narrow window slits, in order to emphasize the corner, rising from floor to skylight, as a vertical. There is a clear hierarchy in

Corner detail with light-towers for the assembly room

[45] Bernd Foerster, Troy University, "Only what matters, an architectural review", The Unitarian Universalist Register Leader, Rochester 1964, pp. 22–25.

View of the south
façade

Corner view from the drive side

View of the short side from the street

the relationship of "servant" peripheral sections, though here used for various purposes, and the "served" dominant centre. Its windowless, dark gallery shows in the external joints, contradictorily is part of the interior and is covered by the skylight towers. This gives the visitor the impression that light is falling behind the actual boundary of the space, the boundary wall, and dissolves its border. The wall of the room is by no means a continuous piece, but a juxtaposition of individual elements, also affected by the heating vents. However, here one can sense Kahn's intention to "insert" this wall in connection with the skylights simply as a dissolving backdrop in front of the space, which stretches out extensively because of the light. This inserted wall with a now almost "provisional" character is also not linked with any other structural elements, it isolates itself and stands in front of them.

In the ground plan and subsequent analysis the complete position of the skylights is shown for the first time; their outermost lines are above the gallery of the church. Thus an ambiguous intermediate area characterizes the intended "twilight" of the pair of opposites, joining and dividing.

In the analysis of the reconstructed ground floor plan (without extension) it can be seen that in designing the Unitarian Church Kahn, as is illustrated by his frequently published explanatory sketches for this building, started his design from the centre. The beginning of the design process is in the middle, that is to say the centre of the church room. This analysis is restricted to the development of the central space, [46] and reveals Kahn's thoughts about using precise geometrical and proportional relations to symbolize *primeval beginnings from the middle*.

---

[46] At the author's above-mentioned seminar in 1990/91 at the Technical University in Braunschweig analysis of the Unitarian Church was undertaken by Titus Bernhhard, Susanne Gehlhaus, Iris Jürgens, Roger Liebig and Elmar Torinus, who were students at the time. It forms the basis of the following presentation.

Skylight in the interior

Corner lights and ceiling cross in the interior

Fig.29 The centre is a square of defined dimension relating to the axes of the space. It represents the zone where the four arms of the Greek cross penetrate the concrete shell roof, inclining to the axes. As a circle the dimensions of the square have the radius R1.

Fig.30 Starting from the horizontal axis, the quarters of the starting square "extend" proportionally downwards or upwards vertically (in relation to the drawing). The geometrical construction of this extension as a major Golden Section[47] can take place on both sides, but can also be mirrored. Here the projection acquires the radius R2 equals R1 x 1.618 (major Golden Section) through the new arc. The top and bottom lower inner wall lines are established in this way.

Fig.31 The same "growth process", as an image of the geometrically dependent extensions, happens in the next step. The square of the previously established radius R2 here forms the basic measurement for the next-larger major Golden Section with the radius R3, which is constructed in the same way. The resultant arc establishes the next, important wall position. Here we are dealing with the left-hand and right-hand outer lines of the central space, so that, with the given constructive wall structure, the overall dimension can be fixed. The thickness of the wall is not determined by construction, but unusually by the integrated heating system.

Fig.32 After establishing the outline of the church space, the question remains of the distance of the sections that "circle round" this space. The gallery attached to the assembly room can be explained with its upper and lower limit by the extension of the starting square from figure 29. The measurement R1 is doubled and gives R4 as the inner line of the gallery, which as it were defines the line of the skylights.

Fig.33 The last outline to be established is that of the gallery's right-hand and left-hand wall. The basis for this is the measurement R2 in figure 30, which formed its enlarged Golden Section in the following figure 31. Here this starting measurement "grows" with the diagonal of its square as root 2 major and thus defines the new radius R5. This radius also directly fixes the line of the gallery on the short sides of the central space.
The four skylight towers of the assembly room now derive from the starting square in figure 29 and the gallery outline that was established last; as already described, these reach beyond the actual border of the room.

Fig.34 The final figure of the central area illustrates that Kahn distances himself in his "diagrams" from the rigid geometrical figure, as in the designs for the Trenton Bathhouse or the Richards Building. There is no doubt that centring continues to be in the foreground, but now a new *directed quality*, as in the Esherick House, plays a larger part, which develops from a *static-centred* to a *dynamic-centred sense of space*.

---

[47] "Major" defines the proportional enlargement of a geometrical figure in contrast with "minor", its reduction.

Fig.29

Fig.30

Fig.31

Fig.32

Fig.33

Fig.34

Fig.29–34
Ground plan analysis of the central hall of the First Unitarian Church from a square starting figure to the outline of the access ambulatory

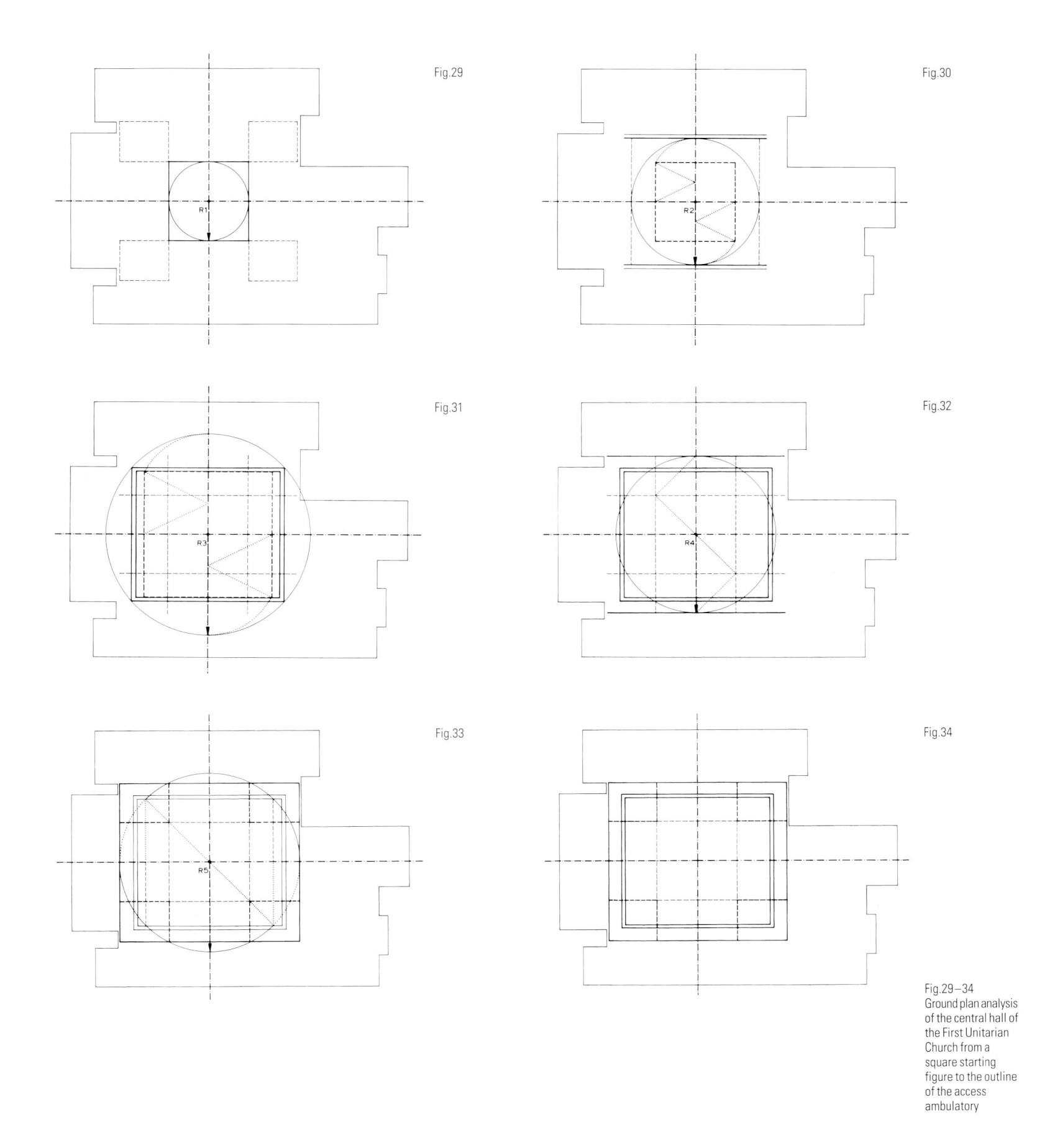

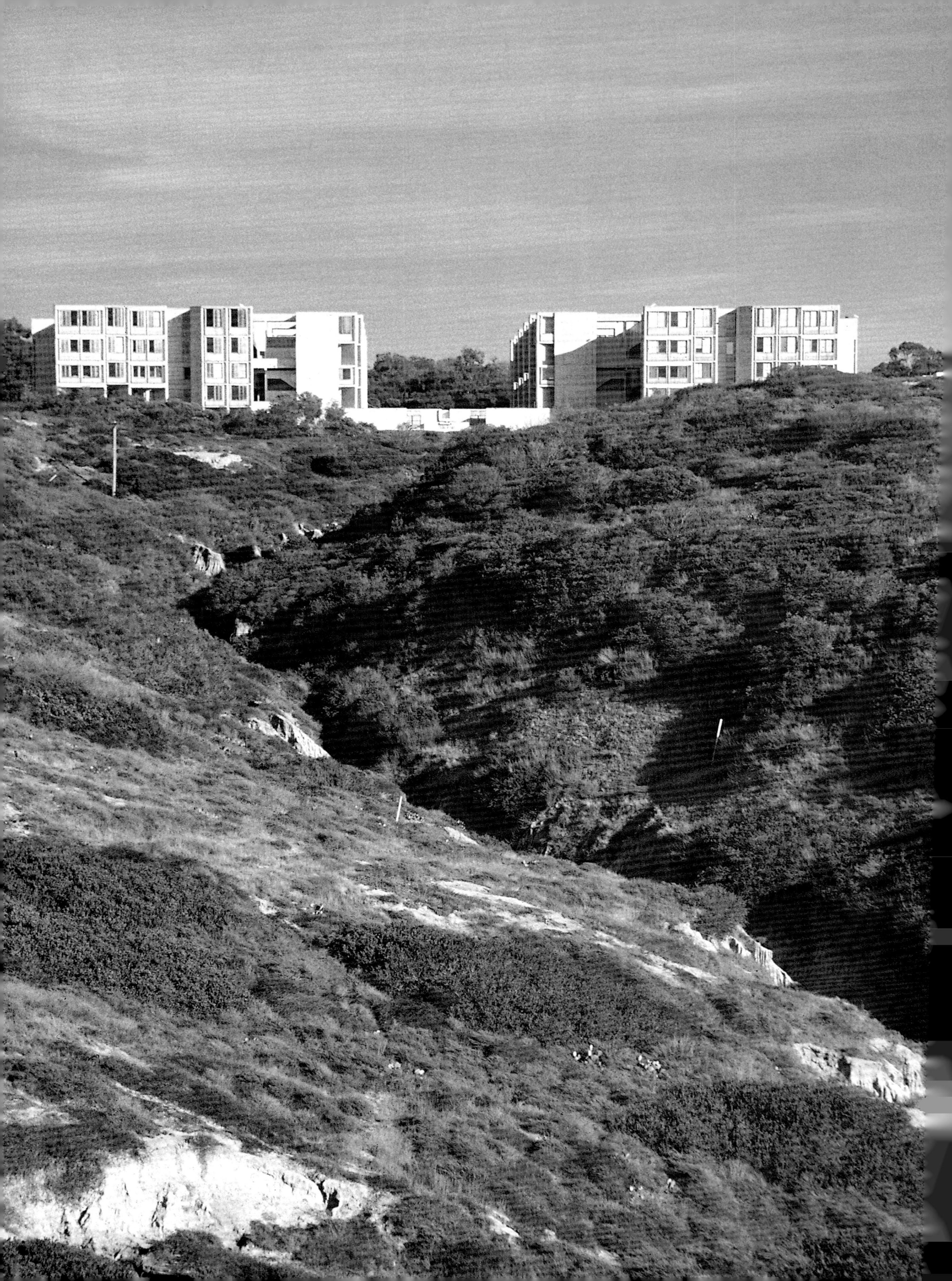

Salk Institute for Biological Studies
1959–67 San Diego California USA

Dr. Jonas Salk, inventor of the vaccine against poliomyelitis, wanted to set up a major biology research centre in San Diego. The city put an extraordinarily beautiful, indeed spectacular site at his disposal, on the edge of a cliff in the northern suburb of La Jolla. Kahn provided Salk with various versions of a design for the laboratories from 1959 onwards, and also for a meeting and discussion centre and accommodations for the researchers (these will not be discussed here).[48]

Fig.35 In 1962 the final concept of the design was fixed. It arranges two similar laboratory wings symmetrically, thus creating a gap, a *courtyard*, between them. The courtyard is flanked by separate rooms for the researchers, so-called "thinking cells", grouped as independent buildings, linked by bridges and their own stairs in each case with the large laboratory space. They are recognizable in the ground floor area in their outline, which is set in the floor. The idea of dividing these rooms from the labs came from Salk, who wanted "monks' cells" for the scientists' meditative research work. Between the thinking rooms are light-wells that cut deep into the site, lighting the labs at basement level. Both laboratory wings have three – a condition imposed by Salk – support-free floors with structural floors between them and exterior vertical access areas relating to the courtyard steps with lateral light-shafts for the basement. It was not until 1967 that the courtyard emerged in its realized form, with its zoning, material and the fountain and pool designed by Kahn. This last version with all important elements is shown for the first time in the reconstructed ground plan here.[49] The other two areas of the overall design conceived by Kahn, the "Meeting House" and the housing, were not built. But in 1994 McAllister, who was significantly involved in the first building, designed an extension for the laboratories that was built. This solution, ultimately preferred by Salk, caused considerable controversy in the American press as it destroyed the natural access to the site that Kahn intended, an existing eucalyptus grove. The following observations are based on the plans for the laboratory building and courtyard actually designed by Kahn.

As in the designs for the Trenton Bathhouse and the Unitarian Church, Kahn used the motif of the centre for the Salk Institute. Additive indiviual parts flank an "empty", rectangular, thus "directed" space. Both are mirrored, so that the resulting dominant symmetry produces two parallel figures linked via a new centre. This connecting space, the courtyard, becomes the actual centre through the emphasis laid on its axis. A large, support-free laboratory space – later organized by its users themselves – can be designed in only a very limited way in architectural terms. Thus Kahn concentrated all his powers on the periphery and especially on a careful design for the courtyard opening on to the short sides. The courtyard, or here better: open square, appears as a third figure, equal in value in its dimensions to the closed, introverted laboratory figure, and yet conflicting; it links up with the appended studies for the scientists, which face the main direction in which one's eye is turned, towards the sea. This movement, as it were enmeshing with the square and orienting away from the labs, makes the square and study buildings undoubtedly the main element in the complex, while the labs, less in the ground plan than the built architecture, "hide" behind it as second-rank elements. Similarly to the contradictory use of "servant" and "served" elements in the Richards Building, in the Salk Institute the "servants", the group of study buildings seem dominant. Here is becomes clear that Kahn is no longer holding on to this strict concept and that the sheer size

View of the laboratory building from the cliffs on the coast

Fig.35
Ground floor plan of the Salk Institute with central square area

[48] For this see publications by Scully, "Louis I. Kahn", 1962, p. 27 and Daniel S. Friedman in Brownlee/De Long, "Louis I. Kahn, In the Realm of Architecture", p. 434, in which these early figures are discussed in detail.
[49] This is based on a copy of Kahn's original working plan for the design of the courtyard from the Louis I. Kahn Collection.

of the building's individual elements does not define the hierarchy. It is also clear that serving elements like the wide-span beams in the laboratories with their mezzanine floors are integral to the actual body of the building and blur the original servant/served concept. Kahn is now interested in more complex connections, as already illustrated in the Esherick House.

Main access is from the road to the east of the building and from the car-parks via an existing grove of trees, which, as mentioned above, was removed when the building was extended. Before entering the "square" it is necessary to get past a first "barrier", a little plateau flanked on both sides by carefully shaped orange trees. From here, in other words from a certain height, the first extraordinarily impressive view across the axis of the platform to the sea is revealed. The platform's up and down in rapid succession makes it clear that Kahn intended to close the square on the entrance side, but did not want to spoil the dominance of the wall formations on the long sides. The natural "wall" of low trees on the plateau at the short entrance side on the narrow entrance borders the space at about the level of the opposite horizon, the dividing line between sky and sea.

Another element, a stone bench occupying the full width of the square, prevents direct axial access. Visitors are forced to enter the square via the sides and its diagonal points, revealing Kahn's intention to relate the inherent monumentality of the symmetrical figure at this place only to the *ordered structure* of the building and not to distance people from the building by making heroic gestures. There is no question that the *ordering* of the buildings in symmetry seems to be the correct answer to this natural point of relation. The square shows itself in all shades of colour in daylight and glares dramatically in the evening sun. This "staging" of an exterior space particularly emphasizes the importance that Kahn allots to it: the metaphysical effect of a *transcendental space* can clearly be sensed, both in terms of this and of another world, without exception determined by the elements and the architecture with its strongly ordered structure – an Olympus. This impression is supported by a symbolic element within the axis of the square, a narrow stream of water originating as a fountain on the entrance side and flowing into a pool at the other end. The life symbol of flowing water relates to the activities of the workers in this institution and is connected visually with the distant sea.

The Salk Institute figure is based on division into three, which firstly determines the arrangement of the lab block, with labs, study buildings and adjacent access elements, and also, aligned longitudinally, an administrative building, a lab and a technical area. Two main parts are placed by a third element, the square, and finally this exterior space with two side rows of buildings, the study-rooms, forms a group of three. The square itself is divided into three central areas, marked with small indentations in the Travertine paving. At the side of each three stone benches in the same material as the entrance barrier "grow" into the ground. They define the precise border of the centre of the square and prevent the "lack of focus" in its outline that would be produced by different lengths of the study building's diagonal wall slabs. Although the study buildings have four storeys, and are taller than the labs, here as well a division into three can be seen in the heights of the individual floors: from top to bottom in the rhythm A–B–A–C. This vertical

Access platform with view over the central water channel to the sea horizon

Main access to the square with "barrier"

View of the short side of the right-hand wing

Study building with pool at the end of the square

View of the laboratory wing with administration section from the site of the accommodation building that was originally planned

Fountain with water channel and walls of the study buildings

View of the study buildings oriented to the sea

Square and concrete walls of the study buildings with stone benches

dynamism, with the highest floor at the uppermost point, varies the otherwise regular façade structure and, in combination with the different length of the wall slabs and their strong verticality, produces an overall view dominated by contrasting rigidity and movement. This vertical dynamism, with the highest floor at the topmost point, varies the otherwise even façade structure. In connection with the varying lengths of the walls with their strong sense of verticality, the overall view is dominated by the contrast between rigidity and movement.

In the western view of the building as a whole the walls of the study building blend into a unit with the base of the square area from which they grow, also adding extra clarity to the stage set-like laboratory façades behind them, which almost make themselves independent in their blatant horizontality. It is not even the laboratories themselves that form the actual background – their deeply recessed and shaded façades dissolve into glass in a way that is most unusual for Kahn, leaving only the support structure visible – but the almost windowless service floors, which are provided only with slits. Even these façades reflect Kahn's contradictory use of his servant and served spaces, a concept that is veiled here to the point of being unrecognizable.

The shuttering on the concrete surface of the vertically oriented study buildings have very carefully executed ridges, and the shuttering in the broadly based shapes of the laboratories remains horizontal.

The extraordinary detailing and the quality of execution, particularly on the surface, is a remarkable feature throughout the Salk Institute. In the square Kahn uses two contrasting materials of almost equal value: hard stone and soft wood. Here the two stone qualities, concrete and Travertine, almost fuse into one: Kahn matched up their light colour by adding volcanic ash to the concrete mixture. Wood is a "filler material" in the study building façades and the administrative area, with clear, glazed joints separating the materials from each other. Honesty and "truth" in the use of materials and their architectural combination are given priority here. Over 30 years after the building opened the surfaces of the building are still of the utmost quality in terms of material, and give evidence for Kahn's longing to *integrate truth of form and material*.

The façades of the administrative areas, but also the above-mentioned legible columns in the labs, show that even construction with an eye to externally illustrated honesty played a part in this design, similarly to the Richards Building. Different spans for the diagonal façade walls make the necessary heights of the bearers in the façade visible and produce vertical shifts in window formats, as in the laboratories in Philadelphia. The diagonal wall bulkheads, which are certainly derived from Le Corbusier's "brise-soleil" walls in Chandigarh, are integrated into the outline of the building. Their edges produce systems of lines on the façade, which in combination with the triple layering of the wooden windows produce a sculptural effect. In contrast with Le Corbusier's diagonal wall elements as the exclusive protection against the sun, here the diagonals to various directions are used additionally as an element in rooms that widen towards the sea.

Kahn's design for the Salk Institute shows clearly for the first time his interest in modulating a site and linking a building very firmly with areas below ground level. His light-wells, cutting in deeply on either side of the lab areas, illuminate their basements and make the study buildings tower-like in part, as their shafts combine with the basement storeys. These incisions are comparable with the light-wells in other designs; however, here they are not independent architectural forms, but remain subordinate. Kahn uses the difference in

Laboratory building with stairwell volumes

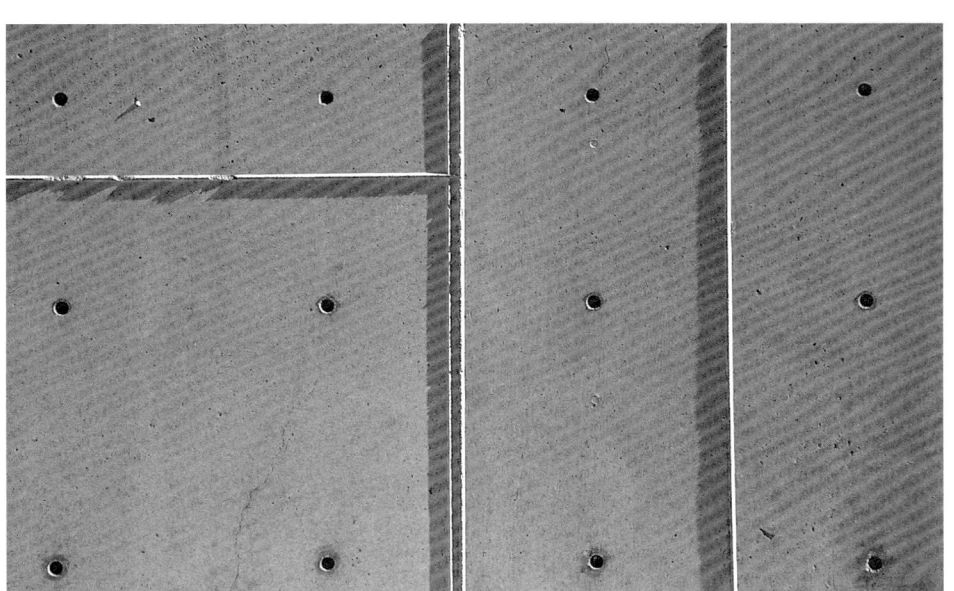

Arcades and administration bulkheads

Detail of the concrete surface

View through the arcades of the study buildings

height with enthusiasm, as can be seen from his detailing of various pools and steps on the break in the site that he created. He forms a cascade to conclude the upper square area and link up with the lower plateau and the adjacent natural surroundings.

The compositional order of the Salk Institute reveals its essential features in a sequence of individual analyses, mainly vertical in our drawings. External outlines of the building, the incisions into the site and also individual parts of the building, like for example steps, are chosen as reference points that have quite obviously determined the genesis of the design down to the final disposition of the sub-figures. Examination of the ground plan immediately shows Kahn's wish for geometry that ties everything together; going well beyond the simple symmetry of his original considerations, the geometry uses a complex combination of sub-levels, the frames, as demonstrated in the previous descriptions. Since the design is so large there has been no "fine tuning" of the investigation, although verifications of measurements by using working plans or possibly a full measurement of the realized building would have been necessary to confirm the assertions made here. And yet in this design as well is it reasonable to assume that Kahn intended to tie all the parts into a dependent ordering system of geometrical figurations.

Administration
head buildings

Detail of the study buildings and their loggias

View from a loggia to the row of study buildings

Fig.36　The initial figure for the design is a square of yet undetermined dimensions that has to establish fundamental external outlines. This square, here identified by its diagonal, "oscillates" – on the present sheet – around a defined width in a horizontal direction. This defines peripheral areas on both sides, in this case the cuts into the site for the illumination of the basement floor.

Fig.37　A new rectangular overall outline, a frame, is defined on the basis of the suggestive movement of the square. It has a vertical axis that divides the field into two halves. With the aid of the Golden Section the two halves can now be zoned in such a way that narrow lower and upper peripheral areas can be separated from the broad central field; to achieve this, the lower strip of the overall area, that divides areas off by the Golden Section, is transferred to the upper peripheral area and vice-versa. Here too it would be possible to speak of a field that is now shifting in a vertical direction, however, as a remainder area it results from the previous geometrical sequence. The upper and lower peripheral zone of the rectangle as a whole identifies the depth of the administrative and the technical building areas as being of the same length. The width of this end building, which belongs to the laboratories, emerges in the subsequent steps.

The position of the columns within the central field of the rectangle as a whole, with their external contour oriented towards the centre as a border for the lab zones, can be defined using a ratio of 1 to root 2. They form the mounting points for the broad-span Vierendeel trusses, which form their own storeys. The width of the columns is fixed precisely via the centre axes of the two halves, i. e. by quartering the field as a whole.　Fig.38

After the complete external outline of the complex had been arrived at and the main figure divided into head, body and end, it was possible for figurations of the centre, i. e. the square, to follow. In this step as well the stairs' positions for the study buildings with their external outlines were determined by the Golden Section construction. The major Golden Section, i. e. the longer side of the area, is set by the depth of the centre field, so that the proportional relationship of long side to short side emerges quite simply.　Fig.39

Fig.36

Fig.37

Fig.38

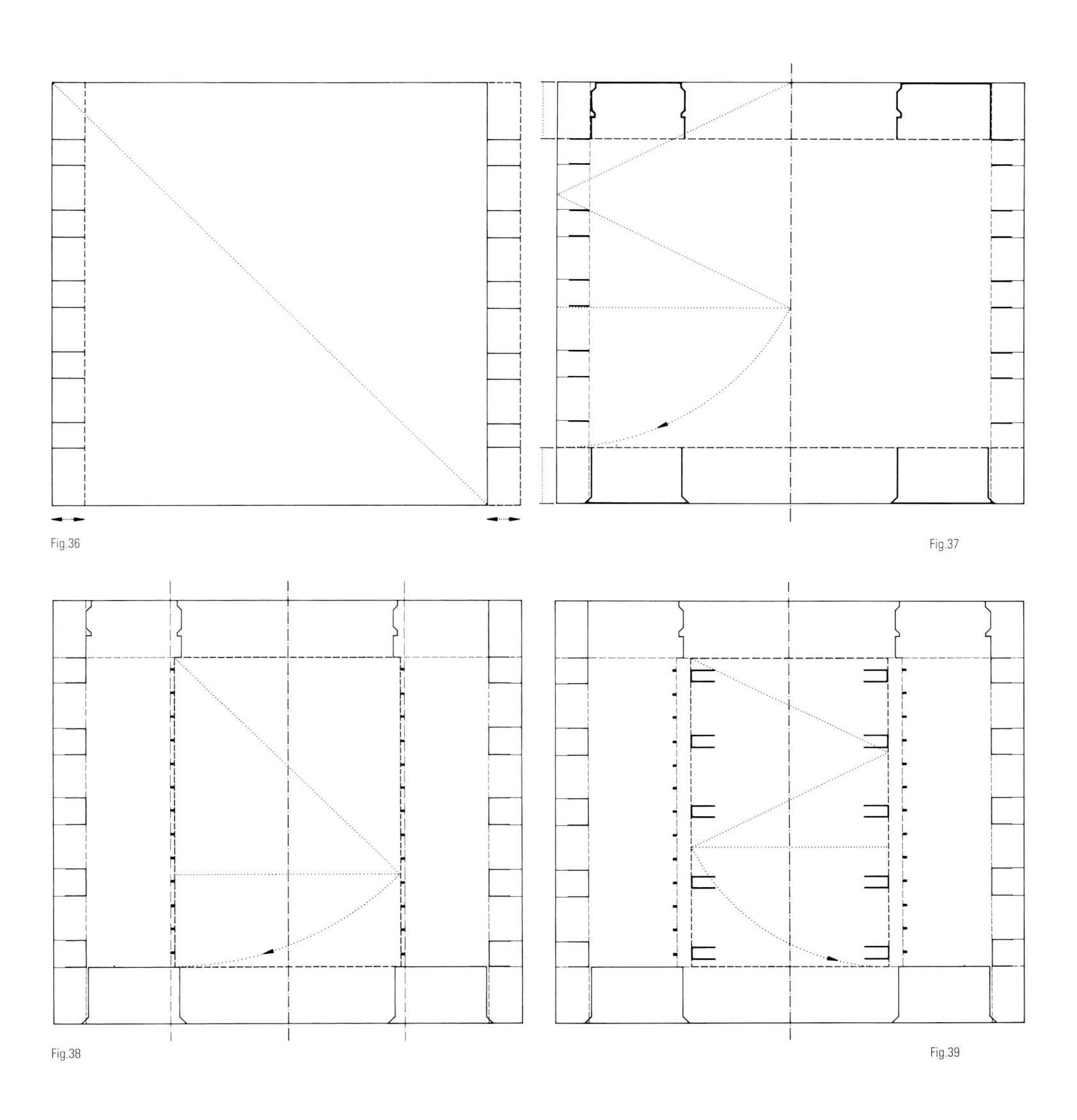

Fig.39

Fig.36–39
Ground plan analysis
of the Salk Institute
with an "oscillating"
square starting
figure

Fig.40 Here too it is the axis of the rectangle as a whole which plays a crucial role in fixing further outlines. As in figures 38 and 39, in which the proportional figures of the Golden Section and root 2, so important in Kahn's work, appear, an equally important frame, the double square, defines the borders of the inner staircase outlines. The distance established in this way, from the outer edges of the columns to the inner edges of the stairs, fixes the position of the columns along the outer walls. Here this distance has to be measured off inwards from the outer edge of the figure as a whole. Within the lengths defined it is now possible for the laboratory building itself to find its width, halving the distance from the outer edge of the columns to the outer edge of the stairs. However, it is the dimension of the service floor that finally decides the overall width, as the labs come in as far as the edges of the columns. The central double square also identifies the limits of the light-wells, thus marking crucial figures within the square.

Fig.41 Once the staircase outlines of the study houses are fixed, double squares with new dimensions can be established in the left- and right-hand peripheral areas. They define a new horizontal line along the upper service areas, and this is the actual border that concludes the square at the top end on the entrance side, in the form of a plinth for planting. This line also fixes a bordering wall within the service section as well.
The short distance from the steps to the external outlines is used for four lift shafts. They link the labs with the group of individual figures on the periphery of the square.

The final border of the external stair-wells and lift shafts can be fixed geometrically only after the upper outline of the square has been established with the aid of a root 2 frame. This geometrical figure is thus added to the external outlines of what has so far been called the centre field. It produces the border on the opposite side of the vertical access area that flanks the labs on the outside. Fig.42

Finally the fundamental structure of the study buildings is illustrated. Once stairs and peripheral outlines have been fixed, square figures of defined dimensions are added, superimposed on the size of the eye of the staircase. They acquire their setting or frame from the double square arrived at in Figure 41 that "holds" the group of study buildings "in position" with the central axis (which appears in the form of a gutter). Fig.43

Fig.40

Fig.41

Fig.42

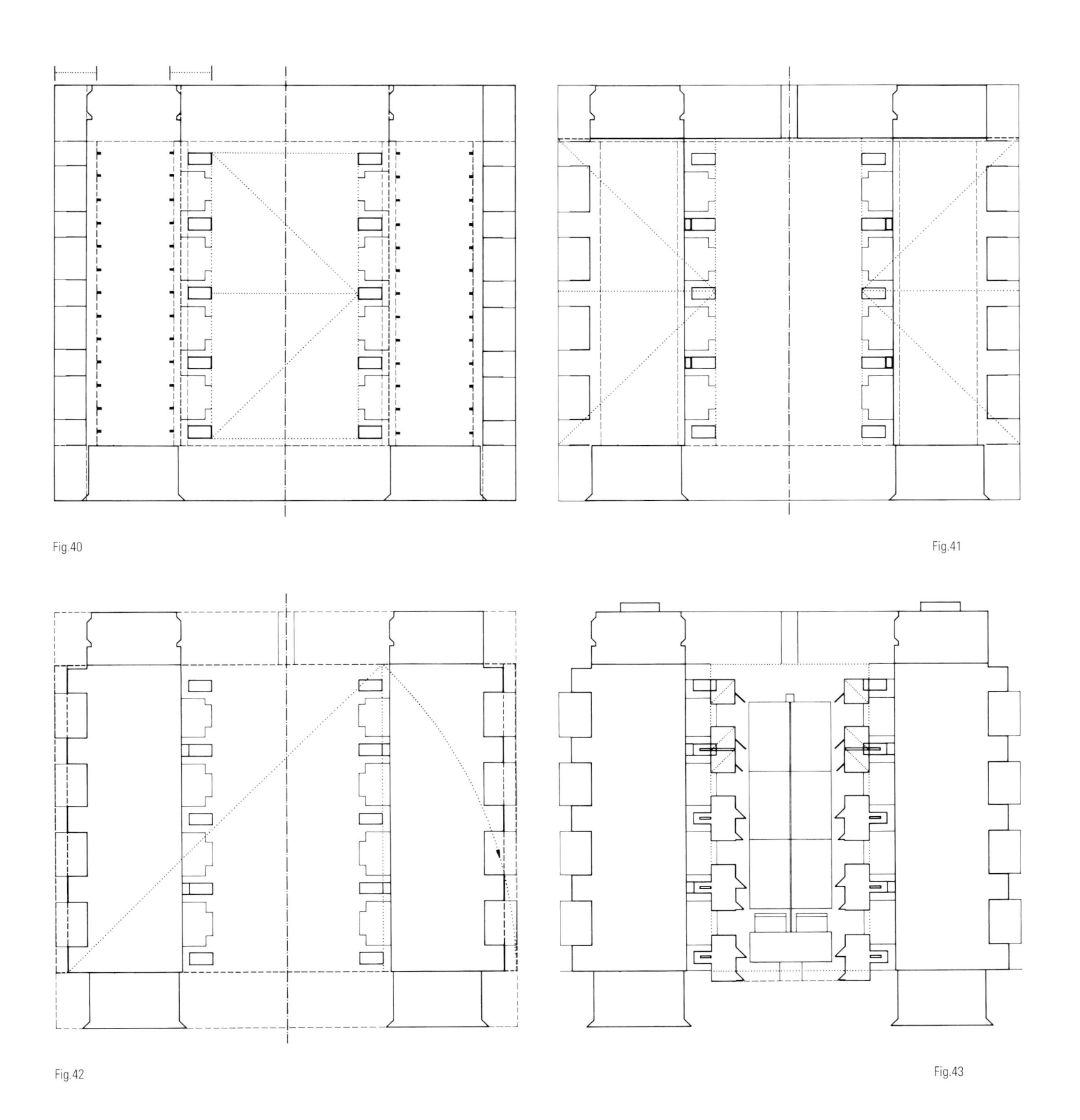

Fig.43

Fig.40–43
Ground plan analysis
of the Salk Institute
to the final outline
of the building and
the square area

View with river landscape

Fisher House
1964–67 Hatboro Pennsylvania USA

The final concept for another extraordinarily remarkable house by Kahn for Dr. Norman Fisher and his family in the rural suburb of Hatboro, north of Philadelphia, was designed by 1964. Kahn had made the first sketches a few years earlier, and the house was finally completed in 1967. The clients were very patient throughout the lengthy planning process, as they were very impressed by the architect's personality and the ideas he presented from the very outset, as Mrs. Fisher has told the author.

The house is on an idyllic site facing north-east towards a river. This orientation makes the disposition of the building particularly difficult, since it is not possible to arrange the living area on the south-western side and at the same time to capture the attractive view of the river landscape.

Fig.44 The building is based on a tripartite cubic composition, arranged according to the external circumstances. The ensemble is made up of independent individual volumes that do not develop from additive or grid structures, but are combined in a free arrangement.

The living area of the building is parallel with the access road, at the end of the drive, on the edge of a slight slope on a visible cellar base, and its southern corner blends with the cube of the sleeping and bathrooms area, which is shifted by 45 degrees. This gives the impression that the buildings are colliding, a new design element in Kahn's thinking. This *free disposition* can also be seen in other designs of this period. The shift follows the points of the compass precisely, so that the building seems to be fixed in place only by this. A third cube, considerably smaller than the two dominant ones and containing technical equipment, flanks the access to the northern garden area and places the composition along the long straight line of the drive. Another cube can be identified as a quasi-autonomous figure: the kitchen block is almost isolated in its position within the living area, as it was inserted into the surrounding sections and besides that does not reach up to the ceiling of the building. Thus the Fisher House can be described as a four-part ensemble of cubic individual volumes, enriched by the fireplace, which as a segment of a circle forms a fifth element.

Kahn decided that the living-room should face north-east to provide a view of the landscape, in other words he opened up the façades to a side that did not face the sun. Here the walls are generously provided with flush areas of glass; the realized version with large windows in the dining area does not fit in with Kahn's original concept.[50]

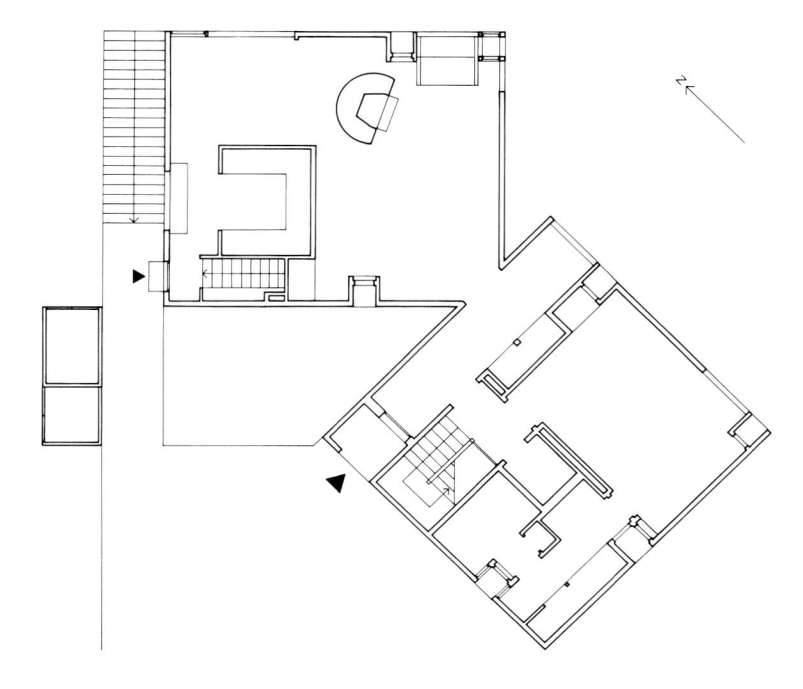

In contrast with this, the façades on the access side have deep indentations with recessed windows, similar to the notches in the Esherick House; these give overall sculptural form to the façade as a voluminous mass. It is striking that Kahn uses these cubic indentations as independent elements and not, as in Rochester or even in the Esherick House, within a continuously layered façade. They stand partly freely in the space along the exterior wall and are an integral part of the cubic composition as independent figures, and not only as windows: they form *lighting spaces*. On the north-eastern side Kahn combines the flat windows with the notches. In the living-room in particular this produces a three-dimensional window sculpture that combines external surfaces and lines in a Mondrianesque way. It is carried on round the corner and inside – surfaces closed with wood or open – works as a body invading the space: the volume dissolves. This is an area in which to linger on an integrated bench, almost outside among the wonderful scenery, with the fireplace in front of it inside, a direct experience of nature fully intended by Kahn. The fireplace block, a free-standing sculpture in the room, has a rustic materiality that stands in contrast with the smooth walls, and is a zoning element inside the living cube. It divides the living and eating area inside a spatial concept

Fig.44
Ground floor plan of Fisher House

---

[50] Ronner/Jhaveri, "Louis I. Kahn, Complete Work 1935–1974", Fisher House, first floor plan 1964/66.

Detail of the large corner window in the living area

that was originally free-"flowing", almost Miesian. It is slightly skewed, which makes it particularly striking within the right angles of the ground plan, and increases the impression that the building is *moving*, though braked by the straight of the drive. In the Fisher House as well Kahn designs on the aggressive principle of a figure that is rigidly bound into geometrical order, suggesting dynamic events.

The second main volume with its two storeys contains the sleeping area with bath and dressing area on the ground floor and other bedrooms and a guest-room on the upper floor. It also contains the main point of access to the building, while another entrance, or better exit, is to be found near the kitchen in the other part of the building. The main entrance, in the form of an enlarged notch, similar to the windows, swings to face the visitor because of the shift in the building, and becomes a clearly defined space because of its basic square form. Here it is particularly clear what a huge effort Kahn made to give all the sub-areas of the ground plan structure a uniform character and to bind them together as a geometrically determined "family of forms". The entrance area inside the building is a narrow, directional tangential space, closely related to the external space, with the living-room immediately adjacent. This area too is not a "leftover space" as a hall, but a zone that is clearly determined in its outline and by the inherent geometry, in other words a designed zone. Thus the striking feature of the interior of the Fisher House is that the rooms are highly independent in character, as a copy of the outward appearance of a design approach that takes *pre-existing patterns* like the pure cube as its ideal. And yet Kahn combines two "ideal bodies" in a contradictory fashion, flowing together because they are the same height and forming a continuous façade in homogeneous material: wood. This makes the façade seem almost infinite. Unlike Esherick House it is designed to be looked at on the diagonal, like the dissolving corner of the living area and the window configurations that refuse to relate to any symmetrical axis. The homogeneity of the exterior material intends to produce a sculpted mass that, in contrast with the stone façade of the Unitarian Church makes the observer uneasy in this case because of the thin-skinned timber structure. The incised notches contradict the skin-like character of the exterior walls. The complete absence of structural elements in the façade, i. e. Kahn's stubborn refusal to give any explanation about the construction, also contributes to this entirely intentional sense of unease. This design can definitely not be described as working on the servant/served principle. Kahn does separate the apparent main function of living/eating from subsidiary functions, but the size of the individual volumes alone, particularly their height, and the material quality of their exterior appearance, produces an equal validity that eliminates any hierarchical character. Thus with the Fisher House Kahn once more invents a new form within his developed design canon by varying his resources.

Looking at the ground plan figure of three rectangular areas, of which one seems very close to a square, the question arises of what their common origin could be. The development of the design to the final plan intended to be built, its genesis, will be examined step by step, in order to establish the logic of the internal structure, its system of order.

Closed façade from the street

Position of the three cubes in the garden

Building volumes' relations, main entrance on the right

View of the main volume of the house with entrance

The two main sections penetrate each other

Main entrance

Corner window
from the inside

View from the
sloping north garden
with generous
window formats

Fig.45   The origin of this design consists of two squares of equal size in a defined dimension. Their position is fixed firstly by the right angle to the access road and secondly by precise orientation to the points of the compass. They are at an angle of 45 degrees to each other and overlap at a point that will be described in greater detail.

Fig.46   The "distortion" of the squares begins. Square 2 expands on two sides by the fixed dimension X to form a larger square. A rectangle extended by 2X derives from square 1. Dimension X defines peripheral zones in which the notch-like window elements are to be found. Thus their borders on the interior side indicate the existence of the original square in each case. The position at which the two squares penetrate each other can now be precisely identified: the diagonal of the initial square 1 divided the new side length 2 in a ratio of 1 to root 2. This is another unambiguous reference to the original squares.

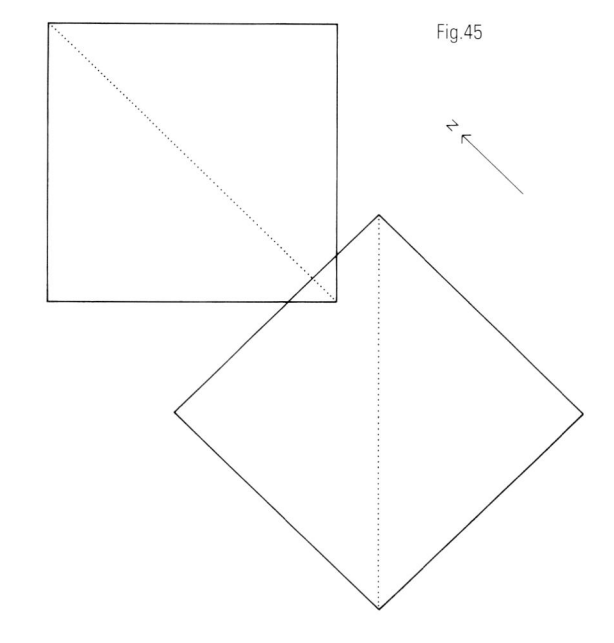

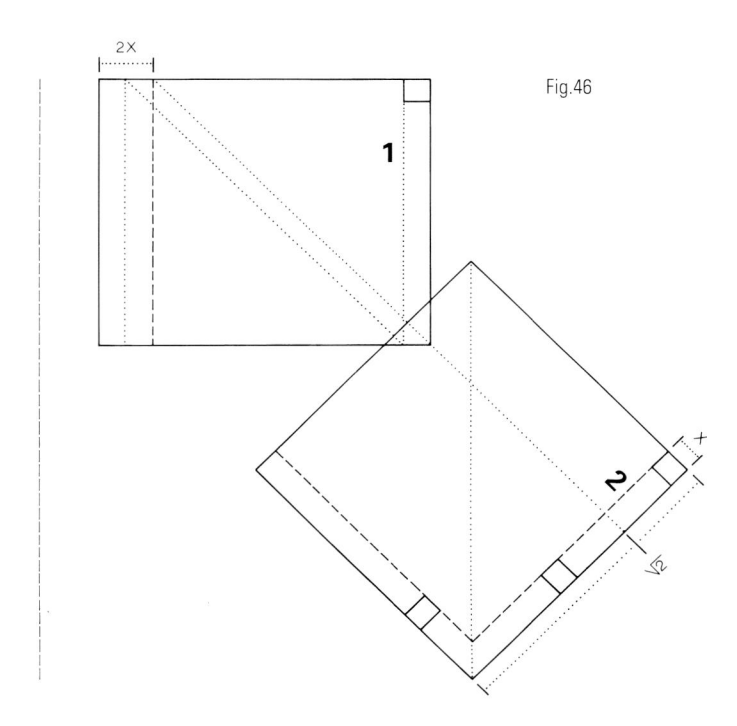

Fig.45–46
Ground plan analysis of Fisher House with two squares at the start

Fig.47 Square 2 also loses its clear square shape. It is extended by the thickness of a wall on the eastern outer wall. Kahn was interested in copying the pure square outlines intelligibly within the ground plan, but also in giving the final building a complex structure. Here it is particularly clear that the interior and the exterior lines of the exterior walls can be just as important for the ordering figures, as all other limiting outlines in this building create exterior lines.

The newly extended outline, with its diagonals, intersects with the diagonal of the penetration axis of the two areas. Thus width A emerges as a zoning factor. In figure 2 it defines the dividing line between the access area with its cupboard elements and the sleeping area and in figure 1, applied to the left-hand outline of the initial square, it defines the width of the kitchen block. This subsidiary zone acquires its long side B from its point of meeting with the diagonal of the shifted initial square. The extension in dimension 2X thus represents the rear access area to the kitchen.

Fig.48 In the two rectangles with precise outlines that have now been identified, the areas with the side lengths A and B are subsidiary. While in area 1 length B forms the border of the kitchen and the cellar steps, in area 2 it gives a wall position that has a crucial impact on the internal structure as a shaft. The length of the shaft is equal to length B, and thus represents a square border and fixes the position of a lighting element. As line B is continued, wall lines emerge in width X that make cupboard installations possible on both sides.

Fig.49 The third volume can now be defined as a next step which was not realized until later, and in a different form. Again position and dimension can be derived from the starting square in Figure 45. The geometrical construction of the ratio 1 to root 2 gives the distance of the building from the edge of the drive and thus one side of the third element. Here an arc of a circle with the diagonal of the starting square as a radius meets the extended line of one side and fixes the position of the third body at this point of intersection, and also, as an extension of the drive, the steps to the garden north of the house. The same construction method, but with a radius of half the starting square, describes the second border of the building, its opposite side. This involves the proportion of the Golden Section. While the area proportion 1 to root 2 is depicted clearly in the line of the stairs, the Golden Section proportion is retained "merely" as a reminiscence in the exterior outline of the third volume. The area of its first sub-element is also determined by the root 2 proportion. A square supplementary element dependent on the established width completes the outline of the third volume. Both proportional relations prove as it were the existence of the original square and its crucial role in the genesis of this figure.

Fig.50 Essential ground plan configurations have now been developed, so that wall thicknesses of a definite dimension can be inscribed in the two main volumes. The last important figure in the plan to be fixed is the fireplace, whose angle and position can be presumed to be part of the figurative geometry system. Its centre as a circle is fixed by a square whose side length divides the final living-cube in the ratio of the Golden Section. In contrast, the diagonal of the front intersecting edge relates to the geometry of the initial square. By extending this line to the outer edges of this part of the building it is possible to establish that it cuts the square exactly at the centre third points. A final square determines the outlines of the access area as a line connecting the two sections of the building in the outside area.

Kahn developed a new building type with the Fisher House. Autonomous forms of the building volumes, which are virtually pre-existent and stand only for themselves, independent of the functional pre-conditions, are connected with each other "directly", i. e. without other connecting elements like bridges, walkways or halls. This new form of communication between building volumes is explored by Kahn in various designs, but was realized only in this design which in this respect is unique.

Something else that is new is the formulation of a *lighting space*, a window element that does not appear bound into a wall structure, but is used independently and singularly. All parts of the design are generated from the ordering system of figurative geometry that Kahn applies consistently even in this design.

Fig.47

Fig.48

Fig.49

Fig.50

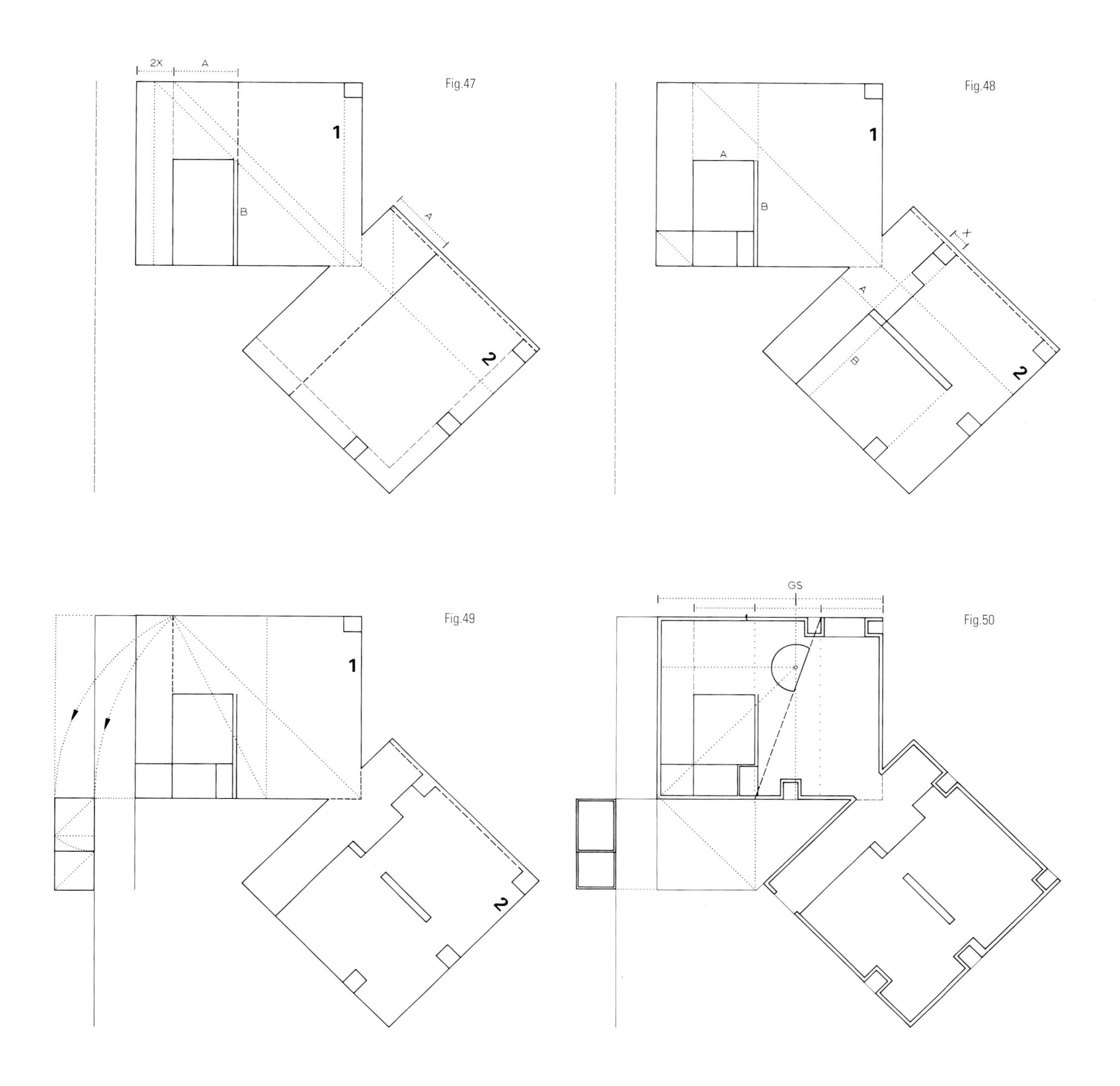

Fig.47–50
Ground plan analysis
of Fisher House to
the final relation of
the three sections

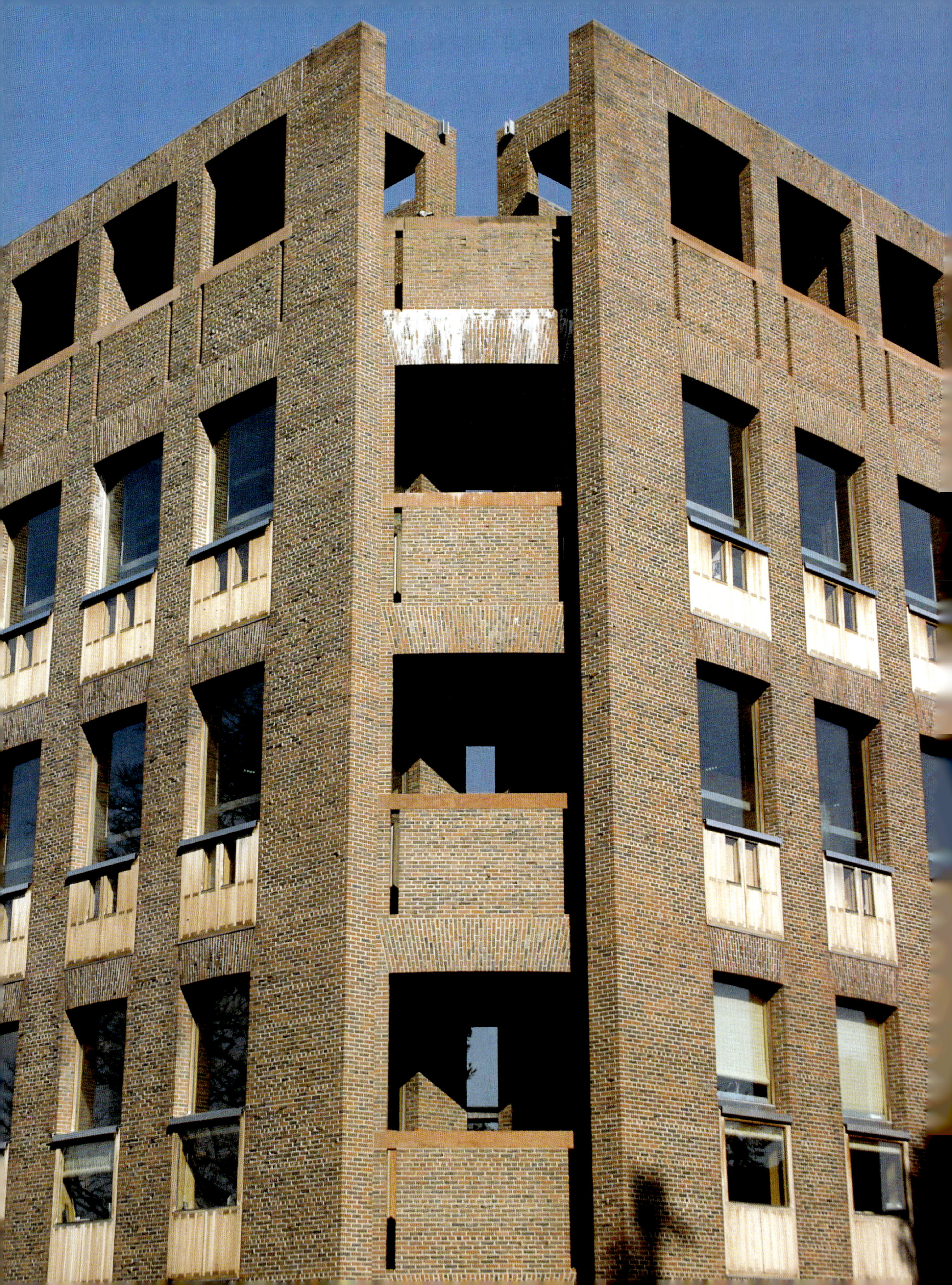

Phillips Exeter Academy Library
1965–71 Exeter New Hampshire USA

Louis Kahn was chosen to design a new library for the Phillips Exeter Academy, a prestigious private school in the north-east American coastal state of New Hampshire, in 1965. The final design was competed in 1969, after many intermediate stages and a difficult design process. The building was finished in 1971.

He had a generous site on flat land at his disposal. It was surrounded by neo-classical buildings conveying a solidly conservative atmosphere. Kahn decided on a centrally disposed building, planned as a dominant solitaire that would not relate directly to its neighbours. The only gesture towards them was the material, a dark, bluish-red brick with a romantic appeal brought about by integrating irregular, faulty products in the façade. This rustic treatment of masonry was a popular design device for neo-classical designs on the East Coast in the last century. Kahn used

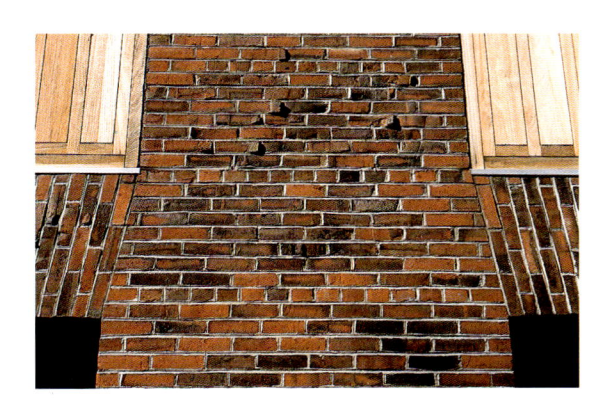

Romantic, rustic masonry with defective bricks

untreated wood for the windows, which was fitted into the openings of the masonry in panels, partly with shutters that could be opened and closed from the inside. The central interior was dominated by very carefully handled smooth fair-face concrete: the choice of material was directed by a desire for conservative correspondence in the exterior and for concealment of modernity in the interior.

The exterior of the building suggests that it has five storeys, as there are five outer rows of openings. The three central rows have particularly high openings with wooden shelvings in the lower part, thus subtly indicating that there are two storeys behind. The upper floor in each of these three rows is set back like a gallery. Thus the building as a whole has eight storeys, which Kahn again subtly hides with a system of openings dependent on the masonry that widen as they rise.

Detail from a corner view with "bursting" corners

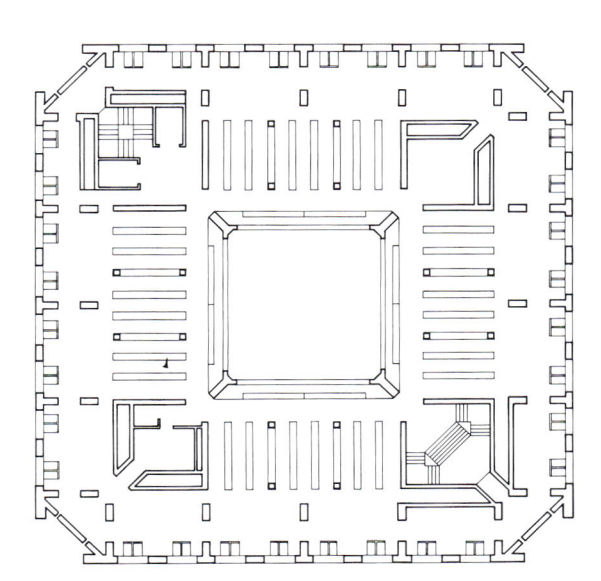

Fig. 51
Typical floor plan of the Phillips Exeter Academy Library

The ground plan envisaged a circular distribution of functions. The fourth floor can be taken as an example. In the centre is the hall area, with natural lighting from above; the books are stored on open shelves in the central ring. Stairs, shafts and rooms for technical equipment are arranged at the corners of this zone. The outer ring contains the students' reading zone with desks along wooden compartments with opening windows. The ground floor has a low arcade running round it that is to be seen as an approach to the interior, like a "transition zone" between inside and outside, as Kahn deliberately omits a sharply defined main entrance. It is only on getting past this relatively dark corridor that the visitor can identify the entrance to the building, which is astonishingly placed on the north side, facing away from the campus and its other buildings. Thus the arcade represents an access ring that "catches" visitors coming from all directions: this is the actual main entrance. Before it is possible to get into the area where the books are it is necessary to go to the first floor, using an almost baroque staircase; it is only there that the magnificent hall begins. Of course this "way upwards" is intended as a *symbolic ascent* into the "Olympus of knowledge", a gesture that Kahn uses for various institutional designs (Richards Building, Indian Institute of Management) and which is here emphasized almost to the point of monumentality by the form of the steps. The top floor is presented as empty on the outside, a "crown" for the building (similar to the parliament building in Dhaka). It is a roof garden with seminar rooms arranged in the interior.

Fig. 51

Corner view of the building

For the ground plan of the Exeter Library Kahn returns to figures from his significant early phase in the late fifties, like the Trenton Bathhouse or the laboratory towers in Philadelphia. The complex, mobile ground plans of his previous period (Unitarian Church, Esherick House, Indian Institute) are again replaced by the archaic, centred primal form of the square, which despite its "distortion" is retained as an intelligible entity in the realized building. This rediscovery of the initial form indicates Kahn's increasing interest at this time in the symbolic form of the square as an image of universal and even metaphysical connections. The complexity of an ordering structure that finds expression in the ground plan figure is not longer in the foreground: *purity of the original form* is represented directly. The ground plan of the Exeter Library, with its double axial symmetry and centring of an "empty" middle shows almost too vividly how much Kahn celebrates the *autonomy of form* and not form devised by mankind, but *form that has always been there*. But here Kahn changes the square in a completely new and unique way: he is not only illustrating primal form, but primal force as well. The restricting lines of the square are burst open, the ground plan is broken up by centrifugal forces, and the parts strive outwards from the centre. The hall frame, the great concrete central structure, has diagonal cross walls indicating a marked sense of diagonal dynamics. All the corner configurations inside the building that were previously closed by walls are broken up into individual volumes by the diagonal line, and this is further intensified by the diagonal asymmetry of the staircases with their shafts. The outer walls of the building strive outwards and are held together by narrow connecting walls in the corners, like prestressed elements. It seems as though Kahn is trying to illustrate the moment at which the building "bursts apart", as these slender, stretched connecting elements give the impression that the outer walls have reached their final state of extension. They are given slits, they burst apart and convey their condition of tension to the outside world. And so what is being shown here is not so much a question of cutting off the corners, as frequently described in other studies, but a force thrusting out from the centre, suggesting a primitive condition, that of connected outside walls.

The similarity of the façades also confirms that the centre was extraordinarily important for the concept of the building, as the centrifugal force dictates approximately identical parts on the periphery. Kahn illustrates processes suggesting movement even in the façades. The rectangular format of the arcades changes into a square by the top roof garden storey, thus producing a vertical dynamic in the façade. Here Kahn demonstrates an old masonry construction for the window lintel with outward-thrusting sills – a good example of how a traditional building method can acquire a new character. The outline of the outermost lintel block in each case fixes the width of the next-highest window, thus producing wall surfaces that get narrower towards the top. This makes the façade into a kind of puzzle picture, as two impressions can be given in turn: either piers tapering towards the top (with window panels between them) or a coherent perforated façade as a wall slab with incised, changing windows.

The hall façades also give rise to different feelings in the observer. Their large circular indentations, behind which the walls of books appear so impressively, also show a motif of dissolving

Detail of entrance at the corner of the building

Position of the building on the site

surfaces. The stable mass reduces its volume to a minimum as a result of the circular excision, so that stability and frailty enter a border zone of unity – a Mannerist principle.

Rigidity and movement also confirm an aggressive element in the Exeter Library design, which can be considered as an aspect of particular quality in Kahn's work. Primal form and primal forces, thrusting outwards from the energy field in the centre ("Big Bang"), create a universe of knowledge here that is bound into the ordering structure.

This design marks the end of Kahn's complex geometrical late work. Grid structures and simple proportional relations are once more in the foreground, as in his important early phase. The system of figurative geometry acts as a counter-force to the suggestive centrifugal movement in the ground plan structure described above, so that the impression of movement is held in a *balance of tension*. These centrifugal forces in the ground plan will be illustrated in the following.

Façade of the eight-storey library, reduced outside to four main storeys and the roof garden

Access arcades as an encompassing circle

Night view of
the illuminated
staircase

Window with
wooden shelving
for the reading
areas

Two-storey
reading-room zone
on the periphery

Fig.52　A square of defined dimensions is the starting-point for the genesis of this design figure. Double axial symmetry and axes of long extension indicate the centred position of this square, a quarter of which represents a grid module.

Fig.53　A quarter of the central starting square forms an axially symmetrical structure extending to four by four elements. The length of a double grid field of the side now represents the relative size for the construction of a line that cuts this length in the ratio of the Golden Section in the inner grid field. Added to this is the intersection point of two arcs of a circle both from the diagonal and from the side of a grid field. The found line develops, relating to the axial centre, into the centred square. This square represents the actual centre of the building.

Fig.54　A new frame surrounds the derived centre square: extensions of a defined dimension are added at the corners, diagonals that represent the width of the corner columns of the hall. Their width defines the actually visible outline of the space.

Another centred square is produced using the same Golden Section construction as in the last step, but here is related to the outer grid field. This square limits the inner gallery.

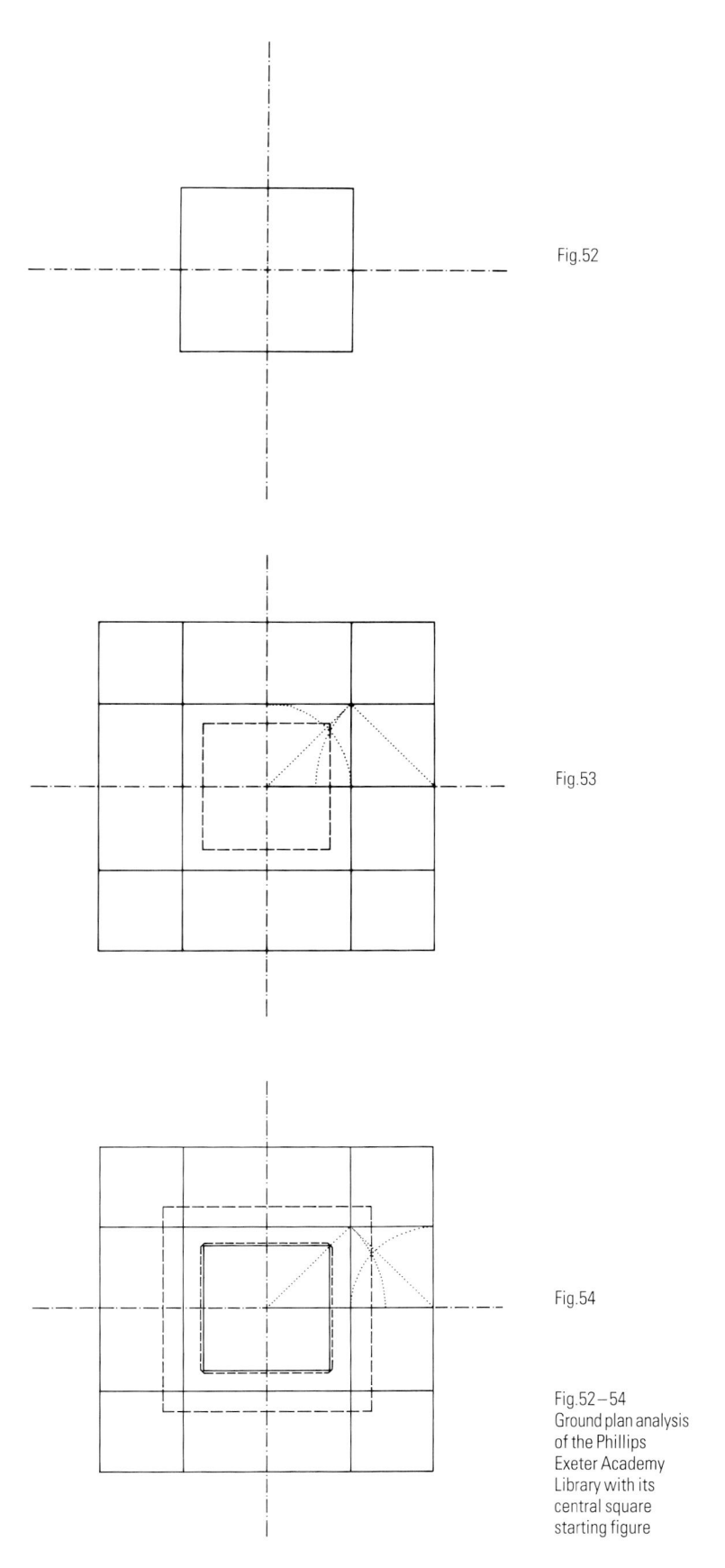

Fig.52

Fig.53

Fig.54

Fig.52–54
Ground plan analysis of the Phillips Exeter Academy Library with its central square starting figure

Fig.55 It becomes clear that the length of the large diagonal columns in the central hall are related to the grid lines of the starting square from figure 52. A gallery around this central room on the normal study levels cuts into four grid squares that are now becoming important at the corners. So-called "cores" emerge within these square corner figures, access elements and shafts.

An arc of a circle is drawn around the centre up to the intersection points of the axis with the aid of the diagonal thus produced. The arc start from the centre of the axis and extends to the outermost lines of these cores. Here the geometrical construction of root 2 major is used. The centred square line applied to the intersection points now forms the final external outline of the building.

It is particularly clear in this geometrical figure how the building develops outwards from the centre. The sequential development stages from the beginning to the final outline remain intelligible, and it is already possible to sense the centrifugal dynamic of the ground plan as a suggestive force.

Fig.56 The outlines of the four core figures in the corners are becoming increasingly more precise. These core bodies break up on the diagonal and extend by length X, which corresponds to the dimensions of the gallery. Here the break-up of the geometrical structure can be seen, and the core bodies form independent elements that are no longer tied into the grid structure. Zones emerge between the cores, still keeping the grid in mind. The bookshelves are placed in these zones, following the lines of the grid. The lengths of cross walls of a defined dimension are now established in the corners of the figure, deriving from the extension of the diagonal cores and following the old grid line tangentially. These walls can now be placed an equal distance apart along the external line in relation to the main axes.

Fig.57 The final lengths of the cross walls arranged on the periphery are defined by the structurally necessary width of the secondary walls of the outer core areas. In this way the outer zone of the reading area is being created, which further breaks up in the ground plan that was ultimately realized (figure 51). The outer walls have the same dimension as the bulkhead walls and form four similar individual areas articulated with niches, as the corners of the overall figure break up in this step. But as the parts are to be kept together in a state of tension, in balance, Kahn adds indented diagonal walls running within a line of the square. They prevent the figure from disintegrating completely.

In the book stack four columns, arranged in a square in each case, indicate the old grid structure and suggest progressive partialization of ground plan structure fixed within a system of figurative geometry in the previous stages.

At first glance the Exeter Library is a very simply structured, symmetrical form in its outward appearance. But viewers who wonder what processes, that are not directly perceptible but still tension-laden, are concealed behind this carefully designed architecture will find that their eyes remain fixed on this building, on its façades and details for a long time. Closer examination reveals complex connections that above all reveal one of Kahn's main intentions: that of developing architecture drawn from a universal language, from a lasting vocabulary not related to its time, and giving it symbolic character and vibrant tension. As has just been demonstrated, it is *order*, understood comprehensively, that forms the basis for this in Kahn's work.

Fig.55

Fig.56

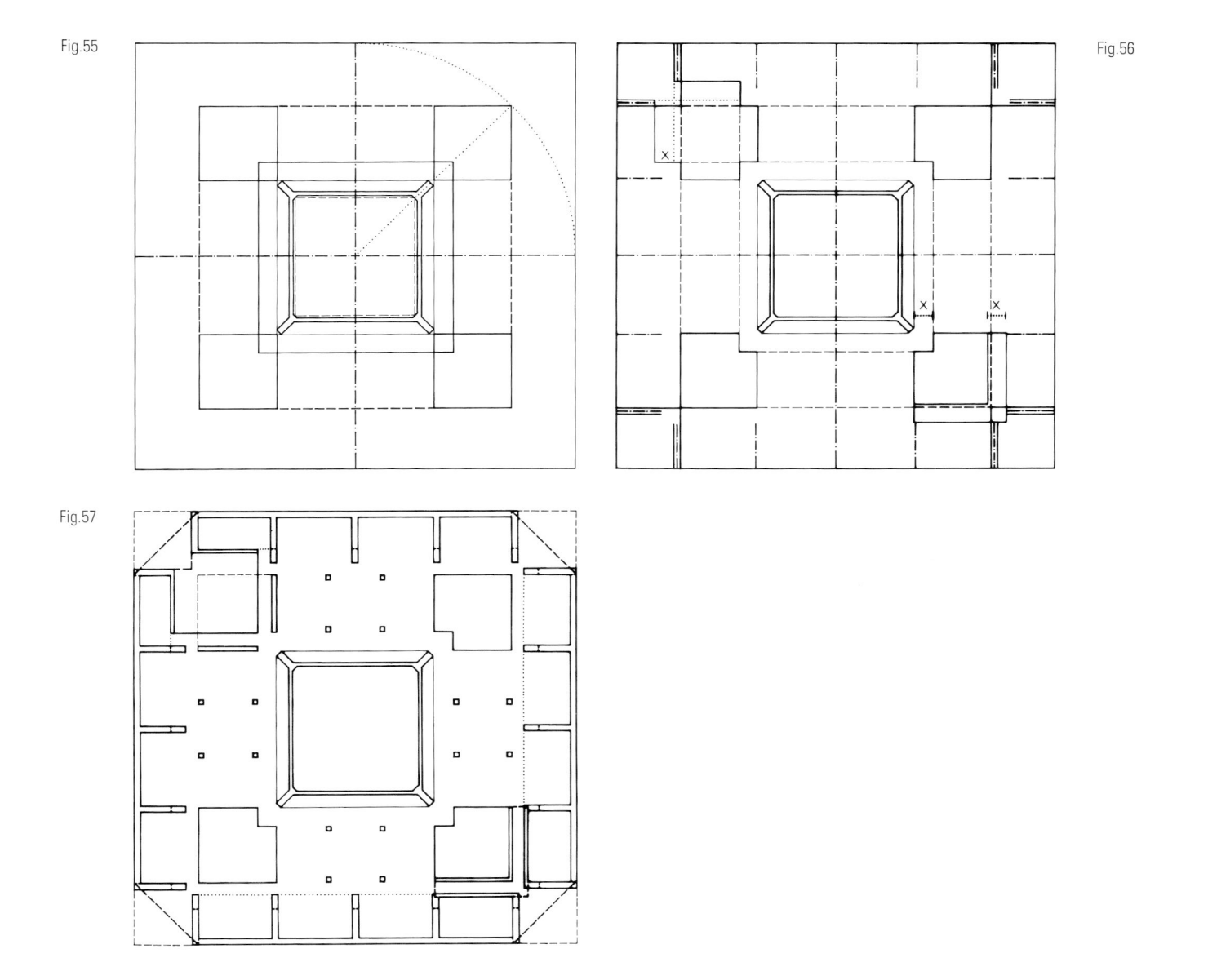

Fig.57

Fig.55–57
Ground plan analysis
of the Phillips
Exeter Academy
Library to the final
ground plan figure

Entrance portico

Kimbell Art Museum
1966–72 Fort Worth Texas USA

The private art collection of Mr. and Mrs. Kimbell in the southern American state of Texas was to be housed in its own museum. Louis Kahn got the commission in 1966 and began to work out his first ideas in the following winter. These were based on an unusual requirement derived from visual relationships with other buildings: the building was not to be higher than 40 feet (about 13 metres). It was to be at the end of a park with existing trees, surrounded by roads on three sides. The final disposition, dated 1969, provided car access from the back road on the basement level, and the main entrance was to face west towards the park on ground floor level. Access from the park and tangentially from the side roads was via an entrance courtyard. A delivery yard and green areas terraced towards the south were arranged on the north side, also at basement level.

The museum design also shows Kahn's return to the simplified forms of his significant early phase. Thoughts about the roof structure, which is necessarily horizontal here, led him to elemental units of the kind that first dominated in Trenton and the Richards Building. This unit considerably affects the structure of the building and almost represents its root. It is formed by a concrete shell construction based on a segment of a circle, in other words a tunnel vault. Additive elements again have an important part to play here, and it should also be said that the character of the design was thus highly dependent on the construction. *Form like construction* could be the formula for this design, which predominantly gives the impression that an engineer is showing his skills, to which August Komendant had made a not inconsiderable contribution.

Fig.58 The ground floor plan shows that the building is symmetrically structured in three parts. In the middle are the entrance courtyard, the foyer and a symmetrical staircase as a connection to the basement, behind this an administrative area and the discrete way up to the library. On the left of our diagram are the area for temporary exhibitions at the front, then a café by a light-well and an auditorium at the back. The whole area on the right is intended as an exhibition area, with two light-wells placed in the centre of it. Offices, other side rooms and access from the parking area were accommodated in the basement. It is clear that all subsidiary figures fit in with the structural principle of the tunnel vault, in other words conform to an internal modular dimension. On the other hand the support-free structure gave a great deal of flexibility within the exhibition area. Between the individual roof elements are small areas in which technical installations can be fitted in the roofspace.

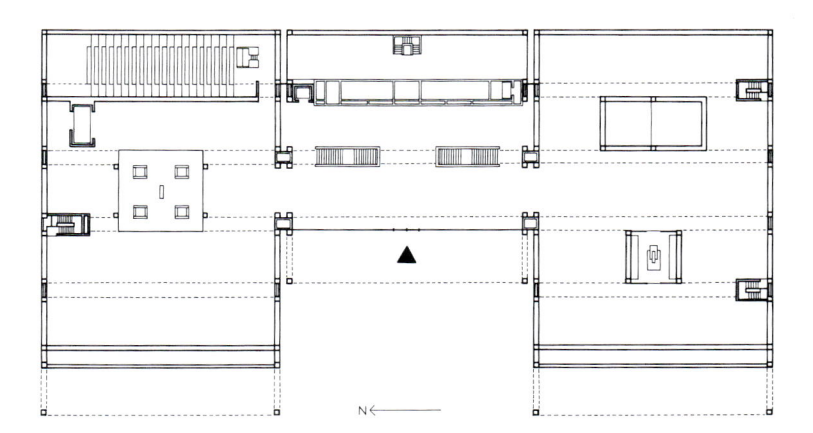

One particular feature makes the Kimbell Art Museum a very independent structure within Kahn's *œuvre*: it has a horizontal quality that is actually very alien to Kahn. He made a virtue of necessity on the basis of the conditions described and dramatized the horizontal element by means of its length. This is particularly marked in the interior of the building, and the visitor is confronted with it in its "pure" form even in the exterior: this basic building block of the whole structure, or better the drama of its construction, is celebrated freely and unobstructed by walls or secondary buildings as a portico on the two side access areas. The piers acquire the character of columns by indications of base, shaft and capital, and the point at which the vault tunnel rests upon the pier becomes a point of unusual detail.

But by doing this Kahn is showing another aspect of his architecture, always very important to him, that of retaining and perceiving the *wholeness* of parts that help to shape the design. The undisguised length of the concrete shell continues to be visible in the entrance "canopy" as

Fig.58
Ground floor plan of the Kimbell Art Museum

Portico and museum form an entity

Overall view from the park

Central access area

Grove of trees at the main access area, providing a natural roof

The two vault elements that impinge on the external space link the building with the terrain. They form the "transition zone" that is so important in Kahn's work, not yet interior and no longer exterior, or both. It is a preparation for the visitor and a space to linger that Kahn designed very consciously with sculpturally cubic stone benches meant as a fixed component of the architecture, not as furniture. Here it is possible to relate different areas: the exterior as an available free parking area, the closer, very carefully designed surroundings of the museum and the all-important vault aspect. Vault, pier, material and the loggia style of this architecture create an atmosphere reminiscent of the Italian Renaissance, but trying to transform it, particularly in combination with the garden and exterior and their material qualities. This intensive detailed planning of the approach areas goes back to Kahn's work with Harriet Pattison and creates an extraordinarily significant museum exterior. A visit to the museum is staged even from a distance: the loggia element is visible as a destination. On the way visitors see the balanced height of the steps, the zoning of the area with non-slip material by means of Travertine framing, in other words rough and smooth material to represent areas to which different weight should be given, and the slight upward slope of the site on subtly differentiated planes, finally the archi-

well as in the portico. In addition, daylight is used in a very particular way, staging these important forms presented in the outside area with the passing day and the interplay of light and shade. In the interior the museum areas are lit be impressive, diffused zenith light, which, as has been much described, is reflected indirectly via the vault. But this ceiling toplight has another function: it means that visitors constantly have the whole of the vault in view. The perception of this whole gives the museum, which is in fact on the small side, a splendid sense of space that is expressed particularly well in the library on the upper floor, which is accommodated exclusively in the vault.

tecture gradually "turns into stone": all this can be experienced as building up to a climax. The special quality of this design lies in its *tactility*, the feel of this approach to the building with its different areas and the functions associated with it. Two symmetrical fountains also evoke a Mediterranean atmosphere.

Tangential access to the museum

Outside portico and sunken sculpture garden

Rear view of the museum from the sunken parking area

Kahn creates a large entrance courtyard. This is an unusual gesture in comparison with his other main entrances, which tend to be concealed, but the courtyard is comprehensible in the context of the exterior space described. Just before the entrance to the building the courtyard acquires a natural low roof of Japanese cherry trees, standing in a homogeneous gravel bed. Visitors are required to walk over the soft, crunchingly coarse gravel area and to experience the daylight filtering through the crowns of the trees, before being drawn into the wooden and stone floor area and the controlled top daylight of the museum interior.

Fountain and pool in front of the symmetrically arranged porticoes

If one considers the side exterior walls of the museum building, one is aware of a tendency to *homogenize* different materials. The materials are similar in character but different in colouring: concrete for the structural system and Travertine for the wall fillings are set flush, and so the vault elements, clearly intelligible in their support structure seem to fuse into a coherent mass with the walls. This is reminiscent of the Salk Institute with its combination of concrete and Travertine, but for the museum Kahn does not try to give the concrete the same colour as the marble. Here an element of *ambiguity* emerges, similarly to the puzzle picture effect of the Exeter library: the additive concrete elements can be seen as tied into a continuous mass, but a dominating elemental structure can also be discerned, which is held together "only" by filler walls.

The piers for the elements seem to grow out of the concrete base of the bottom floor, but then the two areas are separated by a base strip with fine joints. Different arch radiuses in the side vault frames and the wall area suggest dynamics: it remains unclear whether, in the form chosen, this frame in the zenith is thrusting downwards or rising.

The language of additive, quasi-autonomous element figures chosen by Kahn when designing the Kimbell Art Museum could have been influenced by a contemporary phenomenon in the art world, although this cannot be directly proved. It is the Minimal Art movement which started in the early sixties, although this descriptive concept was not accepted by the artists involved. One of the outstanding exponents of this movement was the American artist Donald Judd, influenced in his turn by the German Bauhaus artist Joseph Albers, who was teaching at Yale and also inspired Kahn. The spiritual closeness of this art to Kahn's architecture was confirmed by Judd in a conversation with the author, in which he referred to Kahn as "one of the really important architects", of whom he thought a great deal. Judd made an interesting move in the early seventies from New York, which was very close to Philadelphia, to the southern state of Texas, half a day's journey from Forth Worth, and set up a permanent museum of his own work there. The link between this view of art and Kahn's architecture, as well as a fascination with simplified, additive bodies that could often not be reduced any further as a kind of *final point of abstraction*, was certainly his understanding of the universal language of geometrical structure and its proportional quality.

Concrete sculptures by Donald Judd in Marfa, Texas

Portico with side access path

Pool and exterior area

Portico with bench

Façade detail in the loggia area

93

Façade detail on
the short side

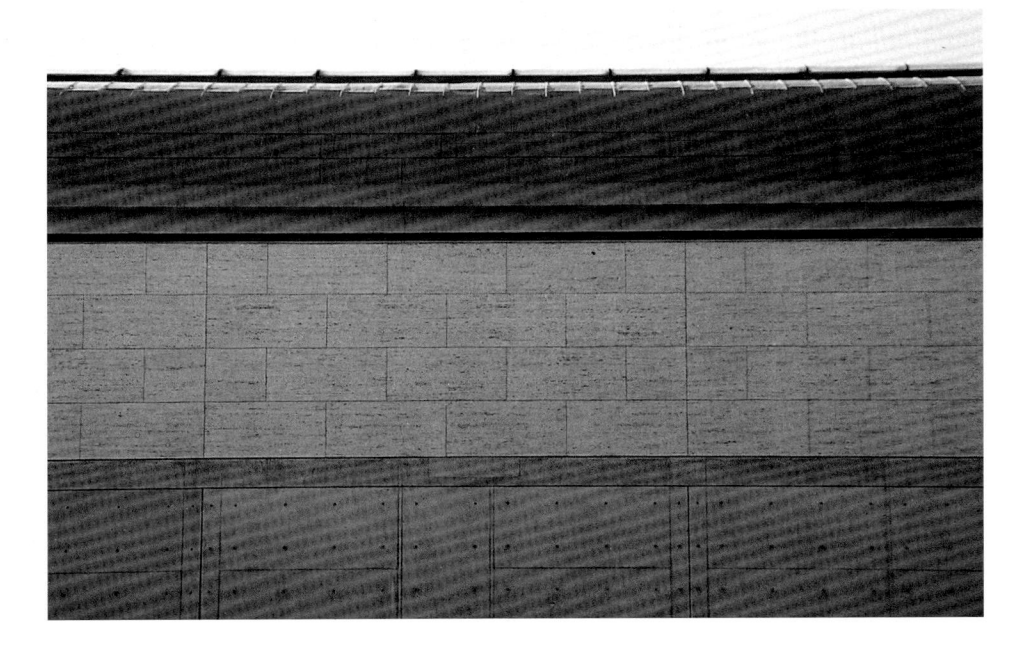

Materials in the
exterior area

Delivery yard
façade detail

Skylight at the peak
of the ceiling shell

Library area in the
upper storey

Fig.59 Exceptionally, the following analysis begins with a geometrical figure that does not agree in part with the existing lines of the building, but that must be valid as a crucial preliminary consideration.

Fig.59 A double square of defined dimensions, placed as a rectangle, is the starting figure for the Kimbell Art Museum. It forms the basis of a symmetry that determines the structure of the building throughout.

Fig.60 A process of movement begins: the double square overlaps itself by the width X. Thus the final length of the interior is already established. The following steps show the extraordinary importance of width X, which has an effect on the whole structure.

Fig.61 The overlap width X can be detected in the symmetrical arrangement of two staircase figures in the rear third of the centre of the space.
A wall thickness of constructionally determined dimensions is now added to the established outline. Kahn fixes the structure of the building by dividing it into three. Three zones are formed using proportional figures after fixing the exterior wall: a rectangular figure placed symmetrically in the centre and two rectangular figures added to the exterior walls on the short sides in a ratio of 1:1.618 (Golden Section). The spaces in between are in the form of narrow strips.

Fig.62 The central role played by the overlapping width X for the structure of the building can be seen from the fact that it determines the width of the vault elements in the roof. Six elements, starting with the outside edges, are distributed along the short side, so that narrow, strip-like intermediate zones are produced in the longitudinal direction as well. They make up the flat roof surface as the distance between the barrels, and the installations areas in the interior. The strips arising from the division into three start to form spaces by zoning the rear interior area.

Fig.63 After fixing the roof structure, which shapes the disposition of the interior, the building now acquires its final outline. Both outside and interior areas are reduced by one vault element, with the sixth now being allotted to the exterior. Thus it can be assumed that Kahn originally intended this sixth element for the interior as well. It is certain that the portico elements of the exterior area were given the same proportions as the building as a whole, as described in the analytical sequence. Here too one vault element is allotted to the exterior space, with the border between exterior and interior, as in the two portico figures, running along the line of the element.

Fig.64 All the sub-figures that are crucial to define the interior derive from the dimensions of the elemental structure described. Light-wells are arranged in the symmetrical axes of the two side areas, forming squares and taking up the outline of the structure. Different functions are zoned off in the rear area, including an administrative element in the middle and the auditorium on the left, each with the width of a vault element plus distance strips. Narrow side rooms for technical equipment are formed along the portico elements.

The Kimbell Art Museum primarily focuses on pattern and structure. However, here the structure does not follow a given formal "law", it also does not establish spatial hierarchies on the "servant/served" principle (as in the Trenton Bathhouse), nor does it spring to life almost automatically by lavishly detailed technical solutions (as in the Richards Building). Instead of this Kahn tries here to develop structure and space as a whole, so that a sequence of these unities will finally form a new, higher unity for the overall space. Here the formal idea of the barrel vault struggles with the structural idea to dominate the expressive gesture, but the outcome of this struggle remains undecided.

Fig.59

Fig.60

Fig.61

Fig.62

Fig.63

Fig.64

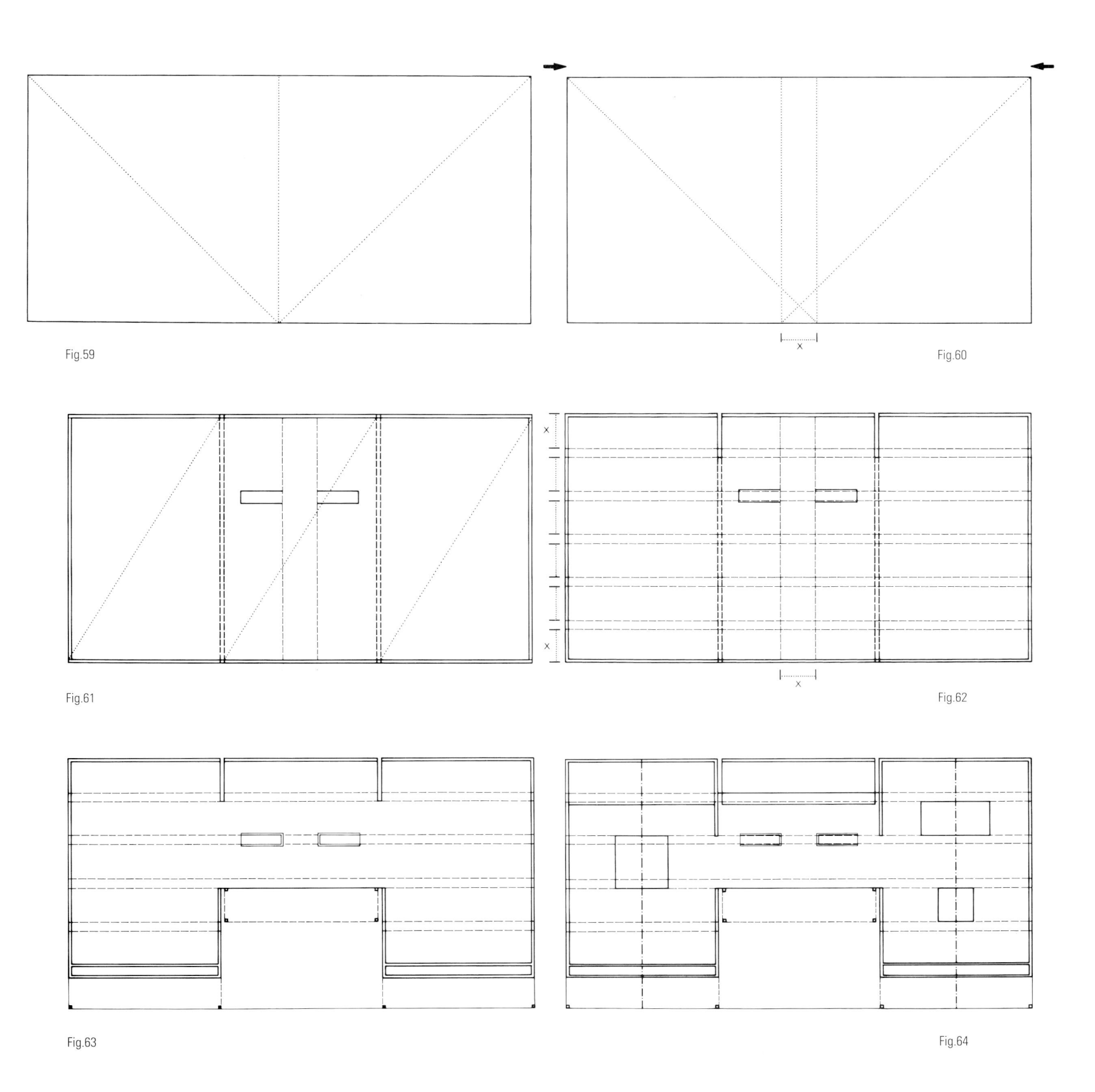

Fig.59–64
Ground plan analysis of the Kimbell Art Museum from the starting figure of a double square to the final figure

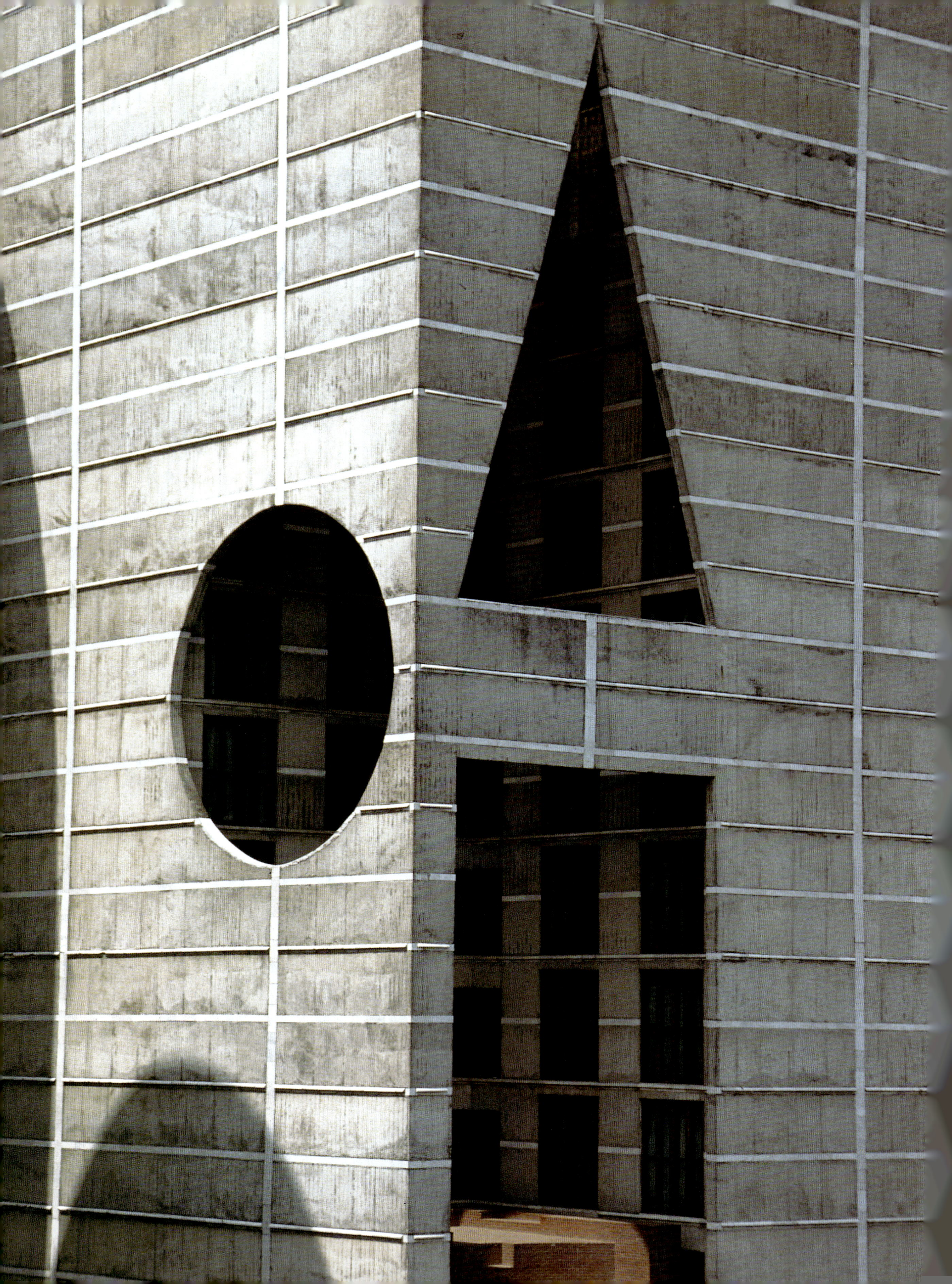

National Capital of Bangladesh
1962–83 Dhaka Bangladesh

Fig.65 Kahn's first visit to Dhaka was in January 1963. The basic scheme for the National Capital of Bangladesh sketched at this time shows two groups of buildings facing each other, relating axially; its approximately final disposition was arrived at in December 1963. It demonstrates Kahn's precise conception and his extraordinarily decisive attitude to an idea that fascinated him: that of mastering a very large building mass. He created a composition at the lower edge of the site with a central prismatic volume as the place for the parliamentary assembly together with linked garden and courtyard areas on two sides and flanking diagonal residential areas. Building work on the revised parliamentary complex and the residential zones on each side in fact started in 1964, but the outbreak of the civil war in 1971, difficulties in execution and Kahn's indecision about the roof design for the hall led to a delay of many years. The main building was not approaching completion until about 1982. Nevertheless, a parliamentary city did come into being, complete in itself and strictly hierarchical in its structure, with diagonally linked residences for employees and ministers and public service facilities on either side, gardens and a ceremonial square for the president on the north side as well as the central, crystalline parliament building for 300 members, in the middle of an artificial lake. The parliament building is ringed by four sets of secretarial and ministers' offices, lavish recreation and catering areas and a mosque with its main entrance on the south side.

Kahn placed a highly symbolic mosque, which was as firm a requirement for Muslim ceremonial as other elements, at the forefront of this complex, intended to be a "national symbol of the beginnings of a democratic society". Kahn stated that "Assembly is of transcendent nature".[51] He thought that when walking through the main entrance with the prayer room above, the building acquired an appropriately spiritual character.[52] Thus Kahn calls the parliament building a "citadel" for the legislative assembly. The assembly building is surrounded by water and thus tends to reflect historic Mogul architecture, yet the name "citadel" is not intended to give it the quite unmotivated character of a fortress. The secure, strong qualities of the citadel are transferred symbolically to a spiritual one initiated by the mosque and embracing the building as an entity.

Façade detail of one of the secretariat buildings

The different buildings of the complex, linked in a circular shape, move round a centre similar to the sanctuary in Rochester and emphasized in its significance. *Concentricity* is a constant motif in Kahn's designs, from the Trenton Bathhouse to the Exeter Library. Concentrated in this way, the arrangement leads to an urban "total form" as a whole and to a monolithic structure, showing Kahn's *antagonism of the integration of autonomous figures*, taken to an extreme. The overall figure is tied together by the homogeneity arising from concrete as material and the contrasting light marble strips, alternately casting shadows, like reliefs. Thus the parliament building is separated from the surrounding squares and accommodation areas, which are kept in brick. This produces a quality that shows up in the Indian Institute building in Ahmedabad, was anticipated in the Unitarian Church and reaches its extreme in Dhaka: the *monolith as a new structural form* of individual figures that nevertheless cohere with the whole. All the buildings mentioned are dominated by a material that embraces all parts, making them an integrated whole, and enter into a charged dialogue with a secondary material – marble in Dhaka and concrete in Ahmedabad.

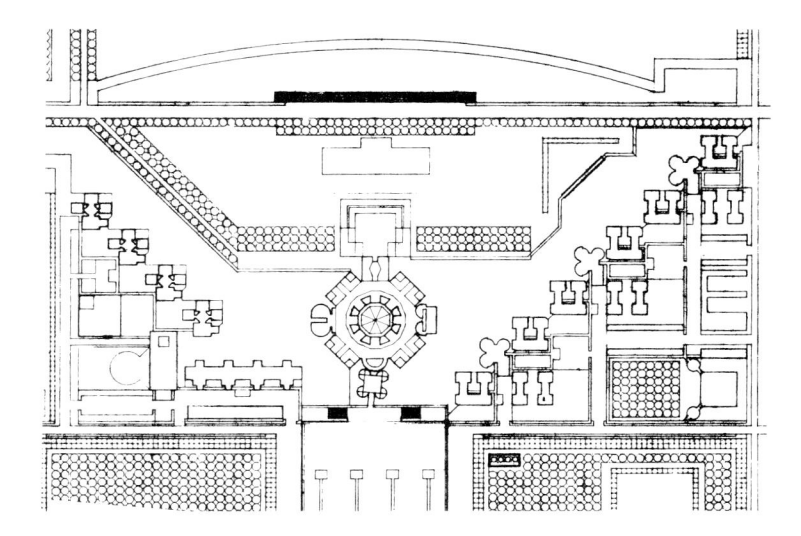

Fig.65
Main access level of the National Capital of Bangladesh

Assembly building in Kahn's lake, catering building front left

[51] Wurman, "What will be ...", p. 105.
[52] Alessandra Latour (ed.), "Louis I. Kahn, Writings, Lectures, Interviews", Rizzoli International Publications, New York 1991, p. 195; Kahn is referring to the parliament building in Dhaka.

View from the President's Garden with show staircase and central main access lobby

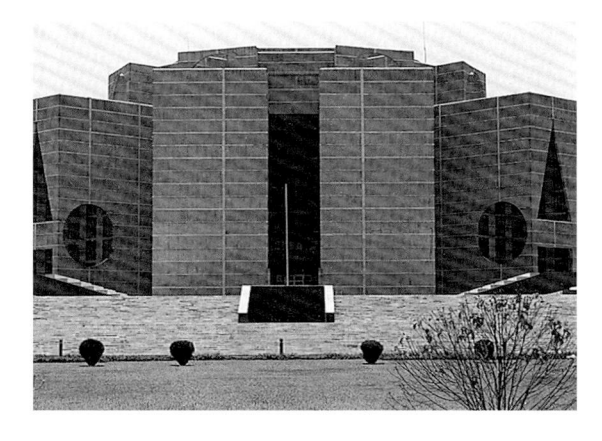

Fig.65a The external lines of the diagonally arranged, rectangular secretarial and office areas in the parliamentary complex can be put together as a square embracing all the sub-figures, whose centre seems to determine the geometry of the pure circle. This is how Kahn's formal concept of the general beginning of a design should be perceived, a concept that was implemented directly and in principle here for the first time as a "primal figure" and a "mandala". The figure of the mandala, a diagrammatic image of universal connections in the form of a "cosmogram" will be presented in the exemplary analysis of the Indian Institute of Management (see p. 178 f.).

But close examination of the geometrical and structural basis shows a subtle but significant "distortion" of this simple initial figure: the building is anchored north-south, and the circle *extends* by a distance that can be established geometrically in this direction, between the parade-ground and the presidential garden opposite.[53] It distorts the figure as a whole and divides it into two halves, so that the rectangular office areas on the periphery find their counterpart not on the axis, but slightly shifted. As well as this, there is a sense that the symmetrical individual figures are being *blown apart*, with the exception of the hermetic appendix of the mosque, which falls on to a line running almost precisely east-west, disturbing the axial symmetry. In the façade this is clearly illustrated by the fact that the "skin" bursts open in the centre, and suggests, heightening the stretching process at the centre, the dynamics of outward-thrusting, i. e. centrifugal forces.

Without particularly bringing out structural elements, the appearance of the individual buildings in the complex shifts between massive volume and a delicate thinness of skin. This leads to new light spaces, the province only of light and shade, with expressively symbolic openings that lend a mystical quality to light itself. These "light spaces", binding themselves in with the mass of the buildings and yet detaching themselves as spaces with their own, autonomous façade figures, are an architectural innovation developed by Kahn. The impressive shadow drama of its façade figures double in the secretarial and office area, their geometrical openings cut out with surgical precision, stands in sharp contrast with the concrete cubes, which are almost white in the sunlight. The openings shape the overall form of the building, although contradictorily they do not express functional areas that lie directly behind them, but reflect an image of *independent, ambiguous spaces*. Despite the fact that they are completely integrated in the simplified volume, which stands out precisely because of the sharp-edged exterior line, these zones remain a component of the exterior space in the twilight between sun and shade. They define *light volumes* – spaces designed without exception for the moderated light, and acquire independent, emphatically anti-functional openings. Their archaic and symbolic character intensifies the intended spiritual "aura" for the building as a whole.

This circumstance confirms that the extraordinary form of the opening figures makes sense, even though the geometry, which has a life of its

Assembly building with hostels in front

[53] Student work by Annett Janeczko and Martina Hille during a seminar by the author at the TU in Braunschweig, in which the "distortion" of the inner circle is demonstrated geometrically.
For this see: Florindo Fusaro, "Il Parlamento e la nuova capitale in Dacca di Louis I. Kahn, 1962–1974", Officina Edizioni, Rome 1985, p. 75.
As well as the incorrect building dates in the title (correct: 1962–1983) there is a very crude geometrical definition of key lines in various projects by Kahn, showing a generally square schematization that is not presented in further detail; it ignores the above-mentioned shifts and deliberately introduced inequalities in the Dhaka parliament, and neglects Kahn's intention in all his projects of building tension into his structures by using the contrast between rigidity and movement.

Fig.65a

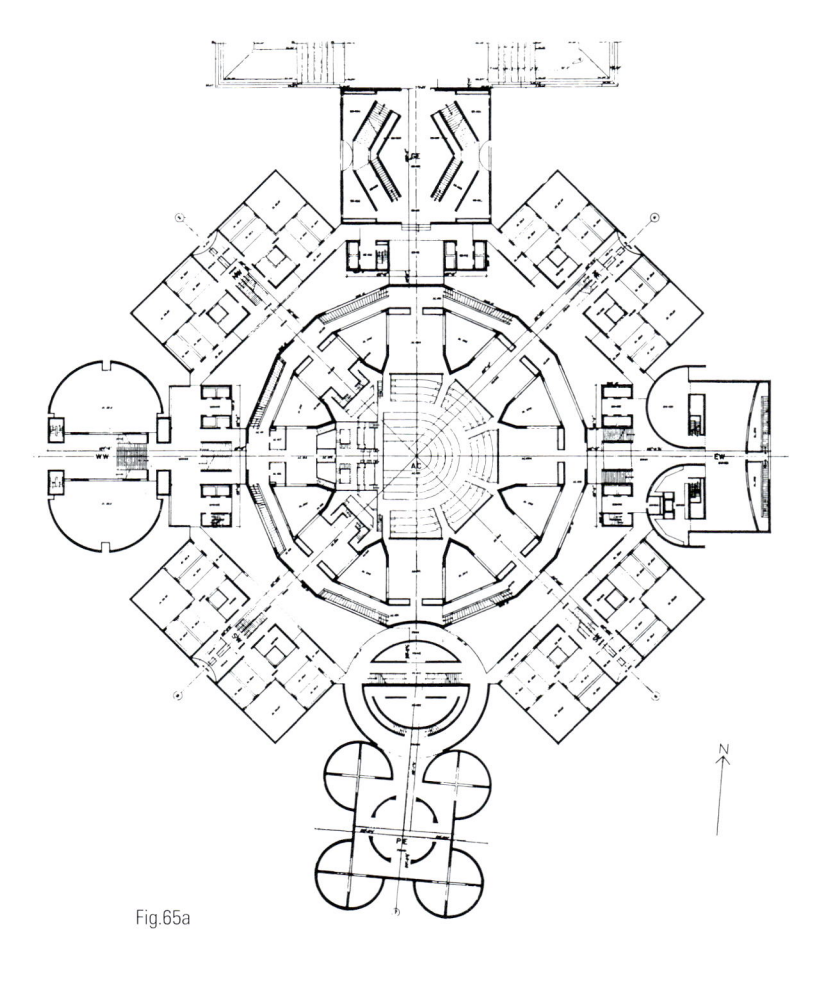

Secretaries' hostels

Ministers' hostels

Central Assembly Building with assembly chamber lighting crown

101

own, has been persistently misunderstood by critics.⁵⁴ The figures are divided into two in the façade, which corrects the impression that there may be two storeys by positioning at the centre of the side a circular incision as a rising cavity.

As "façades for nothingness" the openings identify zones that from the outside belong to shadow as the ally of light, negative light, as it were. Their drama positively harasses the viewer into a definition of the status and quality of light in creating architecture. They are the equivalent of the cylindrical light shafts of the mosque, which break up the corners and exclusively reflect the light of heaven into the prayer hall, a kind of hollow column for light.

View with staircase lobby left, office building centre and recreation area right, with "exploding" joints

Kahn explained the form of the openings as especially resistant to the danger of earthquakes, and tried to calm pragmatic spirits down with this. He also had the main building constructed in concrete for statical reasons relating to the terrain; this material is alien to the country and requires its own manufacturing methods. He also combined the "masculine" material with marble incrustations and their apparently "feminine" character.

While Kahn's long-standing engineering advisor Komendant felt that the parliament complex was a structural and formal, in other words an architectural mistake,⁵⁵ Scully praised Kahn's Asian architecture as "one of the most successful examples of modern architecture on the subcontinent".⁵⁶ Curtis describes the design as an experiment in creating archaic building structures that attempt to fuse the concrete historical models of European culture with those of India in the form of the cosmogram.⁵⁷ Dunnett sees their megalithic magnificence and refined simplicity as a tension-laden pair of opposites.⁵⁸ Banerji, similarly to Curtis, sees the Dhaka parliament building as a return to man's archetypal memory, which is hard to decipher, where architecture is ambiguous and open to misunderstanding, and here, according to Banerji, "does not soothe the senses ... the devil and the angel of Kahn's ideology seem dramatically exposed."⁵⁹ Banerji also asserts that the "tragedy" of the project can be seen in the painful process of its creation, and that Western European romanticism is mixing with Eastern mysticism. He goes on to say that this combination, removed from the rationality of Western thought structures, was easy to understand for "Eastern people", especially as internationalized functionalism was imported to Eastern countries both as an abstract term and as a concrete realization.

Contradictions remain an essential component of the architecture in Dhaka as well. Kahn consciously uses them as means of building up inner tensions, like the calculated move away from axial symmetry evoked by dynamic processes, the distortion of basic geometrical figures and diagonally shifting elements. This not only has an effect on the disposition of the ground plan, but also shows views of the buildings as an ensemble that is compact, yet moving, almost "dancing" around a centre, particularly as the viewer continues to move. The contrasts of divided and linked partial figures, massive cubes against perforated membranes and the combination of both noble and ignoble material, in order to enhance the claim of autonomy in terms of the functional linking also enrich the repertoire.

It becomes clear from the following analysis of the parliament buildings that Kahn followed very consciously the above-mentioned process of distorting his original figures of square and circle. The genesis of the design, in the process shown here, illustrates how Kahn fought to balance the retention of pre-existing forms and the creation of a more complex geometrical structure.

---

[54] Komendant, Kahn's design engineer, said critically in 1975: "The large round openings ... raise questions nobody is able to answer intelligently" (Komendant, "18years ...", p. 86, and Alexandra Tyng found them "too dramatic" in 1984 (Tyng, "Beginnings", p. 50). Robert Venturi explained the openings in particular as "overformalized" in an interview with the author in 1988 and used the figuration of the openinings ironically in the façade of his "Wu-Hall", a student club house with refectory at the University of Princeton, New Jersey.
[55] Komendant, "18 years ...", pp. 85–87.
[56] Scully, "American Architecture and Urbanism", New York 1969.
[57] William J. R. Curtis, "Authenticity, Abstraction and the Ancient Sense: Le Corbusiers and Louis Kahns Ideas of Parliament", in: Perspecta 20, The Yale Architectural Journal, Yale University, New Haven, Rizzoli Publications Inc., New York 1983, pp. 190–194.
[58] Dunnett, "City of the tiger", Architectural Review 1980.
[59] Banerji, "Learning from Bangladesh", The Canadian Architect, Oktober 1980.

Façade details in different lights

Catering area for assembly employees inside the hostels

103

Exterior view of the Assembly Building from the public area

Assembly Building with President's Garden, adjacent to the north, on the left

The starting figure for the parliament building is a square standing on its tip. It defines the shape of the building as a kind of frame. The entire genesis of the basic figure ensues within this frame as a geometrical process comparable to biological development. Axial relations are important here, in this case not as parallels to the sides but as diagonal axes. They set the "genetic" directions in this figure.

Fig.66

Zones are defined by a grid structure made up of nine squares within the starting figure. This figure of division into nine also pre-exists as far as Kahn is concerned, as it is a simplified primal figure of the above-mentioned mandala, and a motif that runs through all Kahn's work. Structure and a diagonal axial cross form the essence, a *genetic scaffolding* from which more complex subsequent figures emerge.

Fig.67

Half the length of a diagonal is now divided in the proportion of the Golden Section. Its geometrical structure can be explained as follows: the half diagonal forms an equilateral triangle with its central, halving vertical. Half its hypotenuse, as an arc of a circle, cuts the arc of the short side of the triangle (cathetus). A line runs through this point of intersection, dividing the half diagonal in the ratio described. The shorter section of this division forms the minor Golden Section, radius of a circle developing around the central point. This is the centre and becomes the starting figure for the inner hall building.

Fig.68

The next thing to emerge is the geometrical connection between the framing outline of the square and the central circular figure. The arc of a circle with the side length of the square cuts the diagonal at a point that is its root 2 division, and thus defines a new radius of a circle that surrounds the inner circle. Golden Section and root 2 proportion once more appear, as in all Kahn's designs, as a communicating pair and form a tense and irrational element within the rationally developed basic structure.

Fig.69

Fig.66

Fig.67

Fig.68

Fig.69

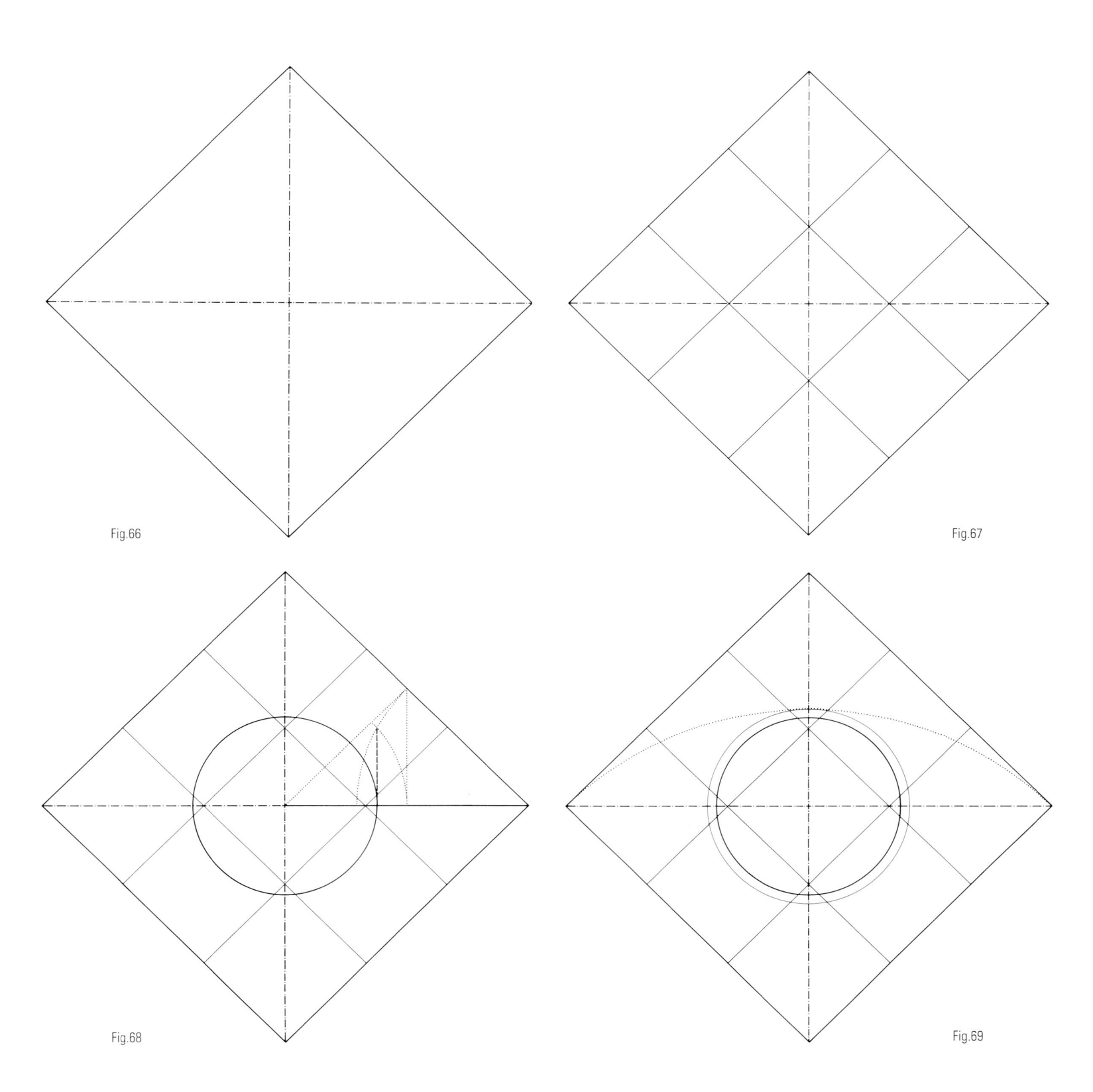

Fig.66–69
Ground plan analysis of the National Capital of Bangladesh with its diagonal square as a starting figure

Fig.70 The crucial process that lies behind the whole structure of the parliament building is that the inner circle, enlarged by the thickness of a wall, is now *exploded*. It extends in a north-south direction by a distance that is determined by the outer circle. The tangents at the points of intersection with the vertical axis fix the distance between the circles in the way they cut the outer circle at two points in each case. Thus the original circular figure of the hall building develops into a form like an oval and suggests a distortion process with centrifugal forces, although they are directed in this project, in contrast with the usual equally undirected forces. Not only the circle is distorted, but the axes parallel with the sides that are associated with it also shift together with the two centres of the radii in a north-south direction.

Fig.71 It is remarkable that the framing outline of the square, does not change with the extension of the circle in the centre of the square. All the processes of movement up to this point have taken place within the bounds of the square and retain the original figure in its totality. Another root 2 division can now be constructed with the shifted axis positions and their slightly changed lengths. The axis forms the diagonal of an imaginary square, the length of whose sides cuts the diagonal as the arc of a circle. Here a line running parallel with the sides of the initial square is added; this forms an outer peripheral zone and divides the area of the square into three fields: an outer "ring", the oval figure in the centre and a gap that is not further defined.

Fig.72 Starting from the grid structure of the square's division into nine, fields that can be clearly outlined are defined within the outer peripheral zone, showing up as four similar rectangles. They make up the administrative areas for the parliament. It is quickly clear that these zones are also shifted together with the axes, so that although mirror symmetry is retained by the vertical and horizontal axes of the starting square, the orthogonal opposite in each case shows differing positions. The long side of such a rectangular area corresponds to the division of the starting square into thirds. The short side allows outer squares to be divided off, to be used as the actual offices.

Fig.73 As well as the office areas, we can assume that the other zones also started as rectangles in Kahn's design ideas. At this stage Kahn sketched rectangles arranged in a ring, appropriately to the scheme presented. Analysis shows that the three areas on the west, north and east sides are squares of the same size, as adjacent narrow zones of this width actually exist in the realized building as access areas. These narrow access zones overlap partly with the squares whose outer corners bump against the framing line of the starting square.

A circular figure is created in the southern area, which unlike the extending hall figure is compressed, and consists of two segments of a circle with different centres. Extending the central hall circle to form an oval gives the impression that the neighbouring figures are distorted with it, as it were. Here we are dealing with a lavish access element in the zone in front of the separate mosque building. The mosque is shifted as a square of particular dimensions in order to approach a precise east-west orientation; however, the shift also means a consciously staged breaking away from fixed structures.

Fig. 70

Fig. 71

Fig. 72

Fig. 73

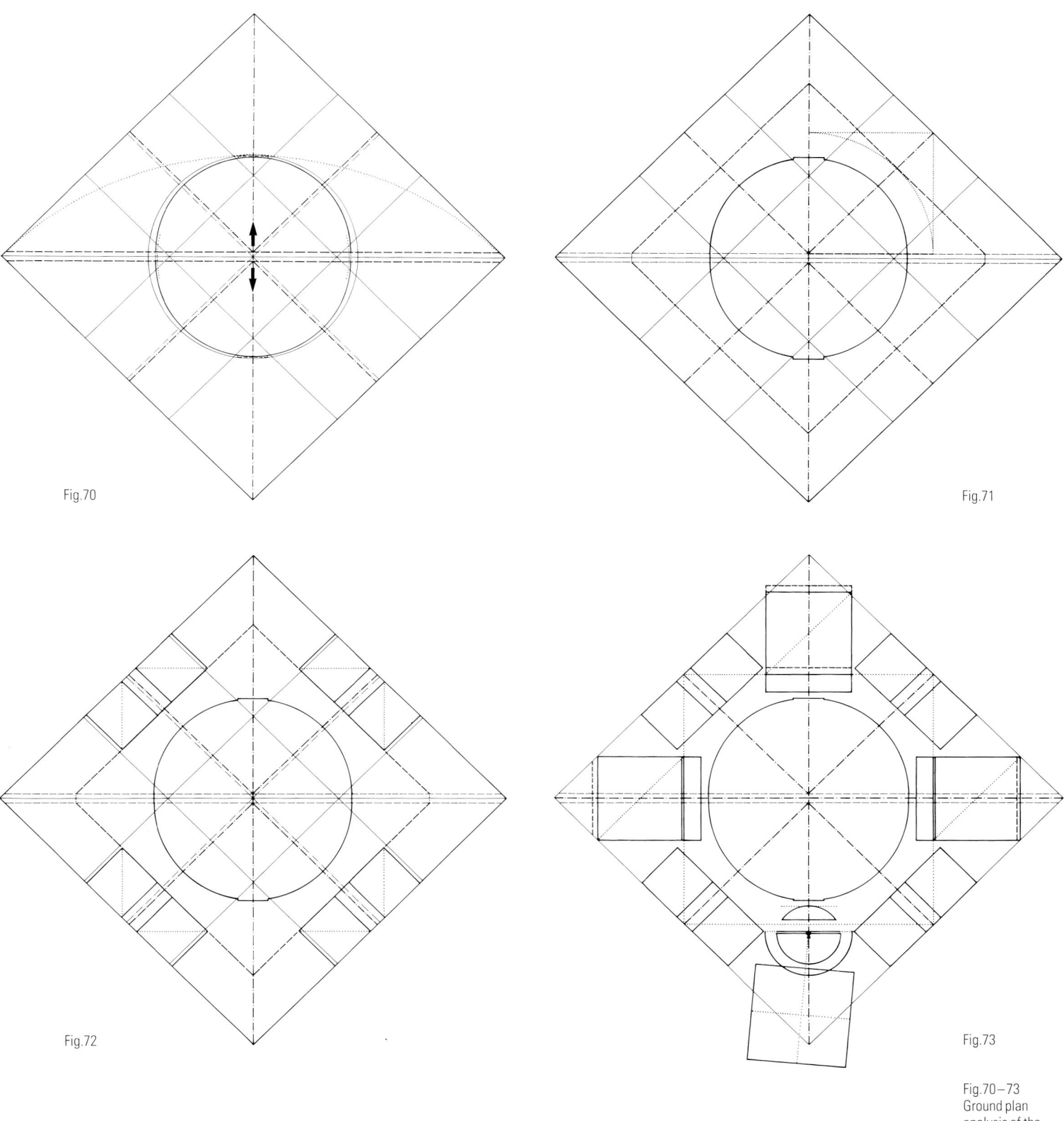

Fig. 70–73
Ground plan
analysis of the
National Capital
of Bangladesh,
continued

Fig.74　All the figures standing next to each other in isolation now acquire a connecting access corridor in the interior.

While the administrative buildings seem fixed as a copy of the grid structure, further distortion of the squares occurs in the corners of the enclosing square. The northern square is an extraordinarily large entrance hall with show staircases, and shifts outwards by the distance of the access figure, while the mosque building in the south forms four circles within the outline of the square that combine at the corners with a central square figure. The absolutely dramatic break away from the frame of the starting square occurs only in the north-south direction, thus supporting the oval's direction of movement from the centre. All the other figures distort within the frame and acquire independent – autonomous – form. Kahn chooses partial circular segments as forms in order to indicate the special function of these parts of the building; on the west side they are generous lounge areas for ministers and catering areas on the east side. However, the choice of the circle segments, as well as performing a functional task, clearly illustrates the distortion as a *crushing* and *compression* within the corset of the square framing. The exploded distance, the twisting of the central circular figure of the hall, is retained in the interior in both these figures by a central rectangular zone, but also in the realized façade image by a slit.

Fig.75　Thus the figure of the parliament building is almost completely developed in its final shape. The isolated, central assembly chamber now acquires polygonal form as a result of the transfer of the segment already sketched in a north-south direction in previous steps to all axes. This provides access zones or sitting areas with various functions dependent on the particular level. The extended polygon emerges as the final external outline of the hall simply by combining these segments within the ground plan figure. A final circle in the centre with half the radius of the hall indicated the central sitting area for the members of parliament.

Between the hall and the peripheral area is an airspace, a kind of covered exterior area, from whose access galleries the autonomous character and the dimension of the buildings can be grasped in full height. All the sections of the building remain distinguishable as single elements in the exterior, but they are bound together into a unit that forms a whole by the ordering structure of figurative geometry, which cannot be grasped directly but is always present.

The parliament building in Dhaka is Kahn's largest, but also his most extraordinary work. It can be called the culmination of several creative phases, and perhaps reflects in the most impressive way Kahn's concern to develop an all-embracing, culture-linking, indeed global architectural language intended to reach far into the 21st century. But only the future will show whether the degree of absoluteness envisaged by Kahn for an "expression of architecture", as he called it, deviating from the taste of its times, hurrying ahead of the misunderstandings current when it was created, committed to that time, but constantly valid, created by an "imperfect" human individual, whether all these things will have found appropriate form in this building as a complex, innovative work of architecture, and will finally do justice to its high demands, from which western categories are partially withdrawn.

Main access bridge from the south, with access for servants above and visitors below

Fig.74

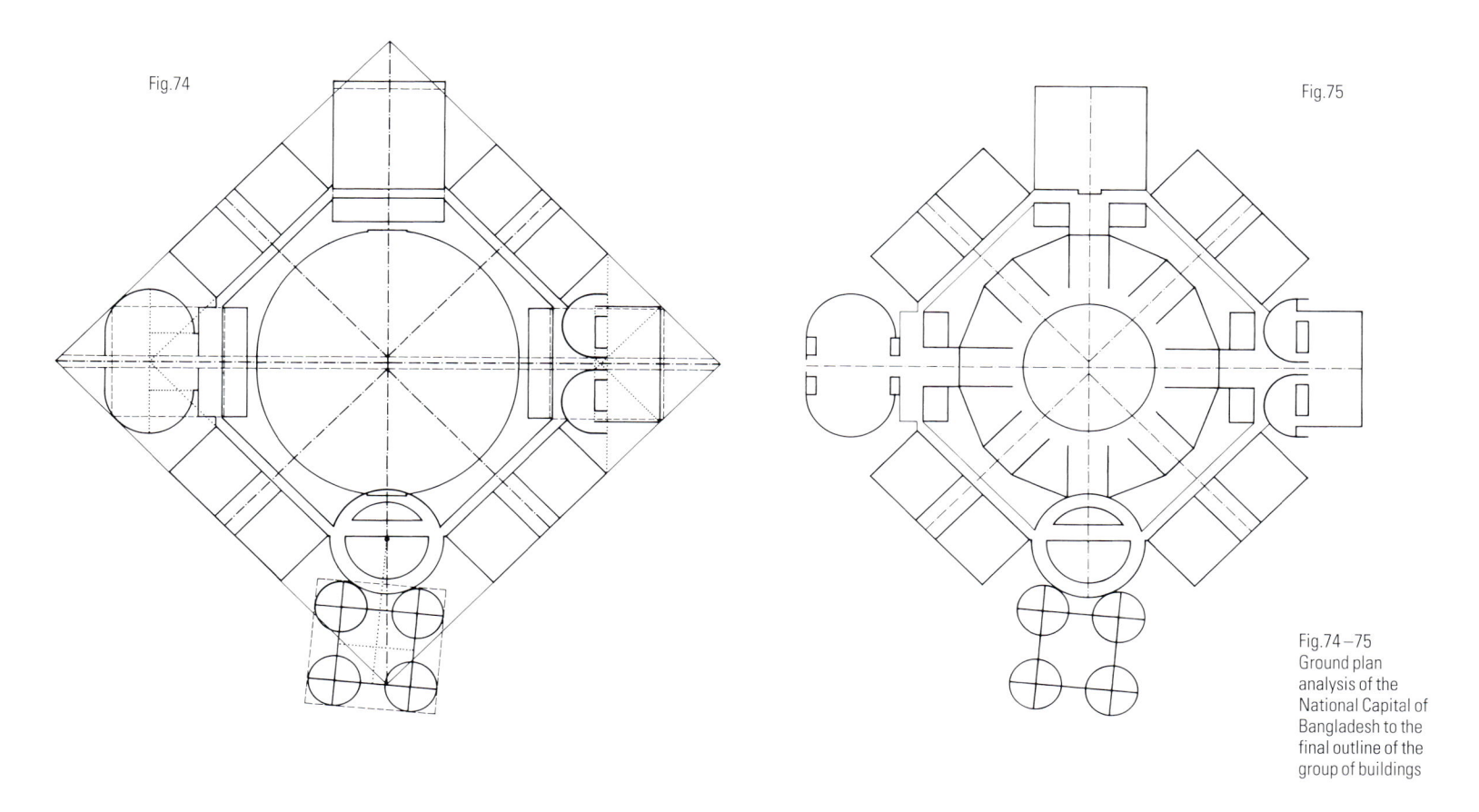

Fig.75

Fig.74–75
Ground plan analysis of the National Capital of Bangladesh to the final outline of the group of buildings

Mosque building swung off the axis

Interior of the
Assembly Building,
mosque forecourt

Staircase within
the presidential
access area

Interior of the
Assembly Building,
access areas

President's
staircase

Mosque interior

"Tent" roof of the central assembly chamber

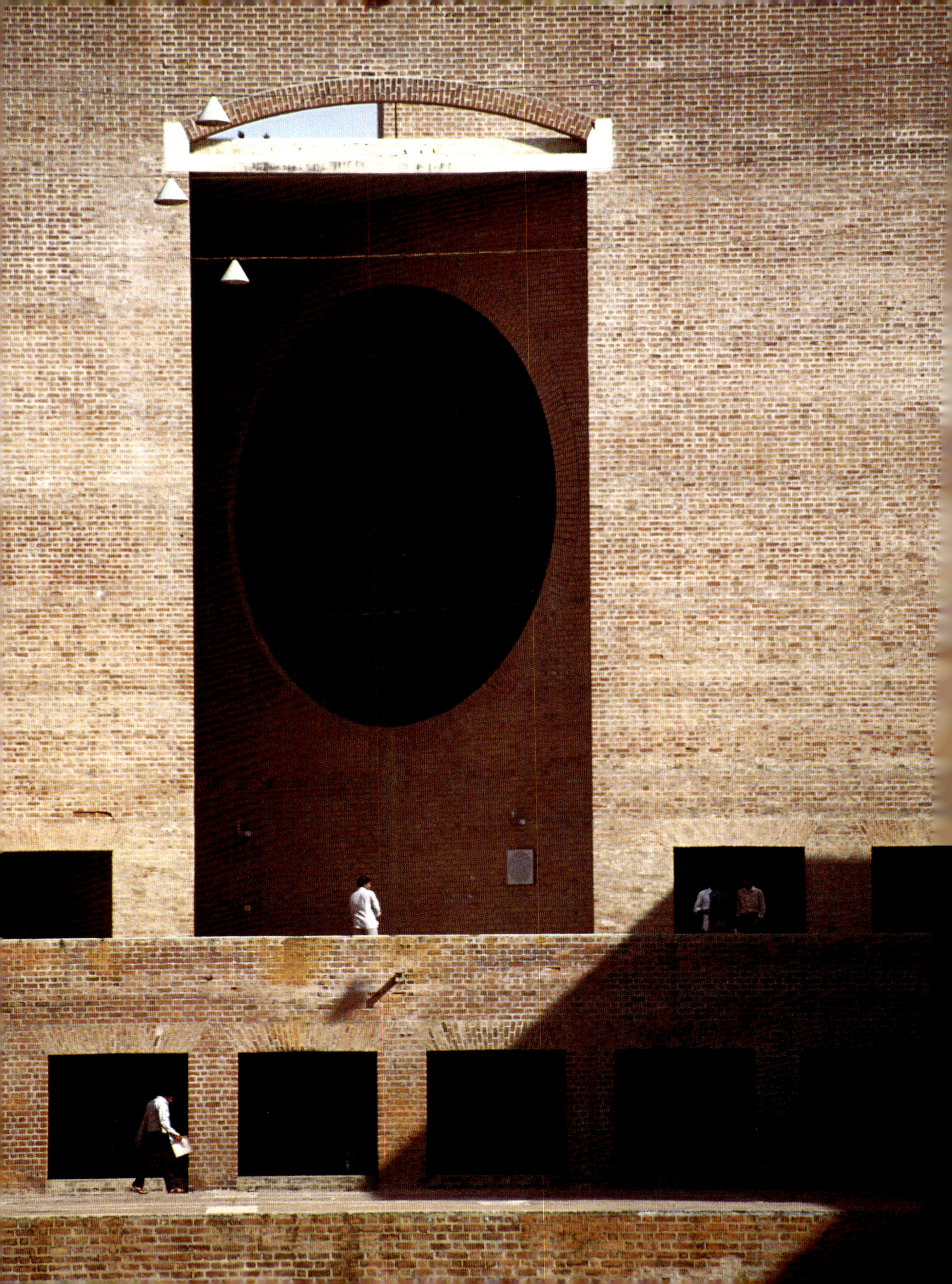

**Indian Institute of Management
1962–74 Ahmedabad India
Exemplary Building Analysis**

This analysis of the Indian Institute of Management examines a piece of architecture based on the concept of multiplicity within a building mass that is coherent in both design and function. The interdependency of individual sections and the complex as a whole are analysed, so that the genesis of the design from a rationally comprehensible initial figure to an elaborate, systematically emerging ordering structure with complex geometry is revealed.

In order to show all the aspects of this design concept of Kahn, including external ones, the presentation begins with the conditions Kahn found on his first visit to the site. Important concepts, sketched intuitively at first and later developed in detail, form the intermediate stages of a design process that extended over 13 years. This is followed by an analysis of a sketch-like, diagrammatic figure from early stages of the design that illustrates how Kahn used ordering principles that continued to retain their validity even in his early considerations. The analysis finally begins with the *starting figure*, and builds up the figurations of the complex as a whole step by step in reversible series. A plan analysis, going right down to the bricks, the microcosm of the building complex, not only gets to the heart of the rational basis of the design, but also demonstrates purely intuitive procedures by Kahn and also reveals insights going well beyond the comprehensible geometrical structure. It fathoms the way in which Kahn thought as a designer and extend to his symbolic and metaphysical views of the Indian world of thought.

THE PLACE

The city of Ahmedabad was founded by the Muslim ruler Ahmed Shah II in 1411. It originated on the banks of the river Sabarmati on the site of a community that was at first reserved exclusively for Hindus. Ahmedabad subsequently developed a predominantly Muslim character with the Bhadra (fortress) on the river and the Jami Masjid (Friday mosque) in the centre. After a decline under Mogul rule the city flourished as a textile processing centre after annexation by the British Colonial rulers in 1817. The original borders of the old town are still discernible from the remains of the town walls; its buildings overlap in their oldest structures, and there is little of historical significance. The most striking feature is the "pols", urban districts strictly separated into population groups. The old town forms the core of the new one, which developed rapidly in the east at first in the nineteenth century, and then to an equal extent west of the Sabarmati. Its image was forced to develop rapidly by enormous population growth, and shows contrasting heterogeneous developments, either intricately broken up or at a large scale and like housing estates, following Western models. These zones are dominated by an architecture that is mostly anonymous and expressionless in its formal language, anti-traditional, but at times follows the achievements of abstract Modernism in terms of quality, with a sense of its own history, alternating with neo-classical Indo-regionalist villas in the bungalow or country house style of the British colonial period.

The contrast between the old and the new town is also reflected in the population structure: old craftsmen's and merchants' streets preserved the centuries-old appearance in explosive, ever-increasing density. In contrast with this, a number of people experienced the effects of urban "functional separation" in monocultures, accommodated strictly according to 20th century guidelines and predominantly belonging to the lower middle class. Poverty took root in the grey area between the two.[60]

The town is still very much dependent on the textile industry, and is known as the Manchester of India, ranking second only to Bombay (Mumbai) in terms of production. Ahmedabad exists as an Anglo-Indian metropolis, shaped by technology and industry, attracting the urban population from the poor peasant surroundings, with both tradition and progress evident in its urban division into two. The population accommodates an extremely heterogeneous spirituality, but was for a long time united in its worship of the heroic leader Gandhi. There are relics of architecture refined by Islam and Hinduism, and a collection of buildings by Le Corbusier that is unique in such quantity outside Europe. Surrounded to the west and north by the desert districts of the Rann of Kachchh and the Rajasthan Thar, the town is exposed to monsoon rains from June to September.

Louis Kahn took account of these external conditions from his first visit to Ahmedabad in 1962 and subsequently tried to assimilate them into the design process.

The site placed at his disposal by the city was on the western edge of the new town area in the rural area of Vastrapur, about 8 km from the centre on the road called Vikram Sarabhai Marg.

The parliament complex in the structure of the city

---

[60] "The City of Ahmedabad", Bulletin of Sanska Kendra Museum, Ahmedabad, 1986; also: Nils Gutschow/Jan Pieper, "Indien", DuMont, Cologne 1986, pp. 318/319 and 338/339, and: Jan Pieper, "Die anglo-indische Station", Antiquitates Orientales vol. 1, Rudolf Habelt Verlag, Bonn 1977, pp. 221–222.

It is set amidst loose residential development; the land between its western border and the next town is an urban development area in which there has as yet been no building, part of a research area centralized by the town. The generous site of 66 acres flat pasture land is well away from any emissions of the inner city and industry, and when planning began it was possible to allow for extensions and the accommodation of other associated units. The main mass of the building could be placed in an approximately central position, thus avoiding disturbance by noise and rush from the access roads, and also at a sufficient distance from the main road into the town.

The site before construction started, with its single mango tree

PHASES OF THE INTUITIVE DESIGN PROCESS

The climatic and geological conditions and the particular mentality-dependent but also spiritual features of the place led Kahn to look for a solution that would represent "the spirit of the commission in a human society that is yet to be discovered". The planning process did not first concentrate on finding an innovative architectural form, but required that the lifestyle of an alien culture be included as an unknown dimension. A building of 170 x 750 square feet (approx. 15900 square metres) had to be designed, intended to contain classrooms, a library, a dining hall, student dormitories, an administration wing, faculty housing and zones for other facilities. It is not possible to establish the extent of Louis Kahn's influence on the constant changes to the programme in the course of planning, but presumably it was not inconsiderable.

Kahn summed up the "new country" of India in one of his first concept sketches on 14 November 1962 (figure 79) by noting "sun-heat, wind, light, rain, dust" in the margin. He formulaically identifies – particularly in the intensification "sun-heat" – the most important criteria as the "primal ground" of the creative process, and the basis of all later influential factors and their synthesis. What can probably be assumed to be the first sketch, on the basis of its vague, schematic, almost visionary character, surrounds the south and west, almost angular line of the site with a soft, swiftly-drawn line and thickening hatching. As possible dense development, this frame acquires a potential access area, indicated by a powerful line on the south-west diagonal. The centre is occupied by relatively randomly placed geometrical figures. An approximate *square* is dominant as a fixed idea from the beginning in the northern centre, between two powerful spots. In the next sketch the northern road edge, drawn as a straight line as a screen or division, condenses as a variant in a site figure that is abstracted as a rectangle for the first time. Kahn pushes the central square to the southern border and groups the L-shapes in the north and east. The next thought again picks up the first solution described and hatches the western edge, simplified as a right angle with a thick line. He is recognizably "testing out" a theme, leaving the constellation of a main square in the northern centre surrounded by secondary geometrical figures oriented west as a group and fixed in the subsequent sketches as a crystalline orthogonal figure with diagonal lines running from south-east to north-west.[61]

Fig.76

Fig.77

Fig.78

Fig.79

It becomes clear that the first thing Kahn did within the considerable scope of the commission was to "dissect" the mass on the basis of a structuring distribution, inherent in the programme, of school buildings, student dormitories and faculty housing in an apparently hierarchical configuration of three. The dependent disposition of the parts – with the attempt, intended as an orientation aid, of "leaning" on an edge – moves within the bounds of the polygonal site "frame".

Further sketches illustrate developing detailing of a crystallizing thought: diagonals radiating from a centre under 45 degrees from east to west.[62] This is impressively illustrated by strong shadow in a photograph that has survived only as a copy of what is presumably the first model study.[63] The central square is now provided with corner emphases that break it up and the diagonals, developed as parts of the building, "wriggle like

Fig.80

Fig.81

---

[61] Fig. 76–79 – concept sketches, 14 Nov. 62; made by Kahn in Ahmedabad; from: National Institute of Design, NID, Ahmedabad.

Fig.76

Fig.77

Fig.79

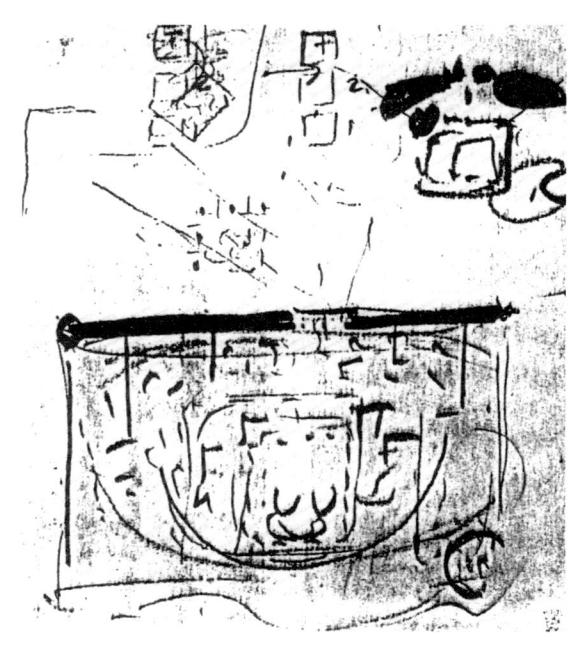

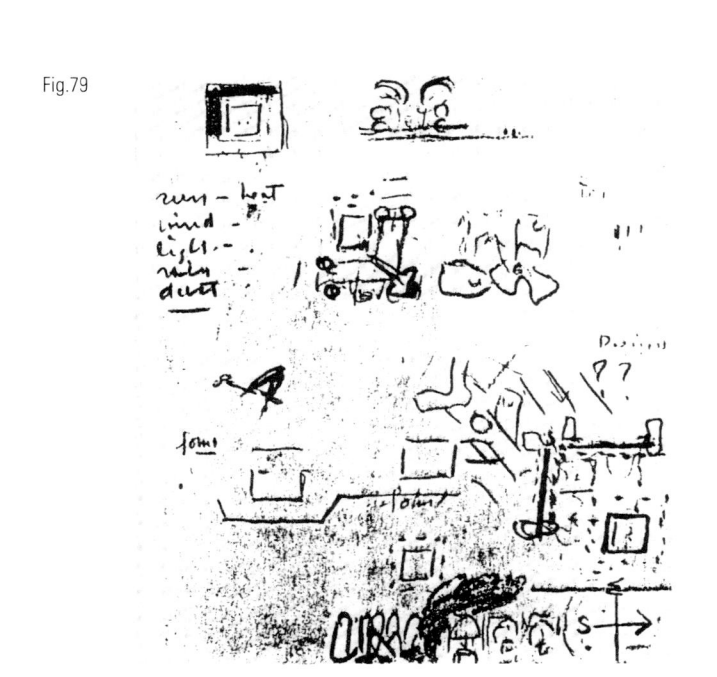

Fig.78

worms", with the eastern end emphasized as a head building. The square that appeared from the first as a main figure is increasingly changed into a horizontal rectangle. Kahn said about this: "I use the square to begin my solutions, because the square is a non-choice. In the course of development I search for the forces that would disprove the square ...".[64]

Fig.82 This new rectangle seems to be put together from parts, composed, and embraces everything in its outline. Starting from this directed figure, the diagonal bodies combine with their western end points and a wall-like border that is removed again in the next drawings.[65] A scheme that is now very concretely developed in its outlines fuses the diagonal elements with their western emphasis, which can be recognized as squares to form a complete rectangle in the outer line. The eastern ends of the diagonals link with the differentiated central rectangle to form a new unit. They form a contrast at a suitable distance, filled by an area that is not further defined, with angled, equal, tightly-packed elements that amorphously form an outer line that is still not at rest.

Fig.83 In the centre, the as yet undisposed part-figures are still crushed together in a rectangular frame, forming a large body of pyramidal, mastaba-like monumentality, considerably higher than the peripheral zones.[66] They are reminiscent of Kahn's earlier fascination with ancient Egyptian antiquity after his trip to the Middle East in the early fifties; its images of tombs and temples can be made out in plan and section variants within the project at this preliminary stage. Additives, based on the geometry of the square, accumulate at the edges, and for the first time a striking diagonal incision appears in the bottom left-hand corner of the rectangle. This can be identified as access to the central area; it appears in subsequent small sketches at various corners, and presumably also derives from the world of Egyptian

Fig.84 architecture. It takes us to the palace architecture in Tell el Amarna, with its gardens and a representation of a bathing pool, combining ground plan and elevation and denying perspective, with a flight of stairs set on the diagonal at the corner.[67] This Egyptian, apparently almost two-dimensional image can be seen as the *primal form* for the initiatory process in this project. The bath complex for the palace in Tell el Amarna, with its extraordinarily placed steps and ground plan scheme is recognizable, because of obvious similarities, as an inspiring figure for Kahn and his subsequent development of the school building.

Fig.80

[62] Fig. 80 – concept sketches, undated, presumably made by Kahn in Ahmedabad; from: the Louis I. Kahn Collection, University of Pennsylvania and Pennsylvania Historical and Museum Commission; also in: the Louis I. Kahn Collection, "The Personal Drawings of Louis I. Kahn in Seven Volumes", Garland Publishing, New York 1987–88, Vol. 4: Buildings and Projects 1962–65, pp. 40–160, nos. 645.1 to 645 195, here p. 42, no. 645.7.
The following sketches from the Kahn Collection are brought together in the microfilm department of the main library of the University of Pennsylvania in microfilms nos. 17 und 18.
[63] Fig. 81 first concept model, 12. Jan. 63, made in the National Institute of Design, Ahmedabad; from: Louis I. Kahn Collection, University of Pennsylvania and Pennsylvania Historical and Museum Commission; Box LIK 113, model photograph, no further description.
[64] Kahn, quoted in: Wurman, p. 254; also in: Ronner/Jhaveri, p. 209.
[65] Fig. 82 – general plan sketch, undated, from: Louis I. Kahn Collection, University of Pennsylvania and Pennsylvania Historical and Museum Commission; also in: Ronner/Jhaveri, p. 209, sketch labelled "IIM. 9".
[66] Fig. 83 – ground plan and section sketches, undated, annotated: "Entrance, Auditorium, General Admin, Faculty, Teaching, Library"; from: Louis I. Kahn Collection, University of Pennsylvania and Pennsylvania Historical and Museum Commission.
[67] Fig. 84 – from: Baldwyn Smith, "Egyptian Architecture as Cultural Expression", New York 1938.

Fig.81

Fig.82

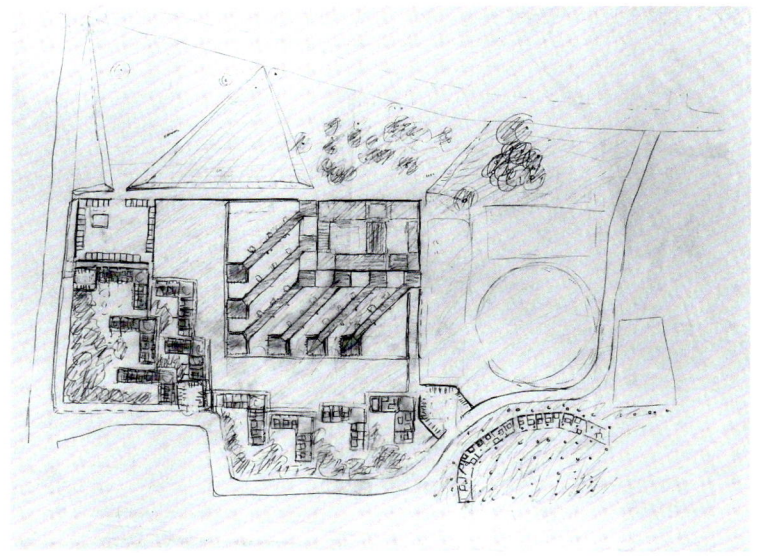

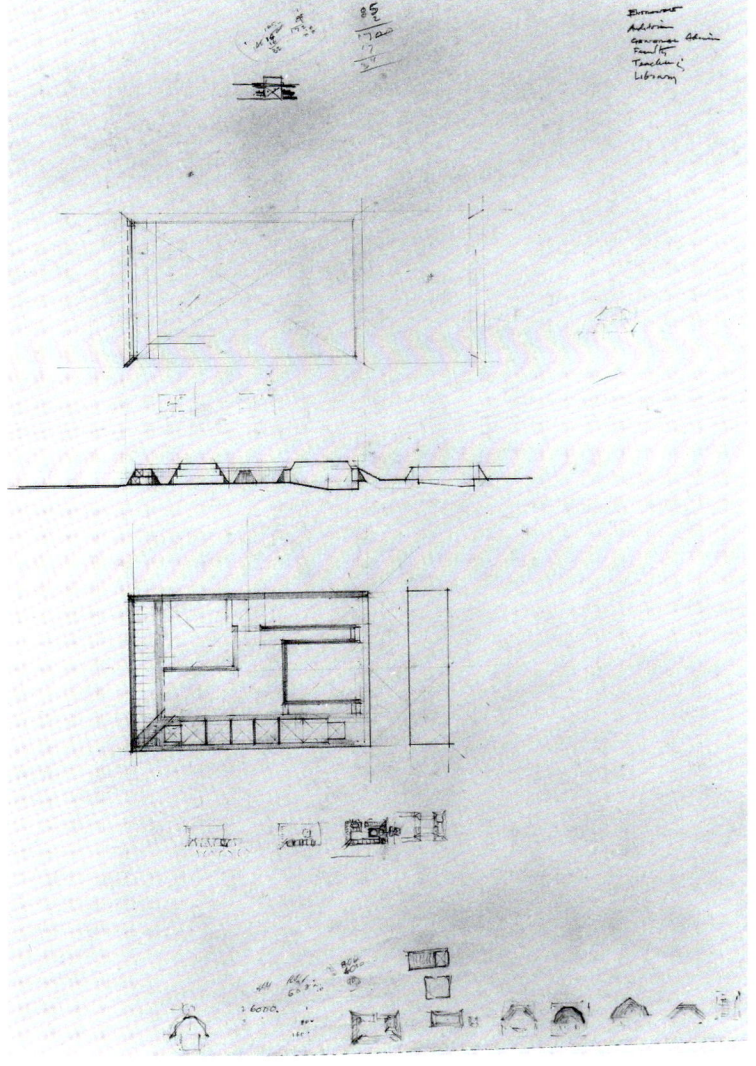

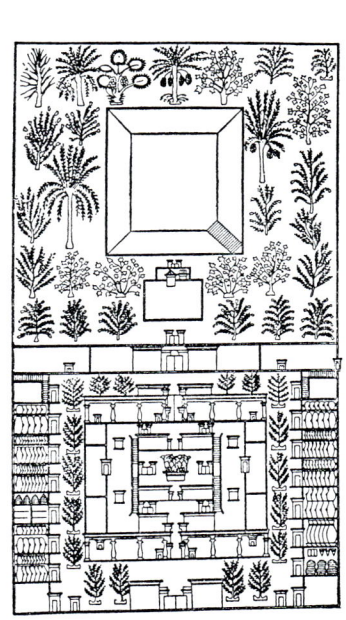

Fig.83

Fig.84

117

Fig.85 This gradually developing scheme now acquires detailing that already elucidates spatial connections and confirms the hierarchy of the structure as just described, no longer in sketch form, but as a precise technical drawing.[68] The centre is formed by a linear arrangement of a centrally placed rectangle, for the school building, with access from the main road in the north-east and from the corners, circularly positioned, with a central volume for the library and entrances cutting in on the diagonal. The "arms" for the student dormitories, running south-west below the 45 degree angle, but remaining orthogonal in their structure, follow the outer edges. Faculty housing, separated from the school area by an area described as a "lake" in the explanation of the model associated with this plan, forms the third area on the south-western edge of the plot, accumulating in a series of diagonal links.

Fig.86 In the view and section drawings of this phase Kahn intensifies the Egyptian-style Mastaba architecture to the monumental form of the centrally placed library.[69] He provides the peripheral zones of the school complex with banked walls borrowed from fortress construction, isolates the complex from the rest of its surroundings by a lake and creates various changes of level. The student dormitories, here extending in a straight line from east to west, are based on the elongated housing structure type. Like the detached faculty housing buildings, all their residential cells face south. Here Kahn's thinking follows the Western idea of "facing the sun", while the structure of the school is derived from its functionality, but also emerges as it does because the found figure sets up such a rigid scheme (see figure 85): the classroom buildings are closely linked with the students' dormitories on the long side to the south, the administration wing to the north and the dining hall and other peripheral zones on the short sides of the "remaining areas". Symbolic small geometries are effortlessly indicated under trees as servants' housing in the south-east and a circular and a rectangular area as a sport and recreation area on the eastern side of the site. The faculty housing also has separate access in the west corner.

These drawings, completed in March 1963, show the state of planning when Kahn again went to India in spring of the same year to present his first ideas to representatives of the committee, Lalbhai and Sarabhai, but also Balkrishna Vitaldhas Doshi. Doshi, who had worked with Le Corbusier and met Kahn in Philadelphia, was the key person in obtaining the Indian Institute of Management commission for Kahn.

Fig.87 The following stage in the genesis of the design can be seen as the most important one: it dates from the second half of 1963, and shows the functional areas in what can be seen as a definitive version. Its crucial feature is a final reorientation of the complex as a whole, following the longitudinal alignment of the plot, and changed by a clockwise turn.[70] There are few fundamental differences for the school building, for which more detailed sketches are provided. Both the corner diagonal incisions as access and also a circular development combining everything around the central, pyramidal library are retained. The administration wing parallel with the road breaks

Fig.86

1

2

3

[68] Fig. 85 – general plan drawing, 12 March 63; from: Louis I. Kahn Collection, University of Pennsylvania and Pennsylvania Historical and Museum Commission.
[69] Fig. 86 – section and view drawings, mid March 63; from: Louis I. Kahn Collection, University of Pennsylvania and Pennsylvania Historical and Museum Commission; also in: Ronner/Jhaveri, p. 210, sketches marked "IIM 11–13".
[70] Fig. 87 – general plan drawing, undated; from: Louis I. Kahn Collection, University of Pennsylvania and Pennsylvania Historical and Museum Commission; also in: Ronner/Jhaveri, p. 214, drawing called "IIM 37".

Fig.85

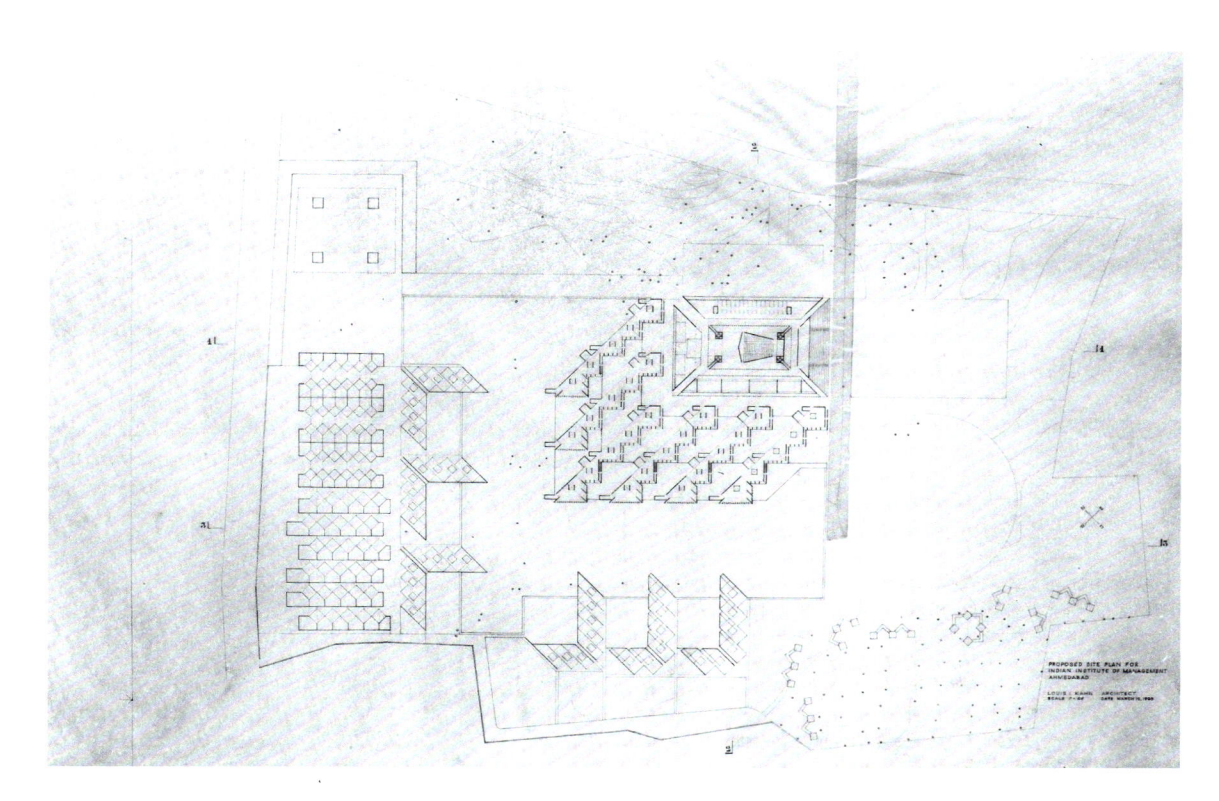

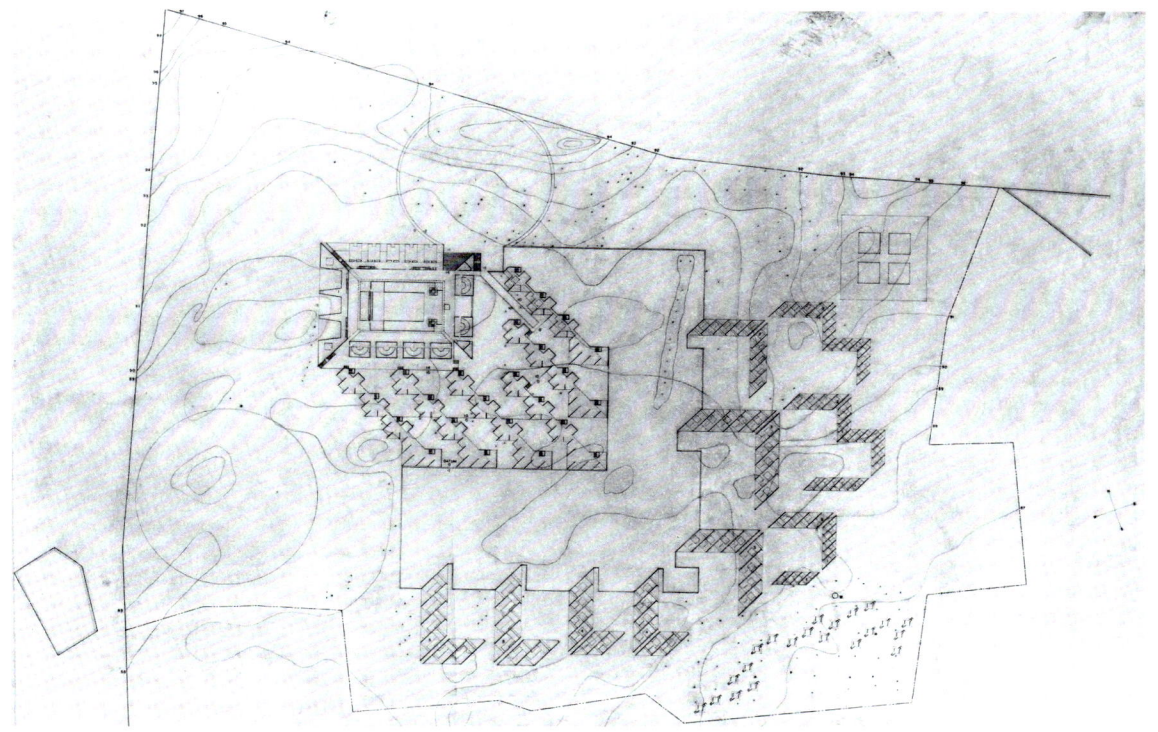

Fig.87

Fig.88 down into five elements; central main and side staircases appear, and various levels are established between interior and exterior, as can be seen from the sections.[71] The student dormitories are now aligned very precisely from north to south, in a mirror image of the first version, at an angle of 45 degrees to the school, thus making it possible to orientate the rooms directly in the direction of the prevailing wind. The buildings bite deeply into the orthogonal line of the lake, on the east side of which the faculty housing is grouped in calmed L-shapes. The constellation of the extended diagonal run of the dormitories now undergoes a crucial change: identical individual figures isolate themselves from four-fold interlinking on a right-angled grid, with the diagonal connection only suggested. The individual figures are made up of two rectangles for the living area, a triangular central corridor area and square "appendices" as service zones, derived from the pre-

Fig.88

vious phase as "tearooms" and seeming almost to detach themselves in their extraordinary independence. The new-found scheme for the *dormitories* also suggests an orthogonal and diagonal approach, forming positive and negative spaces in its chess board-like shape. Built and courtyard zones alternate, consisting originally of three and later four rows and in the other drawings again of three of the sub-figures described;[72] this runs through subsequent sketches as a constant, with slight variations in terms of spacing.

Fig.89

Four different levels, marked as site edges, become discernible: a "bank zone" accompanying the lake on the level of the rest of the surroundings, then the outer dormitories, a ground floor zone with a slight positive change of level covering the full area of the school and the Plus 1 level as the main connecting level between the school and the inner dormitories, which are on the same level, with lavish ramps. Subsequently Kahn concentrated on developing the school building: the administrative area in the north wing changes in terms of the number of office section arms, closely connected with the corridor area, and including first five, then three, then finally four elements. The classroom area also varies, starting with seven, then reduced to six individual sections around the south and east flank.

Next begins the search for a second corner development or corner opening as a diagonal incision, in order to retain the *whole* of a side.[73] The next crucial step is to clear the centre, by reducing the building mass of the library and the shift that results from this. The fact that the library figure wanders in a state of constant change through the open "courtyard" area that is now establishing itself centrally shows Kahn's indecision in positioning this figure, which is dependent on the degree of its importance. Within the open space the possibility arises of placing further figures, like two unequal stairwells, as a connection between the levels. This is followed by experiments with possibilities for lighting the administrative area: first the corporeality of the elements is dramatically emphasized by circular "incision" (see figure 89); then polygonal lightwells, based on functional conditions but subject to the angle of 45 degrees, emerge (see figure 90); their spaces for directed, nuanced daylight degenerate into distance courts in the next phases of the design.

Fig.90

Something that is close to being a final scheme for the arrangement of all the sections of a structure that is now emerging as a crystallized whole is expressed in the next version.[74] Here four administrative elements stand out clearly, linked to the circular development and separated by light-wells, then in their turn seven classroom elements and a differentiated refectory and kitchen area divided into two, with squares inscribed diagonally in a rectangular outline and surrounded by light-wells. The library, linked with the volume of a staircase, is on the eastern side of the courtyard, to whose surrounding corridor access is given by hierarchically structured stairs that cut in on the diagonal. Subtle changes are made to the hitherto rigid grid for the dormitories: their outer row is shifted away from the inner rows by a slit-like distancing piece, but does not abandon the diagonal line. Along the line of the edge of the site, which is succinctly highlighted by this

Fig.91

---

[71] Fig. 88 – section sketches, undated; annotated: "Transverse Section, Longitudinal Section"; from: Louis I. Kahn Collection, University of Pennsylvania and Pennsylvania Historical and Museum Commission.
[72] Fig. 89 – general plan sketch, undated, marked "63" in the margin; from: Louis I. Kahn Collection, University of Pennsylvania and Pennsylvania Historical and Museum Commission.
[73] Fig. 90 – ground plan of the school complex with diagonal access, undated, from: Louis I. Kahn Collection, University of Pennsylvania and Pennsylvania Historical and Museum Commission; other sketches by Kahn for the school figure in: Garland-Publishing, sketches numbered 645.11, dated April 1964, 645.10, 645.45, 645.48–645.50 und 645.55.
[74] Fig. 91 model photograph of the whole complex, Nov. 64; from: Louis I. Kahn Collection, University of Pennsylvania and Pennsylvania Historical and Museum Commission; also in: Ronner/Jhaveri, p. 221, drawings and model photograph "IIM 83-IIM 86".

Fig.89

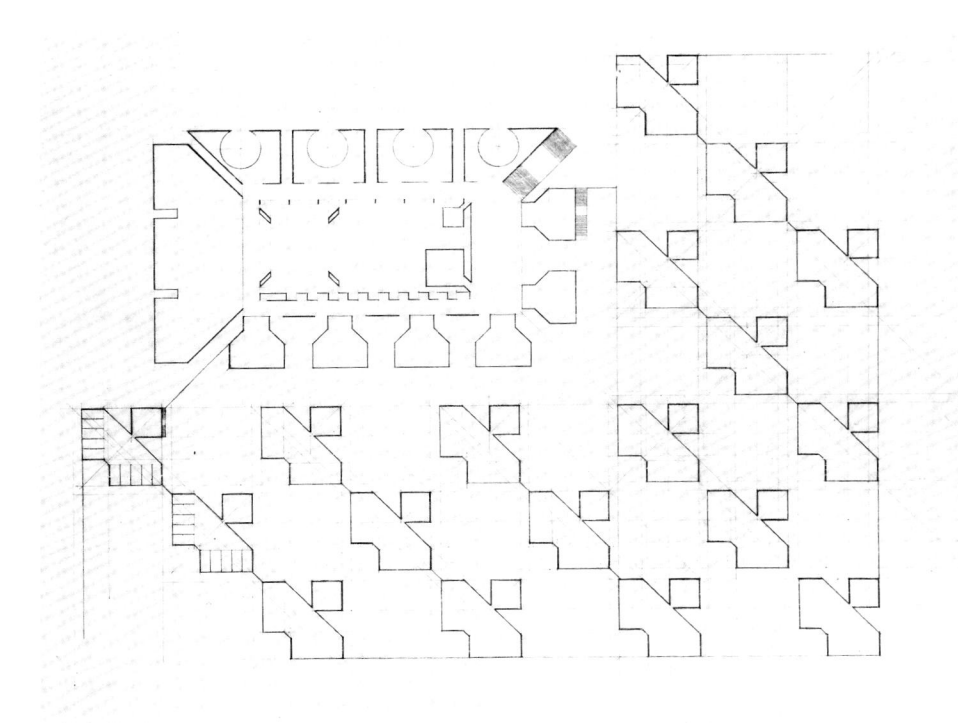

Fig.90

Fig.91

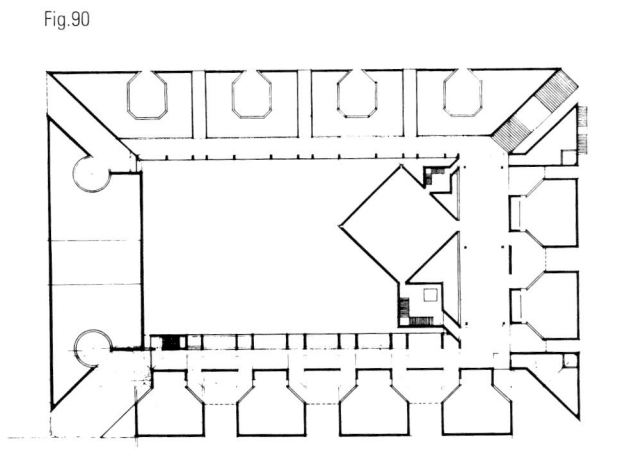

shift, narrow steps are arranged facing the internal, higher plateau on the edges of the dormitories. Base zones, slightly reminiscent of the initial Mastaba forms, are added, thrusting diagonally into the shorelines of the lake, to the outer elements, one storey higher because of the lower level. All the dormitories have semi-circular flights of steps in the middle. Three elements on the north-eastern side, facing the road, look slightly different and are intended as hostels for married students. Their service zones are not isolated, but integrated, so that the straight-diagonal edge that emerges on the road side marks a clear border. A water-tower appears for the first time in the north-west corner of the complex, while a new variant of the servants' accommodation can be made out on the southern border.

Once the dormitory design was complete, work planning and building started in 1966. Kahn concentrated in the subsequent period on developing alternatives for the school area; the version ultimately realized was not finally fixed until 1969. Here the central area underwent a range of changes in connection with the increasingly open inner courtyard, in which there are two walls with arched openings as a structure in which tent roofs can be hung.[75] The number of classrooms is reduced to six, the refectory and kitchen area and the outline of the office areas are simplified, and the complex as a whole acquires double axial symmetry with extended access steps as a last diagonal figure in the north-east corner. At this stage the library breaks out of the enclosed courtyard and overcomes the scheme of a circle that ties everything together that had hitherto prevailed. At the same time as the classroom area and the library were detached, removing their associated dominance as the "head" building, the link with access steps and administration wing was established by a new and significant element, the entrance hall. As a diagonally placed square, it anchors the steps to the access area. The classroom area appears as an unbalanced figure in the ratio five to one, whose single element swinging out of the additive accumulation is reminiscent of the earlier ring constellation. So here we are already seeing signs of a transitional phase, in which a schematic kitchen designed as a conical cylinder is also isolated (to counter anticipated smells). The structure of the water-tower is illustrated for the first time in the diagrammatic geometry of its ground plan (a reinforced concrete structure with central steps and a circular water-tank above them).

Fig.92

In 1969 this phase approached the stage that would immediately precede its realization.[76] The administration wing changes into a purely orthogonal structure with the same dimensions for buildings, distancing courts and window reveals, which cut deeply into the walls. Two semi-circular staircases separate the book zone from the reading zone in the enlarged library block, and this division into two is shown in the exterior by deep niches used for lighting. As a last measure that changes the figure as a whole, all the classroom sections linked to the library by a corridor are placed in a straight line and now enter into a direct dialogue with the administration figure. This important decision now means that the complex as a whole is dominated by two large, parallel walls. Anant Raje suggests that this arose from the influence of a committee member: "… One of the donors was giving an advice for Kahn, he suggested that this should be a straight line, so that it helps open up the court … It was so strong that he immediately accepted it … It was a 'spiritual discipline' to make it into a line."[77]

After Doshi went off to pursue other work of his own, Raje became Kahn's most important colleague in Ahmedabad; he completed the design after Kahn's death in 1974, and with his wife later added new accommodation and training buildings to the complex, borrowing their language from Kahn's design.

In the case of the administration wing the division of the corridor area into access and service zones clearly increased the size of the entrance hall square, making it into a defining figure. Meanwhile the dramatically diagonal area outside the library serves as a light-well for the interior areas underneath it, forming a brise-soleil that is bodily integrated into the outline of the classrooms. The centre of its external wall is related to the access of the courtyard, deviating from the axis of the library and thus conveying the suggestive impression of a *shift*.

Fig.93

[75] Fig. 92 – ground-plan of the school complex, 6 July 66; from: Louis I. Kahn Collection, University of Pennsylvania and Pennsylvania Historical and Museum Commission; also in: Ronner/Jhaveri, pp. 224–225, sketches called "IIM 103-IIM 108".

[76] Fig. 93 – ground-plan of the school complex, 27 June 67; from: Louis I. Kahn Collection, University of Pennsylvania and Pennsylvania Historical and Museum Commission; also in: Ronner/Jhaveri, p. 225, drawings and model photograph called "IIM 109–111".

[77] From an interview conducted by the author.

Fig.92

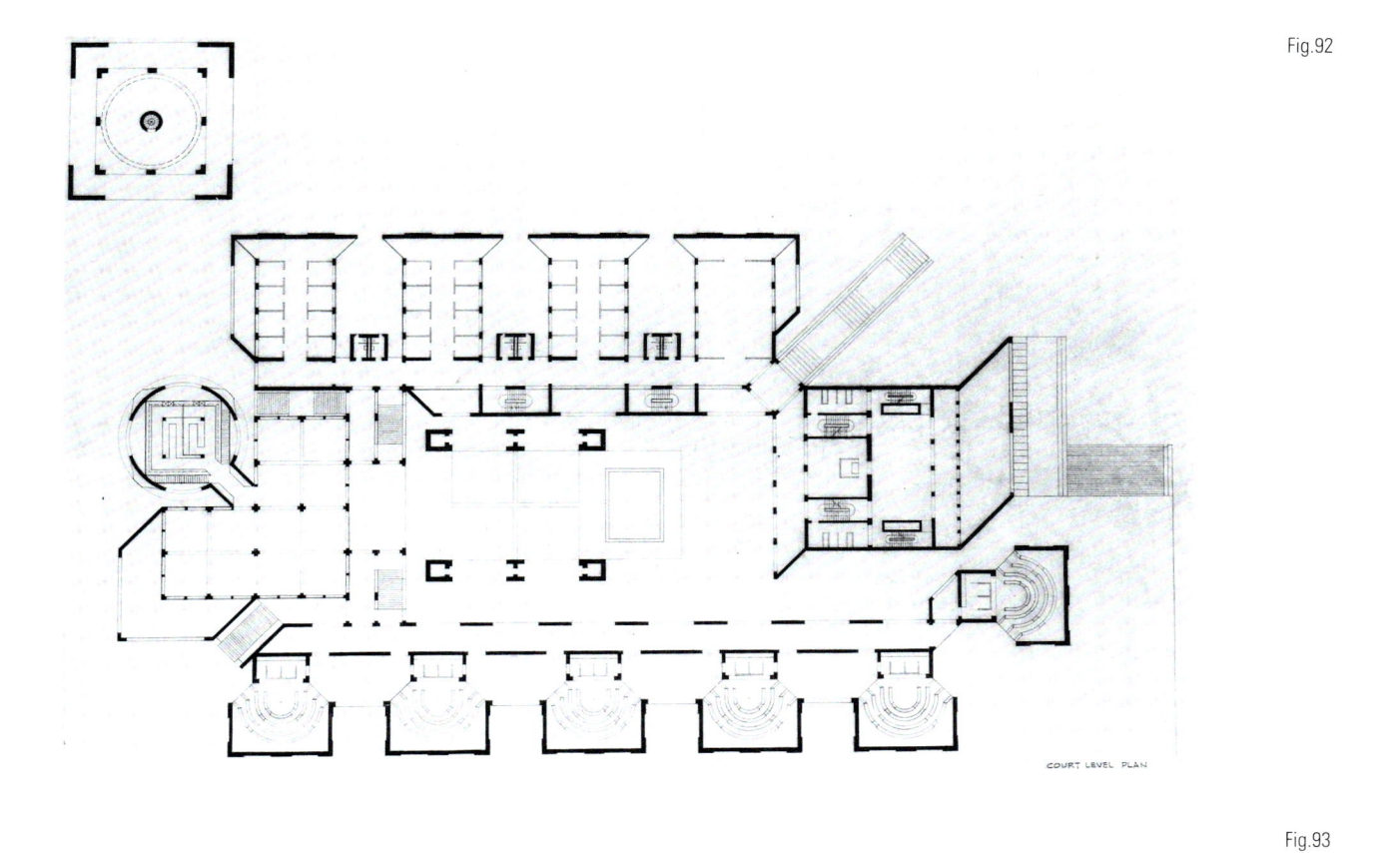

COURT LEVEL PLAN

Fig.93

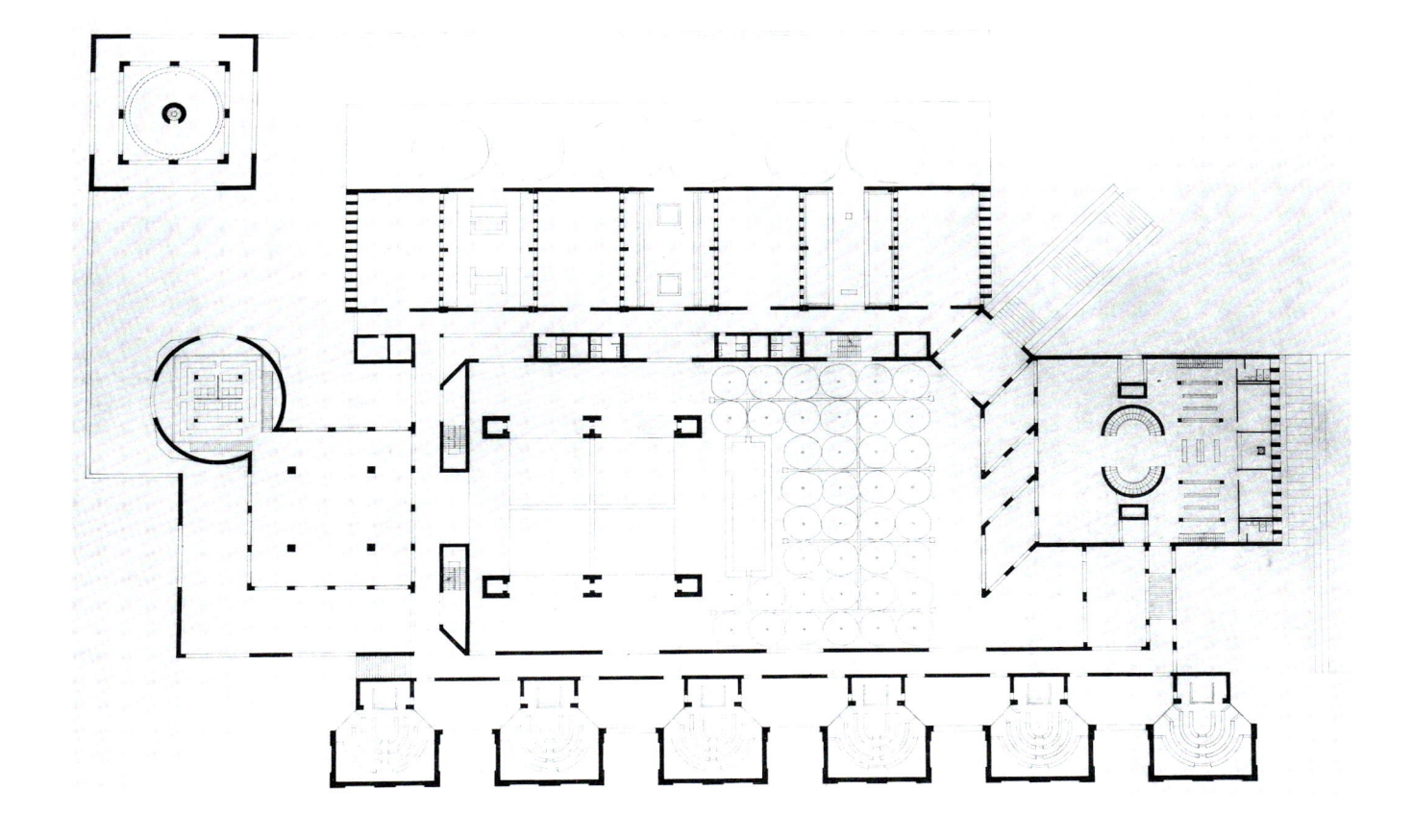

123

Fig. 94 and 95   The scheme underwent very little change in the plans drawn on 23 October 1969,[78] which make the classrooms look as though they are "inserted" into a hall-like ambulatory linking the elements. The classrooms are now linked, via a centred staircase volume built in the courtyard, to an amphitheatre whose axis agrees with the horizontal axis of the courtyard and the ultimately symmetrical dining/kitchen area. All the ground plan figurations presented so far relate to the Plus 1 main access level, which links administration, library, classrooms and dormitories. What is not shown here is a ground floor level, with administrative rooms in all areas, and providing access to the kitchen and refectory. An upper floor in the classroom area with seminar rooms, two upper storeys in the administrative area and three upper storeys in the library as archive and reading areas are also available.

The "final figure" is restricted to the disposition of the school building and the student dormitories, which are alternately dependent on each other. As a product of a design process lasting from 1962 to 1972 it represents an inner potential that continually distanced itself from the starting figure, and was shaped by external influences, but also by intensive harnessing of the spirituality of the task and the place. However, the design was accompanied from the outset by constant features.

The fact, perceptible in the genesis of the design, that these were kept is indicative of a general line of design thinking that will be described in more detail later. The principle underlying this design starts with the division of an indeterminate building mass defined only in terms of its function into a strictly hierarchically formulated "triad" of school complex, dormitories and faculty housing. It uses structural variations but follows the chosen canon in a disciplined fashion, establishing a further hierarchy within the main structure of the triad, the school, whose interdependent parts are framed within a further constant, the centring rectangular outline that binds everything together. The search for the *middle* as the centre leads to the constant starting figure always used by Kahn, the square. It concentrates, as a double axial symmetrical form, on a centre point with the components of a whole that is framed within the geometry circling on its periphery. A continuous feature in the development of the design is the formation of the orthogonal school centre, with dormitories relating diagonally. Their appearance, in structured serial accumulation, oscillates between an orthogonal quality in repose and a moving diagonal quality and makes school and dormitories dependent on each other through tracks and outlines.

THE REALIZATION PROCESS

It was not possible to follow the gradual, linear planning approach in the actual building phase. Realization was driven by an urgent need to complete the building on the basis of external necessity, and the degree of difficulty was considerably underestimated in the agreement made between Kahn and the committee in 1962.[79] They planned to build the whole complex in three years, finishing in 1966, with six site visits by Kahn. Further problems turned out to be the organization of planning activities: Kahn's preparation of the design with only one Indian representative in Philadelphia, finishing the drawings, planning work and project management at the National Institute of Design in Ahmedabad under the direction of Doshi, and supervisory project direction by Kahn himself with large intervals. Communication and sending plans by post turned out to be cumbersome, and telephone calls were subject to major technical hitches. In addition the unstable political situation in India, marked by disturbances, curfews and strikes, and the resulting financial difficulties, both for the client because of missing subsidy and Kahn because of lack of fees,[80] caused serious delay in building progress and led to a planning and building period of over thirteen years. Miscalculations about the time needed to complete the building and bad planning by Kahn – he went way beyond the bounds of the programme – also contributed to this.[81]

---

[78] Fig. 94, 95 – ground plan and section drawings of the projected but not yet realized final stage, September/October 69; from: Louis I. Kahn Collection, University of Pennsylvania and Pennsylvania Historical and Museum Commission; also in: Ronner/Jhaveri, p. 228, drawings called "IIM 123-IIM 124".

[79] "Correspondence", Box LIK 113: letter from Kahn to the committee dated 10.11.62 and letter dated 18 April 1969 from Kasturbhai Lalbhai to Kahn, in which six visits are mentioned. No contractual agreement for the project as a whole has surived. Kahn in fact travelled to India 17 times, which does not concur with the agreement, also in connection with the Dhaka project in Bangladesh.

[80] Kahn Collection, Box LIK 113, letter dated 21 Dezember 1973 from Doshi and Raje to Kahn, discussing major price inflation and the lack of financial support from state and government, and pointing out that committee members are trying to raise contributions from industry.

[81] Kahn Collection, Box LIK 113, letter dated 3 September 1965 from Lalbhai to Kahn, rejecting a concept that exceeded the prescibed area by 50 %.

Fig. 94

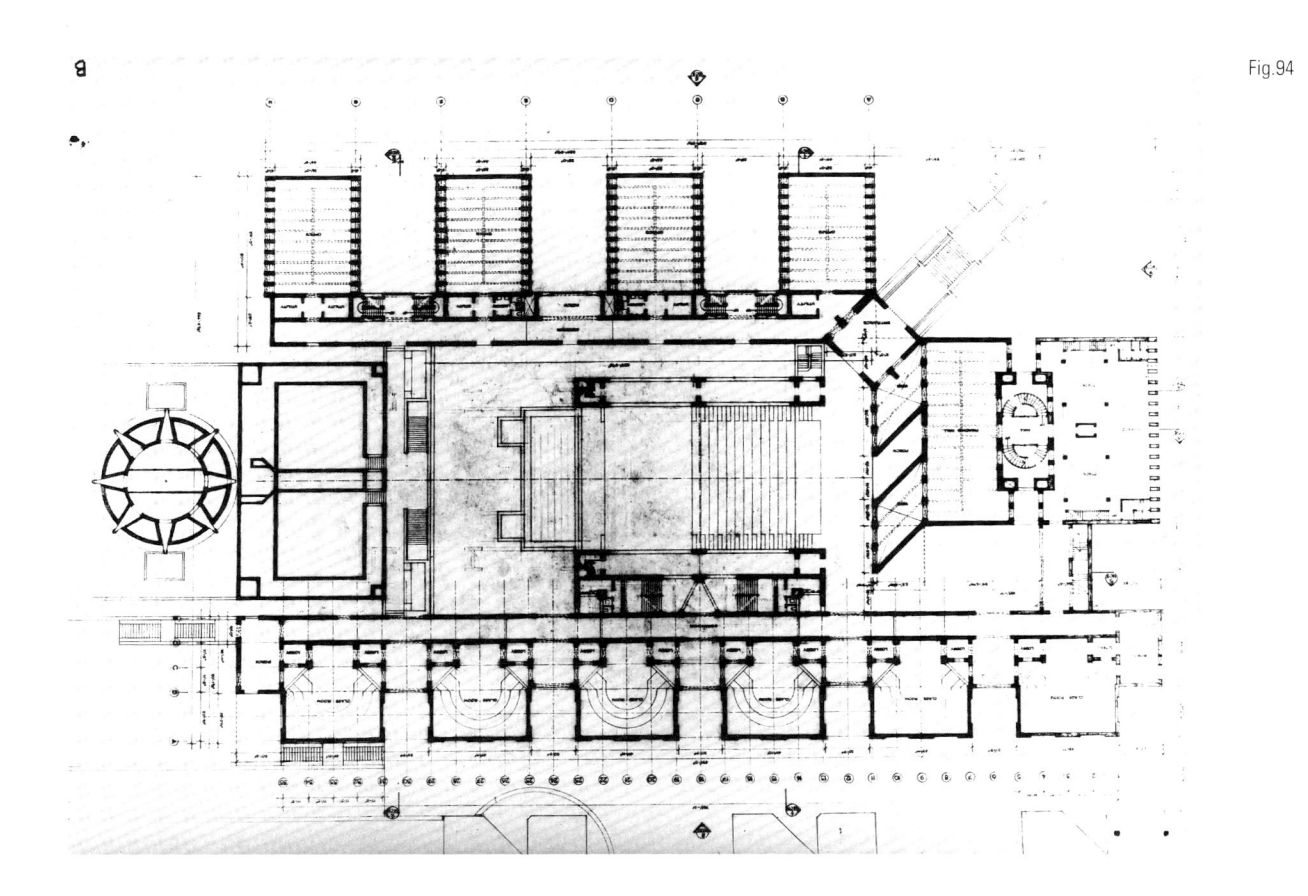

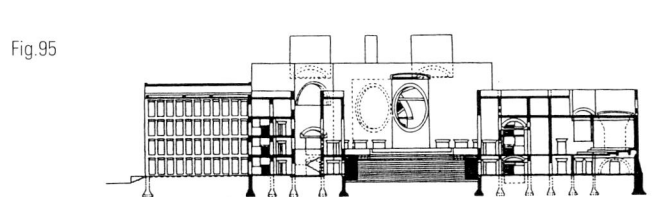

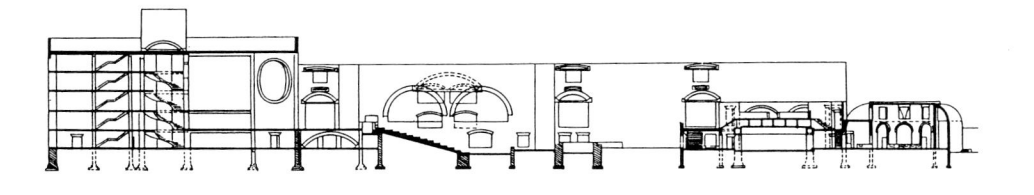

Fig. 95

Outline of the buildings from the west

125

The realization of the dormitories – four-storey in the outer peripheral area and three-storey, with an air-space over the common rooms – began in spring 1966. The residential buildings followed, also with three storeys, in the inner zone, on a slightly raised level, on soil from the partially excavated lake. The two-storey faculty housing, with lavish terraces, on the periphery of the grounds, was built in the next two years. The water-tower was completed from 1967 to 1970, containing water as a reserve, but also for cooling the air-conditioned offices. Work on the school complex started in 1969, with a base floor for side-rooms and offices in the classroom and library area, the double-storey classroom area on the first floor with a lavish lobby in front of it, and small seminar rooms with roof terraces on the upper floor. The library, with access from the base on the main level, three storeys in the front area with the large reading-room and five storeys in the rear area, was built at the same time, along with the administration wing with four storeys in all and access corridors in front, and the main access steps leading to the first floor with the entrance hall and conference room above it as a link. The last part of the design conceived by Kahn to be built remained the three four-storey dormitories, different from the others, on the north-eastern periphery. These were originally intended for married students, but after a decision was taken to build external accommodation for couples they were adjusted to match the function of the others.[82]

The complex as a whole, as planned by Kahn, was completed in its present form in summer 1975, with the last work on the courtyard and the exterior area; Kahn was able to view the completed buildings on his last visit in March 1974.[83] The courtyard was open, and the school building, now U-shaped, had no connection between the classrooms and the administration wing, and so Kahn, in a last attempt to close the courtyard, sketched the figure of an independent theatre building on 15 March 1974, along with stone formats and patterns for laying them on the inner platform that this would produce.[84] The dining/ kitchen area that was originally to have closed the courtyard to the west was built outside the complex after Kahn's death, as there was fear of pollution by cooking smells.[85] The theatre, with baldacchino and pool, a direct connection between the classrooms and the library, and the lake surrounding the dormitories were not realized. The increased danger of malaria, but also the very lavish use of water for no practical purpose in an arid region, led to this decision by the committee.

Subsequently Anant Raje, working from his office on the campus, extended the complex by adding the dining facilities in the area fixed for them by Kahn south-west of the school building. He also built more faculty housing in the south-east, working with his wife, and, again following Kahn's structural basis, designed the "Management Development Center", an advanced training establishment in the north-eastern corner of the site. From 1989 onwards Raje built an events and congress centre to his own design, borrowing from the formal vocabulary and particularly the material quality of the existing buildings, consisting of hand-made Ahmedabad bricks.[86] The choice of brick was not based primarily on Kahn's preference for this old material that he had frequently used in previous work, but on traditional production and use inside India. The brickworks, especially in the Ahmedabad region, which has rich deposits of clay, used the traditional open-air manufacturing process based on a mixture of heat from wood fires and the sun; this provided a lot of jobs and led to reason-

Kahn and Vikram Sarabhai on 15 March 1974

[82] Ronner/Jhaveri, pp. 216–232. Also: Brownlee/De Long, pp. 369–372.
[83] Kahn died on 17 March 1974 in undignified circumstances in a washroom in the lavatories at Pennsylvania Station in New York after returning from Ahmedabad, with a stopover in London-Heathrow, where Tigerman, a student from Yale, met him and found him very changed and tired. His wife was unable to identify him until a few days later. For more detail on this see Esther Kahn in Wurman, p. 283 and Stanley Tigerman, ibid, p. 299.
[84] Ronner/Jhaveri, p. 232, sketches and descriptions called "IIM 147 to IIM 149". Also: the author's interview with Raje on 19.2.91, in which the opening of the courtyard was discussed and Raje talked about Kahn's agreement to the open court at this visit, even though Kahn – as mentioned in the text – tried to close the court until the last.
[85] Ronner/Jhaveri, p. 232, description of "IIM 147".
[86] Interview by the author with Raje on 19.2.91.

able prices. Brick was seen as a rough material, made by hand and imprecise in its dimensions, and was rendered when used in Indian buildings; here it was left untreated, and divided the opinion of the residents.[87] It was interpreted by Raje in its rough, direct manifestation intended by Kahn as a possible symbol for preparing for the ordinariness and wearing quality of life.[88] Kahn's view of the beauty inherent in the natural material does not refer just to its character, but also to the harmony of material and form as a response to an *expressive wish*. This has to follow its own definition in terms of correct – and therefore beautiful – use, and develops here in an architecture that creates large openings, meeting the primary requirements of air circulation and the provision of shade.[89] The so-called *composite order*, consisting of a masonry arch carrying off compression forces and a concrete lintel taking up tensile forces, does justice to what Kahn thought to be an equally valid combination of different materials. Different qualities and characteristics unite without dominating each other, and shape the appearance of the façades as a newly discovered configuration.[90] Kahn's early and insistent fixing of measurements of 4.5 x 9 x 3 inches[91] for the brick to be used in 1964 supports the proposition that this brick was intended as the module for the whole geometrical order of the Indian Institute of Management.

The incompletely realized school complex with courtyard open to the west

The irregular, hand-made Indian brick as module

[87] While the author was staying on the campus in 1990 and 1991 conversations with students revealed a generally very positive attitude to the architecture of the complex, and the "emptiness" of the inner courtyard in particular, but critical voices were raised about the omnipresent unrendered red brick; it was thought that its dark, rough surface would start to be depressing after living with it for a year or two.
[88] Interview by the author with Raje on 19. 2. 91.
[89] Wurman, p. 252, "Louis Kahn Defends – an Interview" (wrongly dated 31 May 1974!): "I asked the brick what it wanted, and it said I want an arch, so I gave it an arch". (Kahn quotation, extract)
Tyng, p. 29, interprets Kahn: On determining the qualities of the materials, the question arises: what would the material want to do with itself? Also: Kahn Collection, Box LIK 113: Interview by Marshall D. Meyers, a long-term collaborator of Kahn's, with Kahn in August 1972 about the harmony of natural materials.
[90] Ronner/Jhaveri, p. 223, Kahn quotation: "The brick was always talking to me, saying you are missing an opportunity. The weight of the brick makes it dance like a fairy above and a groan below. Arcades crouch. But brick is stingy, concrete is tremendously generous. The brick is held by the concrete restraining members. Brick likes this so much, because it becomes modern."
[91] Kahn Collection, Box LIK 113: programme, handwritten notes (to his then colleagues in Philadelphia?) with various instructions and a rough sketch of the project. From this Kahn quotation (interpreted by the author from his holograph):
"Must select brick B 4 (before, author's note) end of September to have adequate supply B 4 (before, author's note) July 1964.
Brick – 4 ½ x 9 x 2 ¾ or 3
2 x 4 ½ x 4 ½
2 x 4 ½ x 9."

GROUND PLAN ANALYSIS OF A PRELIMINARY STAGE

Fig. 96 and 97

The design first started to be fixed geometrically in a drawing that emerged in the period of March to July 1963. It shows a detail from an essentially diagrammatic scheme of the school complex[92] as an unambiguously identifiable, self-isolating centre figure in rectangular outline with staircase access cutting in diagonally on the corners and an inserted library block. The outline can be geometrically verified as a double square. There is no doubt that an imaginary single square exists as a preliminary stage of the double square, as recognizable in the previously described figure 81; its short life shows clearly in the small number of surviving sketches. It is the figure of the design process' start, and it changes rapidly to a rectangular figure following the long side of the site, but suggested previously as a "neutral form" in a kind of raw condition with the symbolic gesture of "non-choice" (Kahn). Its square geometry is illustrated simply by the shortest connection between two corner points under an angle of 45 degrees, in other words the diagonal. The existing staircase figures with their access lines running diagonally to the middle indicate the importance of this diagonal quality. As the design proceeds this figure is articulated more clearly as the courtyard, and symbolizes the notion "centre point" in axial symmetry with inscribed, equally centred outlines. Its geometry is also assumed to be dependent on or in proportion with the figures that have just been described, and as before will be examined in terms of corners, tracks and diagonal relations. The question of the process by which this form came into being, its genesis, is raised by the figure in the centre, clear in outlines, but yet not forming a "pure" square, and later emerging as the library. We also have to establish the relation of the parts to each other, and all the internal dependencies. To this end the analysis examines the preliminary study of the square that has just been described. It is intended to prove geometrical order, which has existed from the beginning, as a fixed component of the genesis of Kahn's design.

Fig. 98

The overall figure of the school complex, developed in spring 1963, contains the described double square of unknown dimension with double axial symmetry as the central figure, and the symmetry axes 1 and 2, as they are known here, as the primary geometrical fixing.

Starting from the central crossing point M the diagonal MD of the halved square ABCD below axis 1, as a radius of an arc of a circle, meets the intersection point R of axis 2, through which a "floor track" can be drawn parallel to axis 1. A crucially important distance ratio RC to CB is now produced as the division of a section of the line in the ratio of the Golden Section. This proportion as a *cosmic law*, derived from relations in natural systems, is expressed in the irrational number ratio *1 : 0.618* or *1 : 1.618*. The track found through point R crosses, at Golden Section distance to the parallel square side DC, the extended diagonal through the centre point M at point V. After mirroring this point over both axes 1 and 2 the new enclosing square STUV is formed, in order to mark the inner outlines in tracks ST and UV and the exterior outlines in TU and SV of emergent function areas.

Fig. 99

In the following step the Golden Section construction is repeated over the quarter bounded by the axes 1 and 2 of the newly established square STUV. The diagonal WU, formed when this quarter is halved and used as the radius of an arc of a circle, establishes point Z at the intersection with axis 1, in order to define a track of the right-hand and left-hand exterior outline of the whole complex, parallel to axis 2 through point Z, and mirrored.

Fig. 100

The connection of these outlines with the square sides TU and SV leads to a rectangular figure whose new long sides, divided at points P1 and P2 in the ratio of the Golden Section, produce the left and right-hand boundaries of the inserted volume of the library.

Fig. 101

Diagonals running through P1 and P2 determine the points of intersection with axis 2 C1 and C2 as borders of the inner lines of the function areas. The points of intersection with the longitudinal outer lines D and F produce the tracks of the diagonal accesses at the corners and their extension to the point of intersection with the short sides of the overall exterior outline, points E1 and E2. The overlap zone X is formed and as well a rectangular figure for the school complex, suggestively moving and "oscillating" by the distance Y, with an area proportion of the Golden Section emerging precisely as an ideal figure in the ratio of L1 to L2.[93]

Fig. 102

---

[92] Fig 96, 97 – Centre of the school complex, from: Louis I. Kahn Collection, University of Pennsylvania and Pennsylvania Historical and Museum Commission; see also Fig. 85; also in the context of the whole complex in: Ronner/Jhaveri, p. 210, 211, drawing and model photograph called "IIM 10" und "IIM 27"; also: microfilm 18.

[93] An outline in the ratio of 1 : 1.618 for the height to the width of its sides, defined in the text as a figure, is considered an area proportion – in the Golden Section, for example.

Fig. 96

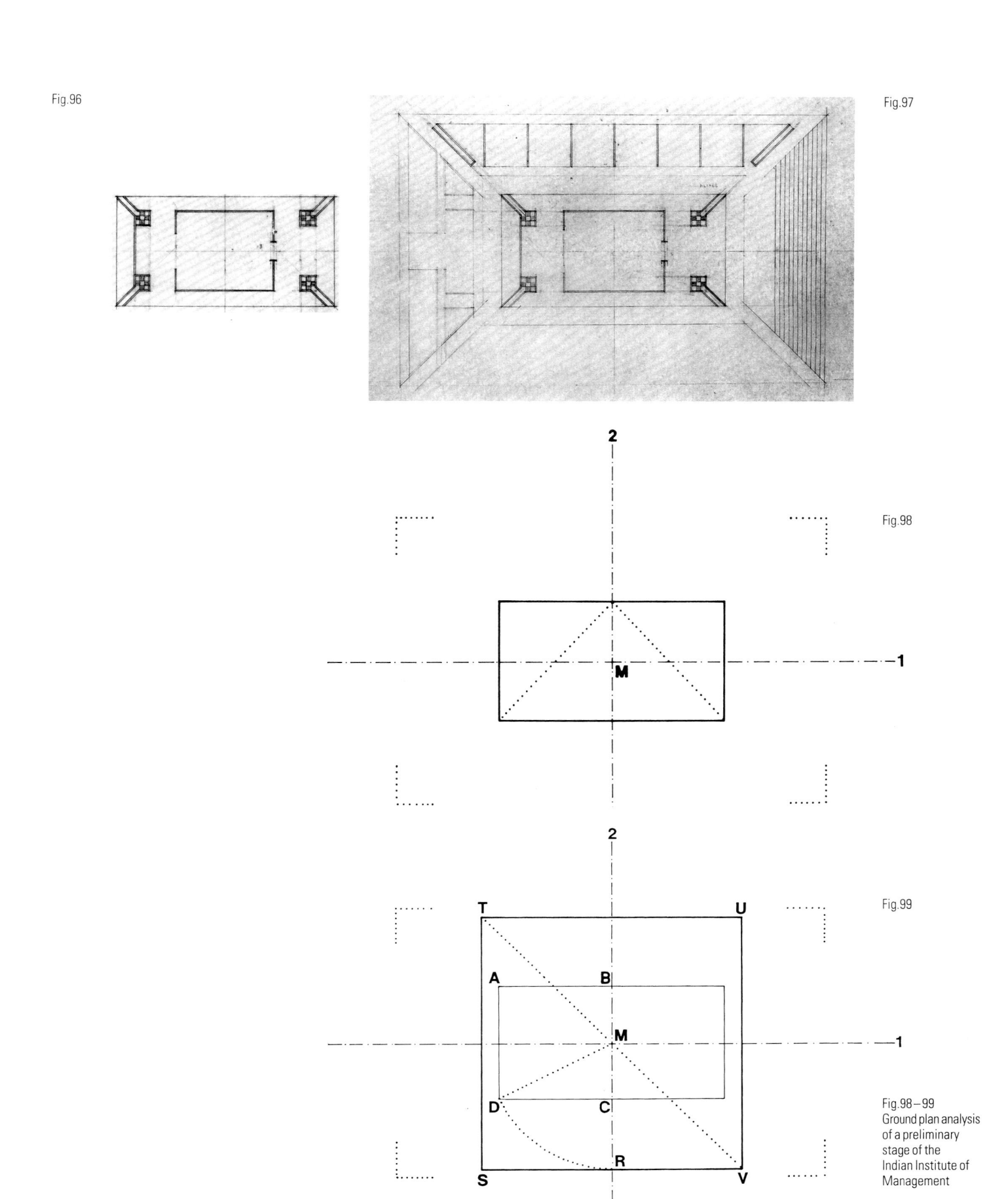

Fig. 97

Fig. 98

Fig. 99

Fig. 98–99
Ground plan analysis
of a preliminary
stage of the
Indian Institute of
Management

Fig.100

Fig.101

Fig.102

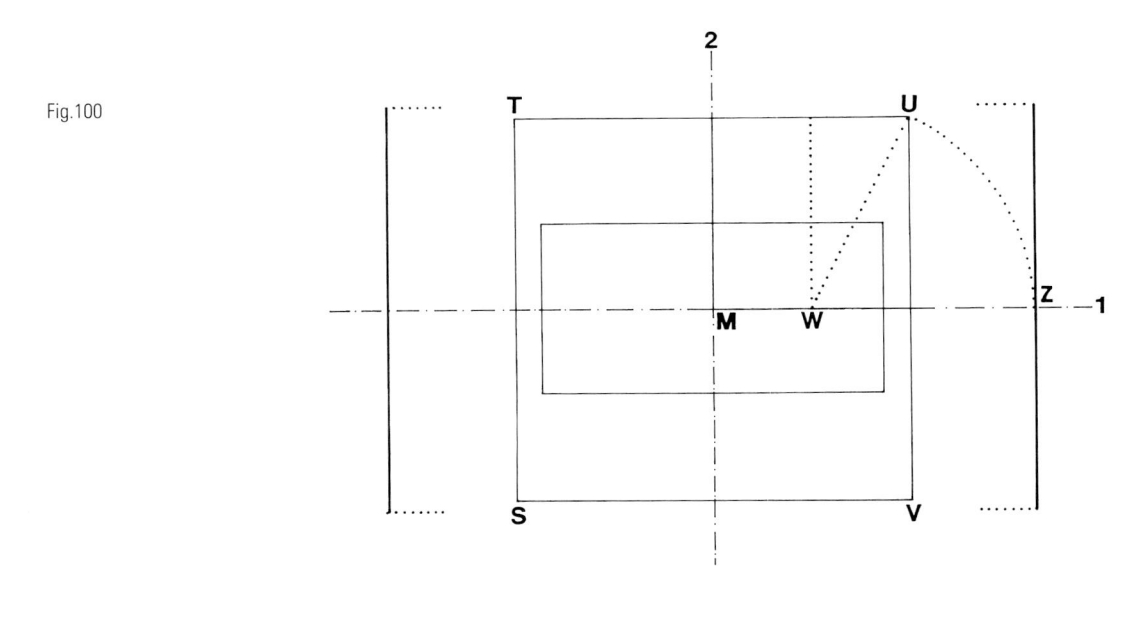

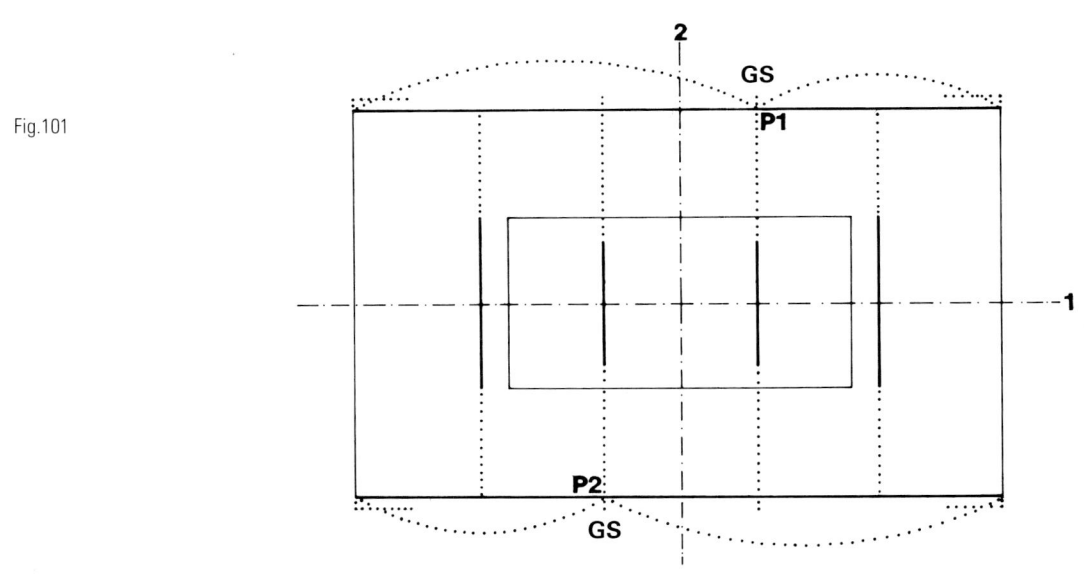

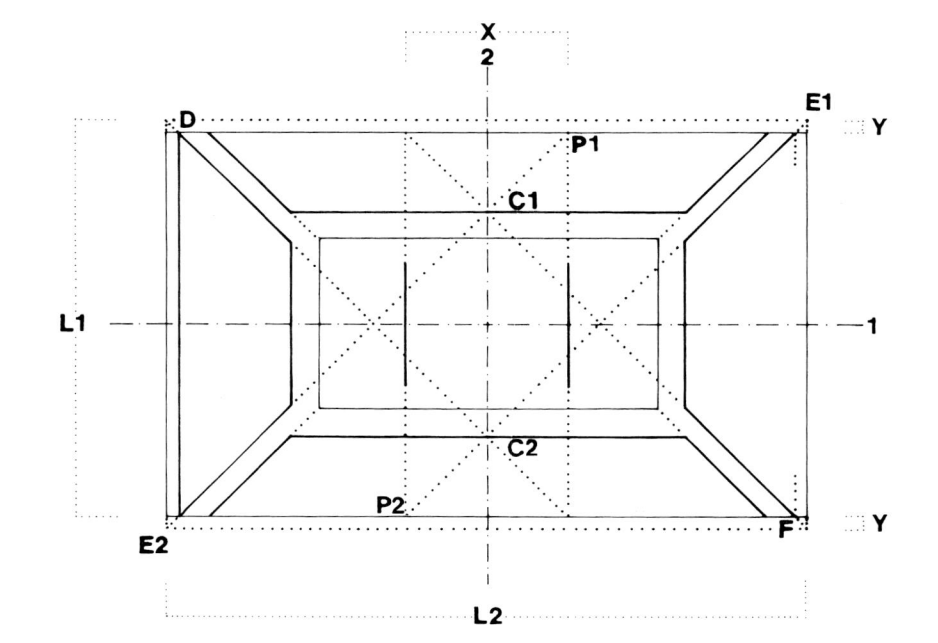

Fig.100–102
Ground plan analysis
of a preliminary
stage of the
Indian Institute of
Management,
continued

Indian Institute of Management
School Complex

CENTRE AND COURTYARD

The above analysis of an early preliminary stage of the project shows the existence of a figuratively developed geometry, interdependent, expanding and hierarchical, as an illustration of an immanent order. It is there so that all the parts of the whole relate to each other. It is comprehensibly demonstrated by the method applied above. The following analysis of the realized design reveals figurative geometry to be an integrative system.[94]

Fig.103

28 design variants for the project were condensed down to a few main phases in the previous discussion. They show a *double square* of still undefined dimensions as a *"set position"* from the outset. It exists as a continuing motif throughout the whole design process in all schemes. Thus this geometrically precisely articulated rectangular figure emerges as the starting-point for analysing the architecture, most of which was indeed realized. The double square and the single square before it can be seen as symbols of a centre: the middle, so significant in Kahn's work as a whole, embodies a *beginning* in the purity of its geometry, and at the same time raises questions because of the neutrality of its shape ("nonchoice").[95] It is present as an exemplary initial figure in many realized designs: the central figure of the 1955 Trenton Bathhouse, a construction of double axial symmetry, adopts the square centre as the design motif for the adjacent sections of the building (see figures 8 and 9). In the parliament building in Dhaka, started in 1962, the "brother geometry" of the square, the circle, is subtly alienated from its original geometry in the central hall, but remains in the viewer's memory as a pure circle (see figure 65). All the projects are basically designed "from the middle", conveying the idea of centrifugal emergence as a *copy of a universal act of creation*. Its origin results from bringing all the elements together to circle around an imaginary concentration point, and retains form-finding within the final figure as an intelligible process "from birth".

The directed figure of the double square as an outline-forming rectangle contains the non-appearing, latent square as a figure that is "present" in one half. This character of an outline that is not immediately visible but can be sensed is extremely important for the concept and method of plan analysis. Recognizing the figure that is present within the tracks and edge-relations of a ground plan thus turns out to be seeing *hidden images* of the real design. Its existence has to be explored: it is without exception based on geometry, and could be more accurately – because more generally – interpreted as closer to the *truth* or to things that are *eternally valid*.

The present square of as yet undefined size now seems visibly integrated. It is showing its symmetrical axis and is mirrored as a double. Its outline, floating in unrest, starts to *move*, a suggestive phenomenon. Its characteristic is that an identical geometrical figure is to be inscribed in two positions a certain distance apart at the same time. The distance "X" emerges as a difference, resulting from the vertical shift, not yet precise in terms of extent and number, but fixed geometrically. Its length has to be added to the moving double square at the top, i. e. closer to the top of the page, and to the bottom long side, and produces a shifted field that moves away from the pure geometry of the square, practically "distorting" it. The result emerges as a rectangle in a new outline: double square plus added or subtracted shifted distance on both sides. This shifted field creates a modular square with sides "X" by "X" in the top right-hand corner of the figure as a whole, by transferring distance "X" to its long side. It is characterized by its diagonals here and with its multiple in addition determines the sides of square and double square as a precise division ratio. Thus the shifted field is explained as a modular extension of a structure inherent in the square and its double of 7 times 7 and 7 times 14 divisions respectively. The 1 : 1 or 1 : 2 ratio blurs with the plus 1 addition of the shift to 7 plus 1 equals 8 or 6 plus 1 plus 1 equals 8 and emphasizes the central overlapping figure of both conceivable squares or double squares. Recognizable as a module, the upper right-hand corner extends its width "X" in the vertical downwards, in order to produce an inner square of the size of 6 times 6 divisions by the subtraction 7 minus 1 equals 6. A narrow field of width X now emerges, framing the central area and added to the top, right-hand and bottom sides of the double square. Its horizontal symmetrical axis runs dependent on the newly formed 6 plus 2 equals 8 divisions on a precise centre line and confronts the previously described movement of the figure with the *rigidity* that comes with symmetry.

Fig.104

---

[94] The analysis is based on original plans from Philadelphia and Ahmedabad and measurements of the building on site.
[95] Kahn felt that the neutral figure of the square as a beginning symbolized the question of what the building that was to be designed would make of itself, as a dialogue designer-design; see A. Tyng, "Beginnings", pp. 44–45.

The outline thus created by this figure of the oscillating double square defines the courtyard of the school building. In the realized project the courtyard functions as a place of assembly and through the walls of the adjacent building forms a central space which is open, directed and empty. It represents the spiritual meeting centre, contemplative and meditative in terms of concentration, but also communicative.

Fig.105 The modular square of dimension "X" simultaneously becomes a *grid* by horizontal and vertical addition. It fixes, as described above, the courtyard square with 7 times 7 equals 49 fields and its double, with 7 times 14 equals 98 fields. It also serves as a correction factor, by shifting the simple double square grid by one field: the grid, extending by one field in each case, acquires 7 plus 1 equals 8 fields in the vertical and 7 times 2 equals 14 minus 1 equals 13 fields longitudinally as a zone marked off on the right. A new rectangle ABCD emerges, unambiguously definable in its outline: the ratio of 8 to 13, precisely legible from the number of fields equals 0.615, which corresponds approximately with the minor of the Golden Section of 0.618.

As an area proportion, ABCD forms the frame of the newly emerged overall field in the ratio of side to height. Within this field, 3 area ratios can be "counted" on the basis of the shifted distance in grid modules: 8 to 13, 7 to 14 and 6 to 12. So-called "commensurable" proportioning,[96] in other words forming ratios of sizes relating to a starting measurement, is produced by the use of complete, "rational" numbers (result 0.615). It deviates from the "irrational" ratio, developed by geometrical construction, only slightly in individual cases (result 0.618). But considerable differences do emerge in the systematized application of interlinking irrational ratios, which are "incommensurable", proportions that build up without a common measurement.

The field that is isolating itself on the right outside the Golden Section frame ABCD contains the modular corner square, whose inscribed diagonal indicates *growth*, as in the previous figure. It enlarges itself in double mirror image into a group of four and leads to a new square, placed like diamond and linked with the Golden Section outline in its vertical symmetrical axis. The frame ABCD thus appears as an "interlinked" subsequent figure, which is appropriate to the idea of growth. It is geometrically very closely linked to the modular square and its blurring fourfold expansion, whose internal, transverse diagonal square indicates a special element in the orthogonal system that will be important later.

Two elements now define the borders of different areas: the all-embracing Golden Section frame ABCD functions as an outer border; in contrast with this, the outline that emerged from the shifted figure of the double square defines an inner area of 6 times 13 grid fields. Their distance apart, not yet measured, is the width of a grid square. This blurs the vertical symmetrical axis of that width? because of the open peripheral zone on the left, while the horizontal symmetrical axis lies on the track of the 4th field as the centre of both areas. The Golden Section square ABCD halts the shifting movement of the double square and stops in the longitudinal direction because of the small diagonal square in a fixed position at point B, which blocks movement, so that ambiguity is created: harmonious figures based on rational numbers like the square and its double lose their repose, they *oscillate*, and dynamic, inherently moving figures based on irrational numbers like the proportions of the Golden Section remain *rigid*. The described figurations in their positions now indicate an architecture that is becoming concrete. Its axes, wall tracks and edge relations are logically generated from the derived geometry. The important outline of the area proportions of the Golden Section determines the forthcoming design.

School complex with administration wing left and classroom group right

[96] "Commensurable" (according to Euclid) means "sizes that are measured by the same scale, and incommensurable are those for which there is no common scale". Euclid, "Elements", in: Wittkower and Naredi-Rainer.

Fig. 103

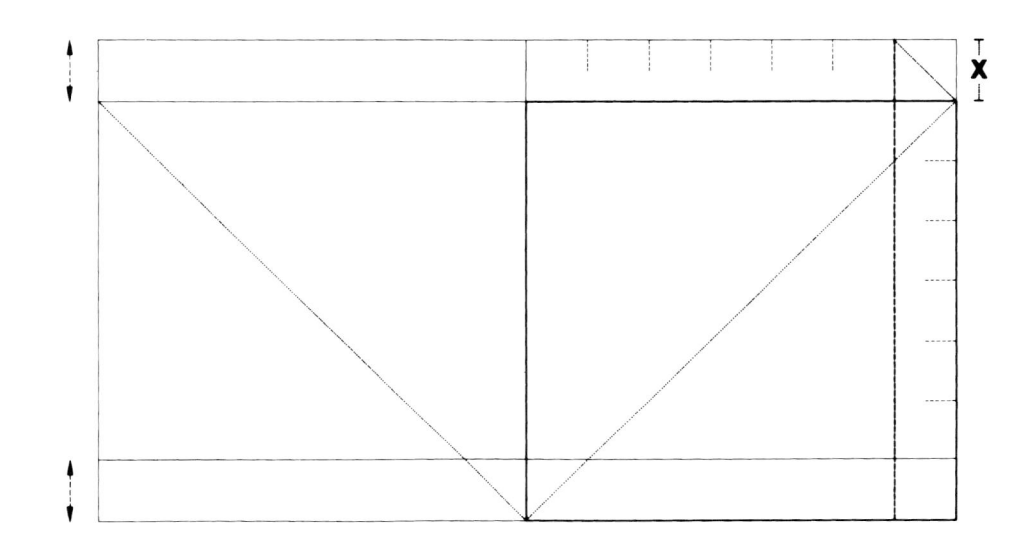

Fig. 104

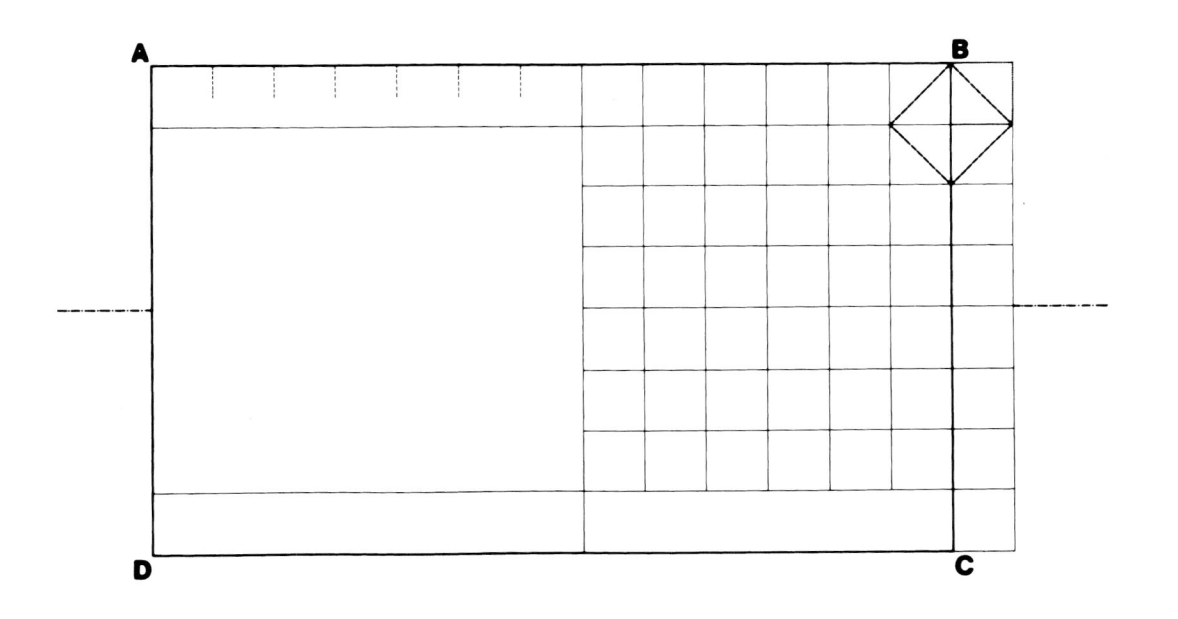

Fig. 105

Fig. 103–105
Ground plan analysis of the IIM with its starting figure of a double square as courtyard

Fig.106 The Golden Section rectangle ABCD continues to remain visible as a figure: walls with fixed measurements of 1 foot and 7 inches (48.2 cm)[97] are placed on all the tracks so far established. In the realized architecture they are massively built in brick,[98] and measure 23½ inches (60 cm) in the figure of the diagonally placed *entrance square*. Its position as an entrance hall at the upper right-hand corner of the whole figure defines the access situation, as seen in the preliminary steps and the genesis of the design in its various phases. The central axes of the walls that join on at the end points of the diagonal square relate to its symmetrical axis and run on the grid track. They fuse with the square through its walls, which follow the grid diagonal axially, to form a wall continuum. In contrast, the walls of the upper and lower Golden Section outline ABCD follow the grid, with either their outer or inner edges taking up the grid track. The edges do not disappear in the mass of the wall, but remain clearly present as border lines. This differentiation seems important: it is not the walls linked with the entrance square in its symmetrical axes that follow the grid, but the edges of the walls whose position was determined by shifting the original double square.

At this point the geometrical assertions made so far will be supported by arithmetical proof. Fixing its dimensions in measurements and number shows that the grid is dependent directly on the entrance square. The primary measurement is that of the outer outline of the entrance square, 32 feet 8 inches (9.96 m, in other words almost exactly 10). Two half walls – 2 times 30 cm – have to be subtracted from that to fix the axial track of the grid, giving 9.96 minus 0.60 equals 9.36 m as the diagonal of the grid field "X". The length of its side converts to 6.61 m and will be taken as 6.60 m in this analysis in comparative overall measurements of the realized building that have still to be discussed.[99] From this we can derive all the measurements of the wall tracks in the entrance square: the external outline with a side length of 9.96 m gives a diagonal of 14.08 m, thus about 14, and the spatially effective inner track with a length of 28 feet 9 inches (8.76 m),[100] and its diagonal of 12.38 m. These relations of measurements and geometry will be analysed in detail after all the sub-parts of the whole project have been discussed. We will then get back to the origins of the relation system of the measurements used (see p.173).

The established measurements make it possible to determine the dimensions of the courtyard and the access zones in the adjacent areas, hitherto described as shifted fields. They show their own lengths within the grid, to be counted by addition: the courtyard outline in the grid ratio 6 times 13 now means 6 times 6.60 equals 39.60 m minus the wall tracks 0.24 and 0.48 m gives 38.88 m. 13 times 6.60 m are 85.80 m minus 0.24 equals 85.56 m, and the access areas as interior measurements at the top 6.60 minus 0.24 gives 6.36 m and at the bottom 6.60 minus 0.48 gives 6.12 m. In the continuing analysis these measurements will have to be verified with regard to the building plans in feet and inches and the measurements acquired by surveying the site.[101]

According to this, the precise area ratio of the Golden Section in its grid lengths 8 to 13 is (8 times 6.60 =) 52.80 m to (13 times 6.60 =) 85.80 m equals 0.615 and can be interpreted as an approximation to the value 0.618. But if one considers the wall running centrally on the short side and chooses the inner outline of the courtyard, then half a width has to be subtracted: 52.80 m is divided by 85.56 m (85.80 minus 0.24), giving a ratio of 0.617, which is very near to the Golden Section. It can be assumed that the precise position of the walls with their outlines in each case as clearly comprehensible figures is crucial for the precise proportional disposition of the different parts. As a comparison, both the geometrical and the arithmetical proof will be shown to support the proposed ideas, and it will be illustrated in detail at linking point B in particular.

[97] Indian measurements are a leftover from British colonial rule and based on the foot, equals 30.48 cm and a twelfth of it, the inch, equals 2.54 cm; there are twelve inches to a foot. These measurements go back to Vitruvius, who speaks in his "Ten Books about Architecture", book 3, chapter 1 of "measurements for all buildings ... that are derived from the limbs of the body": finger (inch) = 2.54 cm, palm =10.16 cm, foot, a sixth part of the height of a man = 30.48 cm, ell = 6 palms or 24 fingers = 61 cm.
Measurements have been metricated except in contexts in which the original terms seemed necessary.
[98] The significance of the brick and its measurements as the smallest unit in the system of geometrical relations is presented in detail on p.173.
[99] For the significance of the decimal system as an attempt to combine the two systems of measurement that divide the world, feet/inches and cm, see "Modular Origin". Also interesting in this context are Le Corbusier's explanations in his "Modulor", pp. 116/117 and 180/181, in which the "regulators" derived from the division of the Golden Section are established as valid in proportional dependences as an all-embracing "harmony" for both systems.
[100] The measurements given were taken from copies of the working plans from Raje's office in Ahmedabad – in the possession of the author – "A 1–2, 3 Feb. 1970, Administration Wing", and "L 1–2, June 1969. Library".
[101] In February and March 1990, then additionally in February 1991, the author measured parts of the complex, revealing different measurements within the plans, incorrect dimensioning and changes during realization, but showing that geometry and the realized building agree precisely in part.

The symmetrical axis Z, running on its track in the third vertical grid field of the courtyard, is important in the next steps of the analysis. It is now shifted, gently and scarcely perceptibly, by the walls on the long sides, which are emerging and differing in their position. This process is the first indication of a possible principle of subtle *refraction* leading from symmetry to asymmetry.

The frame of the field made up of 8 times 14 grids now expands and produces new consequent geometries from the previously existing figurations. It emerges from mirroring the original double square over the square figure emergent on horizontal axis Y, now with 14 times 14 grid squares. In the growth process of the "geometrical organism" it represents the next-largest figure of a further stage and is illustrated here by the its inscribed diagonal square. Equal divisions to those under it occur above the mirrored axis Y: a length of 7 grid fields in the vertical above Y encloses the zone of the upper access corridor with 1 grid field and 6 more. These acquire, parallel with the courtyard figure, a central division on the track of their third field. The diagonal entrance square already suggests further diagonal relations and remains constantly perceptible as a scale.

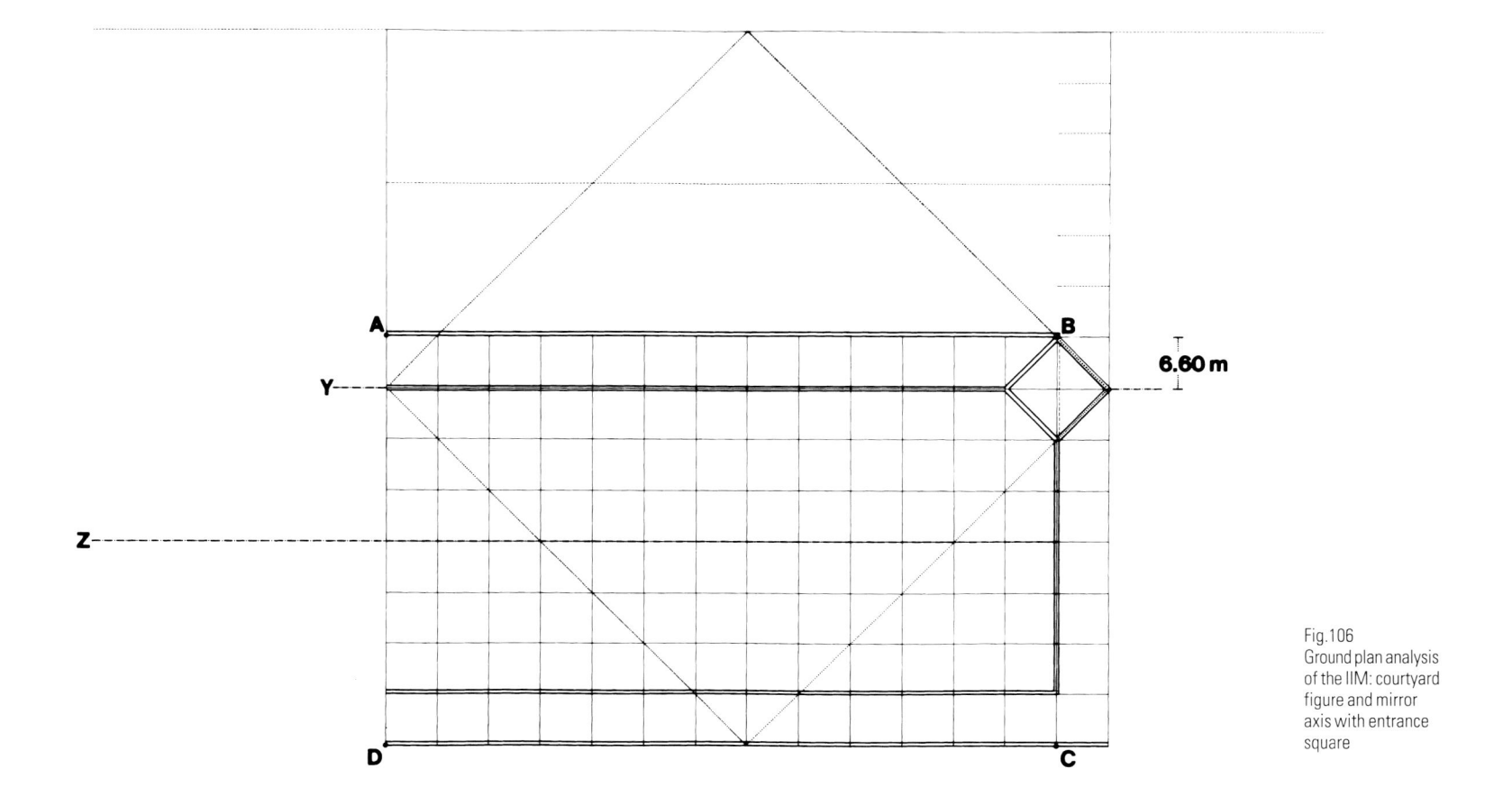

Fig. 106
Ground plan analysis of the IIM: courtyard figure and mirror axis with entrance square

ADMINISTRATION WING AND MAIN ENTRANCE

The centre, so important in Kahn's work, is a double square in the case of the courtyard figure. These simple initial figures can be determined geometrically and arithmetically, so that a dependent *growth process* of the sub-geometries can already be clearly discerned. The courtyard and its surrounding areas constitute the first fixed figure in its limiting contours. Its central position and the walls that surround it, continuous on three sides, suggest a corporeal volume, with the sub-figures developing in the next steps forming "extremities" that are added on to this hollow body. Here the special position of the diagonal square at point B has a signal effect in terms of the access areas, which were originally intended to be on all four corners. It remains the only main entrance at this point that is so favourably placed for the access road.

After the courtyard and its surrounding zones have been defined the figure of the administration wing is now built up on this.

Fig.107 The end of the upper access area is fixed by a wall that is shifted off the grid track on the left-hand edge of the courtyard outline. The distance by which it is shifted emerges after comparing measurements[102] as half a thickness of the 23 ½ inches (30 cm) wall and defines the shift of the Golden Section figure ABCD outside the grid, in order to accommodate the wall line that is visible from the exterior space. When the imaginary – because it is not present in the built reality – grid is abandoned, the Golden Section figure is transferred to existing wall lines that can be grasped visually. Proportional relations thus become evident. The internal walls of the access corridors are the "actual" boundaries of the courtyard; their function is not declared as belonging to an intermediate zone both inside and outside (the original oscillating double square).

In the further development of geometrical figures dependent on each other the diagonal entrance square, operating as "generator" above the mirror axis Y with its own defined dimensions, creates from within itself the figure of the administration wing as an elementally repetitive structure no longer based on the initial grid. This will be explained on a larger scale in the next steps.

Fig.108 A first administration element is generated from a *framing square* of the diagonal entrance square. It runs round the corners of the interior wall track of the diagonal square, which in its dimensions, both in terms of measurements and geometry, is to be described as its root 2 major (the larger in each case). The most important condition for the further genesis of the sub-figures in terms of defining their dimensions is revealed when the entrance square and the measurements of its wall tracks are considered in greater detail: the above-mentioned wall thickness of 60 cm (23 ½ inches) has to be subtracted twice from the exterior measurement with a side length of 9.96 m, in other words about 10 m. This produces an inner track of 8.76 m (28 feet 9 inches),[103] whose root 2 major, the full length of the diagonal, can be established as 12.38 m. The dimension of the square space that is experienced on entering this part of the building is conveyed, immediately discernible as a spatial border, with the measurements of its wall tracks and diagonals (the measurement connections of the entrance square are discussed in detail at the end of the analysis).

The length of the diagonals of 12.38 m is transferred to the corners of the square by parallel shifting, so that the next largest framing square (major root 2 of the diagonal square) appears, with a side length of 12.38 m. It is clear in this detail figure that the upper boundary wall of the courtyard, which joins on to the diagonal square horizontally, does not run centrally along the grid track. Because its cross-section is less than that of the wall that joins vertically – 0.48 rather than 0.60 m – Kahn avoids to choose the centre of the wall, in order to maintain the same distance from the grid track to the outer line and also the symmetry of view for the diagonal wall on the courtyard side.

Fig.109 The grid is continued by the width of a field of 6.60 m above the horizontal line AB. It serves as a support line on the vertical axis of the diagonal square for the 12.38 m square that has developed from this. Its lower line does not follow the grid track, but shifts upwards by about 0.2 m (8 inches), following comparative measurements.[104] This difference, as a Golden Section outline, in the inner wall of the access corridor visible from the courtyard suggests that Kahn corrected this geometrical-proportional figure. The short sides AD and BC of the figure ABCD (see figure 106), which is perceptible in the realized architecture, are thus extended from 52.80 m to precisely 53.00 m. Thus the ratio of the short

---

[102] The measurements used were based on working plan "A 1–2, Feb. 1970, Administration Wing" as one of the last to be valid. It was made available to the author as a copy by Raje in Ahmedabad.
[103] Working plan "A 1–2, 3. Feb. 1970, Administration Wing".
[104] Working plan "A 1–2, Feb. 1970, Administration Wing"; these deviations were also confirmed by on-site surveys in 1990 and 1991.

Main entrance hall
("entrance square")

Administration and classroom access lobbies as areas relating to both the inside and the outside

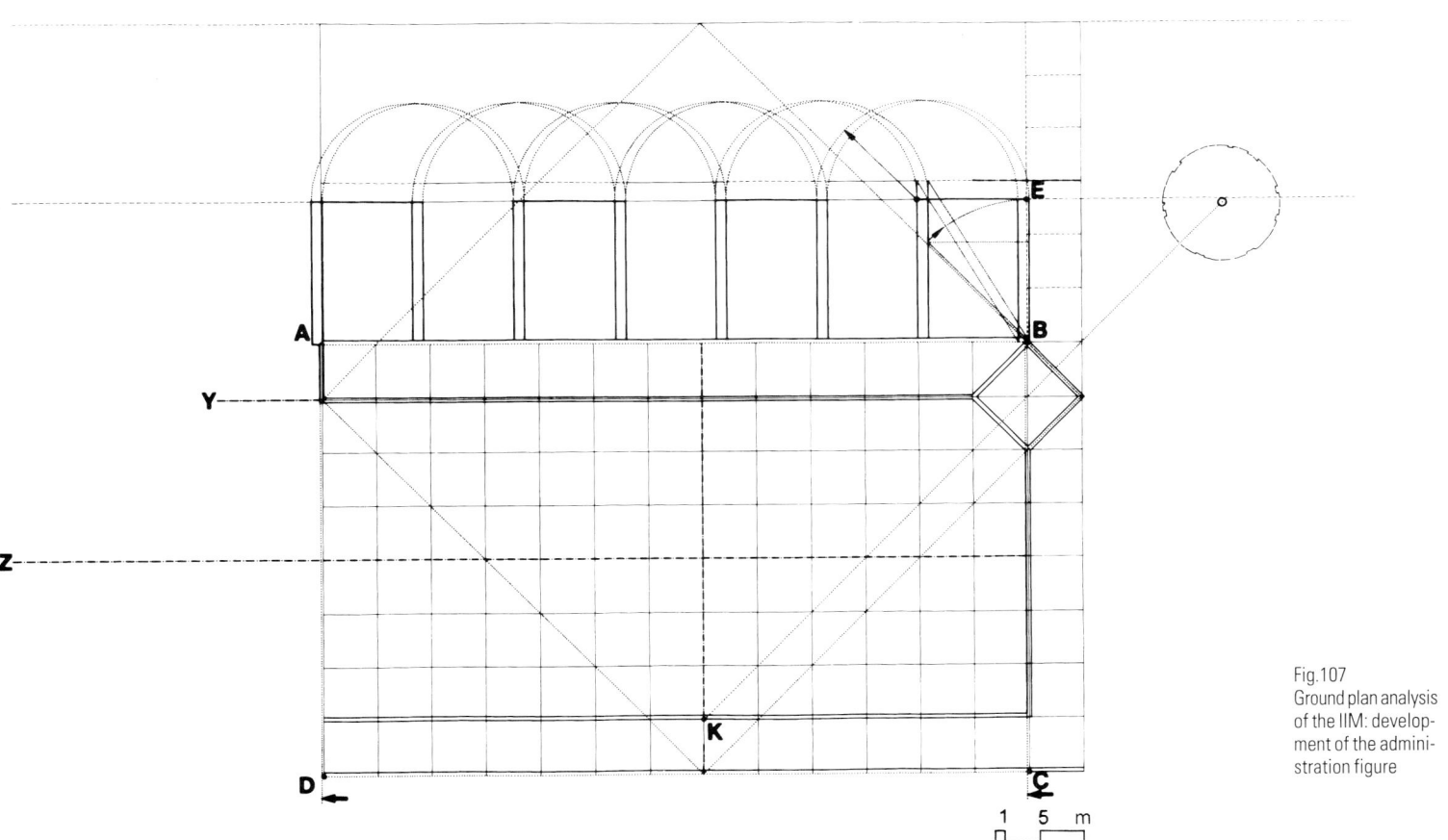

Fig. 107
Ground plan analysis of the IIM: development of the administration figure

side of 53.00 m to the long side of 85.80 m gives the almost precise value of 0.618. The attempt to achieve proportions as close as possible to the Golden Section for the figure ABCD shows Kahn's intention of making the access corridors a component of the courtyard. Despite the extraordinary dimensions of this complex, which are almost outside human scale, the geometry of the related sub-figures – emphasized in their significance – is intended to appear as an illustration of the design's genesis.

The 12.38 m square can be emphasized as the origin for the administration figure. Its diagonal moves on the radius of a circle to the right, so that at intersection point E with the support edge the upper track of an administration "element" emerges, by the geometrical construction of the area figure in the ratio 1 to root 2. The joining or interlinking of these squares at an angle of 45 degrees to each other as primary geometries via the point of contact B again directly indicates the process of genesis and illustrates the *growing* or *growing together* of abstraction transformed into reality in continuous outlines of building volumes.

Fig.110 The important horizontal track of the third grid field above the entrance square combines with the left-hand side FG, extended upwards, of the root 2 figure at point H to form the new rectangle HIB'F. Its side to height ratio is approximately equal to the Golden Section. This suggests that both proportional figures are directly linked with their starting figure, the entrance square: the Golden Section figure HIB'F relates to the grid in the diagonal entrance square and this to its centre track, i.e. the axis of the wall (see figure 108), while the root 2 figure GEB'F results from the inner track of the diagonal square (see figures 108/109). Thus the wall width of the entrance square reveals itself as the dimensional key to the geometrical connection of the two figures (see p. 173 for a detailed description of all dependences in terms of measurements and geometry for this significant figure).

The subsequent shift by the area HIB'F to the left to the intersection point of its diagonals with point G gives point J on the horizontal of the grid through IH. Its vertical now defines the outer line of one administration element and its distance from H the depth of the outer wall as a shade-providing window reveal. Correspondingly the diagonal running through point G to track HB' fixes the right-hand side wall of the figure geometrically. This element, approximating to the final shape, may be considered as the product of an attempt to synthesize both the root 2 and Golden Section figures. It leaves, similarly to the overlapping of double square and Golden Section frame in the starting figure for the courtyard, comprehensible fields of difference as suggestive moving figures caused to *vibrate* by shifting and oscillating. It is because of this that we start to assume the existence of a principle of systematized geometrical connections, running through all the architecture and open to derivation.

This element can now be clearly determined in its outer lines as a sub-figure of the administration wing. It breaks down into three vertical strips: the two peripheral zones as products of the shifting process and the interior zone as an area left over from the root 2 rectangle GEB'F. Finally walls 1 foot and 7 inches (0.48 m) wide are added to the upper and lower line. The element does not remain in its original position following the vertical track of the grid, but shifts to the right by half the width of the wall and takes up the outer track of the vertical wall that joins on below the entrance square. This achieves conformation of the wall lines and closely fused prisms begin to emerge in a crystalline fashion at the point of contact.   Fig.111

The distance GH is defined by the difference in measurement between the Golden Section figure HIB'F to the root 2 figure GEB'F (see figures 109/110) and effectively the distance of the horizontal grid track from the upper outline of the building. It appears in the shape of a staircase figure placed outside the neighbouring area of the administration element as a "distance courtyard" (see figure 111). Its width corresponds with the internal area of the administrative element, so that the courtyard is defined as a "negative" exterior space in relation to the "positive" architectural body, and relates the peripheral zones to both one area and the other as a *puzzle picture*.

Next comes the simple geometrical construction of four administration areas as an additive structure (see figure 107). The peripheral lengths of the previously generated elements are mirrored from the corner points over the radii of their circles. They accumulate as intersection points on the horizontal track running through point E, giving their outlines, which extend to the bordering wall of the access corridor, as vertical parallels. The grid network, previously restricted to

Fig.108

12.38 m

Fig.109

12.38 m

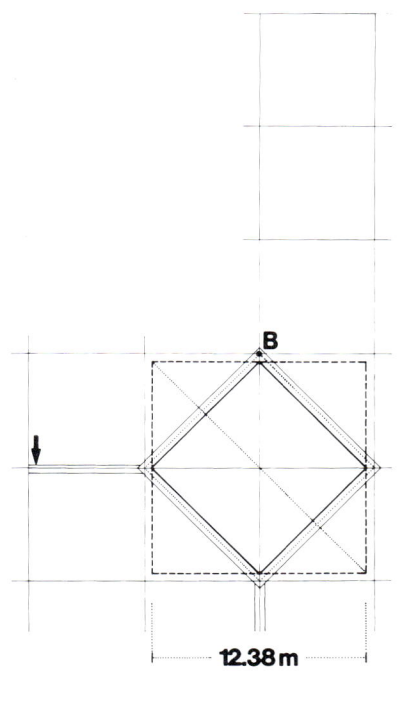

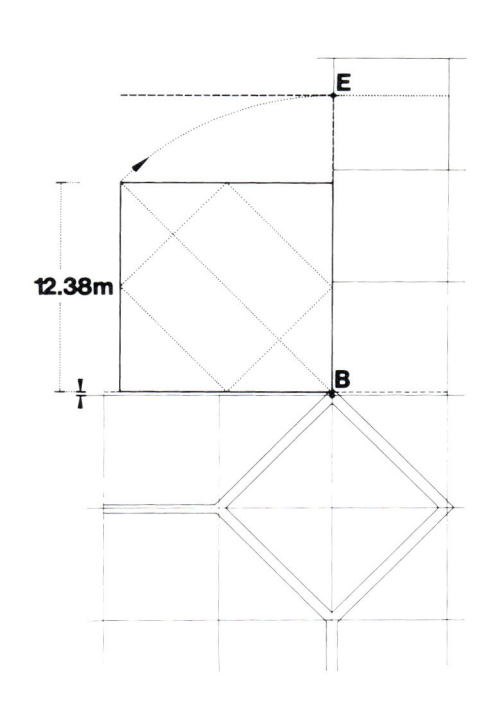

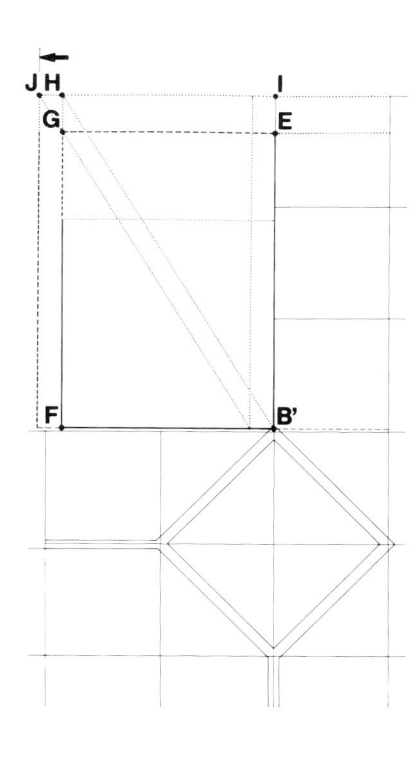

Fig.110

Main entrance with steps placed axially to the existing mango tree

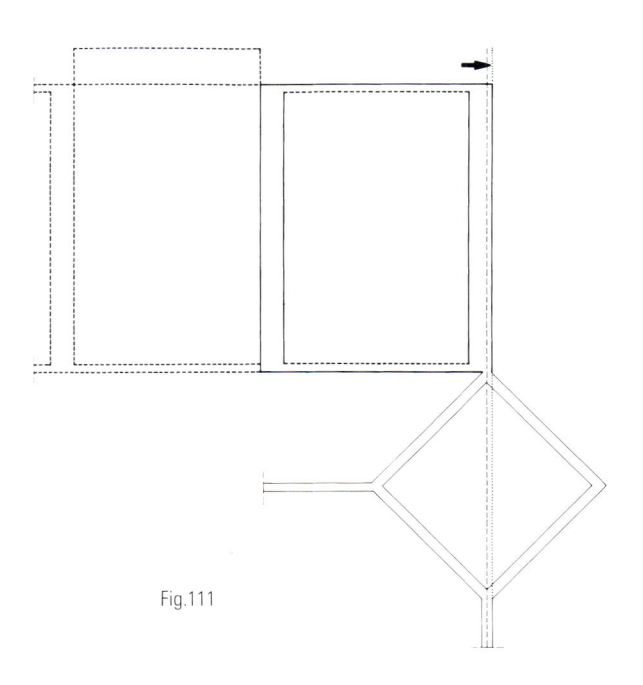

Fig.111

Fig.108–111
Ground plan analysis of the IIM: development of the administration figure from the geometry of the entrance square

Administration wing with four individual buildings joined at the base

the width of the courtyard with 14 fields leaves the administration figure through its outer wall, "breaking out" on the left edge and deviating from the left-hand outer line of the corridor. The subtle differences involved in its tracks, comprehensible as traces of the process of genesis, are the result of three phases that are different but still build on each other. The emphatic shift, the move away from the linking line of the access corridor suggests dynamics: the arrangement of the isomorphic figures is ambiguously perceptible; it is as if they are gliding along a rail, ignoring neighbouring geometries. Elements overlapping each other in their peripheral zones are soon prevented from *distortion* or "drifting apart" to the sides and breaking through framing borders by the rigidity of equal distances. The access corridor also works as a clip, resisting the administration figure's tendency to fall apart, and anchors itself with the diagonal entrance square, which suggestively absorbs pressure and tensile forces, swinging between formation and deformation.

Missing relations become obvious in the symmetrical axes of the individual figures. The administration unit asserts itself as an independent figure with its vertical symmetrical axis. It seems liberated from the hitherto latent dominant symmetry of the courtyard double square with 2 times 7 grid fields. The existing starting grid and its rigidity are consciously neglected in the shift, but the figure itself "persists" in symmetry, so that here too the dialectical principle of rigidity and movement is followed to an equal extent.

The overall figure examined so far is marked by the formation of strips or an accumulation of markedly horizontal, oscillating zones that interlink within the square enclosing 14 by 14 grid fields. Its horizontal tracks running out beyond the outer lines (see figure 107) indicate that the figure is extending (growing) to the left and right and relate to the orientation of the site. The diagonal figure, which with its dotted lines contains the sides of the 14 by 14 grid, acquires a new diagonal axis parallel to its bottom right diagonal track at a distance of one grid field. It starts at a point on the dividing axis of the courtyard, runs through the centre of the entrance square and meets an existing mango tree, which is touched by the extended horizontal track of the upper administration area. The existence of this tree in an axial position is not just a sign for the main entrance there, but gives it symbolic character as the *natural generator* of the growth process of figurative geometry, as will be seen in the following analysis.

WATER TOWER

Previous steps in this analysis have vividly shown the dependence of the sub-figures of the courtyard with is surrounding corridors and the administration wing. The system of figurative geometry that is clearly developing here shapes the structure of this architecture by Kahn in all the subsequent stages as well.

The upper horizontal line of the administration wing is interrupted in the courtyard areas by protruding steps linking the outside area with the courtyard, which lies higher. In the genesis of this figure its width was established as the difference between the geometrical root 2 figure and the Golden Section figure. The meandering of this seven-fold administration element and the associated meshing of the administration wing with the exterior via its courtyard zones and the attached steps can be defined as an upward "stretching" or "craning", i.e. a vertical movement. It contrasts with the previous dominant horizontality of the overall figure as a countermovement, which is also expressed by the fact that the administration elements are aligned vertically, rather than squarely and statically.

Fig.112

With its newly found overall length the administration figure extends over the width of the courtyard and the access corridors to the right and left, making it possible to "break out" of the still dominant rigidity of the 14 times 14 grid field square by means of a new square LMNO that attaches itself to the upper horizontal track of the outer line of the steps LM. With the help of the geometrical root 2 construction its diagonal LN creates the rectangle QMNP. When the left-hand edge of this rectangle is extended upwards, this gener-

The set-back corridor wall in the administration office buildings

Administration wing with corridor sections in front, indented at the end

Fig. 112
Ground plan analysis of the IIM: dependence of subsequent figures on the centre

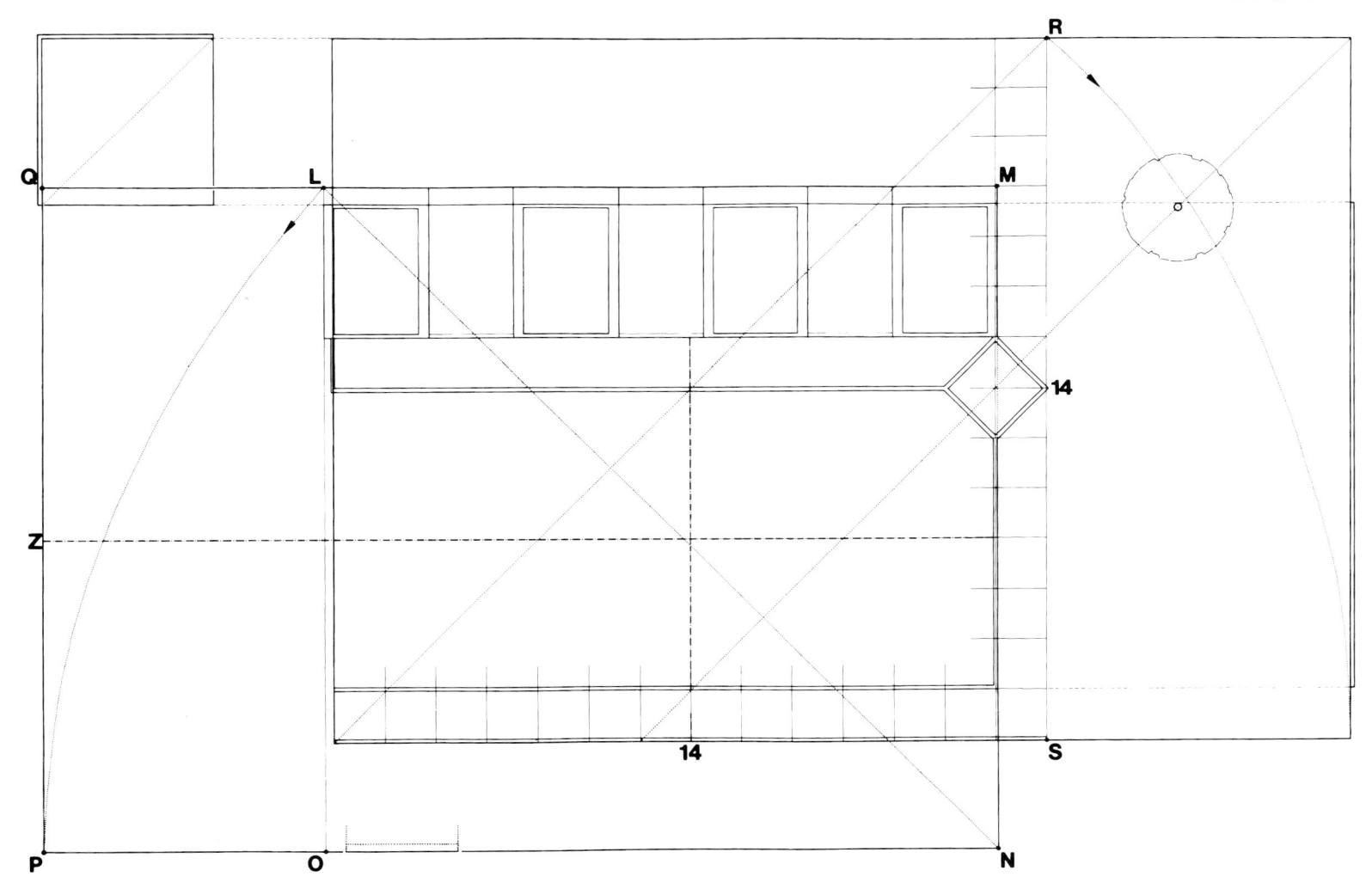

ates the inner wall track of a new ground plan figure for the whole complex, the square ground area outline of the water tower, which provides drinking water and cooling water for the air-conditioning units. The intersection point with the upper horizontal track of the 14 by 14 grid field square fixes the outline and position of the tower, but its dimension is determined only when the upper administration outline is accepted as the lower limit of the new figure; the dimension can then be constructed geometrically via the diagonal as a square.

The gradually built up process of the genesis of figurative geometry is intelligibly retained in the realized architecture through the subtly differentiated outer edges of the administration wing, the access corridors and the courtyard. The resulting root 2 rectangle proportion also suggests a dynamic directedness, unlike its minors and majors extending within the square as static figures. It limits both the external contour of the whole complex and the wall track of this isolated element. Nevertheless it is crucial for the anticipated overall disposition of all sub-figures when fixed geometrically.

Points L and O remain significant here. Their special quality is that they are "non-existent", and neither relates directly to a figure. But they have a key function in the geometrical determination of the extension figure root 2 rectangle QMNP by the starting figure square LMNO, by their definition of the left-hand, crucial side of the square. A similar extension process involving an existing figure that shows its edges only partially in realization occurs in the case of the 14 by 14 grid field square. Its diagonal crosses the vertical symmetrical axis of the courtyard double square at the upper edge of the courtyard and ends at point R. The extension process towards the right to the root 2 rectangular figure creates a vertical edge as the border of the full field. This identifies the exterior wall line of an access ramp whose length is defined at the top by the end of the administration figure and at the bottom by the side of the access corridor that faces the courtyard. Now, with this new field border on the right, the diagonal entrance square in its horizontally central position is more strongly weighted, supported by its conspicuous right-pointing tip. The vertical track running along the ramp marks the border of the root 2 rectangle whose intersection point with the horizontal through point R determines the upper corner of the figure as the end point of the diagonal axis of the entrance square. This integrates the tree and its position firmly into the geometrical system and raises it to the status of an architectonic element. Conversely, the placing of the complex as a whole is now dependent on the existing natural element, and now that the tree is fixed by diagonal and tangent the complex seems like a kind of anchorage. The architecture had previously seemed to be floating on the site, relating to no topographical elements, but now its geometry relates to a natural phenomenon and thus enhances its status, which indicated the symbolic importance of the mango tree in Indian society.

With its shifted distance of 6 grid fields, the 14 by 14 grid field square now forms the described root 2 rectangle in a ratio of the rational numbers 20 to 14, i. e. 1.428, in commensurable proportion, deviating in this lack of precision from the precise value of 1.414 that can be established by the geometrical process in the left-hand extension figure. Here we can again sense Kahn's interest in using and combining the possibilities of commensurable and incommensurable proportion, in order to avoid the danger of paralysis presented by a rationally developed figuration. A vague edge of a stairway can be made out by point O. Despite its vagueness it still relates to the lower outline of the root 2 rectangle QMNP, and indeed confirms its existence. This outline forms a bottom border for the whole school complex and in subsequent steps shows its geometrical relation to the stairs, linked with the exterior space, in the administration courts. This parallel also underlines the existence of the imaginary rectangle QMNP, whose left-hand outer line, as the end of the horizontal courtyard symmetry axis, indicates an extension figure that extends up to it, and is still to be described.

Water tower

Access ramp to the
Plus 1 level of the
student dormitories

Library in the centre
as end building with
diagonal entrance
building on the left

143

LIBRARY

The library figure confirms the highly significant grid module described in the analysis. What becomes very clear is the play between fitting into the ordering structure and breaking it down in terms of individual characteristics, involving each individual section of the building.

Fig.113 The 14 by 14 grid square extending to the right by 6 grid fields as a root 2 major figure is a rectangle of commensurable proportion. It is illustrated here with 20 by 14 "countable" fields. A rectangle on the right with 7 by 14 fields overlaps the 14 by 14 grid square in the centre over the whole vertical strip of the diagonal entrance square. Thus its lower half marks the overlapping of a 7 by 7 grid square with the original courtyard double square from the starting figure. This border of this 7 by 7 grid square is formed by the horizontal symmetrical axis of the entrance square, in whose centre the wall axis of the vertical right-hand courtyard frame intersects. The square acquires its bottom outer line in the outer track of the access corridor and its right-hand edge in the left-hand outer edge of the wall accompanying the ramp. It defines the overlap zone, one grid field wide, as the forecourt of the new rectangular library figure, which is linked with the entrance square. Its 4 to 5 side ratio is derived from a reduction of the area in a ratio 7 to 5, i. e. root 2, which encloses the forecourt and the ramp. The forecourt now follows the diagonal quality of the entrance square, whose border wall with the library is doubly related to both figures. This shift of the forecourt makes the library seem like an oscillating structure "stuck" to the entrance square, and is reminiscent of the vertical movement of the courtyard square, involving the emergence of the access zones and the grid module.

This diagonal quality of the library forecourt area, implying both movement and rigidity – or pausing – is the first directly comprehensible illustration of a movement process in the genesis of the design. This clear emphasis of the measurement of a single grid field fixed in this way is intended to indicate its key function within the conditioning system of figurative geometry, so that the diagonal, distorted wall remains a sign by which the inherent grid can be recognized.

The impression of movement in the forecourt area is reinforced by the process of linking up or fusing with the entrance square and the administration wing. The indentation in the access corridor at the end of the administration area could be explained by the turning of the entrance square, and could express force in a state of tension.

A main access staircase emerges from the access points marked diagonally at the corners in early sketches and schemes (see figure 97). It is attached to the entrance square and extends as far as the border line of the administration area extended horizontally to the right. Its outline protrudes considerably, and gives the impression of a lever intended to turn the tension-laden administration/library figuration, but it is held firmly in position by its axial relationship with the existing tree.

The tree now appears as a natural generator: as a *power provider*, it directs energy via the stairs – which are recognizable as a vehicle – into the distributing entrance square and the firmly linked part-figures in order to extend the geometrical figurations, dependent and built up on each other; this can be interpreted as a natural growth process. The staircase, extraordinarily and almost exaggeratedly emphasized in comparison with Kahn's other work, suggests symbolic importance rather than the function of a main entrance. This is especially true as the entrance square, which is closely linked with the staircase figure, does not provide entry to any interior space. The entrance square zone is in fact a transition, a way of crossing the border from exterior to interior space.

The diagonal on one grid field is the key dimension within the ground plan for establishing the initial grid. It finds its equivalent in the diagonal walls of the library forecourt, as the side wall of the entrance square. In this way it combines the horizontal symmetrical axes of the courtyard and the library, which are shifted in relation to each other. The main entrance to the library follows this diagonal track and builds up, along the central grid line as axis, a symmetrical staircase figure for vertical access to the upper storeys. The vertical track of the second grid field from the left within the outline of the building or – including the forecourt – the symmetrical axis of the rectangle, which now includes 6 grid fields, is the edge in contact with the steps. The shifted contour of an arc of a circle with the radius of one side of a grid field is now added on symmetrically in the ratio of the Golden Section of one field, and the edge is determined as the inner radius of the flight of stairs by a double square dependent on the Golden Section. This fixes the dis-

Diagonal library
walls with entrance
building behind

Diagonal walls in
the library forecourt

Fig. 113
Ground plan analysis
of the IIM: development of the library
figure and the main
entrance

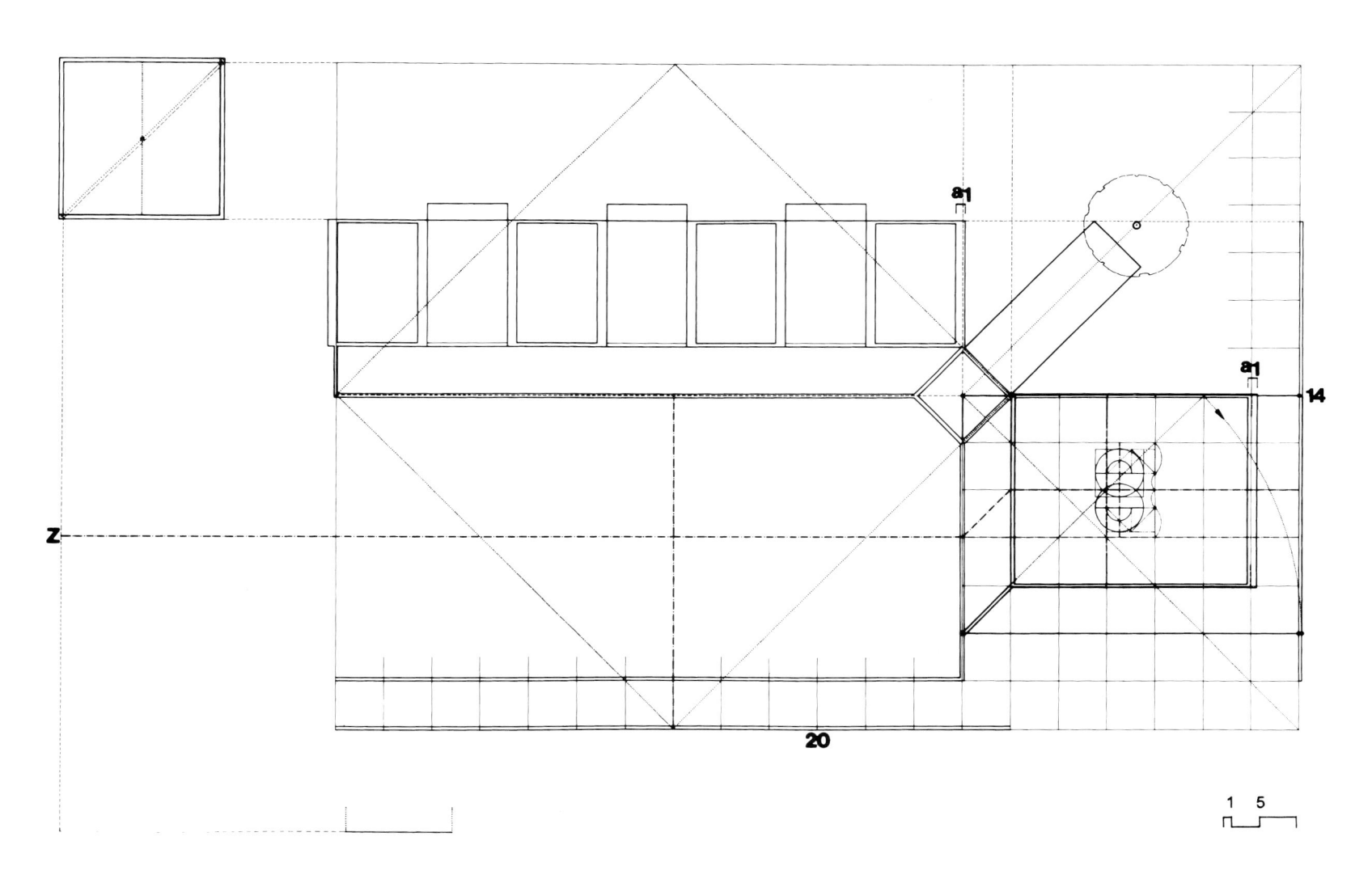

145

tances, leads to overlapping of the circles, and identifies the outer halves of the arc as staircases.

The library walls follow the grid in different ways: in the case of the links with the entrance square the grid track is on the axis of the wall. Furthermore, the left-hand outer edge agrees with the grid track in the interior wall of the forecourt. On the right, opposite the ramp, the wall becomes wider to the extent of the indentation a1 which was added to provide shade for the administration elements. This, similarly to the other parts of the figure developed so far, breaks out of the grid scheme as a "distortion".

The outer wall of the water tower emerges as the final outer line of the whole complex on the left. Its left-hand and upper wall were added on to the outside of the geometrically established internal line and have to be added on to the inside of the other two sides. This produces a shifted centre point with a new vertical axis.

In the above observations it has become possible to recognize the principle that on the one hand the grid is built up as an almost independent basic pattern and the figure is then consequently – logically – related to it. On the other hand this pattern is covered up, indeed questioned, by deviations, like shifts by the width of a wall or measures that have been established by precise geometry. The outlines of the ordering figures help to bind the parts of the design together as a process of duty, and support the rational and the irrational – i. e. interdependent – process of genesis. However, abandoning the schemes as a conscious deviation reinforces inner tension, as a free choice.

CLASSROOM AREA

The school complex as a whole was discussed in the description of the step-by-step development of the design (see figures 79–95). It is a rectangular-circular figure with the function areas disposed in a way that began to emerge at a very early stage, and was differentiated later. The classrooms were arranged on the southeastern periphery, i. e. under the library, and directly connected with the structure of the student dormitories to close the circle of the school.

The classroom figure is also bound in with the inherent geometrical ordering system. To this end the grid net that has hitherto dominated the creation of courtyard and library is extended downwards. In the library entrance area 7 by 7 grids emerge, with an overlap zone of one grid field, which is the important shifted distance of the library axis from the courtyard symmetry axis Z. This shifted distance here illustrates the *primal dimension*. Both squares, the upper one with its border track on the courtyard axis and the lower one with its contact edge on the library axis, cover a total area of 7 by 13 grid fields in their outer line. The overlap denotes the symmetry field of one area of activity. The outer line of the outward-thrusting steps in front of the administration buildings is part of its upper boundary. The right-hand edge is formed by the wall of the access ramp. The stairs depth a2 proves to be the distance from one grid track to the outer line of the administration wing, and this is a crucial measurement for the position of the classroom area. It is added at the bottom of the outermost grid track and defines a new line UV, which is in contact with the outer wall of the library. The aim of this reduction by length a2 is to abandon the rigid grid system without negating the general ordering system that ties everything together, so that – comparably with the genesis of the administration figure – every sub-figure of the complex as a whole acquires quasi-autonomous character as an "individual in the group", with new symmetry axes. The newly established line UV, gives its Golden Section major TU as a length that can be established by measurement and by geometry. Thus the rectangle TUVW can be completed as a limiting framework for the width of the classroom body. The difference measure a2 now exists underneath the classroom area, and can be found in the width of a flight of stairs. This reveals a parallel in terms of dimension and con-

Fig.114

View from the entrance hall into the unfinished inner courtyard

Fig. 114
Ground plan analysis of the IIM: development of the classroom figure and the water tower

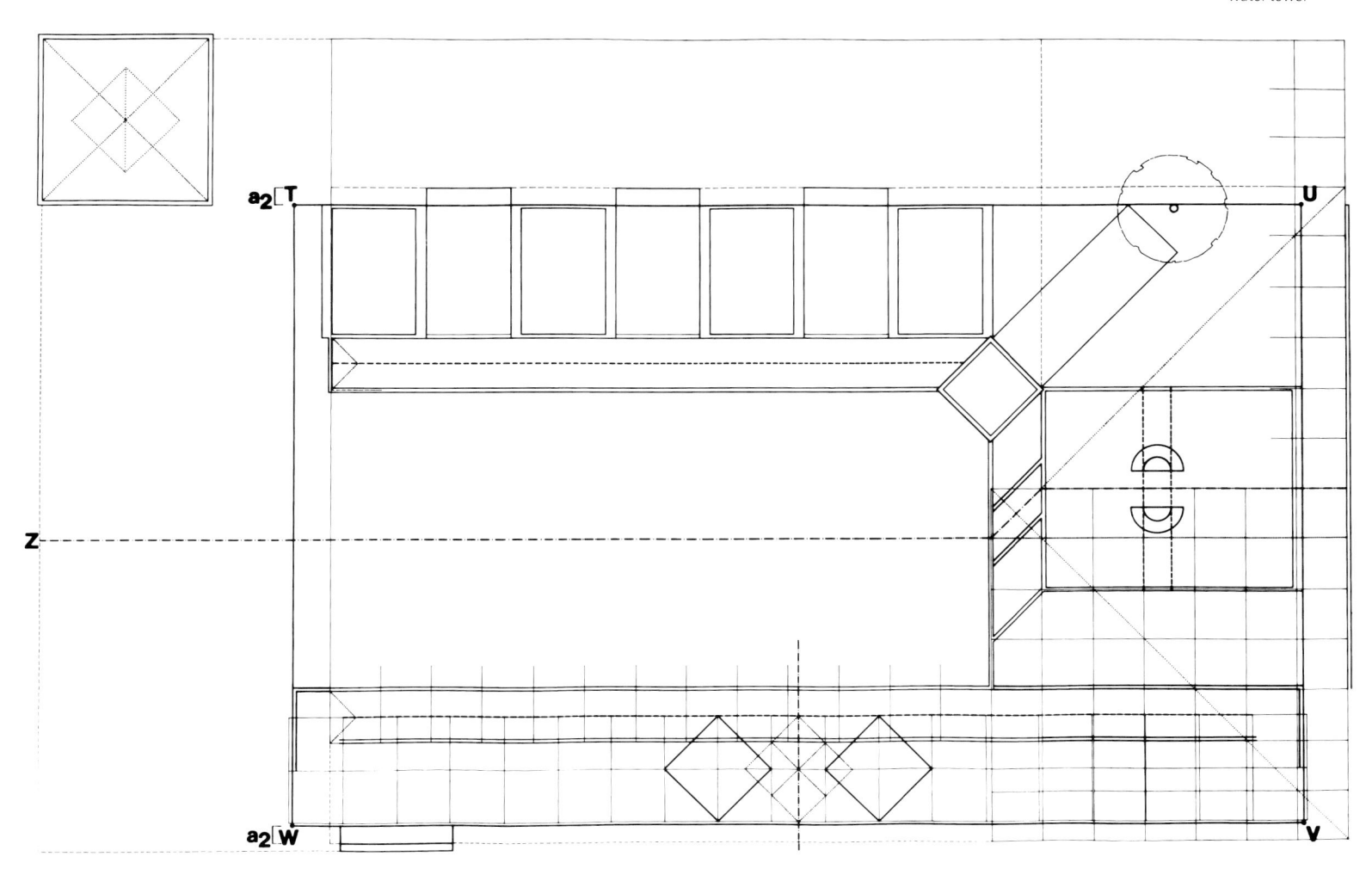

tent: staircase figures below the classrooms and above the administration area.

Once more we can see that Kahn is interested in using both commensurable and incommensurable proportions to vary his themes of geometrical order. Here he combines the grid structure in commensurable ratios and the geometrical construction of the rectangle TUVW in incommensurable ratios. A hierarchy of the two systems emerges: the sequence of genesis is indubitably constituted in the dependence of the classroom figure on the library and administration wing. The existence of staircases of width a2 above the administration wing and below the classrooms and their geometrical dependence support the correctness of the links that have been assumed. It makes it possible to perceive an upper and a lower outline comparable with the figure of the double square at the beginning of the analysis, "merging" by the rectangle TUVW. The aim here is to suggest a link with the exterior and consciously to move the viewer's eye to and fro.

The centre and vertical symmetrical axis of the classroom block can now be determined through the length WV, which is now tangible. A diagonal square divided into four is arranged on this axis in such a way that its upper point touches the middle line of the grid field that has so far been designated as an access corridor. The middle line is the upper border track of a new grid emerging from the diagonal square and its division. Its structure defines the position of the individual classroom volumes precisely within the established length WV. It clarifies its difference as a newly emergent grid in its overlap with the courtyard and library grid. Here too the figure's relation to the figure of the entrance square is obvious, the latter serving as generator of the almost organic growth process within the rational system of figurative geometry. The entrance square allows us to sense the sub-figures' tension between dependence and autonomy. Thus the crucial feature of the generated, differentiated grid systems remain their references to the wall tracks of the entrance square. Its axial tracks produce the courtyard grid, its inner tracks produce the administration figures and the outer tracks the grid-related positions of the classrooms.

Inside the library the proportionately developed semicircular flights of stairs are visible; their inner radii form vertical tracks that keep to the grid and run to the outer lines of the figure.

The emergence of the centrally inscribed "innards" of the water-tower also seems dependent on the relation dimension of the outer line of the diagonal entrance square.

The width q1 of the new classroom figure grid fixes the position of the two adjacent diagonal squares on the symmetrical axis. Its framing line consists of two grid widths q1 per side, which form the frame for the actual ground plan figures of the classroom as major root 2. It seems important in understanding the generative process to accept a diagonal square arranged at first on the symmetrical axis. When divided into four the square determines the grid measurement and the distances for the classroom sections. Fig.115

The frames of the diagonal squares are surrounded by external walls 19 inches thick. At their horizontal centre they are cut into an upper zone to take the wall widths and a lower grid field area that is not clearly defined at this stage. Fig.116

The originally even outer wall track of the classroom squares is now distorted in its lower half. In the geometrical construction of the root 2 rectangle figure, the arc of the diagonal of the square's outer line intersects with the lower side of the square. From this point of intersection a new vertical track to the middle forms the outer line of each wall. The mirror transfer of this track to the outer walls illustrates the *cutting apart* of the upper and lower halves of the square and produces a shift effect for these walls. From the statically rigid grid there now emerges a contrasting pair: lower half/upper half with powerful horizontal dynamics. Its powers of distortion evoke a sense of being cramped, crushed together and thus a tension evoked by the counterforces within the walls, a kind of magnetism. Fig.117

The outer wall boundaries of the classroom buildings are now established by the tracks of the lower halves of the no longer complete square. Concerning their as yet unfixed upper and lower borders the question now arises of a similar genetic process. The grid-determining diagonal square appears as a figure shifting in a vertical direction. Its vibration distance relating to the grid is 9½ inches, i.e. half the known wall width of 19 inches. In the left-hand classroom section it moves upwards to determine the line of the outer wall and moves downwards to the same extent to find the lower outer line of the wall of the right-hand body. This process fixes both final positions of the outer walls of the classrooms by Fig.118

simply transferring the grid structure. It also produces 19 inch connecting walls in the distancing grid field between the classroom sections, to divide off a narrow zone above and a broad zone below. Their wall tracks are created on the left by the diagonal square thrusting upwards with its grid lines running out on the corners, both in its lower outline on the left-hand outer wall and also in its upper one on the right. The right-hand diagonal square, moving downwards, produces only the lower outline on its left-hand outer wall – in this case the central connection of the two classroom figures.

An enhanced process of movement can be sensed: it is not only the original square of the classroom starting square that is distorted both horizontally and vertically, but along with it a "band", the connecting wall starts to *oscillate*, as the positions of the connecting walls change in each case. They are fixed both above and centrally on the grid track.

Fig.119 In this process of vertical movement of the central diagonal square, the thrusting to and fro to determine the outer contours, its own tracks are "blurred". The wall tracks of each of the two walls placed below 45 degrees with a classroom area are defined by oscillating the diagonal square – a reminiscence of the diagonal figure at the beginning. Halving the q1 grid measurement produces a grille. This in its modular measurement takes up the overlap zone of the diagonal squares from the initial phase of the classroom genesis (see figure 72) and marks the borders of the diagonal walls. Their ends fuse with the wall tracks of a zone that takes up the module measurement and identifies the access area. The walls of this area follow the grid lines with differing widths, with a great deal of variety: the lower outer edge of the horizontal boundary at a width of 19 inches runs on the grid track. Against this the vertical is made up of a whole plus a half wall width, i.e. 9½ plus 19 equals 28½ inches. At the point at which it meets the diagonal it protrudes in order to place the intersection point on the grid line with geometrical precision. The walls' different relations to the grid produce a horizontal space emphasizing the direction of access. Its 19 inch boundary wall lies centrally on the grid and forms the upper conclusion of the corridor area. In contrast with this a wall width is produced on the lower border of the classroom whose outer line is derived from the root 2 track of the side wall added at the same distance from the grid. Its in-

Fig.115

Fig.116

Fig.117

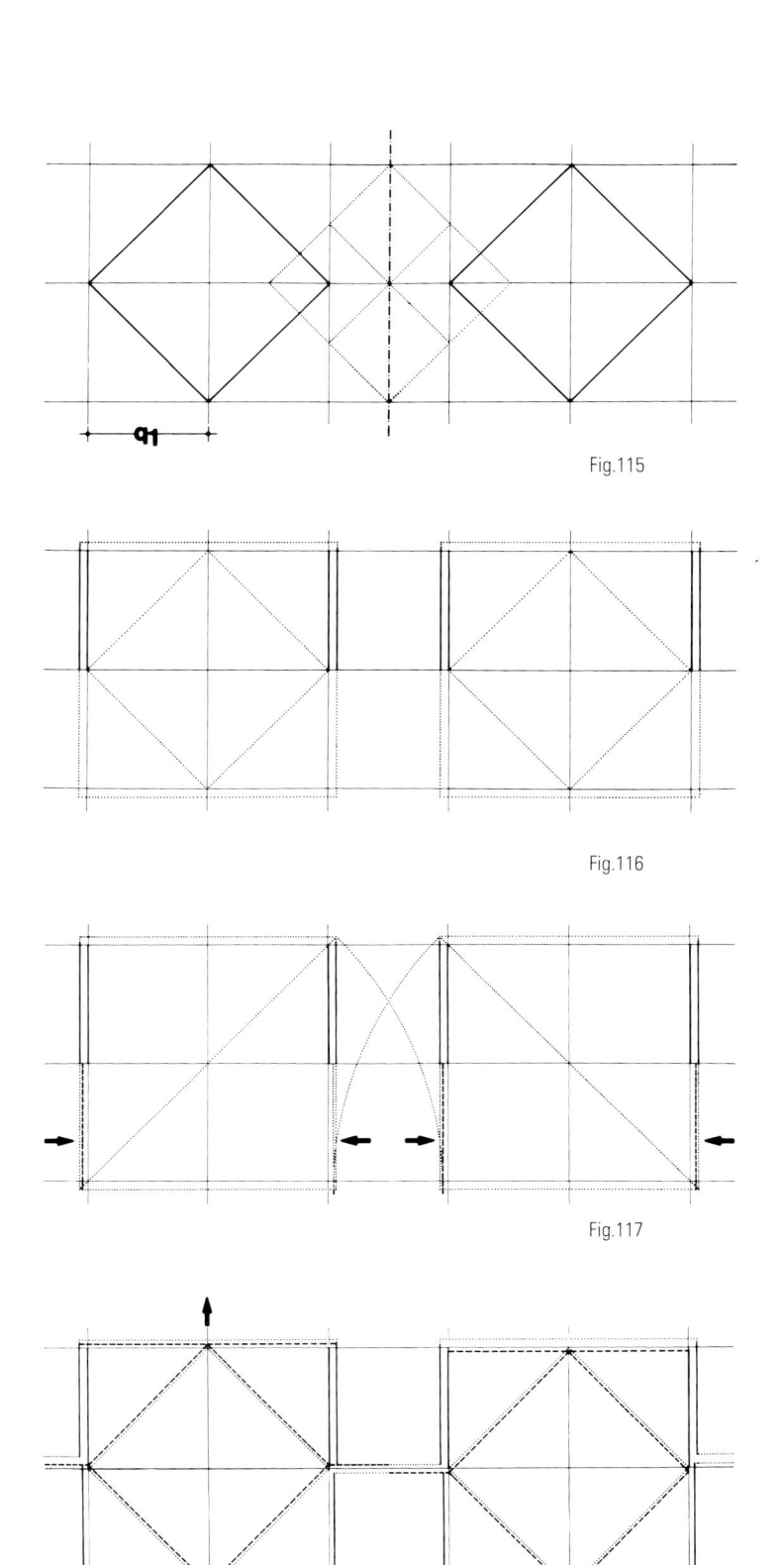

Fig.118

Fig.115–118
Ground plan analysis of the IIM: development of the classroom figure

ner outline is created by the oscillating diagonal square.

The outlines of the classroom figure are now almost completely developed. The fact that it is cut apart horizontally appears to be a consequence of a differentiated, interdependent interior/exterior relation. An interlinking connecting wall between the classroom sections, together with the access areas adjacent on both sides for the classroom areas and triangular light-wells for the basement floors, produce a new, symmetrical figure that can almost be described as independent. Thus figures that do not belong together should accordingly be seen as linked. Clearly a mutual interdependence of the elements is intended, something that could already be seen in the genesis of the administration figure.

Fig.120 The existence of an initial diagonal square as generating figure is now confirmed. The diagonal square follows the grid and the developed wall tracks. The dimensions of its "oscillating width" correspond with the visible diagonal structure of the ceiling joists in the classroom area. It can be seen as an "anchoring" or "blocking" of both the horizontal and the vertical forces in the distortion process – hence diagonal – to create counterforces. The lower part of the classroom building on the exterior side is further distorted: the module measurement half q1 of the grid structure – shifted by its own half – is projected on to the outer wall in axial relation to the inner grid and developed as a niche. In a mutual relation between inside and outside the internal joist structure meets the complete wall sections, now functioning as columns. In contrast, the wall zones in between seem "thinned out" as a result of a suggestive stretching process caused by the diagonal structure of the joists. These niches, measuring 9 ½ inches, can be seen as a reinforcement of the distortion of the side walls described in figure 117. They additionally underline the different characters of the classroom area, dissolving into a "hard" outline on the corridor side and the variably structured "soft" exterior side. Its façade shows the puzzle picture of the niches: as a brick-filled "opening" between the outer walls that form a complete cube as they rise, but also as a wall forming a border for the volume with protruding piers that dramatize the corners in particular.

The mirror of these two school buildings designed and realized above the symmetrical axis of the overall outline of the classroom area leads to additions on both sides. Thus the distance to the nearest adjacent figure can be established by the simple geometrical construction of an arc of a circle. The oscillation of this interlinking, which has the effect of a continuous *membrane*, starts to emerge as the connecting walls are completed. As in the genesis of the administration figure, here too we can see that Kahn is determined to build up tension within the archaic geometrical figure with the aid of subtle distortion processes. The contrasting pair, rigidity and movement, is expressed in a joint figure that is given individuality. But at the same time Kahn causes the appearance of this figure's *primal image*, pure geometry, to dominate and enhance the degree of its autonomy.[105] Therefore the process of refracting and changing the square can be interpreted as a sculptural procedure, which in the suggestive perception of movement of the parts, as an inner tension, "freezes" and thus maintains the genesis of the sculpted form.

Classroom block façade articulation

---

[105] The frequent appearance of simple geometry in Kahn's work has often led to misunderstandings in most publications: the previous lack of a precise analysis of the inherent geometrical order led to the over-hasty opinion that Kahn had been interested only in – "highly symbolic" – presentation of "pure" geometry, which rapidly – because it can always be interpreted subjectively – produced exclusively philosophical and metaphysical interpretations. What was overlooked was that the *distortion process* that we have examined should be evaluated as a fundamental qualitative aspect of Kahn's architecture.

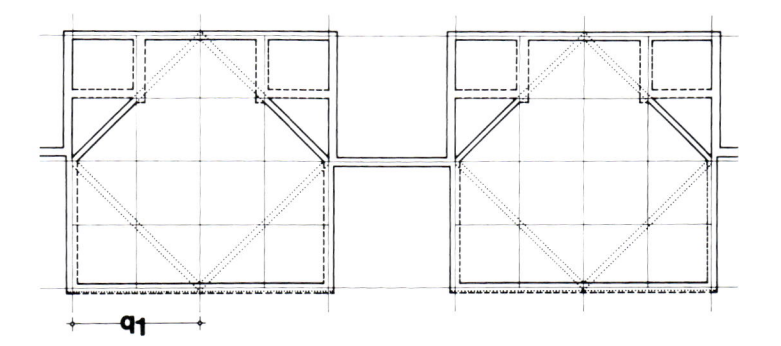

Fig. 119

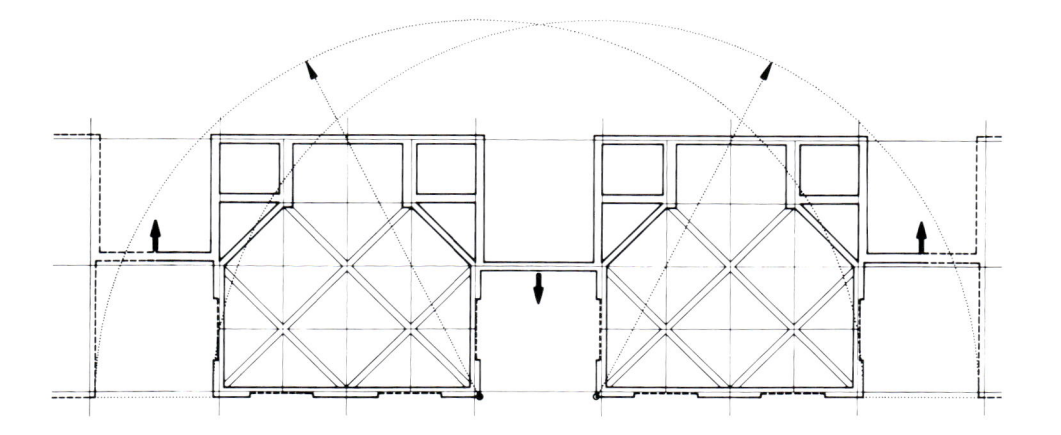

Fig. 120

The "oscillating" connecting walls between the classrooms

Classroom façade

Fig. 119–120
Ground plan analysis of the IIM: development of the classroom figure

151

Fig.121 The classroom figure grows and extends by a simple geometrical arc construction from the centre out to the sides. It includes six classroom volumes and five intermediate zones. Its end is bracketed on the right and left as conclusion and framing of the classrooms by a corridor zone running round them, on the track of the Golden Section frame TUVW. This finally produces seven intermediate zones. They expand as a fusion with the upper gallery to form the lounge area. This gives the effect of individual volumes being inserted into an existing access area with the lower outer wall of the lounge area, which is clearly moving to and fro. Its end fields take up the position of the preceding wall and in their vertical limit fit precisely into the track of the Golden Section frame via the root 2 arc construction. This correspondence suggests that a process of alignment by measurement was undertaken in terms of the TUVW rectangle proportion and the outer diagonal square of the entrance as the determining grid form. This shows in small differences of measurements between the realized architecture and the idealized geometrical construction using the diagonal square: the modular measurement q1-half contains, according to the working plan,[106] the clear grid measurement 11 feet 5 inches (3.48 m). Double this, i. e. 6.96 m, should

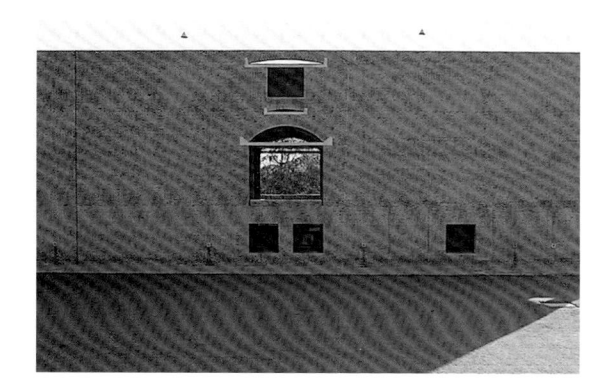

Courtyard with library and classroom wing right with access building in front

Access area wall in front of the classrooms with large "perforated" openings

have agreed with the half diagonal of the entrance square, but differs from its actual size of 7.03 m by 7 cm. Thus we have to speak of an "approximation" to the dimension of the diagonal entrance square. This was presumably welcome as a deviation from or disturbance of rigid structures and was adapted to superordinated proportional figures. And yet there is no doubt that the entrance square, as becomes clear from the principles of the genesis of the whole design, is crucial as a dimensional relation value for the beginning.

The corridor area is halved as a result of linking the classroom volumes and the access area (see figure 120). This leads to division also in the lobby of the administration figure, producing sub-spaces there which belong either to the function area or to the access corridor. Thus the access area to the classrooms, although it is firmly bound into the whole, has to be allotted to the extensive lounge area. This situation is reminiscent of the division of the courtyard from the access corridor around it, which was also not clear (see figures 106/107); their combination by a framing rectangle in the proportions of the Golden Section means that the corridor appears as both an interior *and* an exterior space.

The internal figures of the library and the water tower now acquire their final shape. A dedicated space with 19 inch wide walls is allotted to the radii, fixed in their geometry, of the semicircular stairs. Its openings to the outside area in the dimension of the internal radii of the stairs provide lighting for the access zone and indirectly incident light in the library rooms. This space divides or explodes the library volume into two function areas: one is the two-storey reading-room in the upper storey, with diagonal walls and enormous circular openings, and also indirectly lit, which provides access to the meeting room above the entrance square. It also divides off the stack with reading niches at the back.

A new element relating to the wall of the illumination niche in its outer line combines the library with the classrooms as an access area with stairs and is aligned axially to the last classroom building.

The outline of the entrance square's dimension can now be inscribed centrally into the water-

[106] The precise measurements arise from the last valid working plan "C 1–2, October 1969, National Institute of Design", signed by Raje, whose copy is in the possession of the author.

Entrance to the classroom access lobby

"Perforations" inside the classroom access

Fig.121
Ground plan analysis of the IIM: development of the classroom figure and the water tower

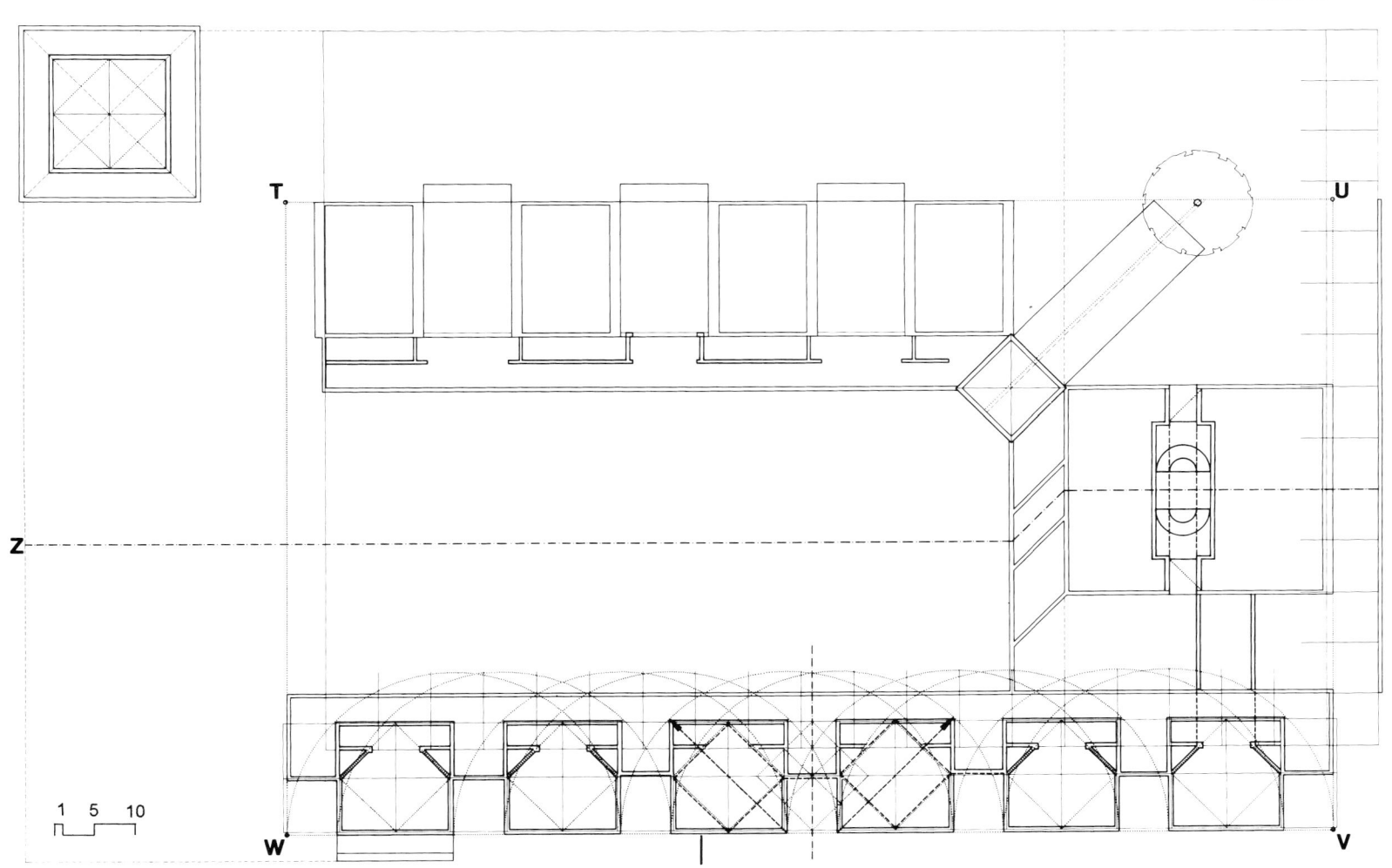

153

tower with its wide base storey for technical equipment. This is framed by 19 inch wide walls and works as a tower-housing for the water-tank which is at the very top.

A final, very slight correction is now made as the final move to fix the complex as a whole on the site. It is of symbolic significance: the trunk of the existing mango tree, which had previously been centred on the diagonal axis of the entrance square and the adjacent staircase figure now shifts off axis. It acquires tangential relation to the said axis and the horizontal track of the lower border of the water-tower, which effectively forms the upper conclusion of the administration wing and a point of contact with the main entrance staircase.[107]

This gesture reveals the full "genetic" process of the architecture as a principle: a complex build-up is followed by a subtle change or refraction, but this does not make the genesis any less comprehensible.

DINING HALL AND KITCHEN

The school complex and its three major function areas, administration, library and classrooms, are now fixed. A fourth group of buildings is now added, the refectory and the kitchens, following the concept of forming a closed circle. The figuration of the outlines of this area was the last version of the design Kahn contributed for the project, but it was not actually built. Although it is not part of the built reality, this figure still remains crucial for the original concept of the design. Kahn intended to close the courtyard as a circle, but this was ultimately rejected by the clients.

Fig.122
On the basis of its exterior line, the entrance square, which is already important for the genesis of the classroom area, also determines the constellation and dimensions of the figures still to be described in the courtyard area as a whole. It confirms the logic of a hierarchical sequence within the plan analysis of these subdivisions of the architecture, which are dependent on each other in terms of measurements and geometry. An access corridor relating to the distancing court between two classroom buildings combines the classrooms and the administration wing. The corridor is 22 feet wide, including the 1 foot and 2 inch exterior walls.[108] This measurement relates to the net measurement of the distancing court from the classrooms and thus explains the sequence of this interdependent figuration. The central corridor access is important for the "attachment" of the refectory. Its intersection point with the outer edge of the administration figure is the starting-point of a diagonal that meets the corridor. There a horizontal to be mirrored across the courtyard symmetry axis Z marks the "framing", i.e. the enclosing wall of the refectory and kitchen area. This zone, extending from the inner track of the outer wall of the water-tower fixes the border of the kitchen delivery yard. It defines an area that emphasizes the longitudinal orientation of the school complex, thrusting out like a tongue from the central courtyard, independent – and thus autonomous. Thus the horizontal courtyard symmetry axis Z continues to determine the sub-figures arranged within this area. They are first fixed geometrically by the adoption of the left-hand administration wing outline, in order to arrange a vertical symmetrical axis for two diagonal squares in the dimensions of the entrance courtyard touching the horizontal axis Z. Mirrored across Z, the square of the actual dining area is thus bordered off. This outline put together from two root 2 major squares of the diagonal square produces a root 2 major figure of a quarter of its total area on the left-hand edge. This is centred on axis Z, so that its upper and lower tips are congruent with the corner of the "enclosing square". Here a circle can be inscribed precisely with its centre on the Z axis. The first circle contains the kitchen, closely linked with the dining-room, and suggests – a special form and therefore a special function – a formal and functional contrast with its opposite, the library, which withdraws from compelling axiality, and is not of equal weight in terms of the kitchen. An exciting composition of opposite places for spiritual and physical well-being within the lone "arms" of administration and classrooms that accompany this duality.

The difference between the outer enclosing outline and the inner dining-room creates a distance relating to axis Z for two zones bordered off from each other 6 inches and 10 feet wide.[109] These are dependent on wall tracks that are not shown here. Its dimensions include a last figure placed inside the courtyard, centred on the vertical sym-

---

[107] The author measured the circumference and position of the tree in relation to the stairs and the complex as a whole precisely on site.
[108] The precise measurements are taken from photocopies, in very poor condition in places, in the Kahn Collection in Philadelphia, of the KD4 working plans "Kitchen/Dining", (photographs in the author's possession) dating from August 1971; they arrived in Kahn's office in Philadelphia on 8 September, show the kitchen and dining area in sections, views and ground plans and identify M. S. Satsangi as the draughtsman.
[109] The measurements given are from the KD4 plans.

Entrance section with management-team conference room above it

The courtyard, open to the west, from the Plus 1 level with administration wing right and classroom group left

Fig. 122
Ground plan analysis of the IIM: development of the dining-kitchen area and the amphitheatre in dependence on the entrance square

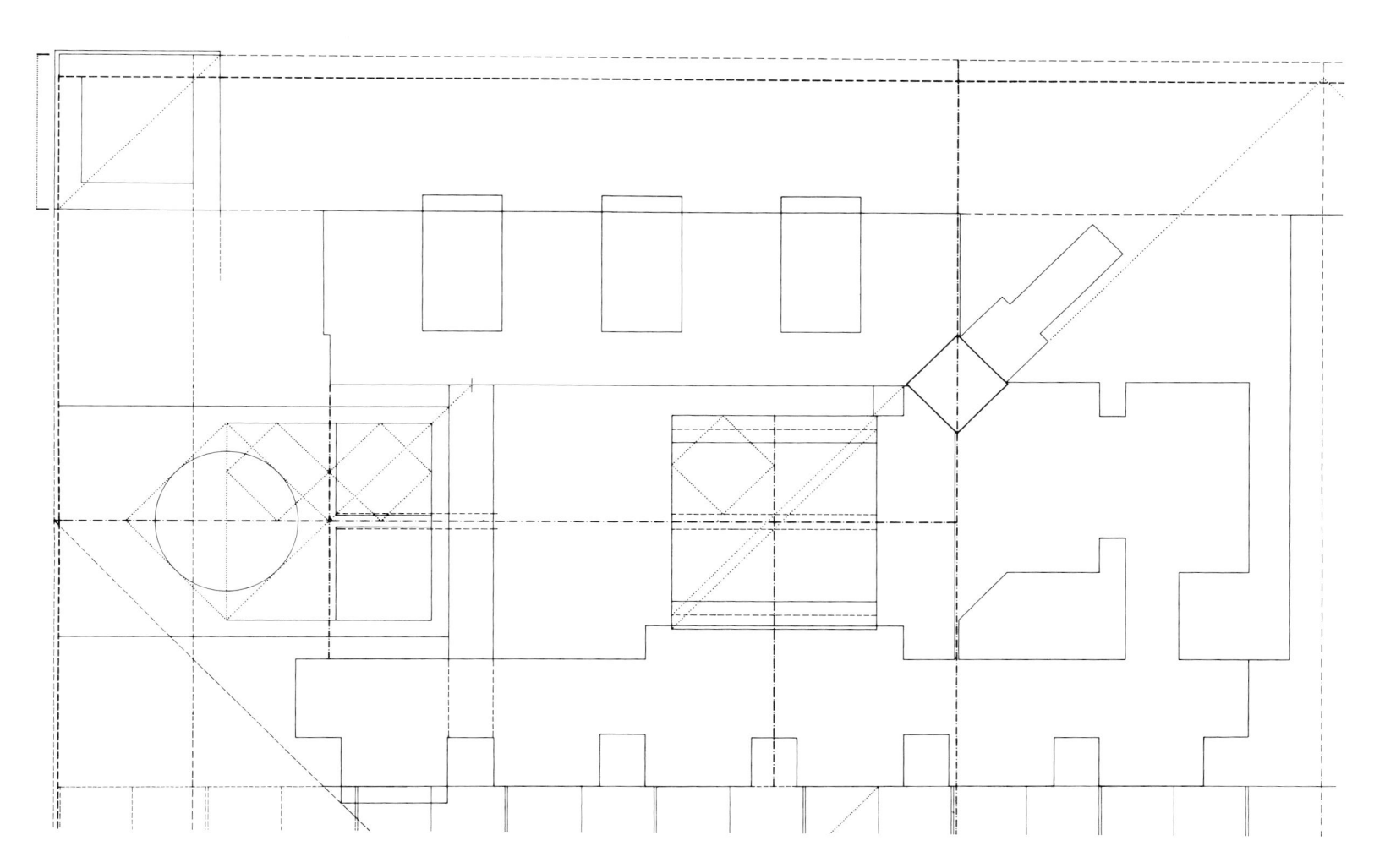

metrical axis of the classroom area. This figure turns out to be a vertically oscillating square, firmly tied into the axiality of courtyard and classrooms in its geometry. Its basic figure can again be understood as framing four interlined entrance square figures, and shows the outline of an amphitheatre with steps for seating and a stage. The peripheral area of the oscillating square created here links with the figure of the classroom area via a symmetrical housing for stairs and sanitary facilities, firmly fused with the corridor and also centred. A small added square – turning back to the starting-point – at the top right-hand edge creates contact with the entrance square as stairs giving access to the courtyard level.

The kitchen-dining area has double axial symmetry, and is a self-relating, closed and rigid figure, contrasting in its "motionlessness" with the dynamic movement processes that we have seen previously. It serves to anchor the various shifting parts of the school complex, which build up centrifugal forces and are nevertheless held in balance. Its strong and autonomous character in this position "tempted" the planning committee, after they had expressed their concern about possible problems caused by kitchen smells,[110] to shift the dining area outside the school complex. Although Kahn's final suggestion placed the circular kitchen outside the courtyard, there was no majority for this solution, even though the elimination of the kitchen had already been proposed in early variants, placing it as a more strongly separated and much higher building, following the roof-lines of the neighbouring buildings.[111] The consequences of these considerations seemed very far-reaching: shifting the dining and kitchen area meant giving up the idea that had been pursued as logical from the outset of a circular complex enclosed on all sides for the sake of concentricity, acquiring direction from the opening on one side. This led to a suggested relation to something significant "outside", logical in its strained axiality. Kahn tried to work against this tendency until his death by suggestion variations, persistently following his original intention to close the courtyard.[112] He finally accepted the committee's decision to shift the dining area and on his last visit to the site on 15 and 16 March 1974 expressed his pleasure with the opening of the courtyard area outwards and the related appearance of the buildings as a composition.[113]

[110] In the interview on 9. 2. 1990 Raje described how committee members raised the problem of cooking smells as something that could disturb teaching and other work when the wind blew in certain directions.
[111] Kahn placed the kitchen on the periphery of the school to avoid problems caused by cooking smells. The committee accepted this at first, but then rejected it. For this see Kahn in H. Klotz, John W. Cook, "Conversations with Architects", Praeger-Publishers, New York 1973.
[112] On 15 March 1974, 2 days before he died, after the final decision to place the kitchen area outside, Kahn sketched a plan allowing the amphitheatre, now changed into a closed theatre section – "theater of performing arts" – to be called "Violin" and to replace the kitchen in closing the courtyard; he identified a new position for the kitchen on a level with the dormitories.
[113] In the above-mentioned interview Raje alludes to Kahn's positive reactions to the almost completed buildings on his last visit to the site.

Indian Institute of Management
Student Dormitories

Ground plan analysis has demonstrated so far that the school complex as a whole consists of a coherent whole made up of interlinked individual figures that are autonomous in character. This shows clearly in the number and dimension of the openings in the differentiated façades. In contrast with this the dormitory group consists of repetitive individual figures in a "structure" that is independent as an entity. Their links with the school complex and the inner hierarchy of its geometrical order are now to be analysed below.

The accumulation of approximately equal individual figures did not exist as an idea from the outset. It results from the breakdown of long "arms" (see figure 87), uneasily combining diagonal and orthogonal qualities in their outline. The structure of the later dormitories was anticipated in the disposition of its function areas and a clear separation of the volumes of stairs and side rooms. Splitting up these arms gave an impression of a merely suggestive *diagonal quality*. The dormitories changed into free-standing individual buildings to take student rooms, an adjacent social area as a corridor and meeting-place with sanitary facilities almost detaching themselves. The school complex and the dormitories started to become congruent in their geometrical order and created "unity" in the structure as a whole, despite the "duality" of their structural character. The genesis of the laboratories was based on overlapping orthogonal grids. Their dimensions vary in the different solutions and produced different numbers of dormitory buildings: starting with rows of three, with 18 dormitories, then with a larger grid measurement and more buildings in rows of four producing 24. Finally, after variations of this arrangement that are not described in detail here, Kahn returned to the first figuration above with differentiated distances (see figure 89). As can be seen here, the dormitory scheme is developed from overlapping square grids at a very early stage in the genesis of the design, and it was fixed in its fundamentally "chessboard" structure independently of the much varied school complex, which was still a long way from the form it would ultimately adopt. The function areas within any given dormitory found their definitive positions: the students rooms on the south-western edge of the building, which were now also fixed at two times five per storey; the centrally located lounge and communication area; and the succinctly separate, almost detached sanitary facilities as square figures. The configuration of these parts was firmly tied into the square. The arrangement of these zones seemed to be subject to climatic considerations, nevertheless the form-finding process for this figure remained "formal": the square derived from the grid is the dominating shape despite subsequent distortions or "de-formations". The process itself – the genesis – was retained until the ideas began to be found.

The entrance square for the school complex did not yet exist in this phase of the project, but it was important for the analysis of the geometrical build-up to the realized dormitory structure. It appeared, after the structure settled and reacted to the variants of the school complex and its peripheries, in the form of a dimensional relation value, at a time when building work had already started on the dormitories[114] (see figure 93). This leads us to suppose that the most important dimensions for the subsequent interdependent genesis of all the subdivisions of the complex as a whole were contained in the figure of the

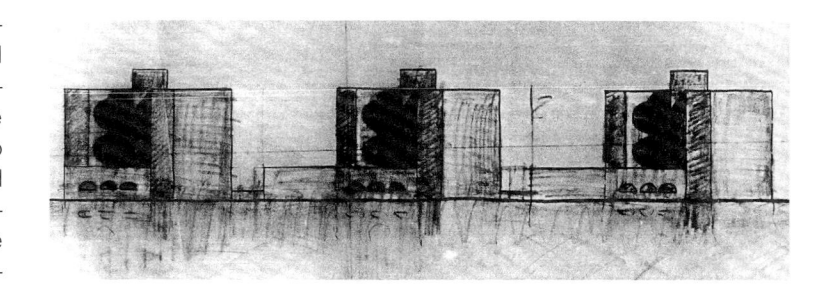

An early sketch by Kahn of the dormitories

dormitories and its cumulative structure. The relation in terms of measurements and geometry between the dormitories and the school building constituted itself to integrate all the figures within a coherent whole by the "invention" of the entrance square. And yet the allocation of the dormitories and their structure to this position should be seen as correct, as the hierarchy of all sub-figures – i. e. the school before the dormitories here – has to be considered when analysing and "deciphering" the internal geometrical ordering system. Therefore it is not the actual building chronology, but the final, almost completely realized design variant, with unambiguous interdependence of all parts, that remains crucial.

[114] It can be ascertained that building work on the dormitories started in spring 1966: Kahn Collection, Box 113, "Correspondence", Doshi to Kahn. Work on the school complex and entrance hall did not start until 1969.

Fig.123 The overall dormitory complex is tied together by a new framing figure. Doubling the defined distance from the left-hand wall of the water-tower to the vertical axis of the entrance square produces the length 1–2. Its right-hand edge defines the border of the dormitory structure field. The extraordinary diagonal position of the entrance square, emphasizing the vertical mirror axis with its upper and lower "tips", is now legitimized, as a centre within the structure as a whole. The length 1–2 produces its root 2 area proportion as a rectangular frame 1–2–3–4, whose position is fixed by "leaning" on the upper inner outline of the water-tower as a relation-edge. In the geometrical construction the square of the root 2 rectangle 1–2–3–4 defines the axis of the ramp that was previously indicated only in its left-hand line; its overall width is arrived at by doubling this half length. It emerges that the ramp and the entrance square and the appended main access stairs are linked with each other geometrically and this "communication" of the parts is continued up to the water-tower. The water-tower is now stripped of its isolation as a solitaire body and becomes an element regulated from the outside within the rational relation system of the figure as a whole. Thus projecting its size on to the lower 3–4 border line gives its precise square dimension with its horizontal continuation across the whole width, defining a zone that sets itself apart from the rest of the frame area.

The grid structure of the dormitories is now compiled from the entrance square as a modular measurement and generated between the lower outer line of the classroom figure and this new horizontal track by simply fitting in five square elements. Linking them together in groups of four describes the outer line of one dormitory. Flush fitting at the top and bottom creates a distance between two groups of four, illustrating the dynamic process of "tearing apart".

Fig.124 This distance apart as a "joint" thus defines the general gap between the groups of four within the dormitory figure inside a double grid. The grid consists firstly of three rows of the groups of four and a square distancing them from the classrooms, then of the even joints. It is held in place by the symmetrical axis of the ramp and the left-hand 4–1 "linking edge" of the frame. The grid extends around the school complex within the boundaries of the 1–2–3–4 framing figure and so far relates only to the edges of the classroom figure and left-hand 4–1 framing border. This produces an almost random arrangement of the grid structure and the 2–3 and 3–4 edges of the frame, which cannot be made to harmonize. The building volumes are positioned in the shape of a group of four of the entrance square module within the grid alternately, like a chessboard. This produces "positive" and "negative" zones of the same area, which relate functionally adequate distancing courts to the sections of the building on all sides. A diagonal that divides the grid and meets the horizontal symmetrical courtyard axis Z at the intersection point of the extended water-tower line, is tangential to the staircase edge below the classroom building on the extreme left, as a stop. It defines the end of the dormitory structure when continued to the bottom frame line. It also announces a diagonal structure that is succinct and contradicts the rigorously orthogonal approach, having so far appeared only in the entrance square.

The overall width of the water-tower reveals itself as a parallel value on the lower side, in terms of the distance between the lower of the horizontals that has already been established, relating to the 4–3 frame edge (see figure 123). Its track separates the outermost row of dormitories from the others and develops strip-like zones of the same width in both the lower and upper peripheral areas of the 1–2–3–4 frame. A comprehensive relation system for all sub-figures becomes clear. The symbolic and simplified ground plan geometry of the water-tower seems to "regulate" the peripheral areas both horizontally and vertically as a "cipher" and relates the upper and lower framing lines 1–2 and 3–4 in a special way. The dimension of the joint between the grid fields is transferred to the inner structure of a dormitory: inserting the diagonal entrance square into the top right-hand corner of the group of four and adding the width of the joint vertically and horizontally creates zoning within the ground plan structure and the functional arrangement of the figure.

We will now examine the structure of a single student dormitory, ignoring the way in which it is tied into the structural or measured geometrical relations of the complex as a whole. As an independent form, the dormitory shows that the hierarchy of its inner structure is dependent on the outer line of the entrance square. Thus the origin of the genetic process, which has already been indicated (see figure 124) is recapitulated.[115]

---

[115] The dormitory was examined by Elke Beccard and Ulrich Gremmelspacher, who were students at the time, during a seminar at the TU in Braunschweig in 1990/91. Their results form the basis for further development.

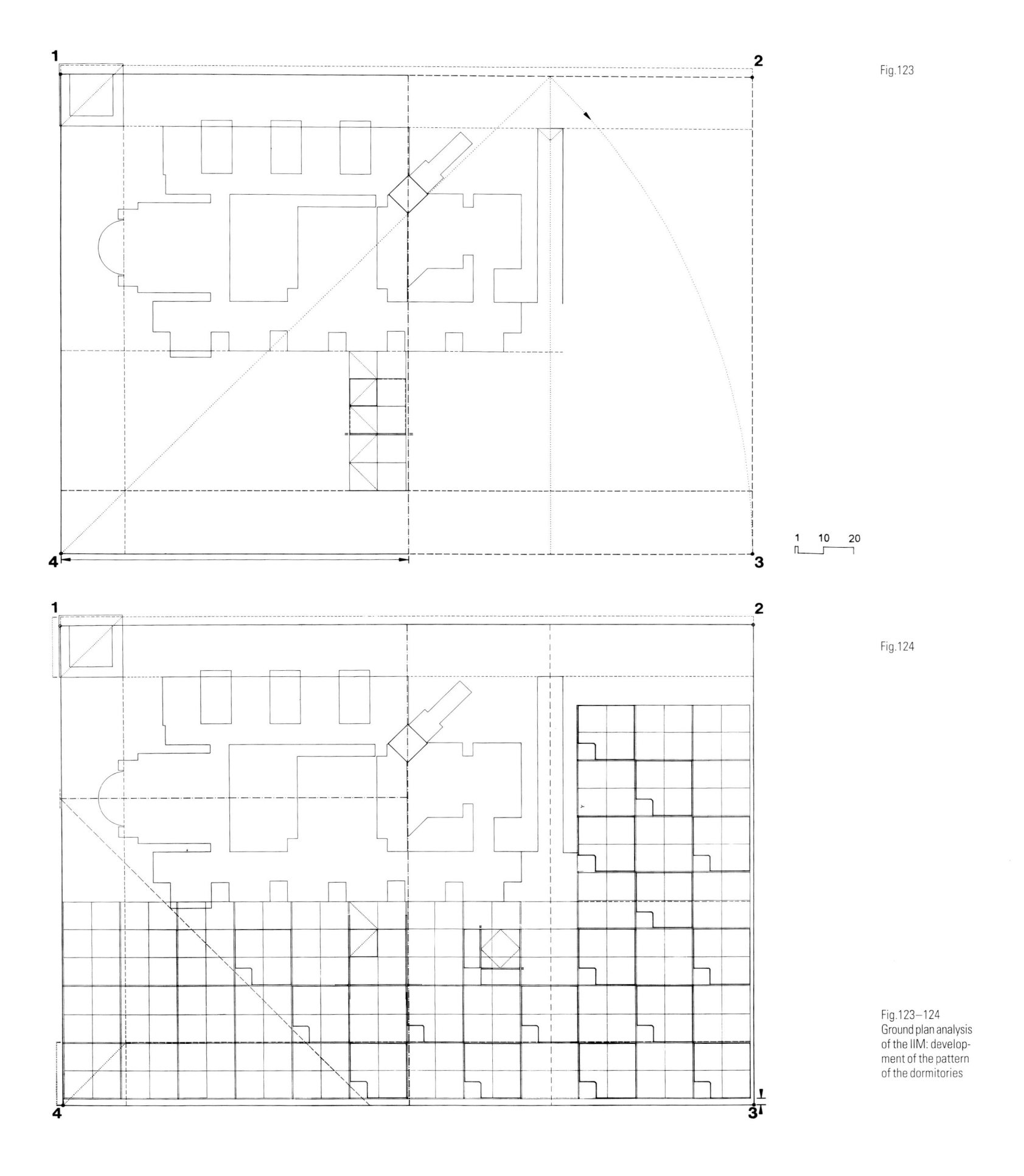

Fig. 123

Fig. 124

Fig. 123–124
Ground plan analysis of the IIM: development of the pattern of the dormitories

Fig.125 The dimensions of the outer line of the entrance square provide the module measurement. Multiplied by four, it produces the original outline of the dormitory structure elements as a grown square. Precise comparison of the side lengths of the apparently congruent squares shows that there are slight differences in the measurements and that the modular square for a quarter of the dormitory was chosen in larger form. A parallel with the genesis of the administration and classroom figure is indicated; its geometrical relation to the entrance square was recognized as absolute, but dimensional tolerances did not permit complete agreement. The side length of the entrance square, at 32 feet 8 ⅛ inches (9.96 m) and the side length of the module square, at 32 feet 11 inches (10.3 m), may be considered valid as dimensions.[116] Thus the difference between the two lengths is 2 ⅔ inches (about 7 cm), which means that both values approximate to the imaginary value of 10 m. As in the figures for the school complex, the principle can also be seen here of creating a new figure within the complex as a whole from the *primal model* of the entrance square. Fitting this square into further, superordinated frames as geometrical relation figures to the whole and as the implementation of the ordering scheme in the actual building nevertheless produces the dimensional deviations, presumably welcome as a variation on a repeating theme – no figure is exactly like any other.

Fig.126 The outline of the dormitory is framed on all sides by the separating joints. Their network of lines produces a double grid so that adjacent areas do not collide. Each second field forms a building shape, this producing a chessboard-like dialogue between the parts. Within a grid field, the diagonally positioned outline of the dimension of the original square is placed over the diagonal axis of the field in such a way that its upper and right-hand edge touches the grid. The resultant root 2 major square creates tracks that define new zones within the grid field. The "regulating" entrance square determines the geometrical proportions within the dormitory ground plan figure as well. The areas produced are structured into hierarchical function areas and build up a diagonal symmetry that includes the adjacent section. Here too a figure swinging ambiguously between diagonal and orthogonal qualities produces a puzzle picture.

Tying the square of the dormitory into the grid and fixing the grid by means of double lines (see figure 124) emphasizes the orthogonal quality. In contrast, the alternate arrangement of the volumes with an "empty area" in between as a distancing court and the disposition of the function areas in cross-corner symmetry suggest an intense diagonal relation.

Fig.127 The zoned peripheral areas now form rectangular figures. But their ultimate shape does not emerge until the joint has been transferred on to the inner, newly formed tracks. Thus rectangles arranged in diagonal symmetry separate themselves off from the students' actual lounge and sleeping areas. Fixing these areas results in a change to the outer line of the dormitories: the short sides of the sleeping areas – facing the next dormitory on the diagonal – form the new outer walls. The distance from the neighbouring part is enlarged via a square corner area that is part of the exterior, so that the courts lying correspondingly on the long sides of the sleeping areas flow into each other. The arrangement of the joints and of the grid areas both outside and inside create a breakdown or a dissolution of these divisions, which were sharply bordered at the outset – the grid is distorted. The perception of unambiguous figurations blurs, so that we can speak of "secondary grids", whose geometrical and proportional dependences betray the compositional intention in the build-up of the figures.

Fig.128 The square continues to be dissolved by further ruthless division or "incision". A diagonal halving of the square left over from the students' sleeping accommodation shows how the overall figure is breaking down into independent parts. A triangle and two added rectangles, whose distancing joint makes the dissolution process visible and causes the areas to thrust apart, remain unalterably fixed in their position, however, through the outer frame of the original square.

The significance of the connection between the dormitory figures, which are woven together in their structure, is revealed by the division ratio of one side. The outer relating edge does not take up its own borders, but that of the corner position

---

[116] The dimensions of the entrance square were taken from the following definitive working plans: "A 1–2, Administration Wing, 3 Feb. 1970" and "L 1–2, Library, June 1969"; the dormitory measurements were taken from the plans: "DA 48, Feb. 1965, Level Plus 1", revised on 29 March 1965, 10 July 1965, 22 July 1966 and 17 Juni 1967; "DA 49, Feb. 1965, Level Plus 2" (exact date no longer legible); "DA 62, DA 74, 19. 2. 65, Details", "DA 99, 19. 5. 66, Details" and "DA 204, Feb. 66, Section", drawn at the National Institute of Design, NID, Ahmedabad; the plans come from Raje's office and are in the author's possession as copies. Comparative measurements of the realized project were established by the author in on-site surveys in February/March 1990 and February 1991.

Fig. 125

Fig. 126

Fig. 127

Fig. 128 GS GS

Fig. 129 GS GS

Fig. 130

Fig. 125–130
Ground plan analysis of the IIM: development of the dormitories in dependence on the entrance square

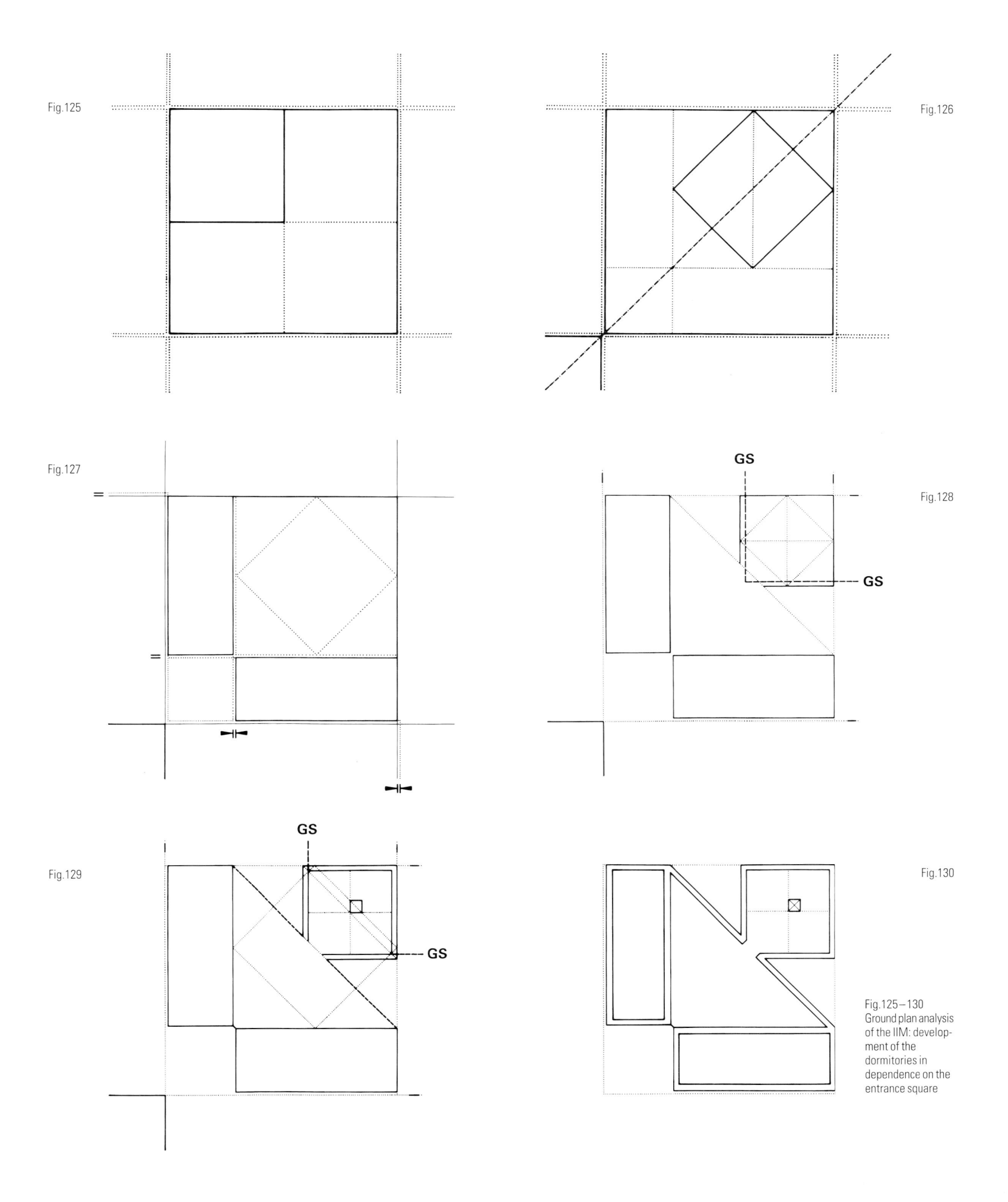

161

of the adjacent figure, which is the width of a joint away. This is how the figures that are falling apart are bound into the scheme of geometrical order, and latently present interrelations between the individual volumes that cannot be perceived directly, are built up once more as they isolate themselves. This happens because the division ratio of the Golden Section is applied to two sides of the dormitory figure. Lines are added vertically at right angles in each case to its points of division to form wall tracks. They meet within the triangular figure and form the borders of a square with side lengths of the minor Golden Section on the right.

The two rectangles and the newly formed corner square now effectively face each other as exact opposites at this stage of the dormitory figure's genesis. Both sub-figures follow the outer tracks of the square frame and in their diagonal symmetry are in balance as if by a distanced *magnetism*. They appear like solitaires within the dissolved frame of the original square, and are linked together by a diagonal line linking the corners of the rectangles. Its intersection point on both sides with the Golden Section dividing lines determines the final size of the corner square. Walls are added to the outside of these in the standard dimension of 19 inches (0.48 m). A minor root 2 diagonal square inscribed inside and relating to the new outline indicates the simple quartering with its axes, and the resulting spatial division of this almost independent volume.

Fig.129　This separated area for sanitary facilities is bound in by adopting the outer tracks of the rectangles as the framing outline of the grid square. The process of breakdown is resisted by fusion with the diagonal outline in particular, and with the diagonal symmetry relating to the right angle, which draws all the parts together again. The walls of the sanitary block, which thrusts into the central triangular zone, are added once outside on the Golden Section line and then inside along the framing outline. Their measurement of 19 inches here turns out to be the intersection point of the Golden Section line and the inscribed diagonal square as a minor root 2 figure. The smallest square outline to appear inside the dormitory figure is formed in the centre of the sanitary area. It is produced as a result of the intersection of the quartering axes and the side diagonals of the root 2 minor square. It also derives as an indirect consequence of the interplay of geometrical dependences of the Golden Section and root 2, and identifies the shaft for the services pipes ("pipe-duct") as a space created especially for this purpose. Thus the displacement of the root 2 minor square outline and of the sanitary area diagonals shows in the lengths of the sides of this little square. The genesis by way of the system of figurative geometry is related to a symbolic figure that works here as a germ cell, whose disposition reinforces the diagonal symmetry within the orthogonal structure as an iridescent element.

The interior walls for the level 0 and Plus 1 dormitories on the periphery and for the level Plus 1 in the central area of the dormitories can now be added. They are 19 inches thick (0.48 m) for the sanitary area, the diagonal and the short sides of the rectangular areas used for social purposes, leisure and access. In contrast, the walls on the long sides are 23 ½ inches thick (0.60 m). These measurements match those of level Plus 1, as described in the genesis of the school complex as the main access level for administration, library and classrooms, with a floor level at the height of 14 feet 10 inches (4.52 m). 　Fig.130

The significance of diagonals in the genesis of the dormitory figure is shown in the figure that follows. After its final outline was fixed the diagonal quality shows in the structure of its interior by means of function elements, whose geometrical construction is determined by a circle, in contrast with previous accounts. Here the diagonal running from top right to bottom left is taken up as a symmetrical axis for the uniform development of these circular geometries. 　Fig.131

In the following analysis the geometry of the enclosing square that includes the outer joints once more turns out to be the key to the design. This will be illustrated from the example of a level Plus 3 ground plan with students' living cells. Its outline is now turned by 45 degrees on to the diagonal axis indicated and touches the top righthand corner of the sanitary block. This "tipping process" leads to a new axis of the Golden Section division running at right angles to it. On this axis (GS) are the centre points of two circles whose radius is derived from the outer track of the sanitary square. Their outlines touch the enclosing square and cut the diagonal of the triangular central area at this geometrically clearly defined position. The segments of circles thus produced represent the inside parapet edge at the border to the triangular, windowless corridor zones, which nevertheless has large circular openings in the diagonal exterior wall. These encourage an intense possibility of vertical communication within the storeys as a result of this visual and acoustic connection and soften the linear quality of the geometry with their contrasting curves. The linking of the contrasting pair of circle and square is enhanced by the distortion of rigid straight lines by placing another central circular element. Its geometrical construction starts from the same radius taken from the dimensions of the sanitary block. This circle has its centre on the diagonal symmetrical axis and is tangential to the Golden Mean division line that runs at right angles to it. As the circles described are congruent in their radius, the centre of the last-named circle – displaced by its radius from the Golden Section axis – must be considered the intersection point of the tangent combining the two segments of circles with the diagonal axis. It represents the centre point of a smaller circle radius whose length is determined by the axis intersection points of the sanitary area.

The result is the vertical access in the form of a semicircular staircase figure. It opens on to the sanitary area and seems to anchor it to the main section of the building as a result of its deep penetration into the triangular space of the sanitary area. The interplay of the imaginary circular formations to be completed via their segments shows the importance of reconstructable axes as ordering lines for figural relations. It allows them to continue to relate to each other and appears within the turned framing square as an independent "foil" projected on to the orthogonal pattern of the dormitory outline, or as overlapping it.

Plan analysis makes it possible to "reveal" the structure of the figurative geometry system completely in its interdependent hierarchy, from superordinated structures down to the last detail. It again documents the principle of a design approach that makes the framing figures at the beginning of the process follow proportional divisions and furthermore to shape the ordering structure by using circle and square, so that it is possible to speak of "primary" and "secondary" order.

Fig.132   At this stage of the genesis of the student dormitory building, the ground plan outlines of levels Plus 2 and 3, where the students' sleeping quarters are housed, can be developed. Here they have reduced wall thicknesses of 14 inches (0.36 m) throughout. The walls are added to the found outlines of the diagonals of the triangular corridor and lounge area and within the sanitary area, as tracks that cannot be derived geometrically, and also to the two rectangular figures of the residential zone. Thus the outer lines are valid for the geometrical ordering system in each case. In the case of the staircases as well a wall of the same dimension is added to the flight of stairs inside, but also to the exterior space in the case of the parapet lines. The starting figure of the enclosing square blurs in favour of a more marked sense of independence for the parts, despite the dominant diagonal symmetry, in the zoning of clearly distinct function areas for sleeping, social purposes and side rooms.

Splitting the halves across the diagonal creates a suggestive interplay of counter-forces: the distorted square of the sanitary area thrusts into the central zone. It thus forces back the stairs, and its massive, windowless figure, mobilizing centrifugal forces, threatens to burst the two halves of the dormitory apart. In contrast with this the two sleeping areas interlink via the floor outline, which protrudes in the façade in particular and a narrow frame profile, whose central window opening has to absorb the forces harnessed in the built reality.

In the next step the sleeping and living areas are differentiated in the individual rooms. The unarticulated rectangles are divided into five to provide a total of ten rooms per floor. The position and dimensions of a narrow balcony depend on the proportions of the Golden Section related to the axes of the dividing walls and the inner tracks of the outermost wall in each case, producing the area of the individual living room. The overall area of one cell corresponds to the approximate area of a double square and makes it seem sensible to provide a separate shaded zone at the front for functional and climatic reasons. The outer dividing wall of this zone consists of a folding wooden door that acts as a membrane; it can be opened fully so that the space can be enjoyed as a whole.   Fig.133

Another Golden Section ratio can be seen in the division of the stairwell as a continuous semicircular airspace for the surrounding flight of steps. Its dimensions of 5 feet 6 inches by 3 feet 5 inches correspond to about 1.68 m to 1.04 m and underpin the inherent geometry.

Fig. 134 The inner structure of the sanitary block is also based on the proportions of the Golden Section. Its reference edges are the tracks of the outer wall and its own division into quarters, and two 14 inch walls are added on. Further divisions continue from these principal edges, to the right to form cells for the WC and the shower-room at the top, and then to provide access to the tea-kitchen area. The top right-hand quarter of the square remains largely untouched; it is not part of the interior, and leads to the floor of the lowest level as a light-well open to the sky; it contains fresh air, walls to prevent people from looking in and the installations duct.

The inner track of the 19 inch outer wall of levels 0 and Plus 1 turns out to be another important reference edge for the geometrical determination of the corner situation arranged in mirror image across the diagonal axis. Its "bevelling" clarifies the diagonal of the square corner position of the outer wall, breaks down the massive quality of the wall and gives the sanitary block in its special position orientation through diagonal symmetry.

Fig. 135 The function zones within the absolute square frame relate in a way that swings between diagonal symmetry and orthogonal asymmetry. In contrast with the way the semicircular staircase "penetrates" the central area, the division of the outer walls of the sanitary block gives the impression of being *blown apart*. Forces thrust outwards, but are held by the enclosing outline of the square. Here the frame of a gauze grille element on the lighting slit takes over the function of holding both halves of the figure together at the dissolved corners.

The geometrical figure of a student's room, which can be seen from its wall tracks, is revealed by the fixing of the dividing walls at 10 inches (0.25 m) as an approximate double square in the outermost, slightly larger rooms. In the inner rooms the double square appears by taking up the inner edge of a gutter on the balcony.

Fig. 136 The ground plan of the dormitory, now completely developed, clarifies all the sub-figures implemented in the realized building and their dimensions, taking level Plus 3 as an example. It defines the placing and the dimensions of the door openings as diagonally symmetrical and moving towards each other, and shows the direction of access within a differentiated semicircle and the spatial connections of all the sanitary facilities needed for 10 students in each case. The parapet heights of the outer walls of the balcony and the wall-to-wall toplights in the students' rooms suggest transparency, which is also intended to be expressed in the 9½ inch inner walls on the corridor with their plastered inside surfaces. Close linking between the cells in both directions can be discerned, as the ends of the membrane-like dividing walls give the effect of piers both inside and outside, as relics of wider walls. Thus the process of breaking up by thinning out, splitting and stretching sharply differentiated sub-figures as an aggressive principle to create "transparency" for massive volumes does not apply only to the ground plan structure. It also includes vertical communication by floor-linking cavities that are semicircular here, to conform more closely with the Indian way of life. This also explains the different widths of the students' cells within one run of rooms, which is expressed by dividing the rectangles for individual rooms by taking up the inner track of an outer wall and not its axis (see figures 133–135): diagonal piers, visible on the exterior façade as well as in the interior, are placed on the lowest floor – level 0. In the case of the dormitories in the peripheral area, arch structures are put in place to absorb forces thrusting in from the outside, spanning the level over two storeys. They relate axially to the central dividing walls, but fit flush with the outer walls on the short sides. This leads to the shift of axis that has been described and in the façade in particular offers very subtle variations on the theme of making a series of isomorphic elements coherent by using larger openings on the periphery.

Rear side of a dormitory with separate toilet facilities

Fig.131

Fig.132

Fig.133

Fig.134

Fig.135

Fig.136

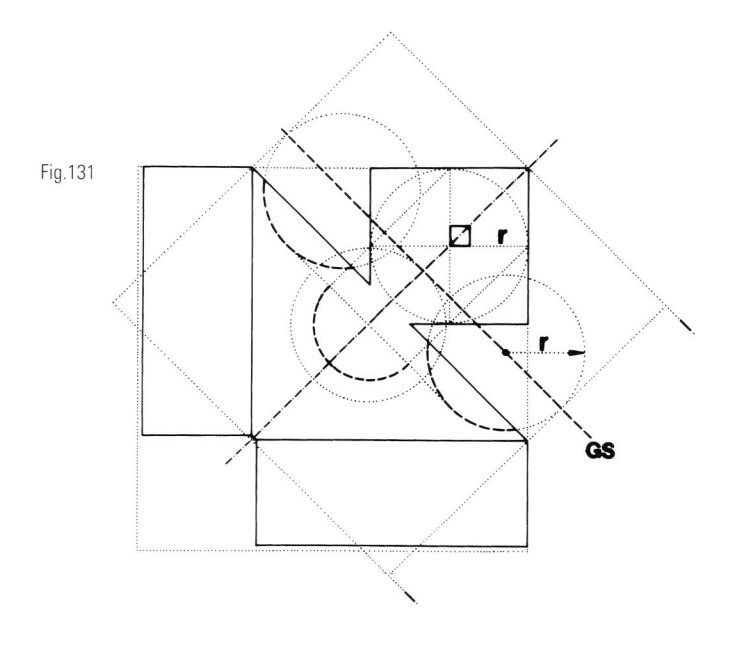

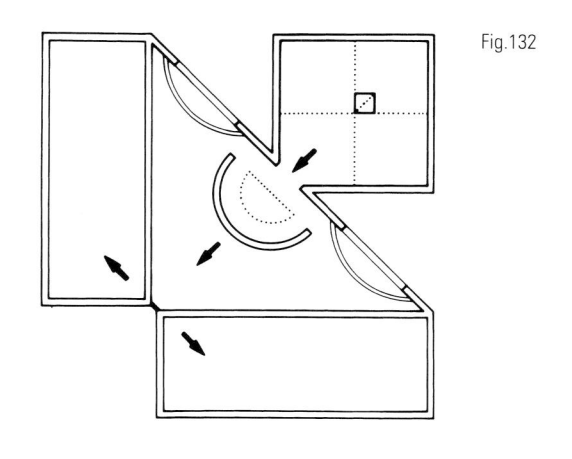

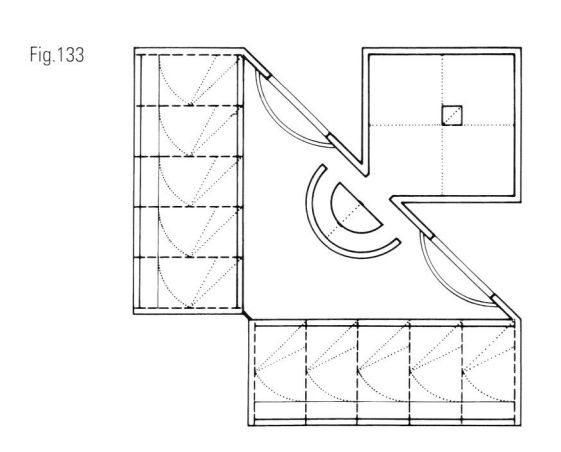

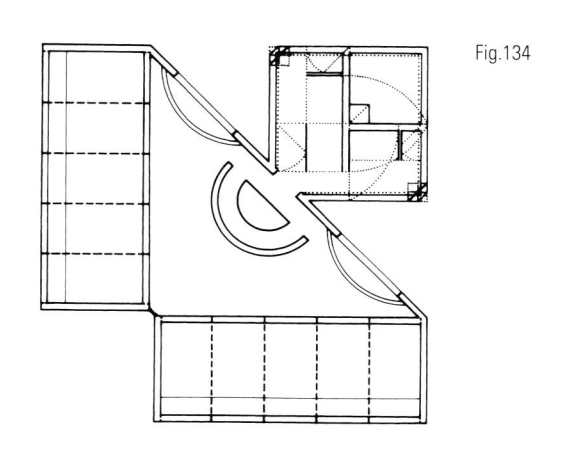

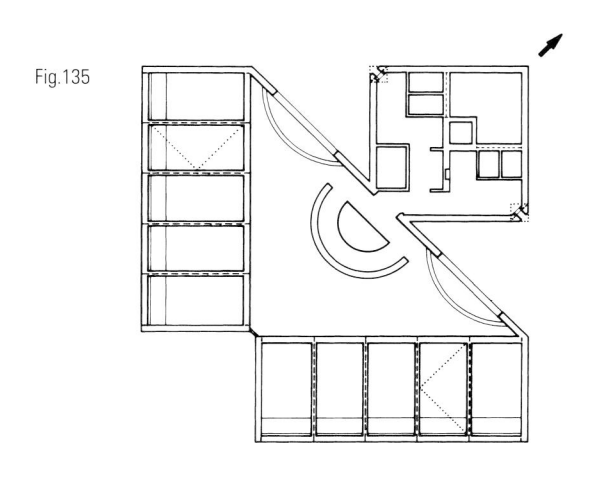

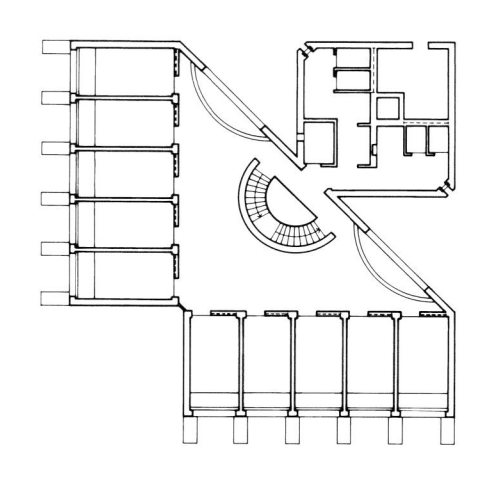

Fig.131–136
Ground plan analysis of the IIM: development of the dormitories to the final ground plan figure

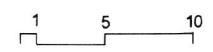

165

Dormitory with two-storey lounge at ground floor level and students' sleeping areas above

Dormitories on the southern periphery

Student accommodation: balconies and piers on the exterior façade

Outer row of dormitories

Courtyards between the dormitories

"Fault" as a difference in site height between the inner and outer row of dormitories, with access steps

Dormitory access lobbies on the Plus 1 level

167

Fig. 137 The genesis of the single dormitory figure leads to its connection with the general structural pattern. Its frames determining the geometrical order are proportional figures that can be clearly grasped. Thus the process of fitting in, i. e. matching the dormitory figures with the frame tracks 2–3 and 3–4 (see figure 124) can be continued. To this end the outer, here lowest of the rows of dormitories, fixed at a total of 18, is "detached" from the constraints of the grid and shifts with the outer track of its piers on a 45 degrees diagonal as far as the 2–3 and 3–4 frame track. On its upper side, facing the adjacent buildings, it is displaced to the size of a pier, minus the joint that is already present. Its upper line marks the "fault" created by the difference in height be-

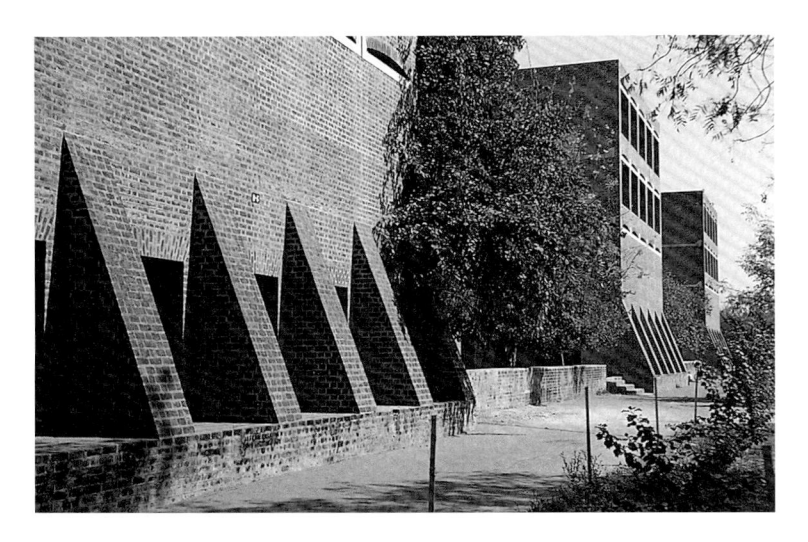

Piers of the outer row of dormitories

tween level 0 in the peripheral area and level Plus 1 in the rest of the dormitory area. There the steps needed to deal with this change of level are placed within the newly defined displacement distance along the sanitary block. It becomes clear that the previously indicated fault between the levels E 0 and E Plus 1, geometrically determined and linked to the water-tower in terms of dimensions, makes the piers and the displacement distance interdependent. It also relates the piers to all the building sections on the edge and fusing with the upper plateau. This is how the new dormitory type for the peripheral area that has "grown" in its outer line by the length of the pier is generated (see figure 136).

There is a clear parallel with a strip-like zone, corresponding in its dimensions, on the upper and lower edges of the 1–2–3–4 rectangle, whose lengths are adopted from the dimensions of existing buildings. It produces a formal relation for the sides and establishes the presence of an oscillating rectangle. This oscillation or vibration occurs vertically by the distance between the fault and the lower outline of the frame or from the outer line of the administration to the inner track of the water-tower. It is similar to the oscillation of the double courtyard square at the beginning. The suggestive diagonal quality of the dormitory structure is further enhanced: an edge that meets the horizontal courtyard symmetrical axis on the right-hand outline of the water-tower, then runs on at an angle of 45 degrees, forms the borders of the structure. Its track cuts off the dormitory grid to the left and is tangential with the outlines of the dormitory piers on level 0.

As so often the disposition of the individual figures in the complex as a whole, following a process of movement intended to overcome an inherent rigidity, remains dependent on the border lines that have been built up within the system. The disposition oscillates in a tension-laden field of *dynamic repose*. Movement in a vertical direction can be seen in an imaginary, framing rectangle, and this also follows the horizontal: the root 2 outline of the 1–2–3–4 frame "vibrates" within the cipher-like ground plan figure. Its fixed displacement runs from the outer left-hand to the inner right-hand water-tower outline to the equivalents 1'–2'–3'–4'. The right-hand outline forms the border of the outermost right-hand wall of the group of three dormitory buildings. The water-tower ground plan, with its simplified orthogonal, double axially symmetrical rigidity seems like a *frozen relic* of these movements. It contrasts with all the other figures, which present themselves dynamically. Its detached position, not directly linked with any other building, indicates its special function within the structure of geometrical order.

In order to determine the last group of dormitories, separating out top right and breaking out of the root 2 outline, we have to consider the square in the peripheral zone that has *grown* and been extended by the length of the piers. Its a–b–c–d outline is surrounded by its diagonal root 2 major square e–f–g–h, in such a way that a figure with a new value emerges as a product of the principle of *rational organics*. The square e–f–g–h performs a mediating function in the genesis of these "special dormitories", which no longer follow the original grid structure, but form an independent group. They relate to a 45 degree diagonal ending on the symmetrical axis of the ramp in the north-east of the complex as a parallel

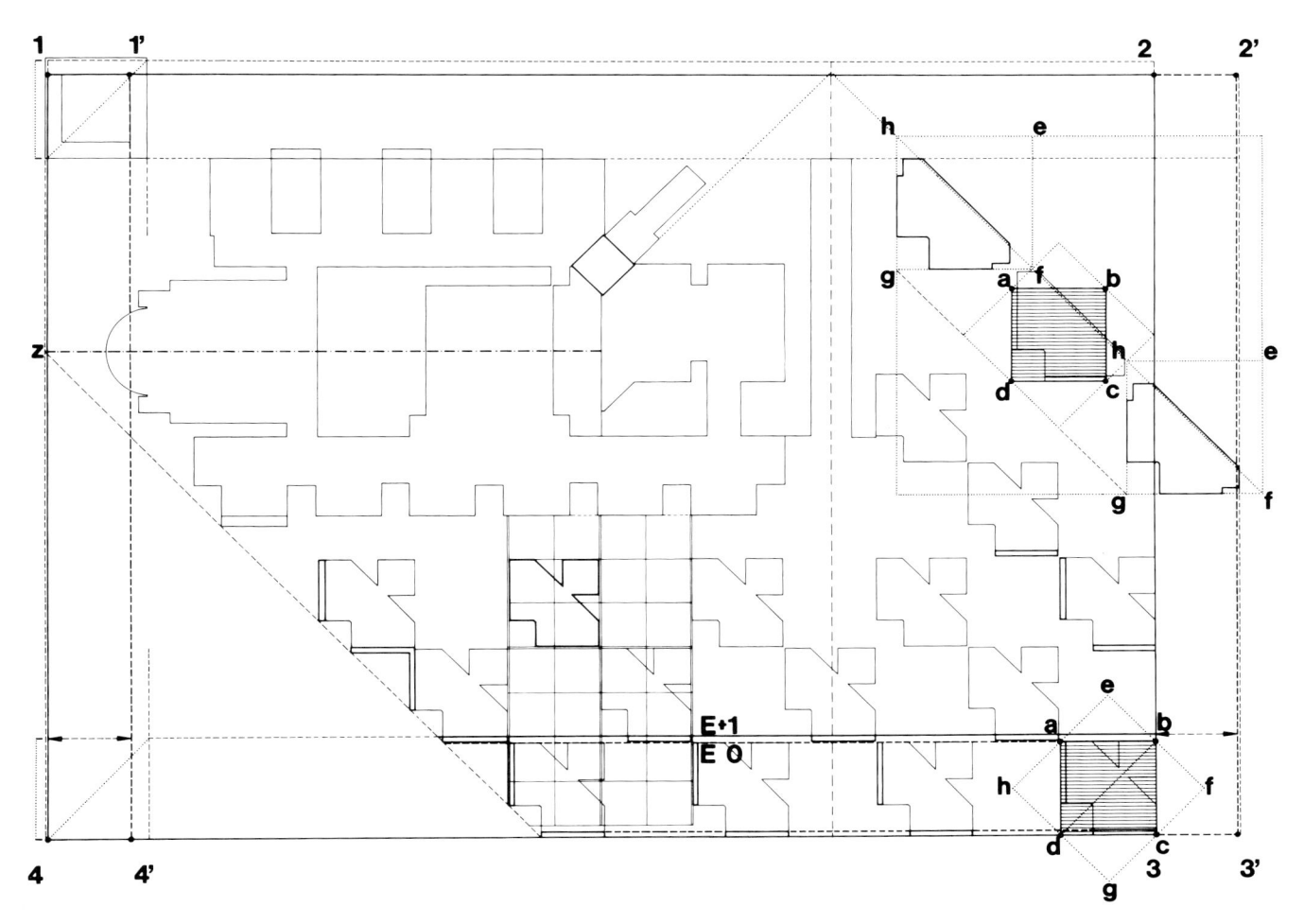

Fig.137
Ground plan analysis of the IIM: development of three special dormitories in dependence on the others, and determination of the framing geometry of the complex as a whole

"Original" dormitory left and extended dormitory right

Group of special dormitories on the eastern edge of the complex as a whole

with the dormitory boundary in the south-west. Three e–f–g–h squares are placed along this line, so that their diagonal symmetrical axis is congruent with the reference edge. In order to fix their position the middle square is turned by 45 degrees and shifted so far that one side lies on the tangent running through the g corner points. In this way both the other squares "tuck" the middle one in between them with their corner points f and h. This tangential geometry means that the combination of three within a surrounding square frame on the diagonal seems open to shifting at will. However, it is placed in such a way that the area on the right outside the 2'–3' line equals the one above the extended administration area. The e–f–g–h squares are cut by this "overhanging" area and fitted into the named outlines. Equally the main line of the diagonal figure serves as the border of the actual body, and triangular figures are formed for the buildings. The process of cutting off the squares is continued on both sides of each square. This reconstructs the symmetry and diagonal orientation of the individual figures and can be seen as a directly perceptible plastic process within the "distortion" as a whole. This process illustrates an almost craft-oriented way of thinking during the act of design, and the handling of essentially corporeal structure.

The inscribed root 2 minor square a–b–c–d is remembered in two shapes that detach themselves to mark the students' dormitories, so that a front view corresponding to the peripheral dormitories, i. e. a south-west façade, emerges. Despite their independent disposition outside the dormitory structure, the special dormitory system is successfully integrated by taking up this façade development. Their diagonal wall, again binding all the three parts of the building together, is seen as a defensive wall and clear boundary for the exterior space.

The diagonal wall of these special dormitories is given its articulating "distortion". It does not extend over the diagonal element into the exterior area, but curves inwards. In contrast with all the other sub-figures in the complex as a whole – with the exception of the kitchen building in the courtyard, which was not built – the circle appears in the façade for the first time here. These buildings were given a special form because they were originally intended to have a different function as accommodation for married and Ford Foundation students, but later it was decided not to separate them from the others.

Fig.138

After "plastic distortion" has bound this section into the enclosing shape of the square, the genesis of the diagonal element, marked by convex and concave curves, is based on the example of the "middle" building. The starting-point remains the common orientation with all the other dormitories, with the placing of two "strips" of accommodation towards the south-west, and symmetry running from bottom left to top right. The basic figure for the structure of one building corresponds to the disposition of the sub-parts of a "normal" dormitory (see figure 127). Here the entrance square is inscribed into the top right-hand corner of the square a–b–c–d. This results – as before – in zoning into two sleeping areas and the corridor zone with separating joint. This is fixed in position by the root 2 minor framing square a–b–c–d with its outer piers. Indented by the width of a pier the exterior outline of the a–b–c–d square that is already linking up through "capping" of the ends with the diagonal track forms peripheral figures for sanitary areas on both sides. They are inscribed into a new imaginary square, and identify its centre by quartering. A circle at the centre of this square is tangential to the outer track of the outer wall with known dimensions that unites all the dormitories in their diagonal run (see figures 129–131).[117] The overlapping of the diagonals with the dimensions of the outer wall is to be seen as a conscious shift within the ordering structures, and consequently the radius of the staircase circle can be established. Two intersection points with the circle are defined by halving this circle parallel with the diagonal outside wall, and two intersection points with the diagonal outside wall via lines a–b and b–c. The central verticals at right angles to

---

[117] The measurements for the three special dormitories come from the working plan "AD2, August 1970, First Floor Plan", received from Raje's office and in the author's possession as a copy. Comparative measurements of the realized project were established by the author in on-site surveys in February/March 1990 and February 1991.

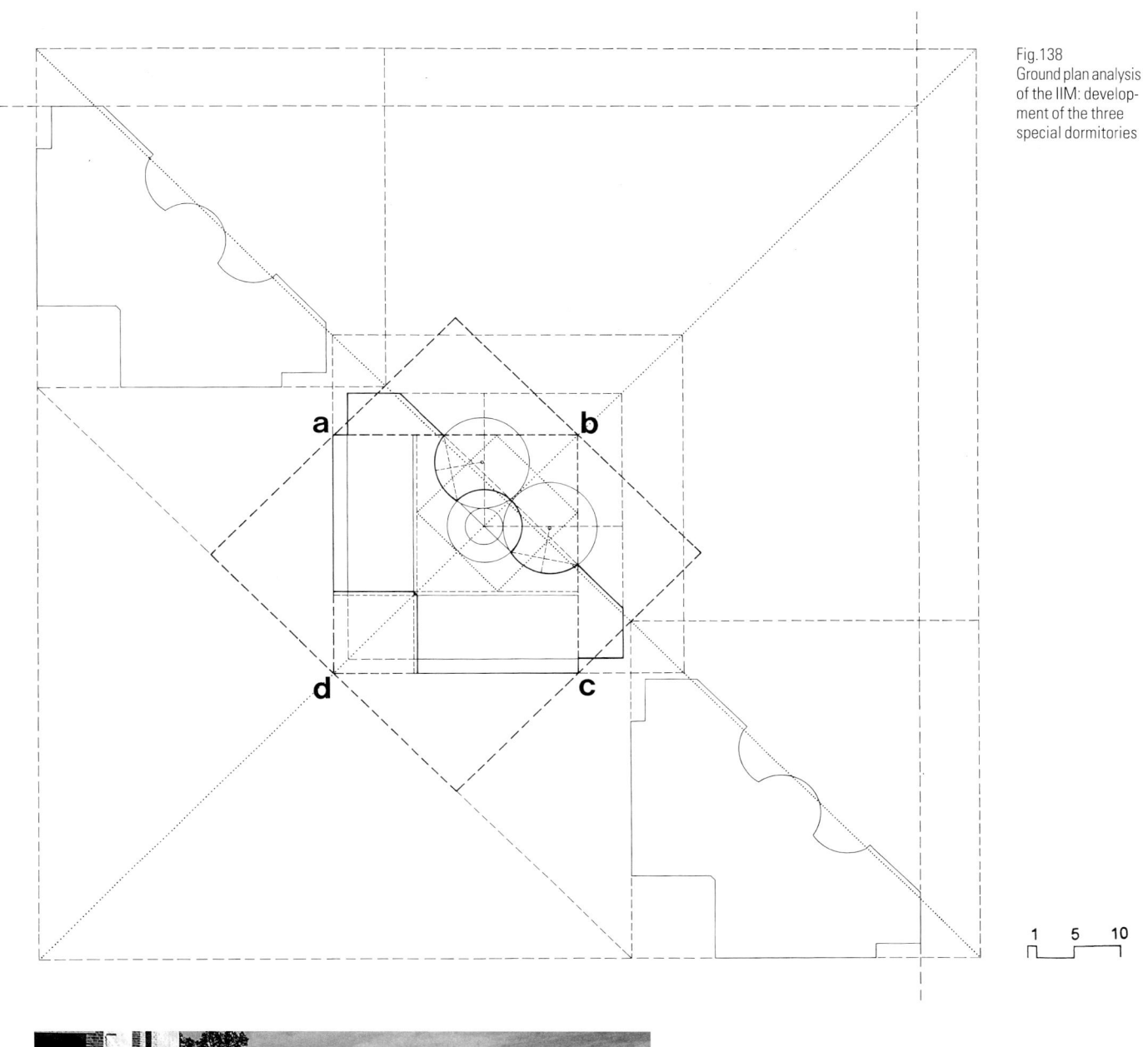

Fig. 138
Ground plan analysis of the IIM: development of the three special dormitories

Sleeping section with balconies of a special dormitory

171

Access side of a special dormitory with circular stairwell

Triangular overall outline of the individual buildings

these points follow the straight lines between them as axes for the central points. Finally the relevant radius of both arcs results from the dimensions of the width of the staircase and its well, which is tangential to the arcs. A double concave circle figuration, now thrusting deep into the central lounge, attempts to include the exterior space in the building and breaks through the defensive, enclosing linearity of the diagonals. Their outline fits the separating parts together again in the attic storey, balancing the circle of the staircase, which curves convexly outwards, tangentially, precisely on the track of the diagonal outer wall. So here again we have a possible reminiscence of the original position with an initially linear outer line, later distorted to a curve, that retains this element in its form-finding design process.

The massive quality of the cylindrical staircase volume shows dramatic penetration, held in tension by the sophisticated circular geometry, of an independent body by the cross walls of an absolute diagonal, which are giving way and moving backwards. They look like ramparts, and seem to be turning away, both here and in the rectangular figures of the students' rooms opposite contrasting pairs are formed between the hardness of prismatic cubatures and curving, moving, dissolving soft membranes. The part-figures are related alternately by the dissolution of their outlines and a symmetry that divides their diagonal façades again. The central, cylindrical staircase tower, which also looms up in the view over the roof, collects the details of the building volumes that develop evenly towards both sides via its symmetrical axis, and at the same time it is an element of separation. Then again the polygonal peripheral volumes of the sanitary areas, isolated by a joint, incline towards each other over the symmetrical axes of the gaps, so that pair formations link up with the adjacent element on the one and on the other side, like a puzzle picture.

This group of buildings, which was realized last in the chronological sequence of the design genesis, shows the most intensive formative process of the whole complex, sculpting the building volumes. We see that Kahn was consistently more determined to distort, and the use of interpenetrating curved ground plan forms suggests a new creative phase eight years away from the beginning of the design.

Façade detail with pressure-bearing arch and reinforced concrete band absorbing tensile forces

Indian Institute of Management
Modular Origin

"The spirit of the start is the most marvellous moment
at any time for anything. Because in the start lies the seed for all things that must follow."[118]

The overall figure of the school and residential complex reveals the square figure of the diagonal access area as its generator because of the square's status in the genesis of the design. This centrally located square determines the crucial measurements and dimensions within the disposition of all parts and those in a position where outer lines relate to each other. The "pure", unsullied square outline of its inner area identifies a unique point of concentration and poses the question of its further significance. The specific dimensions and dependences of its measurements give rise to the subsequent sub-figures through a potential *module* that binds everything together, the size of which is still to be found. Its existence seems necessary for the implementation of all the geometrical proportions described within the realized building.

MODULAR ORIGIN

So far we have examined the "macrocosm" of the architectural world of the Indian Institute of Management as a whole, open to visual experience and directly accessible in its corporeality. It now remains to be asked what degree of detailing is reached by the system of dimensional and proportional order when determining structural elements, wall thicknesses or material connections on a micro-level. The entrance square remains significant here. This figure has to be examined more closely both from the point of view of an extended analytical procedure within a key ground plan position, but also of bringing an elevation figure into the context of the all-embracing ordering structure. With its portal facing the access steps it stands as an example for all the other sub-figures that can stand up to any kind of detailed examination, but would take us well beyond the scope of this book if considered with due care.

The diagonal figure in the main entrance situation remains as a relic of a rectangle that can be accessed diagonally via the corners, originating from the school building in the conceptual phase of the design. In the further course of the genesis it reduces itself to two, and then to one entrance only in the top right-hand corner. Emphasis of the entrance by position and form must ultimately be submitted to semiotic interpretation as a symbolic gesture.

The mango tree that is drawn into the diagonal constellation by the symmetrical axis of the steps firstly reduces the monumental effect of the axis by being placed within, or "blocking" it, and also becomes an architectonic element. But it also, because of its almost "sacred" untouchability – it is forbidden to fell mango trees in India – gives the access figure spiritual character as a natural feature of the Indian character. Its symbolic use, here as a mediator between man with his artificial architectural products, and nature as an existing world beyond that created by man, relates its own image of organic growth to the steps, as a *vehicle* for "spiritual growth" and as shorthand for the institution "school".

As established in the analysis of the whole complex, the idea of growth is transferred as a quasi-organic process to the rationale of the geometrical and proportional ordering system. Figures are generated, they build up on each other and can be precisely described. They begin in the square of the entrance porch with its main access steps, a mediating platform related to the porch and the mango tree.[119] As the birthplace of a hierarchical, rational principle embracing all parts of the whole, it is to be assumed that this extraordinary figure was built up on the same principle. It could be possible, within the scale connections of its outlines and constructive details, to develop a symbolism for the entrance porch – together with its portal, which takes ground plan and elevation

Main entrance with tree, steps and portal

[118] Kahn quotation from: Oscar Newman (ed.), "New Frontiers in Architecture: CIAM in Otterlo", Universe Books Inc., New York 1961; also in: A. Latour (ed.), "Writings, Lectures, Interviews", p. 85.
[119] As can be seen from one of the definitive working plans "L 1–2, Library, Level 14' 10", June 69", the realized platform suggests the width originally intended for the steps, and counts as part of the staircase, not of the entrance porch.

into the third dimension – following the mango tree and the steps as a "triad".

The starting-point for the assumption of a highly symbolic entrance square built on previously formulated modular combinatorial numerical analysis is the grid fixed by the outline of the courtyard and the access corridors around it (see figures 104/105). Its side length for one field of 6.60 m (21 feet 8 inches), given a standard wall thickness of 0.60 m (23½ inches), produces an outer line for the entrance square of about 10 m (32 feet 9 inches), which is confirmed in the working plans.[120] The square, with a converted side length of precisely 9.96 m, very close to the metric 10, suggests the conjecture that it was not feet and inches but metres that form the basis of the unit of measurement. This could reveal Kahn's intention of using a combination of the two world-dividing measurement systems to indicate a common one that would bring the Anglo-Saxon and the rest of the world together.[121] This area, now 10 by 10 m and its diagonals of about 14 m contains, in its halves, i.e. the quarter square and the figures 5 to 7, the smallest root 2 relation of rational numbers that is still imprecise and undefined in terms of dimension and scale.[122]

The wall thickness measurement of 0.60 m, subtracted on both sides from the outer length of 9.96 m, gives the internal track measurement for one side of the entrance square of 8.76 m in length (28 feet 9 inches). Measurement of the entrance square on site showed at level 0, the lower entrance level (plus 4 feet ½ inch), an inner track measurement of 8.76 m and at the Plus 1 level (plus 14 feet 10 inches) 8.65 m, i.e. both show a deviation.[123] This difference of 11 centimetres (4⅓ inches) that cannot be identified in the plans is not a sign merely of dimensional tolerance as result of inadequate care when building – this would not seem plausible given the simplicity of the figure, two identical rooms placed one above the other. On the contrary it emerges as the key to deciphering all the previously unexplained connections in terms of measurement: Kahn intended to create an entrance situation that was an "intersection point" between real and transcendental dimensions!

The imperceptible difference between the two rooms explains their "non-functional" cause, although dimensional relations emerge only after extremely precise analysis. This confirms the interpretation that the difference in dimensions that we have pointed out was Kahn's intentional reference to the inherent system of order, a reference that initiates the decoding of the whole complex. Both these measurements, 8.76 and 8.65 m, are derived proportionally from the abovementioned values 5 and 7 and their root 2 majors. As "growing" squares turned around the smaller in each case by 45 degrees, they enclose them at the corners, meaning that their area is doubled. This shows the relevance of the deciding values with the rational numbers 5–7–10–14–20 as an excerpt from the infinite chain of all root 2 relations for fixing dimensional connections within the figure of the entrance area of the building. The diagonally placed entrance square already indicated the turning process which occurs when inscribing other root 2 squares that build up on each other. Its side length determines the outer line of all the values in the above-mentioned sequence of numbers: the approximated 2 times 5 equals 10 m and following from this its diagonal of approximately 2 times 7 equals 14 and the next largest, the imaginary root 2 square that with a diagonal length of 20 m then frames the 14 m diagonal.

Kahn's interest in incorporating the whole-number rationality of the values 10 and 14 here in the metrical dimensions of the entrance section now appears in the inner tracks of the two entrance halls, placed one above the other. Their mysterious difference reveals a clearly comprehensible sequence of numbers for the integration of ground plan and elevation figures within the ordering structure. As can be seen from the above analysis of the complex as a geometrical construction and from the resulting figuration, all the dimensions are linked – arithmetically here – by the dominating division ratios root 2 and the Golden Section! Firstly, as a derivation of the ideal starting measurement of 10 m outside length, the precise root 2 major value 14.14 m follows as a diagonal and the inner track measurement derived from this of 8.74 m as the minor Golden Section of 14.14 m (realized in level 0: 8.76 m). Then derived from the ideal starting measurement of 14 m diagonal length its root 2 minor re-

---

[120] The plans used were Raje's, "L 1–2 and L 1–7, Library, Entrance Porch and Sections", June and July 1969 and "A 1–2, Level 14' 10", Administration Wing", February 1970; all plans are in the author's possession as copies.

[121] The problem of the world-dividing measurement systems metre and foot/inch was addressed in detail by Le Corbusier in his "Modulor"; he suggested the modulor series of numbers built on the Golden Section as an ideal for uniting the two systems; this must have been known to Kahn.

[122] This could be Kahn's attempt to harmonize the metric and the foot/inch measurement systems, starting with the root 2 relation, with the aid of the two starting proportions root 2 and the Golden Section.

[123] The survey carried out in February and March 1990 was used to compare the built architecture with the working plans available as a basis for the analysis and admitted no central points other than insights previously acquired. After establishing deviant measurements on the ground and upper floors the entrance square and its portal were surveyed in full detail.

Main access steps and Fig. 139 View of the main entrance portal

sults in 9.89 m as outer line (realized in Level 1: 9.85 m) and its precisely realized minor Golden Section of 8.65 m as the inner track of the starting square. The directly perceptible difference of root 2 and Golden Section values, 9.96 minus 8.76 and 9.85 minus 8.65, shows equally in both wall thicknesses of 0.60 m (23 ½ inches), as an "automatic" result on both levels of the entrance building. The outline of its lower square, larger on both sides by 5.5 cm (2 ¼ inches), agrees with the upper one on the outer line of the access side and is thus slightly – imperceptibly – shifted against courtyard.

The inner and outer tracks of the walls of the entrance square as the difference between root 2 and Golden Section now confirm, in their "logical" rationality, the initial assumption of the analysis: they are the modular origin. They create the administration figure in the dimensions of the inner square, and also the classrooms and dormitories in the dimensions of the outer square, and finally the courtyard area in between, using the grid of the middle track square. Thus all the quasi-autonomous figurations with their own symmetrical axes are bound into a common ordering system. The dimensions of the dormitory structure, which were constituted even before the entrance square cropped up, or the precise final details of the school complex, also become explicable: the dormitory outline, identified as a four-fold entrance square in its exterior measurements (see figures 123–125), with a side measurement of 20.06 m (65 feet 9 ¾ inches), when halved to 10.03 corresponds quite precisely to the ideal value 10, or halved, as 2 times 5, as the smallest whole-number module. This underlines the importance of the basic value and the ideas developed here.

The world of dimensional and geometrical order of fixed reference values is continued in the portal figures for the main entrance, linked with the steps and the ground plan. We have assumed a copy of the proportional links of the ground plan lengths. Here the opening of the main portal on level Plus 1, which is associated with the mango tree, will be examined.[124] It is a vertical projection of the "step band" on to the plane of the wall.

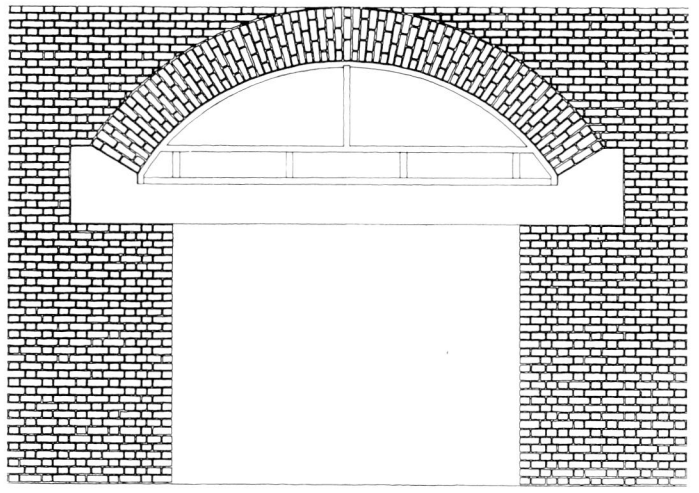

Fig. 139

The access opening corresponding to the width of the flight of steps acquires a symmetrically related arch in the form of the arc of a circle extending over and above the opening. Its outward-"thrusting" masonry structure with a width of 2 ½ bricks is locked in by a concrete beam to absorb the compression forces of the arch; it puts its stamp on all the architecture of the Indian Institute of Management, almost as a formal incunabulum. The contrasting material concrete means that this element shows the flow of forces in the function of a simple lintel. In the façade it traces the position and edge of the particular storey floor as visible outside. Contradictory things are combined: the portal figure binds disparate functions behind the openings together into a unit through its vertical axial symmetry. The window in the arch, on the other hand, provides light for a conference room for the school's management team placed directly above the entrance square. We become aware of the autonomy of the façade through the neglect of merely functional placing in this ambiguity of components that almost work against each other, which informs the overwhelming number of openings in the complex as a whole. Division and simultaneous linking of openings show that the functional notion that the façade is "automatically" produced by a ground plan dispo-

[124] This drawing is a view reconstructed by the author, on the basis of fully detailed on-site measurements; the dimensions of its masonry, especially the brick layers, agree with a longitudinal profile of the layers (in the author's possession) and the proportional relations presented below.

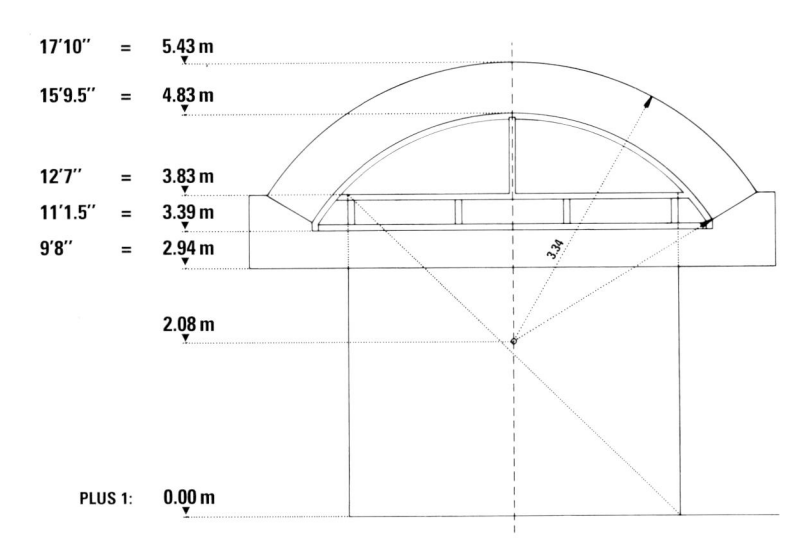

17'10"	=	5.43 m
15'9.5"	=	4.83 m
12'7"	=	3.83 m
11'1.5"	=	3.39 m
9'8"	=	2.94 m
		2.08 m
PLUS 1:		0.00 m

Fig. 140
Dimensional relations of the main entrance portal

sition has been removed. The unifying centring of the window figure and the entrance opening via a vertical axis finds its characteristic form in a small bar at the peak of the arch. It belongs to a window placed far back on the inner line of the wall as an interior application. Its lines contrast with the horn-like concrete abutments, joining them to stand out against the all-homogenizing two-dimensional quality of the masonry wall.

Fig. 140 In order to define the dimensions of the portal outlines, we have to look for the relation to the "ideal" value, the value 10, which generates the ground plan outlines. The minor Golden Section of 10 gives a result of 6.18 m, which is half the realized diagonal measurement 12.38 m (geometrically: 12.36 m) of level 0. Its next minor Golden Section, measuring 3.83 m, creates the width of the entrance opening and of the flight of steps. The fact that the outer arc and the width of the openings are interdependent is proved by the dimension root 2 major of 3.83, 5.43 m (17 feet 10 inches), which is the highest point of the arch and tangential to an imaginary root 2 rectangle unifying the opening and the arch. It is a point that equally presents its height arithmetically as minor Golden Section of the length 8.76 m – the side of the lower entrance square. The outline of a square 3.83 m (12 feet 7 inches) high and wide appears on the upper edge of a second horizontal window profile, whose distance from the lintel of 0.44 m almost corresponds with the concrete beam at 0.45 m and is to be seen as a further indication of the intended interweaving of both opening geometries. It is noteworthy that the centre of the circle does not declare the floor of the Plus 1 level to be the tangent of the circle, in other words that it is not half way up: here too its position results from the relation of the Golden Section with an overall height of 5.43 m (17 feet 10 inches). Its distance from the floor level is 2.08 m as minor and its accompanying major section as the radius of the outer arch, 3.34 m. The point in time at which the height of 3.29 m (10 feet and 9 ½ inches) between the floors, concealed behind the concrete lintel, was established as the distance between the upper edges of the floors cannot be reconstructed and remains open.[125] However, the visible distance from floor to ceiling, the net height between floors, 2.94 m (9 feet 8 inches), is dependent as a major root 2 on the position of the circle centre at the level of 2.08 m. Its distance relates to the overall height of 5.43 m (17 feet 9 ½ inches). Two last measurements are also derived from each other: the value 4.83 m (15 feet and 9 ½ inches), defines the height of the lower arc as the fixed measurement of a distance from the upper arc corresponding to the wall width of 0.60 m (23 ½ inches). This measurement acquires its root 2 minor of 3.41 m, realized here as 3.39 m (11 feet 1 ½ inches), as the upper edge of the concrete lintel placed 10 cm above the floor.

View from the courtyard of the "entrance square" hall portal with conference room above

[125] The dimensions of the height between floors come from plans "L 1–7, Entrance Porch and Sections", July 1969, "L 1–10, Library West Elevation and Sections," August 1969 and "L 1–14, Library Cross Section", August 1969, signed by the National Institute of Design, Ahmedabad; copies in the author's possession.

It should be explicitly stated here that the width of the access opening and the height of the arch, as initial outlines of the portal, are derived directly from the ideal ground plan lengths 10 and 14 m. All the vertical divisions along the symmetrical axis dependent on the radius of the arch are built up on this, like a musical scale. Although the precise implementation of pre-formulated proportions is based on a constant approximation between the decimal and the feet/inch system, a high level of agreement is nevertheless reached.

To sum up, it can be seen that all the measurements defining the outlines of the portal figure are related to the entrance square in a self-conditioning process of genesis. Here the square's dimensional and proportional structure on both levels and its original dimensions of 10 as twice 5 are valid. The measurements are subject to differentiated alternation of arithmetical division ratios of the Golden Section and root 2, and as an expression of complex order are comparable to the geometrical construct of the complex as a whole.

And so the question arises of what measurement, common to both division ratios, serves as basis for the transfer of geometrical and proportional lines, relating to the precise dimensions of the brick, on to the reality of masonry structures, following the division of both the Golden Section and root 2.

The wall thickness of 60 cm (23 ½ inches) results from the difference of proportionally related lengths of the entrance square outlines. It is divided into 2 ½ brick widths, so that as a result of Kahn's early choice of the sides of the brick its width is now 9 inches (22.8 cm) and its depth 4 ½ inches (11.4 cm), with a joint width of 1.2 cm. This alternation of a whole and a half brick forms the pattern of the masonry in all the walls, although the typical hand-made quality of the Indian brick and full pointing of the gaps meant that the brick measurements were of necessity imprecise. Special opening widths like the entrance portal (see figure 139) can be realized precisely by adding in special formats as the penultimate brick in every second layer of bricks in each case and a double half brick to form a vertical joint above the inner springing point of the arch. Thus, when a planned opening dimension is being shaped, but also in the case of every other set of lines or outlines within a related system, it is not the almost randomly changeable width of the brick format that is crucial for fixing proportional relations, but, as in the case of the entrance portal opening, the *height of the brick layers*.

So we are compelled to face the key question about the height of the smallest modular building element, the brick as a *nucleus*. According to plans,[126] one brick plus two joints gives a height of 4 inches (10.16 cm) and in the layer plan one brick plus one joint 3 ½ inches (8.8 cm), from which it can be deduced that one brick is 3 inches high (7.6 cm) and the joint is half an inch (1.2 cm). According to this, all the portal dimensions calculated arithmetically as numerical values of geometrical and proportional order (see figures 139 and 140) follow the common division value of one layer of bricks (here the lowest arch joint of about 1.2 cm must be subtracted from the height in each case):

2.93 m : 33 brick layers = 8.8 cm
3.37 m : 38 brick layers = 8.8 cm
3.82 m : 43 brick layers = 8.8 cm
4.82 m : 54 brick layers = 8.9 cm
5.42 m : 61 brick layers = 8.8 cm

The measurement 8.8 cm (3 ½ inches) as the layer height, made up of one brick plus one joint, defines the *common modular measurement of proportional relations produced both through the Golden Section and also through root 2*. It makes a wide variety of figures possible with the aid of both division ratios within the whole structure of the façade, which is based on brick, and can be expressed through the direct relation of the irrational abstract numerical values:

0.618 (Golden Section) : 0.707 (root 2) = 0.87

This division value, to be defined in the metric system as 0.087 m, means the closest possible approximation to a brick manufactured under the English feet/inches system 3 inches high plus a half inch joint (0.088 m). Given that Indian masonry tends to be imprecise in its line-building a large spectrum of tolerance is allowed to this millimetre deviation. Thus a high level of agreement is to be achieved between arithmetical, geometrical and realized measurements.

The links between Golden Section and root 2 values have so far been proved arithmetically, but this can also be done geometrically and graphically. They are to be illustrated within the root 2 chain of growing squares, relevant to the entrance

Fig.141

---

[126] The working plans "A 2–1, Masonry Arches", April 1970 and "A 2–2, Wall Sections", June 1970, with masonry details, were used as a basis here, drawn by the National Institute of Design in Ahmedabad and in the author's possession as copies, and also the brick layering plan mentioned.

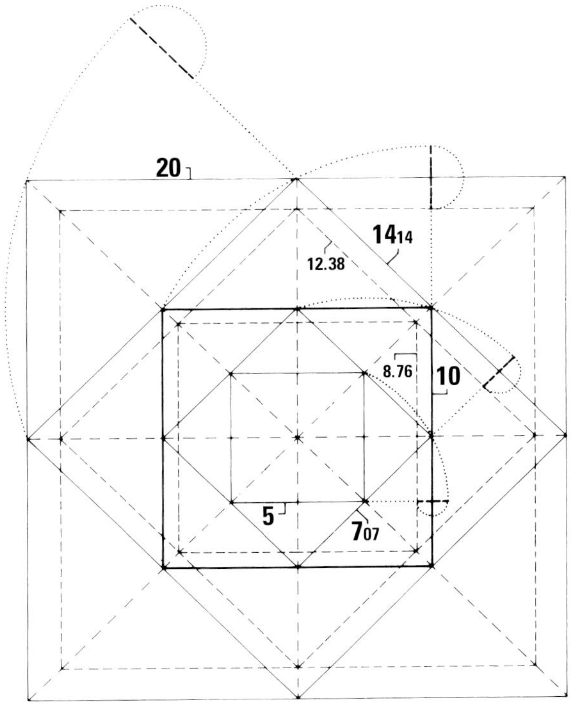

Fig. 141
Geometrical and dimensional relations of the Golden Section and root 2 dependent on the dimensions of the entrance square (value 10)

square, of 5–7–10–14–20 (precisely: 5–7.07–10–14.14–20). This gives the "ideal measurement for the outer line of 10 (m) as an orientation figure.

The arc of the geometrical construction of the Golden Section with an initial size of 5 crosses the intersection point of the "pure" root values 7.07 and 10 and meets the "floor line", 5. Their common point is mirrored via the outline of ten, so that the square dimension of the value 8.76 (inner track of the entrance square at level 0 as minor Golden Section of 14.14) can be inscribed. The next-largest link of the root 2 starting value 7.07 can also by illustrated by Golden Section geometry with the diagonal of level 0, 12.38 (minor Golden Section of 20). Thus the infinite chain of growing root 2 squares is followed by a parallel accompanying series of Golden Section lengths. Conversely a corresponding root 2 value can be reconstructed geometrically for a known Golden Section value. Here, in the combination of square and circular segment constructions we can see the dynamics of a spiral-like figure with Golden Section distances as an indication of a much more complex geometry. The relation of both division ratios with geometrical systems could be further illuminated, as a variety of possible combinations of proportional relations of circle and square constructions exist.[127]

This figure of inscribed, constantly growing squares, touching at the corners, as a root 2 series of explicit numbers can be seen as related to an important diagrammatic representation in Indian religion and philosophy. Its symbolism is to be interpreted as an integrating image of the existing, but not really existing world, and is defined as a "cosmogram" or "psychocosmogram" called "mandala".[128]

The Sanskrit word *mandala* translates as circle, and in the overwhelming majority of cases consists of several squares, usually surrounded by circles or overlapping triangles, placed concentrically over an axial cross. In Hinduism it remains on the graphic-abstract plane and in Buddhism it is amplified in a variety of ways by images of saints and images of the real world. Close linking of circular and square figures is often seen as "squaring the circle" and can be interpreted as the "archetype of the whole" (Jung).[129] In the Indian mind this links very subtly defined zones of the real microcosm with transcendent levels of the universal macrocosm in a concentrated, integrating image of a visually perceptible and imaginary world, which is in every case open to experience. Conversely, in the context of western European culture the mandala is said to appear as a positive reaction to circumstances of physical disorientation.[130] In Indian thinking the mandala does not have a specifically therapeutic effect, but is considered, particularly in Tibetan Buddhism, alongside its purely image-supplying symbolism, as a cultic instrument known as "yantra". But it also serves as a vehicle to support meditation and contemplation, whose religious meaning here requires a short explanatory digression.

Indians acquire true "self"-awareness through a slow inner process of finding themselves, in which psyche and intellect – in contrast with the Western world, which splits these two characteristics – form an equal unity in order to transform the self into a higher, "depersonalized", "pure" awareness of the absolute *(atman)* within an existing world. There it is liberated from life's burden of guilt *(karma)*, but its sum of actions and experiences remains as potential energy for ever. In certain states of the soul universal force and absolute awareness appear as an "inner light", whose immaculate "lightness" fuses subject (I) and object (it). It can be experienced in a condition of meditation and contemplation and in the ideal final condition – within the relativity of life's bonds – it eases the path to absoluteness through

[127] Mathila Ghyka, "Geometry of Art and Life", New York 1977, first edition 1946, and Dr. Anne G. Tyng, "The Energy of Abstraction in Architecture: A Theory of Creativity", dissertation at the University of Pennsylvania, Philadelphia 1975. The central theme of both essays is the Golden Section.
[128] Guiseppe Tucci, "Geheimnis des Mandala", Scherz Verlag, Bern 1972, p. 31; also in: Pieper/Gutschow, "Indien", p. 129.
[129] Carl Gustav Jung, "Mandala, Bilder aus dem Unbewußten", Walter-Verlag, Düsseldorf 1977, p. 116.
[130] C. G. Jung, "Mandala". Jung describes the expressive form of the mandala, strictly ordered and structured in its native cultural circle, as "compensation for a psychological state that has become confused" and declares it to be an attempt at self-healing by nature (p. 115).

Fig. 142

Fig. 143

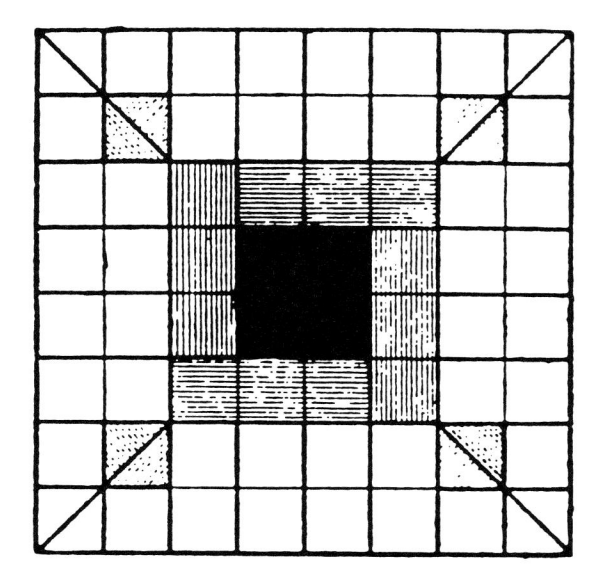

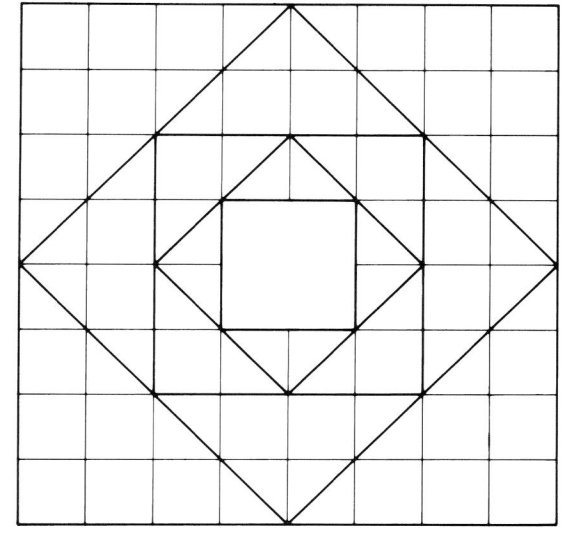

Fig. 142–143
Mandala diagrams

"enlightenment".[131] Thus in Indian philosophy life appears as an intermediate condition that has to be overcome by virtue. Appropriate support is offered in symbols, almost keys, so that inhibiting forces can possibly be discharged through the depth of our understanding of them and the intensity of our approach.

The mandala, as a psychocosmogram, helps with its symbolism to open the doors on the way to "enlightenment". It unites the individual's soul with cosmic forces in its abstract, motionless geometrical scheme as a vital process of endless spatial and temporal expansion and turning around a "world centre" (axis mundi). Its appearance in reality varies as a representation of the mountain (the world mountain meru) and its copy set in stone: centrally planned buildings with a highest point ("mountain-top" with connecting point to the universe). Thus there are numerous mandala schemes in all buildings that mark the border zones between the worlds as cult areas. Abstract, three-dimensional transformations of the universe like the Buddhist stupa can be erected; this is a hemispherical structure on a round or square base, topped by a screen on a square base, with a concluding, emphasized point, or there is also the Hindu temple, individually shaped according to a specially directed faith or a region. Its tower (sikhara) remains common to all sub-species as a mountain symbol, frequently metamorphosed through multiple refraction of the original square ground plan to a circle, thus achieving the above-mentioned "squaring of the circle". This thought is continued in the expansion of the cultic precinct into the area of everyday life as a whole, the city. If it is ideally planned as a mandala then its resident exists on the threshold of the absolute almost automatically and chaos, the source of destructive forces, is confronted with the *ordered world soul*.

In its most common basic structure the graphic scheme of the mandala is arranged in five parts with four equal sides (the four points of the compass) over a diagonal or orthogonal axial cross and the centre *(axis mundi)*[132]. In its natural form it corresponds with India's profoundly symbolic lotus flower, and in many ways encodes the figure 5 in the ritual, named as an example here, of worshipping five gods and the five world elements: *earth, water, fire, air and sphere.*[133]

Division of the mandala square into 8 times 8 equals 64 grid fields (also 9 times 9 equals 81) now takes us back to the starting figure of the root 2 relation chain 5–7–10–14–20 (see figure 141): in a combination of "growing" diagonal squares and an 8 times 8 equals 64 grid division it is quickly seen to be *a diagram similar to the mandala we have described.* Here the initial value of 2 times 2 grid fields with its starting number 5 and its empty centre exists as world axis and centre of microcosm and macrocosm.

---

[131] G. Tucci, "Geheimnis des Mandala", p. 13 ff.
[132] Mandala with 64 squares.
[133] Klaus Fischer, Michael Jansen, Jan Pieper, "Architektur des indischen Subkontinents", Wissenschaftliche Buchgesellschaft, Darmstadt 1987, p. 72; also: Pieper/Gutschow, "Indien", p. 123.

Here, at the end of the process of analysis, this analogy supports the argument that the dimensions of the original square were not chosen at random to generate all parts of the whole complex, but that they exist as an image of a geometrical and proportional relation system whose origin is to be sought in Indian philosophy. The analogy, proved in terms of measurements and of geometry, between the structure of the entrance square and one basic scheme of the Indian mandala seems comprehensible, and so does the symbolic nature of the figure 5 in Indian thought. We must also add the figure 7, significant in Judaeo-Christian faith as a sign of the abundance, wholeness and perfection of the world, for the figures 5 and 7 produce the entrance square.

These last facts lead us to speculate that by inventing the entrance square Kahn did not just constitute a key to the understanding of an all-embracing inherent order, but also of the differing spiritual worlds of East and West, as an intended *integration of intuition and rationality.*

View of the entrance hall main portal from the steps

MODIFICATION OF THE DESIGN

The design for the Indian Institute of Management, as well as the groups of buildings that have been examined, also includes surrounding faculty houses, accommodation for married students, and for servants (see figure 91). Their position is obviously bound into the geometrical structure of the complex as a whole, and will not be considered here as they have been much extended over the years. A visit to the site today reveals something almost like a town, extended by Anant Raje and his wife in the architects' office they have set up there. They have built accommodation, a "Management Development Center" with rooms for instruction and hotel-like accommodation and an auditorium with foyer and conference rooms that was completed recently.

Deviation from Kahn's "integrated" design for the school complex lead to the distinction made between the intended version, on which our analysis is based, and the realized version. Both versions agree to a large extent in the programme for all the different elements. The area required is accommodated in four four-storey administration wings, a library with three storeys at the front and five at the back and six two-storey classrooms with a base storey for office and storage rooms. There are a total of eighteen student dormitory buildings, five with four and six with three storeys in the central area. Five dormitories on the lower peripheral area have a double storey on the ground floor and two other accommodation levels above them with separate sanitary areas. Three four-storey buildings on the upper right-hand periphery have sanitary areas included in the body of the building.

Fig.144 and 145

The most important deviation from the original version is that the axially placed kitchen and dining area is missing. It was intended to form a border for an inner courtyard, but its two storeys would still have related the courtyard to the exterior space and emphasized the hierarchy of the building's composition with the library as "head" and the classroom and administration wings as "body" (see figure 95). The ensuing figure follows the axis of the courtyard precisely and increases the symmetry by doubling, consisting of a dining area facing the courtyard and a circular kitchen with its delivery area with two appendices. Dividing lines between the dining area and the neighbouring buildings that can be identified in figure 144 show the key levels, united here, of both ground floor zones in the kitchen and dining area

Fig. 144

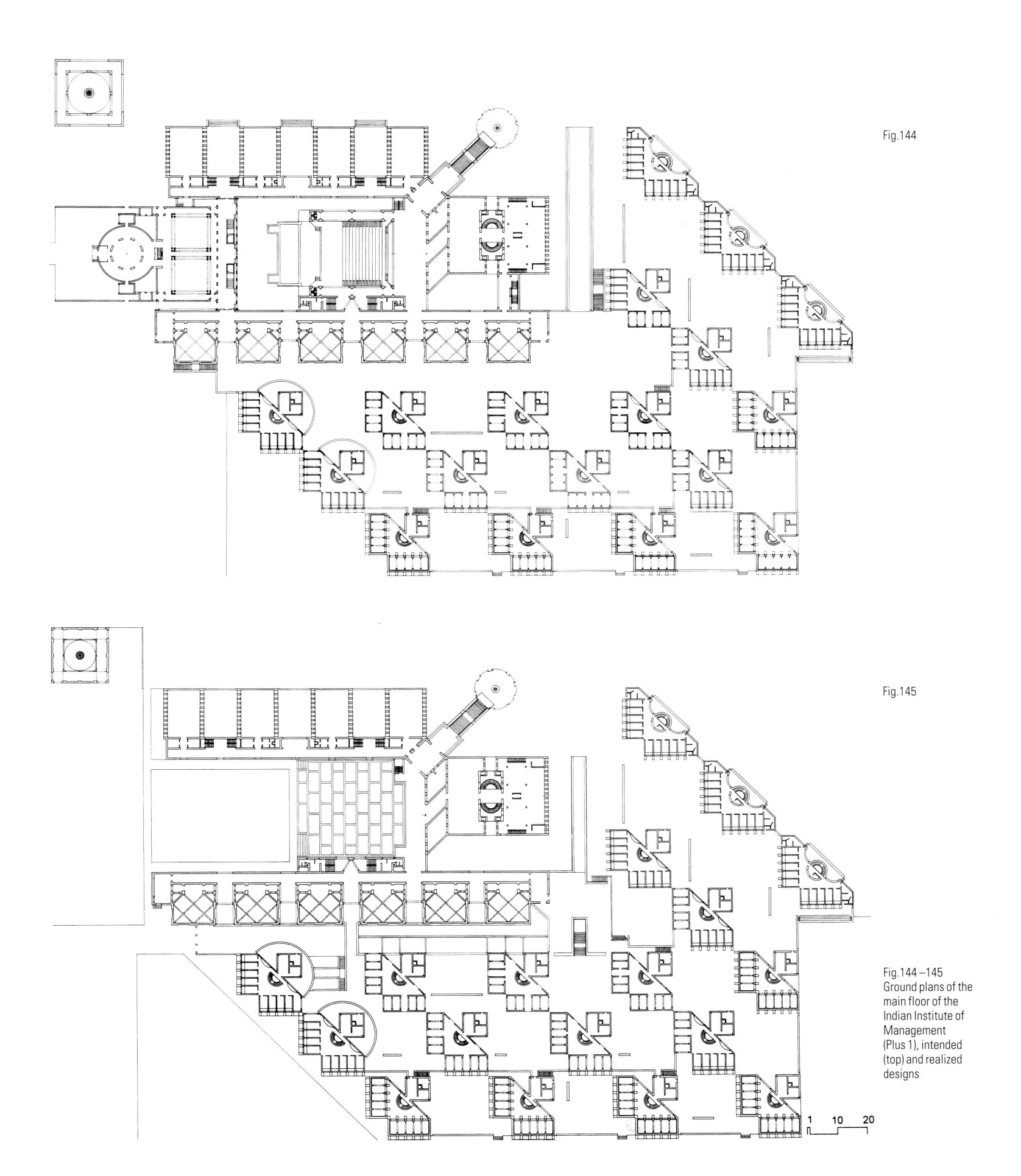

Fig. 145

Fig. 144–145
Ground plans of the main floor of the Indian Institute of Management (Plus 1), intended (top) and realized designs

181

(level 0) and the main access level for the school complex (level Plus 1). They mark the link-points of a circuit with a maximum of transparency providing access to the upper level with a promenade roof (see figure 95). The dining area, enclosed by two squares, indicates separation from the student body and staff. It shows its corners with hollow columns of the support structure above and combines with the kitchen through a service area that is also divided into two. Kahn justified its circular shape, with centralized preparation area, in functionalistic terms as a "ventilator".[134] Along with two symmetrically appended storage rooms, the contrasting but closely linked geometry of circle and square creates intermediate areas that form distancing courts on the basis of the site's slight slope to the west, their slight differences in level involving steps and narrow entrances; they are in direct contact with the delivery area in the west.

The theatre also relates axially to the dining area and the classroom figure with steps isolating themselves in front of it. It has steps for seating and a stage at the centre of the whole school complex, joins on to the open "foyer" area between library and entrance hall and is framed by two narrow buildings that are to be seen as side foyers, with steps for access to the courtyard. Their height is needed as a support structure for a flexible baldacchino spanning the theatre. A pool between the dining area and the theatre links directly with the stage and is set on the edge of a garden with trees as a natural element. A complete "set of furniture" made up of a variety of sub-sections of the complex relating to each other was intended for the courtyard area, as a means of linking the two facing figures of library and dining area (see figure 95).

The diversity of this court explains the façades, modest and sober both in concept and in realization, in the two surrounding circulation areas: both the apertures for access to the classrooms, structured hierarchically appropriately to their use and the somewhat narrow views through into the administration corridor relate to the rhythm of their additively appended building volumes. They produce a calm backdrop, framing the scene on both sides, for a mobile foreground that was not in fact completed later.

Thus in built reality the school complex, without Kahn's intended courtyard arrangement with its important concluding kitchen-dining building structure remains amputated as a torso (see figure 145), and deprived of its finely tuned gradation from the massive head section – the library with its equipment towers – down to the squat kitchen building. Kahn tried without success to shift the kitchen out of the ensemble's context to avoid problems for the administration wing caused by cooking smells.[135] Both a circular chain of buildings, concentrically oriented, that determined the concept from the outset and the all-round access associated with this remained unbuilt. This led to a stiff juxtaposition of monolithic autonomous structures with "mute" façades, behind which are corridors that come to dead ends. The façades, which were simply to be the background to an elaborate staging, thus lose their impact to a considerable extent.

After the border element of the courtyard had been removed, it also lost its "furniture", for financial reasons: garden, pool and the theatre with baldacchino structure were not built. But the courtyard does acquire a new quality of complete emptiness, and the difference in its level is marked by a stone platform ending in the centre in contrast with the green lawns running out of the area. In cross-section the courtyard has three steps: first the Plus 1 level as an "access road" in the library forecourt and then a lightly raised platform on the 0 level mentioned in the analysis (called "Louis Kahn Plaza"). It is reminiscent of the shape of the theatre with, stone slabs laid according to a pattern designed by Kahn on his last visit to the site,[136] and has a diagonal relation based on different step widths. Finally there is an unbuilt open space in the second half of the courtyard on the level of the terrain running off flat to the west, showing the state of the school complex at the time of writing, its final one.

On the occasion of the above-mentioned last visit Kahn proposed that a closed theatre building ("violin") should replace the kitchen and dining area, to rescue the original concept. The open area adjacent to the platform was available for this.[137] But no plans were drawn, so the status quo seemed sealed when Kahn died shortly afterwards.

The impressive emptiness of the courtyard, combined with the bleakness of the excessively large brick walls, cubes with prism-sharp edges and unglazed openings with profoundly black shadows all tend to lay weight on Kahn's intention to de-

---

[134] John W. Cook and Heinrich Klotz, "Architektur im Widerspruch", Verlag für Architektur Artemis, Zurich 1974, p. 233; also: Wurman, "What will be ...", p. 199.
[135] The idea of an external, round kitchen in the final proposed version was originally accepted by the client (also at the time of the Klotz/Cook interview), but later ultimately rejected for the reasons mentioned above.
[136] The paving stones as laid and the steps on either side were surveyed by the author on the site in March 1990. Kahn first made sketches for this in Ahmedabad on 15 March 1974 when shifting the kitchen and dining area. See Ronner/Jhaveri, p. 232, sketch called "IIM 147".
[137] Ibid.

Symmetrical façade figures on the courtyard side in the classroom wing

The incompletely realized courtyard area with stone platform and lawn running out of it

The changed distance between the administration wing and the edge of the water tower

Kahn's longing for an archaic architectural language

velop archaic architecture almost detached from the designer's own times, representing only itself. The opening on one side of its centre now acquires new significance: no longer concentrated introversion, but axial extroversion including the exterior space, and in this new expression appealed to the spiritual mentality of its users.

In the administration wing, changes from the intended version are restricted to the omission of the exterior steps as access to the distancing courts, which are important in the system of figurative geometry. Another exterior staircase on the edge of the extreme left-hand classroom for access to the Plus 1 level of the dormitories is geometrically connected with the steps. Its existence was sacrificed to changes on this level, which also meant that the relation network of the innate, regulating geometry was partially removed. The water tower becomes isolated, by losing its significant original position as a peripheral figure intended to bind the outlines of the imaginary frame for the complex as a whole together; this happened as a result of the new requirements for the size and capacity of the tank, different openings and a new structural approach with three extra outer lines. As has already been mentioned, the Plus 1 level in the classroom area, created artificially with earth excavated for the lake, was not completed. This led to a moat-like dip as a division between the classrooms and the dormitories, with a bridge relating axially to the classroom figure, intended to be the central access point to both zones. The intended interweaving of living and teaching by means of a continuous level with permeable lounge areas between the classroom buildings thus turns into precisely the opposite. This change, a second serious impairment of the original concept leaves behind a banked foundation wall[138] and leads as a substitute for the Plus 1 access along the classroom area to a flight of steps parallel with the bridge with cultivated areas at the side to connect with the dining area, which has shifted to the west. Two semicircular walls of the first two south-western dormitories frame "notches" in the Plus 1 plateau of the dormitory building as light-wells for the students' lounge and sanitary facilities that are only to be found in the lower storey. The ramp axis is retained as the defining edge of a geometrical frame, but its changed outer lines, like the edges of the water tower, lose their relation within the system of figurative geometry. They degenerate into random products, which forcibly reduces the intended status of the ramp vis-à-vis the main access steps to the school building to second rank.

A lining element with steps between the classroom group and the library, parallel with the ramp and close to it, which would have provided sensibly shorter vertical access, is also omitted. Its function in principle as a link within the circular complex as a stretched *stressing element* for a "deviating" figure seems necessary, and indeed the built reality offers an incomplete, unsatisfactory condition that is totally lacking in tension.

Despite the removal of a considerable amount of earth in the area west of the dormitories the lake intended to surround them was never constructed. Kahn wanted to include a natural element in the composition, but it was also to separate the school buildings and the associated students' dormitories from the accommodation for faculty and domestic staff. In reality the lake is unsatisfactorily replaced by a lawn that needs constant watering.

---

[138] The outline of the existing wall can be identified in figure 145 on the outer periphery of the classrooms and ends on the left at the start of the originally intended steps. The depth and nature of the gradation were surveyed by the author in March 1990.

Kahn's Design Principles

Aspects of Kahn's design that are generally valid are often pragmatically described as a "reformulation of spatial understanding" and also imprecisely defined as "geometrical structuralism" or one-sidedly as a "controlled dramaturgy of light". But then poetic criteria like the archaization of architectural bodies or integration of a design into an all-embracing order remain imponderable interpretations, not presented in any further detail.

Here however we emphasize a rational approach that can be tested against existing evidence and tries to avoid speculative statements to the largest possible extent. The analytical rationality of this approach can be unambiguously related to the Vitruvian concept of *venustas* (the graceful, the beautiful, usually today *Gestaltung*, artistic creation, structure, design). Within this field three central aspects, beyond pragmatism and broadening the view of Kahn's work, are at the centre of a complex whole as a selected *essence*, starting by concretizing the above-mentioned concept of *order* and later completed by the newly defined principles of *contradiction* and *movement*.

ORDER

Vitruvius's classification of architecture into three main categories,[139] tossed off somewhat casually, has remained valid until today because it is such a succinct and precise definition. In this order, he identifies *firmitas* as strength (today: construction), *utilitas* as usefulness (today: function) and *venustas*, the Venus-like, as grace (today: artistic creation, design). Here the last concept, *venustas* will be important; its meaning is hard to state precisely – because it belongs to particular historical epochs and phases – and the notion is constantly reinterpreted.

Vitruvius himself related the concept to Greek antiquity and explained it imprecisely;[140] it was not defined until the mid 15th century, by Leon Battista Alberti, where the three terms approximate to our modern ideas of construction, function and artistic creation or design, although the usual wooden German translation, *Gestaltung*, causes difficulties in terms of the notion *Venus-like*.[141] The attempt to interpret grace or beauty leads to Plato's definitions,[142] who presents the beautiful in its perfection only in the idea of an eternally valid substance outside the human mind that cannot be concretized. He makes beauty in the world one of the "ideas", the constant and unchangeable *primal forms* or *primal principles* of things,[143] to which the human beings/artists can relate however transient they and their world may be.

"The beautiful as such is beautiful and for always"[144] defines the categoric concept of *venustas*, while the "immortal is the most beautiful of all that has come into being"[145] extends the idea by ascribing beauty to the eternal itself, in its quality of being eternal, in other words judges it qualitatively. The assertion that "the rightness of a matter, of a thing ... lies in that which was always there and will always be there"[146] equates the immortal with the right, and thus also grants beauty to that which is right. Here at the latest we begin to understand Kahn's statement, which relates directly to Plato, "what was has always been, what is has always been and what will be has always been".[147] It illustrates, against the background of Platonic thought, that the rightness of a thing is to be equated with its *essence* as immortal. This therefore clarifies Kahn's view of the special quality of the eternal.

The "was and will be as forms of time that have come into being"[148] is an image of the continuously moving world of the planets, the limited universe as perceived by man, whose elements are determined by numbers.[149] Numbers for their part form the basis for building up a world order[150] and identify the relativity of human existence and its products as results of creation processes that at best approach the right or the immortal. Numer-

---

[139] Vitruvius (also: Marcus Vitruvius Pollio or L. Vitruvius Mamurra, the complete name cannot be fully established), c. 84–10 BC, "De architectura libri decem". German translation by Dr. Curt Fensterbusch, Wissenschaftliche Buchgesellschaft, Darmstadt 1964, here 4th edition, 1987.
[140] Vitruvius does not directly define *venustas*, but in his second chapter, before dividing architecture into three main categories, he names eight general "basic aesthetic concepts of architecture" (p. 37–43 in the German edition), of which Georg Germann identifies three as fundamental: symmetria, eurythmia, décor. In: Georg Germann, "Einführung in die Geschichte der Architekturtheorie", Wissenschaftliche Buchgesellschaft, Darmstadt, 2nd edition 1987, pp. 18–23.
[141] Leon Battista Alberti (1404–1472), "De re aedificatoria". German translation by Max Theuer, books 2–3 "firmitas", books 4–5 "utilitas", books 6–9 "venustas"; Wissenschaftliche Buchgesellschaft, Darmstadt 1991, unchanged original edition of the 1st edition, Vienna 1912. Alberti thus takes over Vitruvius's categories and states them more precisely. See also: Hanno-Walter Kruft, "Geschichte der Architekturtheorie", Verlag C. H. Beck, Munich 1985, here 2nd edition 1986, pp. 46–52.
[142] Plato, quotation numbers according to the edition by Henricus Stephanus, Paris 1587. German translation by Friedrich Schleiermacher and Hieronymus Müller, here Rowohlt Verlag, Hamburg 1957/1988.
[143] Erwin Panofsky, "Idea, Ein Beitrag zur Begriffsgeschichte der älteren Kunsttheorie", Wissenschaftsverlag Spieß, Berlin 1924, here 6th edition 1989, pp. 1–6.
[144] Plato, Cratylus, quotation 439 d.
[145] Plato, Timaeus, quotation 29 a/b.
[146] Plato, Cratylus, quotation 397 c.
[147] Wurman, "What will be ...", appendix from: "The Notebooks and Drawings of Louis I. Kahn", R. S. Wurman and Eugene Feldman, Falcon Press, New York 1962.
[148] Plato, Timaeus, quotation 37 e.
[149] Plato, Timaeus, quotations 38 c–e and 39 a–d.
[150] Plato, Timaeus, quotation 40 a/b.

ical relations of the elements determining the form and movement of the planets and the universe lead to geometry which, like mathematics, encodes the whole world and is innate in man as a memory.[151] The statement "everyone always knows everything"[152] – i.e. knows the essence of all things inside the structure of the world – then shifts geometry, with its relative classifications, the proportions, into the realm of the eternally valid.

Erwin Panofsky feels that Plato determines the value of artistic creation by the measure of theoretical, and especially mathematical insight,[153] and defines Plato's philosophy as actually a "theory alien to art",[154] as the artist – tool and producer of what has always been (*idea*) – is denied any kind of originality and individuality as ideally expressed in the rule-bound art of ancient Egypt, which Plato found exemplary. Thus in Vitruvius as well the mathematical aspect of artistic creation and the expression of an all-embracing order is found in the concept of *ordinatio* as the measuring of a part of a building in terms of proportions. But it is also present in *symmetria*, as the harmony of a calculated part – modulus – with the building as whole,[155] although these two concepts cannot be directly classified as *venustas*.

For a thinker like St. Augustine in the Middle Ages the concept of *ordo* defined man's world picture as the fundamental order of the world and the cosmos. Ordo is built on the rationality of number and measurement as a starting-point for the explanation of everything irrational. But then Alberti defines beauty in a more differentiated fashion as an unambiguous component of *venustas*, which is precisely described in four of ten books. He places the number *(numerus)* first in his list of criteria, then mentions relation *(finitio)* – containing proportion, which was practically sacred for Alberti – and finally arrangement *(collocatio)*, an understanding of symmetry based on the mirroring quality found in natural forms.[156] Alberti subjects all concepts to a mathematical rationality committed to a natural world order, expressed in the concept of regularity *(concinnitas)*, and believes firmly in the "ideas" in the tradition of Plato's thinking.

Unlike Vitruvius and Alberti, Jacopo Barozzi, called Vignola (1507–1573) derived dimensions, in this case for determining the five column "orders", not from a pre-existent mathematics and proportion reflected in the structure of man, but in his publication about the *Rules* ("Regola delli cinque ordini di architettura", 1562) explained them by empirical observation of the buildings of Roman antiquity.[157] Vignola's rules for modular determination of proportions remained successful in teaching well into the 20th century and have ossified into dogma through oversimplification. Later statements by architects like Jean-Nicolas-Louis Durand in the late 18th century derive from Vignola.

Thus while the ideas theory anchored itself firmly in the theology-dominated awareness in the Middle Ages as the logic of purely divine thought with art as the expression of divine appearance,[158] in the 15th century a writer like Alberti moved their character away from theological fixation and metaphysics. It now exists as a direct component of the human, and particularly the artistic spirit and leads, as in the case of Michelangelo, to a "canonization" of the artist as the image of God.[159]

"Order is", Kahn's brief formula, expressed powerfully and with conviction in its succinct condensation, for a Platonic world picture poetically declares order to be pre-existent. It allows the artist to acquire his creative power from it, sees the introduction of order by intuition as "exercises" by these two qualities and draws a distinction between applied order in the creative work, even in nature, and beauty:

"In order is creative force"
"Mozart's compositions are designs, they are exercises of order-intuitive"
"Order does not imply Beauty, the same order created the dwarf and Adonis"[160]

Kahn's view of implementing this idea of order in realized architecture culminates in the figures of the Egyptian pyramid. Its quasi-functionless absoluteness is closest to the Platonic ideal of the idea in its role as the start of a creative process and as a form that keeps the process itself visible. It means an "intersection point" between the ideas theory and an individually shaped the-

---

[151] Plato, Menon, quotation 85 e.
[152] Plato, Euthydemos, quotation 296 d.
[153] Panofsky, "Idea", pp. 2–3.
[154] Ibid.
[155] Vitruv, "Ten books ...", 2nd chapter, p. 37; also: Germann, "Einführung ...", pp. 18/19.
[156] Alberti, "Ten books ... ", Book 6 *venustas*, p. 293; also: Kruft, "Geschichte ...", pp. 50–52.
[157] Germann, "Einführung ...", pp. 118–119; also: Kruft, "Geschichte ...", p. 88.
[158] St. Thomas Aquinas, "Of being and essence" (written c. 1252). German translation by Rudolf Allers, Wissenschaftliche Buchgesellschaft, Darmstadt 1953, here 1989; pp. 49–50. – "Accordingly spirits must consist of form and being and have their being from one of the first to be, which is only being. But this is the first cause, and that is God."
[159] Panofsky, "Idea", p. 64–72.
[160] "Order is", poetic essay by Kahn, first published in: Perspecta 3, The Yale Architectural Journal, Yale University, New Haven 1955, p. 59.

ory of order on the one hand and the rationality of the built form on the other.

"The pyramids try to say to you 'let me tell you how I was made'" says Kahn[161] and means their genesis, but particularly the order of their structure, geometry, which has become form and is comprehensible. Geometry, as a mathematical product with its world of numbers and proportion as a copy of eternal beauty symbolizes regularity achieved through its precisely formulated criteria.[162] In Kahn's idea of form the "pure" geometries of square and circle are the figures that stand at the beginning of his creative process. Geometry is the immediate expression of order, and as a product of the mind finds its equivalent to nature in its inherent structures of interdependent "growing" figurations and integrates *venustas* with the categories of *firmitas* and *utilitas*, almost to the point of fusion.

"Growth is a construction",[163] growth in the sense of structure and direct relation to the order of nature, informs the complex geometry of Kahn's whole work. Growth can be discerned in the detailed steps of analysis in the sequence of geometrical figurations that build up on each other – usually squares, but also proportional rectangles – thus determining ground plan dispositions for all parts of the design: working against the *loss of the middle*,[164] an eccentricity of beauty and division of the rationality of understanding and the intuition of feeling, a design by Kahn begins with the centred figure of the square as a symbol of the centre. This concentric quality is reminiscent of the ordering figure of the cosmogram, the mandala of Indian origin. The connection of geometry and growth can be understood directly in the endless extending chain of squares inscribed within each other and turned by 45 degrees. Firstly their dependences, as minors or majors of the ratio of 1 : 0.707 or 1 : 1.414 (root 2), constitute sub-figures of the whole complex. Then their geometrically generated rectangles in the same proportion or the proportion of the Golden Section in the ratio 1 : 0.618 or 1 : 1.618 result from an expansion of the rigid square centred on itself as a dynamic growth process. Linking together or fusing the parts of the design that remain independent in the formation of their outlines shows Kahn's intention to achieve almost organic growth.

The relations of the sub-figures to each other are finally built on central ordering concepts of the Ecole des Beaux-Arts, "distribution, disposition and composition",[165] and shed light on the way in which Kahn was affected by the maxims of his training.

Thus *order*, as an elaborate complex concept in Kahn's realized architecture, appears to be directly comprehensible in the rationality of geometry; it shows in its complexity as a system and tries to fulfil Alberti's three criteria of beauty (*numerus – finitio – collocatio*): *numerus* is preferred as a rational number by Alberti; here it is the starting-point of the genesis and acquires symbolic character. On the one hand it embodies the possible cipher for the elements earth, water, fire, air and sphere in the number 5, and on the other hand the Platonic 7, the number of the universe. *Finitio* contains proportion as an important component, which determines architecture as a whole in number and figure.

Collocatio is realized in the concept of order and its symmetry in all sub-figures and the way in which they are bound into the complex as a whole.

Both the parts and the whole, in their implementation as buildings, find the equivalent to order in the ground plan in the abstract expression of cubes, usually prism-like blocks, and in their symmetrical façade figures as images of archaic primal bodies.

CONTRADICTION

The innate order of Kahn's architecture is faced with a play of forces that does not lead to "disorder", but creates a system of inner duality that makes it possible to avoid the paralysis and monotony of geometrical structures. However, when using simple figures in the ground plan and elevation, like grids, but also proportionately determined rectangular figures or "frames", there is certainly a danger that the work will become mechanical or schematic. This can be resisted by emphasizing of architectural complexity by using the aggressive principle of contradiction.

---

[161] Wurman, "What will be ...", p. 1; Kahn's statements "On order", from: Perspecta 3, The Yale Architectural Journal, Yale University, New Haven 1955.
[162] Rudolf Wittkower, "Architectual Principles in the Age of Humanism"; German edition, Beck-Verlag, Munich 1962, pp. 92–95; Wittkower describes "the creation of dimensional proportions by Alberti", which later, related by Francesco di Giorgio Martini to the Pythagorean-Platonic "harmoniy of the universe" (Timaeus), were stated more precisely in the "sacred" seven-number row 1–2–3–4–8–9–27 (pp. 83–87). See also: Anne G. Tyng, "Louis I. Kahn's 'Order' in the Creative Process", p. 277 in Latour, "Louis I. Kahn, I' nomo, il maestro", Rome 1986.
[163] From: "Order is".
[164] Hans Sedlmayr, "Verlust der Mitte", Otto Müller Verlag, Salzburg 1948, here 8th edition 1965, written 1943–45.
[165] Arthur Drexler (ed.), "The Architecture of the Ecole des Beaux-Arts", with essays by Richard Chafee, Arthur Drexler, Neil Levine and David van Zanten, The Museum of Modern Art, New York 1977, pp. 112–114.

Contradiction is an element of Mannerism, which is explained by Panofsky among others as resistance to the rigid, particularly mathematical rules of the Renaissance.[166] The all-embracing drive towards harmony based on belief in the Pythagorean-Platonic number is now subject to alienation, indeed a distortion or buckling[167] of the design principles. Further reshaping of the Platonic ideas theory is brought about by the detachment from mathematical ideas, which sets the heroic artistic spirit of the Renaissance free of ties, and then leads in a further stage to return to the metaphysics of Plato and the Middle Ages. Under Mannerism, an artist's free creative work, condensing in the motif of the *figura serpentina*,[168] shifts away from his own, but divinely inspired, powers *(disegno interno)*[169] but into the rationality of an external order that binds the free forces together. Art is declared to be a rationally organizing cosmos,[170] and in this tension-laden duality shows parallels with Kahn's architecture. Just as the orthodox metaphysics of light of Mannerism is mirrored in Kahn's work as the "reflection of God",[171] distortions, shifts and even buckling can be found within a framing ordering structure.

Kahn's stay in Rome in 1950/51 and his subsequent examination of the ideas of Robert Venturi, who was later to be his assistant and worked in his office in the following year,[172] brought Kahn close to Giovanni Battista Piranesi's (1720–1778) architectural fantasies. His visions[173] are complex structures made up of existing, preconsidered elements that coalesce into innovative units in the form of extreme combinations of contradictions. Mannerism in the style of Piranesi, not designed for realization, led in 1762 to the completion of the "Campo Marzio dell' Antica Roma", an invented collage of bulkily opposed, symmetrically autonomous sub-figures of the ancient Campus Martius in Rome, and remained a rich storehouse for Kahn's designs.

Venturi's manifesto "Complexity and Contradiction in Architecture", written in 1962 and published four years later, resisted the "Mies doctrine"[174] that had persisted into the sixties. It was an uninhibited plea for contradiction as something that was enriching and complex in architecture, presented by Venturi with views of examples from the present day right back to ancient times. Presumably Venturi's commitment to presenting contradictory architecture as a qualitative aspect of complexity remained important and not without influence on Kahn's subsequent work;

Kahn had prepared for such an approach in the Trenton Bathhouse, but did not express it explicitly.[175] Venturi draws attention back to buildings by Frank Furness (1839–1912) in Philadelphia, many of which have not escaped demolition. His banks for the Provident Life and Trust Company, the National Bank of the Republic or his Fine Arts Library on the University of Pennsylvania campus, in which Kahn taught[176] (restored by Venturi from 1988 to 1992) all show eclecticism using ironic formal quotations of opposing elements and a proportional canon that stands classical rules on their head, all exaggerated to the point of being grotesque.

Combinations of this kind stimulated Venturi, who soon moved away from Kahn, who did not accept his view of contradiction in architecture as something that should affect his realized work.[177] In his book Venturi divides contradiction into the categories ambiguity, contradiction, contradiction juxtaposed, the inside and the outside, relation to the whole and double function. In order to illustrate his concept of *ambiguity*, Venturi quotes the Bauhaus painter Joseph Albers, who influenced Kahn,[178] with the words that "the discrepancy between physical fact and psychic effect" is a contradiction that becomes "the origin of art".[179]

The difference between reality and perception and the ambiguity that could possibly result from this lead in Kahn's architecture to the question of whether the formulated Platonic claim of a pre-existent, eternally valid world of order is con-

---

[166] Panofsky, "Idea", pp. 39–40.
[167] Panofsky, "Idea" p. 41.
[168] Panofsky, "Idea", pp. 42–43.
[169] Panofsky, "Idea", pp. 47–49.
[170] Panofsky, "Idea", p. 43.
[171] Cesare Ripa, "Iconologia", Rome 1603; mentioned in: Panofsky, "Idea", p. 111.
[172] These details come from the author's interview with Robert Venturi in September 1988 in Philadelphia.
[173] Hans Volkmann, "Giovanni Battista Piranesi, Architekt und Graphiker", Bruno Hessling Verlag, Berlin 1965. Also: John Wilton-Ely, "The Mind and Art of Giovanni Battista Piranesi", London 1978.
[174] Robert Venturi, "Complexity and Contradiction in Architecture", Museum of Modern Art, New York 1966.
[175] When asked about this aspect of the Kahn-Venturi relationship Venturi replied that here perhaps "the master learned from the pupil".
[176] James F. O'Gorman, "The Architecture of Frank Furness", Philadelphia Museum of Art, Philadelphia 1973. The base floor of the Fine Arts Library, which is now a working library again, houses the "Louis I. Kahn Collection".
[177] Interviews by the author with Mrs. Esther Kahn and Dr. Ann Griswold Tyng in September 1988 in Philadelphia with statements about Kahn's critical attitiude to Venturi's architecture, which he never voiced in public.
[178] Joseph Albers (1888–1976), former teacher at the Dessau Bauhaus, came to Yale University in New Haven in 1950 and met Kahn there. His series of "Square" paintings impressed Kahn, as did his way of writing poems, which has formal similarities with Kahn's poetic descriptions. Mentioned in: Brownlee/De Long, "In the Realm of Architecture", pp. 45–46.
[179] Venturi, "Complexity and Contradiction", p. 20.

veyed directly in built architecture. It remains to be seen whether Kahn's interpretation is dependent on the observer's individually developed ability to perceive or based on pre-existent patterns that are general to human perception. The image of order could be seen either as appearing in archaic forms beyond history or in abstract design of a particular period only. It is also not clear whether the *form* (idea) as a figure at the beginning of a creative process is retained in the final shape, as described by James F. Ackerman in the context of Michelangelo,[180] or whether – following Alberti's *varietas* requirement – the starting figure of the cube on a square ground plan, simple here, represents only itself, because the three-dimensional process distorts it entirely.

Ambiguity in built architecture appears in the Fisher House, for example, whose form shows up as two dominant cubes in the ground plan. However, in the exterior view the volumes flow into each other and form a continuous, uniform mass, given that they are the same height and made of the same material. In the student dormitories for the Indian Institute of Management (see figures 144/145) the geometrical "notches" in the ground plan figures are either cut out of a preconceived enclosing square or the whole figure is presented as a number of individual forms like triangle, rectangle and square. The genesis of this dormitory figure can be analysed precisely in geometrical terms, as we have seen, but remains ambiguous as a final figure.

Another concept described by Venturi is *contradiction*,[181] meaning a deliberately introduced "both-and"-paradox. Usually it expresses contrasting form and function, but also ambivalence related exclusively to the Vitruvian category of *venustas*. A contrast of this kind can be seen in the Exeter Library, where the building's double axial symmetry requires an extraordinary and clearly identifiable entrance, which, however, it is hidden behind a low arcade. Something similar can also be sensed in the main entrance to the Indian Institute of Management in the structure of a staircase axis, which was disturbed from the beginning by a tree placed almost in the centre, and then creates an unexpected entrance gesture by reaching dramatically outwards. The point of reference is neither an interior goal nor a climax in terms of the building, but simply nothing but the open courtyard. Every sub-figure of the complex as a whole in the Unitarian Church and the Indian Institute has its own symmetrical axis, which is toned down in terms of the overall effect by shifting and thus remains significant only for the individual figure. The building is isolated by the concentric symmetry, but the combination and fusion of the parts works against separation.

Contradiction juxtaposed[182] defines approaches and stark juxtapositions of contrasting elements. This is clearly present in the disposition of the central group of buildings in the National Capital in Dhaka, whose sharp individual outlines suggest that each part is autonomous, but all the sections, clad in a homogeneous "dress" and given the same height, form a unit. In the courtyard of the original Indian Institute project (see figures 145 and 95) the dominant library at the end and the low dining area create an exciting juxtaposition, mediated by the flanking side volumes. The juxtaposition of massive building volumes and transparent thinness of skin also appears as a contrasting pair in both designs, with a homogeneous block-like quality contrasting with wide openings revealing the interior of the buildings.

The aspect of *the inside and the outside*[183] arises in the form of a question about the agreement or contradiction between the outer line of a building and its interior, which often involves ambiguity. The exterior of the Kimbell Art Museum has extensive porticoes that mediate between the interior and the exterior and are part of both. But in the Assembly Building in Dhaka the transitional zones with their dramatic façades can be allocated to neither, they are independent spaces, relating only to light and shadow and thus to themselves. The forecourt of the library in the Indian Institute, with its diagonal quality and perforations seems independent and detached and would "like" to be part of the exterior, but its outline links it completely with the library building. Relation to the whole, what Venturi calls "the obligation toward the difficult whole",[184] defines the many-faceted co-operation of part and whole and their interaction and states that the part itself can be a whole or a fraction of a higher entity. Thus in the Kimbell Museum the additive element plays a major part as an *entity*, and appears distinctly both in the exterior and the interior. Here the part fits into the whole as an entity and loses its individuality. In the central Assembly Building in Dhaka as well the individual sections stand out distinctly in their sharp outlines, and "would like" to remain autonomous, but tie themselves into the overall figure – they are of the same height,

---

[180] James S. Ackerman, "The Architecture of Michelangelo", A. Zwemmer Ltd., London 1961, mentioned in: Venturi, "Complexity and Contradiction", p. 44.
[181] Venturi, "Complexity and Contradiction", pp. 23–32.
[182] Venturi, "Complexity and Contradiction", pp. 56–69.
[183] Venturi, "Complexity and Contradiction", pp. 70–87.
[184] Venturi, "Complexity and Contradiction", pp. 88–105.

and are built of the same materials –, blurring into a higher whole. The body of the staircase in the classroom area of the Indian Institute is almost isolated; it relates to itself and the adjacent classroom block, but then disturbs the encircling flatness and dimensions of the courtyard walls and with its very small cubature refers to the break in scale in the outer sub-figures.

The notion of *double function* also acquires special significance. Venturi relates it to "particulars of use and structure", in contrast with the above-mentioned both-and, which is much more concerned to demarcate the relation of a part to the whole.[185] Then again, Sedlmayr and Wittkower describe double function differently. According to Wittkower, one and the same architectural member relates firstly to one thing and then to another, creating a lack of clear perception. The result is a feeling of instability in contrast with clear stability, which has already been mentioned in terms of the doubly occupied hollow columns of the Trenton Bathhouse and the unequal and yet symmetrical rear ventilation shafts of the Richards Laboratories. Something similar can be seen in the Indian Institute in the combination of the administrative area with its courtyards, equal in width and emphasized by prominent steps, with each one acquiring a double relation. In the case of the classroom figures the vertically oscillating connecting wall ties two adjacent buildings together, so that here every second one has a "double" function. This double interlinking can be found in the dormitories and their accommodation façades, which are divided into two; seen on the diagonal, symmetrical in themselves, they allot one half both to their own volume and also to the adjacent volume for new centring and pair formation.

Inversion, as represented by Wittkower presents a variant of double function,[186] meaning similar or dissimilar architectural members placed one on top of the other in a contradictory fashion; they appear separate, but are tied together by the observer's eye, leaping back and forth,[187] something that is implicit in the courtyard façade figures in the administration wing of the Indian Institute of Management. Here the rectangular openings merge with the segmental arches above them to form a visual entity, although they in fact belong to the next storey with the corresponding opening. No unambiguous spatial boundary can be established in the wall layers of the classroom façades: they cannot be definitely defined as broad piers applied to the wall behind them because it is possible, as their bases fuse with the wall, that they form the actual exterior continuum of the wall with closed openings in between. Wittkower calls this ambiguity *permutation*.[188]

"Growing" façade openings in the administration corridor section

[185] Venturi, "Complexity and Contradiction", pp. 34–40.
[186] Rudolf Wittkower, "Das Problem der Bewegung innerhalb der manieristischen Architektur", Kunsthistorisches Institut Florenz (von Thies), p. 626.
[187] Ibid.
[188] Wittkower, "Das Problem der Bewegung ...", p. 628.

MOVEMENT

Rigidity and movement start to relate as duality and a united pair of forces, but also as rival poles. Conflicting and yet connected, the two aspects form a unity in Kahn's architecture and represent – like the general principle of life – the *organic quality* of a system, which can be defined as *persisting dynamics* and discernible tensions. Movement is the result of an order that has been built up and then questioned. No process of movement in architecture can come into being without order and contradictions as shifts, buckling, contrasts of curves and right-angles but also double function.

Wittkower's "*Bewegungsmoment*" (element of movement) as a product of the above-mentioned double function, inversion and permutation, as well as Sedlmayr's double structure, mean suggestive movement of the architectural members as an unstable process that makes viewers insecure: their eyes wander indecisively to and fro and are not in a position to grasp the complexity of the process all at once. The aim here should be a "*pendelnde Gefühlslage*" (swinging emotional state)[189] caused by blurring, indeed almost dissolving clear and unambiguous structures that are also geometrically rigid, leading to an intensified examination of the architecture; this can be seen as an essential characteristic of Mannerist design. The *figura serpentina* means a dramatic expression of the detachment from mathematical and mechanical rigidity in late Renaissance sculpture, and its twisting spirals symbolize a violent breakaway from pre-stabilized thinking in terms of harmony. This lives on as a memory in the subtle processes of distortion within Kahn's architecture, but without moving too far away from the primal forms of Plato and Pythagoras.

The concept of the *marche*,[190] coined in 1828 at the Ecole des Beaux-Arts, means progress in a particular direction in relation to an order. It also means the sequence followed by the composition of the spatial connections, of the parts, also of light and shade on the "tableau" of the drawing, and can be counted as an aspect of movement in Kahn's disposition of parts.

The first directly perceptible movements within Kahn's fixed architectural vocabulary can be seen in the ground plans of the Adler and De Vore houses (see figures 10 and 11); their shifted – moving – and structural, space-creating entities indicate an original grid, and statics and dynamics appear as a pair of forces. Double-functioning, in the form of alternate relations of individual architectural members can be recognized for the first time in the Trenton Bathhouse (see figures 8 and 9), rotating movement around a centre in the Richards Laboratories (see figure 14); movement of the sub-figures within a concentrated whole can be seen when walking or driving round the Assembly Building in Dhaka, which was designed to be effective from a distance. The Indian Institute shows directly intelligible movement of architectural members: the distortion of the library forecourt strikingly thrusts the library building off the symmetry of the courtyard axis and produces twists and tensions, as it is firmly anchored to the neighbouring buildings. The rigid, almost solitaire-like sub-figures of the complex as a whole, symmetrical in themselves, are set in motion by reciprocal interlinking, so that shifted symmetrical axes create *stable unrest* or *persisting dynamics*. Oscillating connecting walls between the classrooms convey an impression of instability. We observe Kahn's continual concern to combine symmetry of the individual figure with asymmetry within the overall disposition.

The dynamic interplay of forces seems to be "tamed" particularly by the system of frames, proportional rectangular figures that are created and fix the position and dimension of the parts. These framing elements, intelligible in most outlines and determining the overall form of the designs are set in motion themselves by oscillating vertically, but also to and fro horizontally, defining stretching and blurring border zones by this vibration.

Mechanical movements can be identified in a number of cases: addition and accumulation of buildings of the same kind produce tension through linking and framing, and refractions, shifts and breaks in level are disturbing as they deviate from a structuring principle based on a grid. Different parts of the buildings burst and split as well as being stretched and shifted as they are linked together.

Movement, created first by double function, unstable and undirected, and then as a physical and mechanical process, directed and undirected, can be illustrated particularly clearly by the plan analysis method, and represents a central aspect of Kahn's architecture. Its origin can be defined beyond the phase of Mannerism by the concept of *beauty of movement*,[191] the harmony of parts and their reaction to each other, which changes, distorts and moves the parts themselves, Vitruvius's *eurythmia*.

---

[189] Wittkower, "Das Problem der Bewegung ...", p. 629.
[190] Drexler, "Ecole des Beaux-Arts", p. 163.
[191] Germann, "Einführung ...", p. 21, on the Vitriuvian concept of "eurythmia".

„Order is"

The investigations described in this book focus on a method for researching rational principles in architectural design. They reveal an immanent structure of figurative geometry, which is not directly open to perception, but is always present as a hidden image of the evident ground plan outlines of existing buildings. The rationality of the designs is expressed in the geometry that obviously determines all their sub-figures. The complexity of their structure constitutes the way in which architecture is built up; it is the image of an all-embracing idea of order that can be broken down in to multiply linked, proportionately bound figures representing areas or frames. Geometry and proportion, here as factors that are entirely dependent on each other, and fused with the framing figurative geometry. They part of eternally valid principles for form-finding, with countless possibilities for variation. They are expressed in the two classical ratio values root 2 and the Golden Section, which are used and combined almost systematically by Kahn, and constantly affirm that the original figure is a square. The dependent chain of root 2 squares appears as a complete synthesis of geometry and proportion, whose larger or smaller (major or minor) value also forms the figure of the square geometrically, and then finds itself doubled or halved in the next value but one as a potentially rational number. Admittedly it is not possible to answer the question here of whether Kahn allots a definite "function" to a particular proportion within a ground plan figure, in other words whether each proportional figure is linked with a statement. The duality or polarity used in Kahn's preferred division ratios of the Golden Section and root 2 appears as a game reserved for the most important figures within the ground plan structure, especially in the quasi-organic growth process that has been described.

In the detailed analysis of the Indian Institute of Management project, the proportional figures concentrate on the extraordinary diagonal position of the entrance square as a starting cell and generator of all subsequent figures. Proportionally related geometrical figures (frames) link together and, combined with grid structures, lead to overlapping. At the same time, similar figures that deviate from each other are produced, with subtle refractions and intentional dynamics: consistently relating parts of any overall figure present *processes of movement* by shifting, stretching and bursting, or even by rotating, and demonstrate, particularly in the Unitarian Church, the Indian Institute and the Dhaka parliament a "trial of strength" by neighbouring bodies with prismatically simplified outlines. The antagonism that arises between the *rigidity* inherent in an archaic geometrical figure and dynamic processes of *distortion* is an exemplary demonstration here of an aspect of Kahn's virtuosity and individuality of approach in handling complex, figurative geometry as an image of an order that is comprehensively understood. The analysis of the ground plans can demonstrate Kahn's constant concern to create order within a whole that includes every single part of the design. The process of architecture includes all details, right down to the brick as a module; this means that the microcosm is penetrated, and suggests an analogy with an organic growth process, because it is dependent and hierarchically structured, and starts with the "nucleus". On the other hand, the idea of order acquires a macrocosmic dimension: in the realized, dependent system of complex geometry, a *cosmic legality* is encoded as an image of universal connections. Kahn's buildings in Asia show an attempt to combine "Eastern man" and "Western man"[192] by fitting Eastern and Western thought and culture together. This process of fusion and neutralization is intended as an approach to a *primal image* of architecture,[193] independent of regional influences. This intention is indicated by the inclusion of classical "patterns", such as archaic models and individual, spiritual aspects. Kahn is convinced that there is a historical wealth of architecture, with form-finding principles, eternally valid laws that overcome time and space, and that it is necessary to transform these so that they can be applied to present-day condi-

---

[192] "Ostmensch" (Eastern man) and "Westmensch" (Western man) come from the conceptual world of the artist Joseph Beuys; his intention was to perusade people to abolish these categories, a process that peaked in the notion of "Eurasia".

[193] Kahn's idea of a starting point for all design that would unite everything can be found in his statement that he wanted to read "Volume Zero", the book that had not yet been written, which is to be interpreted as an overwhelming desire to find archaic, eternally valid structures: "... The first chapter I read very thoroughly, and I turn to the first chapter every time I open the book, reading it thoroughly and finding, since I have so poor a memory, new things in it all the time. I know what it is: it is my desire to sense Volume Zero. Volume Minus One. A search for the sense of beginning, because I know ... that the beginning ... is an eternal confirmation. I say eternal because ... eternal deals with the nature of man". Kahn quotation from: Patricia Mc Laughlin, "How' m I Doing, Corbusier?", The Pennsylvania Gazette, Volume 71, no. 3, Dec. 1972, p. 20. Also: Alexandra Tyng, "Beginnings", p. 132. Also in: Joseph A. Burton, "The Architectural Hieroglyphics of Louis I. Kahn," p. 5 and pp. 63–65.
Burton interprets "Volume Zero" as the "primal ground of the psyche, but also relates the idea to the books "On Growth and Form" and "Book of Creation" which Kahn owned (both no longer available), and speaks of Kahn's romantic desire to thrust down into the beginnings of a "world soul".

tions.[194] Cultures on all continents developed similar principles for finding architectural form, without ever communicating with each other. Thus we can assume a kind of *universal spirit* of architecture, which means that consistently comprehensive ideas of order have flowed into built reality as a component of knowledge stretching far back into the past (Indian or Chinese philosophy).

In his original version of the design for the Indian Institute of Management (see figure 144) Kahn was trying to create a "functioning" organism relating all its parts. It was also to be an interpreting, abstract image of natural systems, which can only be imagined in the built architecture (see figure 145), as important parts of the communicating whole are missing. Obviously his aim can be considerably impaired by even minor deviations. However, the fact that the design was realized very incompletely did not cast doubt on the concept, rich in variants but consistently pursued, it simply lead to partial reinterpretation and reformulation of the architectural statement within a reversible process.

Plan analysis leads primarily to intensive illumination of the rational architectural aspect within the genesis of the design. But it opens up insights that go far beyond this field, striding forward in the name of rational observation into the realms of symbolism and of intuitive, associative discovery of ideas and on to the world of philosophical and metaphysical views, revealing the designer's thought structures. Here again we have to preempt the possible misunderstanding that examination of rational aspects alone leads to high-quality results in the design process, and that the sole use of complex geometry means that architecture is a quasi-mathematical product. On the contrary, transformation into dimensional and geometrical figures follows intuitive processes that encircle the problem "irrationally" and represent basic requirements of design (see Kahn's sketch figures 76–80). Both approaches are mutually complementary and achieve their quality by a *synthesis* of intuition and rationality that depends on the personal ability of the individual. Thus the architectural product can never develop its own quality from one of the two aspects considered in isolation.

Kahn's ideas of order reflect Le Corbusier's thoughts about order related to geometry and proportion that are explained in detail in his 1948 publication "Modulor".[195] Le Corbusier's direct inclusion of architectural and historical models, which were evidence of his mediating position between Historicism and Modernism even in his early and significant essay "Vers une architecture"[196] in the twenties, was intensified by Kahn in a new way in the second half of the century. Kahn's perception of Le Corbusier's elaborate and also consciously contradictory architectural structure as a complex whole seems to have been extraordinarily influential. Its character is, as Kahn himself remarked,[197] informed by universally valid principles; it crops up once more in Kahn's work as a parallel and justifies his assertion that Le Corbusier was his actual teacher, alongside Cret.[198]

Kahn had already been intensively introduced to principles of order as requirements for original architectures while studying at the Ecole des Beaux-Arts under Cret, and by his early examination of Wright, whose pupils Neutra and Schindler reflect Wright's ideas of order in their designs, permeated as they are by geometry, module and proportion. Kahn's concern with Mies's claim that architecture is absolute and his perception of Le Corbusier's faith in the significance of the proportion of the Golden Section ("Here the gods are playing")[199] confirm and strengthen his own convictions. Starting with the additive, almost self-explanatory ground plan disposition of the 1947 Weiss House (see figure 4), the 1950 design for the Yale Gallery and especially its independent staircase cylinder, relating only to itself and placed on the symmetrical axis of the building (see figure 6), Kahn creates a new awareness of *autonomy of form* and the value of its category *venustas*. This was strengthened in 1954 in the Adler and De Vore houses with their additive square units (see figures 10 and 11). The logical climax of this intellectual approach is the epochal Trenton Bathhouse design in 1955 (see figures 8 and 9), which reduced to absurdity the meaningless concept of functionalism and became a turning-point of 20th century architecture as a "pure" *venustas* approach.

---

[194] Burton, "The Architectural Hieroglyphics of Louis I. Kahn", pp. 59–61.
Kahn's "cosmo-cultural" awareness shows, according to Burton, in his interest in countless ethnic forms of design, books in his possession on Hebrew and Babylonian alphabets, Egyptian, Mexican and Indian architecture and calligraphy, all of which he saw as based in a comprehensive, common primal language of eternal significance.
[195] Le Corbusier, "Modulor", Paris 1948.
[196] Le Corbusier, "Vers une architecture", Paris 1924.
[197] Wurman, "What will be ...", appendix of handwritten notes, including Kahn's remark: "Mies – Corbusier, who is prettier? Corbusiers work is eternal ..."
[198] Louis I. Kahn: "How' m I doing, Corbusier?" Interview with Patricia Mc Laughlin, in which this statement was made.
[199] Le Corbusier, "Modulor", German edition Stuttgart 1978, p. 238.

The functionalist ideas of an International Style as formulated by Hitchcock and Johnson, an architecture that relates to Greek antiquity and Gothic building from constructional points of view,[200] is effectively countered by Kahn:

1. Construction and exterior wall are not longer separated from each other as a matter of principle, but integrated.

2. The "free ground plan" or "flowing space" of architects like Wright or Mies van der Rohe is dropped in favour of fitting clearly distinct spatial outlines together.

3. Solidity and mass, giving an effect of stability and an earthbound quality, replace thin-skinned, transparent "containers" on stilts, with stone as a solid material creating a three-dimensional quality and weight in the exterior appearance and making the façade independent by "choreographing" light and shade.

4. Obvious clarity in the development of constructive structure and openings reduced to what is strictly necessary yield to an architecture that is not easy to understand at a glance, defined by contradictions and double relations, an architecture that makes the aspect of function as an ambiguous concept dependent on the primary design process.

5. Constructive systems are not necessarily illustrated in the body of the building, and the constructive member itself is not longer a prefabricated, minimized mass product but emerges from a higher design will as a form in its own right.

6. The intrinsic value of building elements is increased in individuality, and standardization and the imposition of norms are reserved for secondary elements that are usually not visible.

7. A building composition that is held in balance by symmetry and carefully placed asymmetry replaces "picturesque" and obsessive asymmetry; individual sections of the building are made completely symmetrical as individual unities.

8. Geometry and axiality create basic orders, but asymmetry and double relations, working as counter-forces, produce an oscillating sense of an unstable condition between rigidity and movement.

9. Material dualities and surface textures with their own legalities enhance the status of material as a form-determining medium and put an end to the neutrality of the surface and its dogmatic whiteness and allow colour variants that are inherent in the material to make their presence felt.

10. The building is no longer a standardized series product but a complex individual entity within a general order.

Brick wall inside a student's room in the Indian Institute of Management

---

[200] Hitchcock and Johnson, "The International Style, Architecture since 1922", The Museum of Modern Art, New York 1932, foreword.
[201] B. V. Doshi, "Le Corbusier – Acrobat of Architecture", undated essay, handed to the author in March 1990 in Ahmedabad to sum up his thoughts and experiences while working with Le Corbusier and Kahn.

Louis Kahn's architecture is driven by an urge to produce order, as intense as Le Corbusier's. Although the path and the result are different, it is described by Kahn's Indian colleague Doshi as a "universal intuition" that is inherent in both.[201] This force, perceived particularly by the Indians because of their spiritual background, helped to bring about the unique meeting of Kahn's and Le Corbusier's buildings in the Indian city of Ahmedabad.

When dealing with Kahn it remains difficult to reconcile his idiosyncratic combination of faith in the metaphysics of a Platonically shaped truth with his fund of historical architectural models and the conflict-ridden synthesis of autonomy and functionality of form and their implementation within the reality of complex geometry.

Considering the rational aspect of Kahn's architecture in this way leads to the essential insight that there is an all-embracing order in Kahn's work, and that it is an order which can be understood: *order is.*

Louis I. Kahn

Geometrical Principles
Notes to pp. 25 (note 20)
and 40 (note 34)

[20] The square irrational value **1 to root 2** (equals 1.414) defines the length of the side in relation to the diagonal of a square.
Two possibilities offered by the geometrical construction of the root 2 proportion are principally used in this book: firstly, the diagonal of the square described in the text, when added to the side, leads – similarly to the Golden Section – to a rectangular figure, secondly, when the diagonal of the square is shifted to the corner position of the external outline, this produces the next-largest "enclosing square". The irrational number values of the small and large line sections of the root 2 proportion are:
    1: 0.707 (minor) and 1 : 1.414 (major)
The principle of quadrature, which was described in antiquity by Pythagoras, Plato ("Menon") and Vitrivius, and was used in the 13th century by Villard de Honnecourt ("Die Skizzenbücher des Villard de Honnecourt", Hahnloser, 1935) and as "quadrature over position" in Gothic pinnacle architecture in particular (Roriczer, "puechlen der fialen gerechtikait", Little book of Pinnacle Correctness, Regensburg 1486), and it appears in the Renaissance in the work of Alberti and Serlio, Giorgio Martini and Peruzzi, also in Leonardo da Vinci and Dürer and is called "one of the finest ratios" by Palladio. The fascination of this proportional relationship derives partly from the simplicity of its geometrical construction using constantly growing, "pure" squares, but also in the combination of rationality and irrationality in its possible numerical values, as every second number in a sequence – as double the last but one – can seem rational. Here for example:
5–7.07–10–14.14–20 etc.
Above-mentioned information and bibliography in:
Rudolf Wittkower, "Grundlagen der Architektur im Zeitalter des Humanismus", and Paul v. Naredi-Rainer, "Architektur und Harmonie".

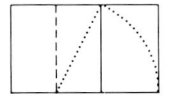

[34] The **"Golden Section"** was defined c. 1500 by Leonardo da Vinci as the "Sectio Aurea", and at the same time by the Italian theologian and mathematician Lucas de Burgo (1445–1514), also known as Paciolus, later called Luca Pacioli, in his writings as "La Divina Proportione" – presumed to have been taken from essays by his teacher Piero della Francesca –; it is also sometimes called "Divine Proportion" in English, and describes the irrational divisions of a line whose shorter part is in the same ratio to the longer one as that of the longer one to the whole; expressed as a formula:
$$a : b = b : (a+b)$$
expressed as a ratio of irrational numbers:
    1 : 0.618 or 1 : 1.618
The simple geometrical construction of the Golden Section, preferred in this work, relates to the existence, always presumed, of the square whose half diagonal, transferred by circular arc construction to the side of the square, shows the line and area ratio of square to rectangle as the proportions of the Golden Section.
Even at the beginning of the Egyptian high culture of the Old Empire in the Third Dynasty, about 2650 BC, we can see, in the first monumental structure in cut stone in the history of mankind, the "Step Mastaba", or step pyramid of King Djoser and his architect Imhotep in Sakkara an approximation of this construction in the ratio of diagonal ground plan length to height, and far more precisely in the ratio of breadth to height in the pyramid of Cheops in Giza in the subsequent period (detailed bibliography in: Siegfried Giedion, "Ewige Gegenwart", New York and Cologne 1965). The Golden Section was a division ratio known in Greek antiquity to Plato ("Timaeus") from Egypt, described by Euclid and Pythogoras, and in Rome by Vitruvius ("Ten Books on Architecture", preface to Book 9), citing Plato and Pythagoras. This was later demonstrated by the medieval mathematician Leonardo da Pisa, known as Filius Bonacci, in a sequence of numbers formed by taking the sum of the two previous ones ("Fibonacci series", also known as the "Lame series" after French mathematician Gabriel Lame: 1, 2, 3, 5, 8, 13, 21, 34, 55, 89, 144, 233 etc.); as the size of the numbers increases. division of two adjacent ones provides a constantly growing approximation to the abstract value of the Golden Section. In the early Italian Renaissance "La Divina Proportione" can be seen in the structure of the Duomo in Florence (Saalman, London 1980). It was promoted particularly in the treatises of Alberti and Serlio and is said to have been behind pictorial compositions by Michelangelo (Linnenkamp, Graz 1980).

The Golden Section was the object of comprehensive scientific examinations in the 19th century. Adolf Zeising in particular ("Schriften zur Proportionslehre", Leipzig 1854–1888) and Franz Xaver Pfeifer ("Der Goldene Schnitt", Wiesbaden 1885) looked, like Plato, for evidence in the whole world system, which led to philosophical and metaphysical interpretations, seeing it as the apparent key to the structure of the universe: it is asserted that this proportion appears in the composition and structure of all living creatures, in the plant world, in the ratio of land to water on the terrestrial globe and finally in the relative planet constellations of the earth-solar system and the distances between arms of cosmic spiral nebulae.
Gustav Theodor Fechner ("Vorschule der Ästhetik", Leipzig 1878) and Pfeifer recognized the Golden Section as the result of a world "law" called the "principle of uniform linking of the multiple" ("natura diverso gaudet"). Multiplicity and "perfect constancy" (as a particular feature and distinction of the Golden Section as a division ratio) and the "mediation" of these constant division ratios can be illustrated mathematically in the simple addition of extreme ratios 0 : 1 plus 1 : 1 gives 1 : 2; 1 : 1 plus 1 : 2 gives 2 : 3; 1 : 2 plus 2 : 3 gives 3 : 5 etc. (Fibonacci series) and leads to the assertion: "The Golden Section is the expression of complete constancy and mediation". From this a natural-philosophical hypothesis can be derived: if the laws of constancy and mediation are to achieve full expression in nature, they would have to be expressed in the Golden Section. Fechner speaks of "man's need of multiplicity in active or receptive involvement ...", here in the sense of diversity and complexity, and allocates the proportions of the Golden Section pride of place in the human soul.
Dr. Anne Griswold Tyng, in "The Energy of Abstraction in Architecture: a Theory of Creativity", dissertation at the University of Pennsylvania, Philadelphia 1975, as a long-standing colleague of Kahn, addresses structural and repetitive systems in architecture as parallels to natural, biological systems. She discusses – here mentioned as examples – the occurrence of the ratio 1 : 1.618 as a distance within the structure of red blood corpuscles and 1 : 0.618 as a reinforcement sequence within the brain in nerve synapses. Here she postulates that "Divine Proportion", the Golden Section, is the probable average value in the universe for repeatable procedures with two possible solutions.
Detailed bibliographies on the subject of proportions (including those mentioned above) in:
Hermann Graf, „Bibliographie zum Problem der Proportionen", Pfälzische Landesbibliothek, Speyer 1958 (only to 1957, completed by Wittkower, „Architectural Principles in the Age of Humanism").
Paul von Naredi-Rainer, „Architektur und Harmonie".
"Minor" and "major" were introduced by the Italian monk and mathematician Luca Pacioli c. 1500 in his work "La Divina Proportione" as a name for the two sections of a line relating to each other in the ratio of the Golden Section with short minor and long major sections (Naredi-Rainer, p. 196).

Bibliography

Alberti, Leon Battista, — "De re aedificatoria", German edition translated by Max Theuer, Darmstadt 1991, unchanged 2nd original edition of the 1st edition, Vienna 1912.

Aquinas, St. Thomas, — "De ente et essentia" (written approx. 1252), German edition translated by Rudolf Allers, Darmstadt 1953, here 1989.

Aubert, Hans Joachim, — "Nordindien", Cologne 1989.

Badawy, Alexander, — "Ancient Egyptian Architectural Design; A Study of the Harmonic System", Los Angeles 1965.

Bailey, James, — "Louis I. Kahn in India: an old order at a new scale", in: Architectural Forum, July/August 1966.

Banerji, Anupam, — "Learning from Bangladesh", in: The Canadian Architect, October 1980.

Banham, Reyner, — "The new brutalism", in: Architectural Review, December 1955.

Banham, Reyner, — "The buttery-hatch aesthetic", in: Architectural Review, March 1962.

Banham, Reyner, — "Theory and Design in the First Machine Age", XXX 1960.

Bauer, Hermann, — "Form, Struktur, Stil: Die formanalytischen und formgeschichtlichen Methoden", pp. 158–162, in: Kunstgeschichte, eine Einführung, Berlin 1985.

Benevolo, Leonardo, — "Geschichte der Architektur des 19. und 20. Jahrhunderts", Munich 1960, 3 volumes, here 5th edition, 1990.

Bissing, Friedrich W. von, — "Das Re-Heiligtum des Königs Ne-User-Re", Berlin 1905.

Blake, Peter, — "The mind of Louis Kahn", in: Architectural Forum, July 1972.

Boesiger, Willy and Girsberger, Hans (ed.), — "Le Corbusier, Oeuvres complètes 1910–65", Zurich 1967.

Boles, Doralice D., — "The legacy of Louis Kahn", in: Progressive Architecture, December 1984.

Bonta, Juan Pablo, — "Architecture and Its Interpretation", London 1979.

Bottero, Maria, — "Indian Journey: Le Corbusier and Louis Kahn in India", in: Zodiac 16, 1966.

Bottero, Maria, — "Organic and rational Morphology in the work of Louis Kahn", in: Zodiac 17, 1967.

Braudy, Susan, — "The Architectural Metaphysic of Louis Kahn", in: The New York Times Magazine, 15. November 1970.

Brooks Pfeifer, Bruce (ed.), — "Frank Lloyd Wright, Letters to Architects", letters to and from F. L. W., selected and with a commentary by Brooks Pfeiffer, Los Angeles 1984.

Brown, Jack Perry, — "Louis I. Kahn, A Bibliography", New York and London 1987.

Brownlee, David B. and De Long, David, — "Louis I. Kahn, In the Realm of Architecture", New York 1991.

Burton, Joseph Arnold, — "The Architectural Hieroglyphics of Louis I. Kahn, Architecture as Logos", Philadelphia 1983.

Burton, Joseph Arnold, — "Louis I. Kahn, personal library", The Louis I. Kahn Collection, Philadelphia, no date.

Chipiez, Charles and Perrot, Georges, — "Geschichte der Kunst im Altertum-Ägypten", Leipzig 1884.

Choisy, Auguste, — "Histoire de L' Architecture", Paris 1898.

Choisy, Auguste, — "L' Art de Bâtir chez les Egyptiens", Paris 1902.

Conrads, Ulrich, — "Programme und Manifeste zur Architektur des 20. Jahrhunderts", Braunschweig/Wiesbaden 1975/1986.

Cook, John W. and Klotz, Heinrich, — "Conversations with Architects", New York 1973.

Correa, Charles, — in: "Vistara, Die Architektur Indiens", Haus der Kulturen der Welt, Berlin 1991.

Curtis, William J. R., — "Authenticity, Abstraction and the Ancient Sense: Le Corbusier's and Louis Kahn's Ideas of Parliament", in: Perspecta 20, The Yale Architectural Journal, New Haven, New York 1983.

Curtis, William J. R., — "Balkrishna V. Doshi, an Architecture for India", Ahmedabad 1989.

De Long, David and Brownlee, David B., — "Louis I. Kahn, In the Realm of Architecture", New York 1991.

Devillers, Christian, — "L'Indian Institute of Management ad Ahmedabad 1962–1974 di Louis I. Kahn", in: Casabella 571, September 1990.

Doshi, Balkrishna Vithaldas, — in: "Architecture and Urbanism, Louis I. Kahn", essays by Louis I. Kahn, Vincent Scully, Stanford Anderson, Balkrishna V. Doshi, Fumihiko Maki, Peter Smithson and Uttam C. Jain; Tokyo 1975.

Doshi, Balkrishna Vithaldas, — "Le Corbusier – Acrobat of Architecture", documentation of experiences in dealings with Le Corbusier and Kahn, no date.

Drexler, Arthur (ed.), — "The Architecture of the Ecole des Beaux-Arts", with essays by Richard Chafee, Arthur Drexler, Neil Levine and David van Zanten, The Museum of Modern Art, New York 1977.

Dunnett, James, — "Sher-e-Banglanagar, The city of the tiger", in: The Architectural Review, December 1980.

Eames, Charles and Ray, — "Eames-Report", study of designers Charles and Ray Eames, Los Angeles, on the situation of the Indian Design Institute, Los Angeles 1957.

Edwards, I. E. S., — "The Pyramids of Egypt", New York 1952.

Fechner, Gustav Theodor, — "Vorschule der Ästhetik", Leipzig 1878.

Feldman, Gene and Wurman, Richard Saul, — "The Notebooks and Drawings of Louis I. Kahn", New York 1962.

Fischer, Klaus and Jansen, Michael and Piper, Jan, — "Architektur des indischen Subkontinents", Darmstadt 1987.

Foerster, Bernd, — "Only what matters, an architectural review", in: The Unitarian Universalist Register-Leader, Rochester 1964.

Frampton, Kenneth, — "Louis Kahn and the French Connection," in: Oppositions, no. 22, Sept. 1980.

Frankl, Paul, — "Die Entwicklungsphasen der neueren Baukunst", Leipzig 1914.

Friedman, Mildred (ed.), — "De Stijl: 1917–1931, Visions of Utopia", essays by Kenneth Frampton et. al.; Walker Art Center, Minneapolis, New York 1982.

Fusaro, Florindo, — "Il Parlamento e la nuova capitale a Dacca di Louis I. Kahn, 1962–1974", Rome 1985.

Gandhi, Mohandas Karamchand ("Mahatma"), — "My life is my message", the life and impact of M. K. Gandhi; Gandhi – Informationszentrum Berlin, Kassel 1988.

Germann, Georg, — "Einführung in die Geschichte der Architekturtheorie", 2nd edition, Darmstadt 1987.

Ghyka, Matila, — "Le Nombre d'or", Paris 1931.

Ghyka, Matila, — "The Geometry of Art and Life", New York 1977, first edition 1946.

Giedion, Siegfried, — "Space, Time and Architecture. The growth of a new tradition" (1941), Cambridge, Mass. and London 1967.

Giedion, Siegfried, — "Ewige Gegenwart, Der Beginn der Architektur", New York 1964.

Girsberger, Hans and Boesiger, Willy (ed.), — "Le Corbusier, Œuvres complètes 1910–65", Zurich 1967.

Giurgola, Romaldo, — "Louis I. Kahn", in: Perspecta 3, The Yale Architectural Journal, Yale University, New Haven 1955.

Giurgola, Romaldo, — "Louis I. Kahn, Œuvres 1963–1969", in: L' architecture d' aujourd' hui no. 142, 1969.

Giurgola, Romaldo, — "Louis I. Kahn", Zurich 1979.

Giurgola, Romaldo, — "Giurgola on Kahn", in: American Institute of Architects Journal, Washington, August 1982.

Graf, Douglas, — "Diagrams", in: Perspecta 22, The Yale Architectural Journal, Yale University, New Haven, New York 1986.

Graf, Hermann, — "Bibliographie zum Problem der Proportionen", Speyer 1958.

Guerin, Jules, — "Egypt and its Monuments", Illustrator, second edition, New York 1880.

Gutschow, Niels and Piper, Jan, — "Indien", Cologne 1986.

Hambidge, Jay, — "Practical Applications of Dynamic Symmetry", New Haven 1930.

Hahnloser, Hans Rudolf, — "Villard de Honnecourt", Graz 1972, first edition Vienna 1935.

Hennessy, Richard, — "Current monumental architecture", in: Architectural Forum, 1970.

Hitchcock, Henry-Russell and Johnson, Philip, — "The International Style: Architecture since 1922", The Museum of Modern Art, New York 1932.

Hitchcock, Henry-Russell, — "Architecture of the Nineteenth and Twentieth Century", The Pelican History of Art, Harmondsworth, Middlesex 1958.

Hitchcock, Henry-Russell, — "Notes of a traveller: Wright and Kahn", Zodiac 6, 1960.

Hichens, Robert Smythe, — "Egypt and its Monuments", second edition, New York 1880.

Hochstim, Jan, — "The Paintings and Sketches of Louis Kahn", New York 1991.

Huxtable, Ada Louise, — in: "The New York Times", 1970; quoted from: Susan Braudy, "The Architectural Metaphysic of Louis Kahn", in: "The New York Times Magazine", 15 November 1970.

James, Kathleen, — "Ahmedabad, Ruins, Cutouts and Courtyards: Louis I. Kahn's Indian Institute of Management", master's thesis at the University of Pennsylvania, Prof. Brownlee, 1988.

Jansen, Michael and Fischer, Klaus and Piper, Jan, — "Architektur des indischen Subkontinents", Darmstadt 1987.

Johnson, Philip and Hitchcock, Henry-Russell, — "The International Style: Architecture since 1922", The Museum of Modern Art, New York 1932.

Jung, Carl Gustav, — "Mandala, Bilder aus dem Unbewußten", Düsseldorf 1977.

Kahn, Louis I., — "Monumentality", essay 1944, published in Perspecta 2, The Yale Architectural Journal, Yale University, New Haven 1953.

Kahn, Louis I., — "On order", in: Perspecta 3, The Yale Architectural Journal, Yale University, New Haven 1955.

Kahn, Louis I., — "New Frontiers in Architecture: CIAM in Otterlo", New York 1961.

Kahn, Louis I., — "Remarks", Perspecta 9/10, The Yale-University Journal, Yale University, New Haven 1965.

Kahn, Louis I., — Interview in: Architectural Forum, July/August 1966.

Kahn, Louis I., — "Statements on Architecture", in: Zodiac 17, 1967.

Kahn, Louis I., — "Silence and Light", in: Ronner/Ihaveri, Complete Work, lecture at the ETH Zurich 1969.

Kahn, Louis I.,	*"How' m I Doing, Corbusier?"*, The Pennsylvania Gazette, Volume 71, no. 3, Dec. 1972.
Kahn, Louis I.,	*"Louis Kahn Defends"*, in: Wurman, Richard Saul, *"What will be has always been – The words of Louis I. Kahn"*, New York 1986.
Kahn, Louis I.,	The Louis I. Kahn Archives, *"The Personal Drawings of Louis I. Kahn in Seven Volumes"*, New York 1987–88.
Kass, Spencer R.,	*"The voluminous wall"*, in: The Cornell Journal of Architecture, Cornell University, Ithaca, New York 1987.
Kaufmann, Emil,	*"Three revolutionary Architects, Boullée-Ledoux-Lequeu"*, American Philospical Society, October 1952; German edition: Staatliche Kunsthalle Baden-Baden und Gesellschaft der Freunde junger Kunst e. V., second impression 1971, published jointly with the Institute for the Arts, Rice University, Houston.
Klotz, Heinrich and Cook, John W.,	*"Conversations with Architects"*, New York 1973.
Komendant, August,	*"18 Years with Architect Louis I. Kahn"*, Englewood, New Jersey, 1975.
Kruft, Hanno-Walter,	*"Geschichte der Architekturtheorie"*, Munich 1985, 2nd impression 1986.
Kultermann, Udo,	*"Kleine Geschichte der Kunsttheorie"*, Darmstadt 1987.
Langford, Fred,	*"Concrete in Dhaka"*, in: "Mimar 6", The Architectural Journal, Singapore, Oktober 1982.
Latour, Alessandra (ed.),	*"Louis I. Kahn, L' uomo, il maestro"*, Rome 1986.
Latour, Alessandra (ed.),	*"Louis I. Kahn, Writings, Lectures, Interviews"*, New York 1991.
Latour, Alessandra (ed.),	*"Louis I. Kahn, Die Architektur und die Stille"*, selected texts in German translation, Basel 1993.
Le Corbusier,	*"Vers une Architecture"*, Paris 1924
Le Corbusier,	*"Modulor"*, Paris 1948.
Le Corbusier,	*"Modulor 2"*, Paris 1955.
Le Corbusier,	*"Œuvres complètes 1910–65"*, edited by Willy Boesiger and Hans Girsberger, Zurich 1967.
March, Lionel and Sheine, Judith,	*"RM Schindler, Composition and Construction"*, London and Berlin 1993.
McLaughlin, Patricia,	Interview mit Kahn: *"How' m I Doing, Corbusier?"*, in: The Pennsylvania Gazette, Volume 71, no. 3, Dec. 1972.
Meyers, Marshall,	*"The wonder of the natural thing"*, interview with Louis I. Kahn in August 1972; The Louis I. Kahn Collection, University of Pennsylvania, Philadelphia, Box LIK 113.
Moessel, Ernst,	*"Urformen des Raumes als Grundlagen der Formgestaltung"*, Munich 1931.
Moholy-Nagy,	*"The Future of the Past"*, in: Perspecta 7, The Yale Architectural Journal, Yale University, New Haven 1961.
Naredi-Rainer, Paul von,	*"Architektur und Harmonie"*, Cologne 1982/89.
Naredi-Rainer, Paul von,	*"Musiktheorie und Architektur"*, essay 1983.
Neumeyer, Fritz,	*"Mies van der Rohe, das kunstlose Wort"*, Berlin 1986.
Newman, Oscar (ed.),	*"New Frontiers in Architecture: CIAM in Otterlo"*, New York 1961.
O'Gorman, James F.,	*"The Architecture of Frank Furness"*, Philadelphia Museum of Art, Philadelphia 1973.
Panofsky, Erwin,	*"Idea, Ein Beitrag zur Begriffsgeschichte der älteren Kunsttheorie"*, Berlin 1924, here 6th impression 1989.
Panofsky, Erwin,	*"Aufsätze zu Grundfragen der Kunstwissenschaft"*, Berlin 1964/1992.
Perrot, Georges and Chipiez, Charles,	*"Geschichte der Kunst im Altertum-Ägypten"*, Leipzig 1884.
Pevsner, Nikolaus,	*"Pioneers of Modern Movement"*, London 1936, New York 1949.
Pfeifer, Franz Xaver,	*"Der Goldene Schnitt"*, Wiesbaden 1885.
Piper, Jan,	*"Die anglo-indische Station"*, Antiquitates Orientales vol. 1, Bonn 1977.
Piper, Jan and Fischer, Klaus and Jansen, Michael,	*"Architektur des indischen Subkontinents"*, Darmstadt 1987.
Plato,	Complete Works. German translation by Friedrich Schleiermacher and Hieronymus Müller, Hamburg 1957/58.
Reed, Peter S., in: Brownlee, David B. and De Long, David,	*"Louis I. Kahn, In the Realm of Architecture"*, New York, 1991.
Ronner, Heinz and Ihaveri, Sharad,	*"Louis I. Kahn, Complete Work 1935–1974"*, Basel/Boston 1987.
Ronner, Heinz,	*"Zur Entstehung des Complete Work von Louis I. Kahn"*, essay, ETH Zurich 1988.
Rothermund, Dietmar,	*"Indien"*, Munich 1990.
Rowe, Colin,	*"The Mathematics of the Ideal Villa and Other Essays"*, The Massachusetts Institute of Technology, Cambridge and London 1982, here 1989.
Rykwert, Joseph,	*"The First Moderns"*, The Massachusetts Institute of Technology, Cambridge 1980.
Sarnitz, August,	*"Rudolph Michael Schindler, Architect"*, New York 1988; original edition: Akademie der Bildenden Künste, Vienna 1986.
Schindler, Rudolph Michael,	*"Selected Writings"* (and other essays) in: *"RM Schindler, Composition and Construction"*, ed. by Lionel March and Judith Sheine, London and Berlin 1993.
Scully, Vincent,	*"The heritage of Wright"*, in: Zodiac 6, 1960.
Scully, Vincent,	*"Louis I. Kahn"*, from the series *"Architects of Today"*, New York 1962; German edition 1962, Ravensburg.
Scully, Vincent,	*"Light, Form and Power"*, in: Architectural Forum, 1964.
Scully, Vincent,	*"American Architecture and Urbanism"*, New York 1969 and new edition 1988.
Scully, Vincent,	*"Works of Louis I. Kahn and his method"*, lecture at the IAUS-Konferenz in New York, 1974; published as an essay in: "Architecture and Urbanism, Louis I. Kahn", Tokyo 1975.
Scully, Vincent,	*"Travel Sketches of Louis Kahn"*, Pennsylvania Academy of Fine Arts, Philadelphia 1978.
Sedlmayr, Hans,	*"Gestaltetes Sehen"*, essay in: Belvedere 8, 1925.
Sedlmayr, Hans,	*"Die Architektur Borrominis"*, original edition Piper Verlag, Munich 1939, new edition Hildesheim 1986.
Sedlmayr, Hans,	*"Verlust der Mitte"*, Salzburg 1948, 8th impression 1965, written 1943–45.
Serenyi, Peter,	*"Timeless but of its Time: Le Corbusier's Architecture in India"*, in: Perspecta 20, The Yale Architectural Journal, Yale University, New Haven and The Massachusetts Institute of Technology, Cambridge 1983.
Smith, Baldwyn,	*"Egyptian Architecture as Cultural Expression"*, New York 1938; in: Fine-Arts Library, University of Pennsylvania, Philadelphia, Furness-Building.
Smithson, Peter and Alison,	*"Louis Kahn"*, in: "Architects Yearbook no. 9", 1960.
Taylor, Brian Brace,	*"Dhaka"*, in: "Mimar 6", The Architectural Journal, Singapore October 1982.
Thies, Harmen,	*"Grundrißfiguren Balthasar Neumanns. Zum maßstäblich-geometrischen Rißaufbau der Schönbornkapelle und der Hofkirche in Würzburg"*, Florence 1980.
Thies, Harmen,	*"Michelangelo, Das Kapitol"*, published by the Art-Historical Institute in Florence, Munich 1982.
Thies, Harmen,	*"Zu den Wurzeln der Modernen Architektur, Teil 1"*, journal of the Braunschweigische Wissenschaftliche Gesellschaft, Göttingen 1988.
Tigerman, Stanley,	in: Wurman, Richard Saul, *"What will be has always been – The words of Louis I. Kahn"*, New York 1986.
Tigerman, Stanley,	*"Mies van der Rohe: A Moral Modernist Model"*, in: Perspecta 22, The Yale Architectural Journal, Yale University, New Haven, New York 1986.
Tucci, Guiseppe,	*"Geheimnis des Mandala"*, Bern 1972.
Tyng, Alexandra,	*"Beginnings, Louis I. Kahn's Philosophy of Architecture"*, New York 1984.
Tyng, Anne Griswold,	*"Louis I. Kahn's 'Order' in the Creative Process"*, in Latour, *"Louis I. Kahn's, l'Uomo, il Maestro"*, Rome 1986.
Tyng, Anne Griswold,	*"The Energy of Abstraction in Architecture: a Theory of Creativity"*, dissertation at the University of Pennsylvania, Philadelphia 1975.
Vallhonrat, Carles Enriquez,	*"Tectonics Considered"*, in: Perspecta 24, The Yale Architectural Journal, Yale University, New Haven, New York 1988.
Venturi, Robert,	*"Complexity and Contradiction in Architecture"*, Museum of Modern Art, New York 1966.
Vitruv (Marcus Vitruvius Pollio)	*"De architectura libri decem"*. German translation by Dr. Curt Fensterbusch, Darmstadt 1964, 4th edition 1987.
Volkmann, Hans,	*"Giovanni Battista Piranesi, Architekt und Graphiker"*, Berlin 1965.
Williams, Robin B.,	in: Brownlee, David B. and De Long, David, *"Louis I. Kahn, In the Realm of Architecture"*, New York, 1991.
Wilton-Ely, John,	*"The Mind and Art of Giovanni Battista Piranesi"*, London 1978.
Wittkower, Rudolf,	*"Das Problem der Bewegung innerhalb der manieristischen Architektur"*, in: manuscript of the Festschrift for Walter Friedländer's 60th birthday, Art-Historical Institute Florence, no. C 1109 q (by Thies).
Wittkower, Rudolf,	*"Systems of Proportions"*, Architects Yearbook 5, Journal of The Warburg and Courtauld Institutes, London 1953.
Wittkower, Rudolf,	*"Architectural Principles in the Age of Humanism"*, London 1949 and London and New York 1952.
Wright, Frank Lloyd,	Complete Works, edited by Bruno Zevi, Zurich 1980.
Wright, Frank Lloyd,	*"Letters to Architects"*, letters to and from F. L. W. selected and with a commentary by Bruce Brooks Pfeiffer, Los Angeles 1984.
Wurman, Richard Saul and Feldman, Gene,	*"The Notebooks and Drawings of Louis I. Kahn"*, New York 1962.
Wurman, Richard Saul,	*"What will be has always been – The words of Louis I. Kahn"*, New York 1986.
Zeising, Adolf,	*"Schriften zur Proportionslehre"*, Leipzig 1875.
Zevi, Bruno,	*"Frank Lloyd Wright"*, Zurich 1980.